Ovid Revisited

Ovid Revisited

The Poet in Exile

Jo-Marie Claassen

```
R  O  M  A
O        M
M        O
A  M  O  R
```

BLOOMSBURY
LONDON • NEW DELHI • NEW YORK • SYDNEY

Bloomsbury Academic
An imprint of Bloomsbury Publishing Plc

50 Bedford Square	1385 Broadway
London	New York
WC1B 3DP	NY 10018
UK	USA

www.bloomsbury.com

First published in 2008 by Gerald Duckworth & Co. Ltd

British Library Cataloguing-in-Publication Data
A catalogue record for this book is available from the British Library.

ISBN: PB: 978-0-7156-3783-8
     Epub: 978-1-4725-2144-6
     Epdf: 978-1-4725-2143-9

Library of Congress Cataloging-in-Publication Data
A catalog record for this book is available from the Library of Congress.

Contents

For Peter and Martin, with love

Preface

Published in time for the bimillennium of Ovid's relegation by the emperor Augustus to Tomis on the Black Sea, this book examines aspects of Ovid's poetry from exile. It is unashamedly diffuse in character, covering topics that range from quasi-historical studies, to stylistics, to literary comparison and various matters between. It offers a wide-ranging overview of the exiled poet and the autobiographical elegiacs of his last years in a compilation of my previously published articles or reviews. Any observed omissions or redundancies must be ascribed to this fact: not only has *Ovid* been revisited, but also the matter of each of the six chapters. My aim is to make easily accessible research papers and reviews published over more than twenty years in a variety of journals spanning eight different countries. These have been abbreviated, rearranged and merged in logical, rather than chronological, order.

Overlaps in the introductions of various articles that form subsections of chapters have been weeded out, as have all foot- and endnotes. A small proportion of previously unpublished material has been added (some passages deriving from aspects of my Stellenbosch dissertation, others are new). Those few articles that were integrated into the fabric of my *Displaced Persons* (London, 1999) have not been reused. I have tried to offer the material in a palatable form, also for non-specialists, with a minimum of references to other secondary material. To make the book more readable, all quotations and excerpts have been furnished with fairly literal translations. These are, unless otherwise acknowledged, my own, and are presented in 'free verse' format where line-by-line equivalence is possible, but as prose where logical English equivalence cannot retain the integrity of the Latin word order over a couplet. Non-specialist readers may feel happier to skip the more technical third sections of Chapters 3 and 4.

The title of the book is a tribute to L.P. Wilkinson's *Ovid Recalled* (Cambridge, 1955), while respectfully disagreeing with the master as to the literary value of the poems. That his poetry from exile is consistent with the rest of Ovid's oeuvre in quality and style has been the under-lying assumption upon which my research was based. My publications from 1986 onward have consistently treated Ovid's poems from exile as the literary, as well as the chronological, culmination of his oeuvre, ascribing the poet's palpable resilience in the face of extreme hardship to the relief that his poetry afforded him.

My earlier research mostly concentrated on the uses to which Ovid put his exilic poetry and his manner of composition, but more recently I have ventured into the twin minefields of literary comparison and armchair psychology. Chapter 6 is a compilation of two papers resulting from research on Ovid's universalisation of exile funded by the South African National Research Foundation, which body is again thanked. Here the degree to which Ovid universalised the sufferings of the dispossessed is assessed by comparing his exilic works with modern exilic literature. Recent events in southern Africa have led to severe displacement of many, so that the topic has increased in poignancy for me.

To take the topics of the other chapters in order: the Introduction considers the phenomenon of Ovid's continued popularity, explaining the importance of chronology in our reading and critical judgement of the exilic poems. Ovid's first readers would have received his missives from Tomis over time and in serial format, unrolling the scrolls and reading the poems in the order in which the author presented them. Hence the Introduction ends with a brief summary of the contents of the *Tristia* and *Epistolae ex Ponto,* divided into five chronological phases, to be read rapidly and in that order. Topics of subsequent chapters range from consideration of Ovid's relationship with Augustus and with his own poetry, to his ubiquitous humour, to his skill as poet, including metrics, vocabulary and verbal play, and to Ovid's use of mythological figures from earlier parts of his oeuvre. Finally, an *Excursus* examines some historicist conjectures about Ovid's exile, ending with adaptations of some recent book reviews, the whole serving to indicate some of the directions that Ovidian studies are taking today.

The number of the chapter into which each source has been incorporated is given in parentheses after each in the list of my publications ('Sources', pp. xi-xii below). In some cases the *disiecta membra* of an article have been redistributed over various chapters. This is indicated merely by listing these chapters after the title and provenance of a particular paper. Readers wishing to pursue any topic in greater depth are referred to the original journals from which these chapters derive. Sincere thanks to the anonymous readers of these journals, who originally each individually contributed to the logical flow and tautness of the respective articles. Thanks, too, to my editor Deborah Blake for advice and encouragement, to Gareth Williams for his careful scrutiny and meticulous annotation of the manuscript and his many helpful suggestions, to Maridien Schneider for years of research assistance, and to my husband Piet, for endless support.

Jo-Marie Claassen
Stellenbosch, June 2008

Sources

My publications are listed by date, title, journal and place of publication. The permission of the editors of each journal to use the relevant material is gratefully acknowledged:

1986: 'International interest in Ovid's exile and the search for Ovid's tomb', *Akroterion* 31 (4), Stellenbosch, South Africa. (Introduction §2; *Excursus* §1)

1987: 'Error and the imperial household: an angry god and the exiled Ovid's fate', *Acta Classica* 30, Pretoria, South Africa. (§1.1)

1988: 'Ovid's poems from exile: the creation of a myth and the triumph of poetry', *Antike und Abendland* 34, 158-69, Tübingen, Germany. (Introduction §3, §5.10)

1989a: 'Carmen and poetics: poetry as enemy and friend', *Collection Latomus, Studies in Latin literature and Roman history* 5, 252-66, Brussels, Belgium. (§3.1)

1989b: 'Meter and emotion in Ovid's exilic poetry', *Classical World* 82 (5), 351-65, Pittsburgh, USA. (§3.2)

1990: 'Ovid's wavering identity: personification and depersonalisation in the exilic poems', *Latomus* 49.1, 102-16, Brussels, Belgium. (§1.2)

1991: 'Une analyse stylistique et littéraire d'Ovide *Epistolae ex Ponto* 3.3 *Praeceptor amoris* ou *praeceptor Amoris?*', *Les Etudes Classiques,* 59, 27-41, Namur, France. (Original English version: §2.2)

1992: 'Structure, chronology, tone and undertone: an examination of tonal variation in Ovid's exilic poetry', *Akroterion* 37 (3&4), 98-113, Stellenbosch, South Africa. (§2.1)

1994: Review article: 'Ovid's exile: is the secret out yet?' R. Verdière: *Le Secret du Voltigeur d'Amour*, *Scholia* ns 3, 107-11, (then) Durban, South Africa. (*Excursus* §1)

1999a: '*Exsul ludens*: punning and word play in Ovid's exilic poetry', *Classical Bulletin* 75 (1), 23-35, New York, USA. (§4.2)

1999b (published 2001): 'The vocabulary of exile in Ovid's *Tristia* and *Epistolae ex Ponto*', *Glotta* 75 (3-4), 134-71, Göttingen, Germany. (§4.1)

2000: Review: '*Ad nostra tempora: carmen perpetuum, carmen aeternum*', on Philip Hardie et al. (eds): *Ovidian Transformations: Essays on Ovid's Metamorphoses and its Reception* (Cambridge, 1999), *Scholia Reviews* ns 9 (2000), 24. Electronic publication from Durban, South Africa. (*Excursus* §2)

2001 (published in 2003): 'The singular myth: Ovid's use of mythology in the exilic poetry', *Hermathena* 170, 11-64, Dublin, Ireland. (Chapter 5)

2003a: Review: Sandra Citroni Marchetti: *Amicitia e potere nelle lettere di Cicerone e nelle elegie ovidiane dall'esilio* (Firenze 2000), *Latomus* 62, 962-3, Brussels, Belgium. (*Excursus* §1)

2003b: ' "Living in a place called exile": the universals of the alienation caused by isolation', *Literator* 24, 85-112, Potchefstroom, South Africa. (§6.2)

2004a: *'Mutatis mutandis*: the poetry and poetics of isolation in Ovid and Breytenbach', *Scholia* 13, 71-107, (now) Otago, New Zealand. (§6.1)

2004b Review: A.J. Boyle: *Ovid and the Monuments: a Poet's Rome* (Bendigo 2003), *Scholia Reviews* ns 13 (2004) 26, electronic publication from Durban, South Africa. (*Excursus* §1)

2006: Review: É. Tola: *La métamorphose poétique chez Ovide*: Tristes *et* Pontiques (Bibliothèque d'Études Classiques 38), *Classical Review* 56 (1), London, UK. (*Excursus* §2)

2007: Review: Jan Felix Gaertner: *Ovid* Epistolae ex Ponto *Book 1, Gnomon* 79, 124-8, Munich, Germany. (*Excursus* §2)

*

1986: *Poeta, exsul, vates: a stylistic and literary analysis of Ovid's* Tristia *and* Epistolae ex Ponto. D.Litt. diss., Stellenbosch, South Africa (published in microfilm by UMI). (Introduction §§4 and 5; §§3.3 and 4.3).

*

Text used for quotations: S.G. Owen 1963: *P. Ovidi Nasonis Tristium libri quinque, Ibis, ex Ponto libri quattuor, Halieutica, Fragmenta*, Oxford, Clarendon.

Introduction

1. Setting the scene: why Ovid remains so popular, and what this book is about

Ovid's versatility may perhaps explain his continued popularity, but fashions in judging of his place in the Classical pantheon come and go, as do fashions in the evaluation of his exilic works. In the 1950s, L.P. Wilkinson's otherwise measured judgement of our poet's oeuvre (*Ovid Recalled,* Cambridge, 1955) still took at face value Ovid's many protestations of the inferiority of his poems from exile and his conversion from flippant player to serious emperor-worshipper. For a long time these poems were considered mainly as historical source material. The British scholar E.J. Kenney, in 'The poetry of Ovid's exile', *PCPhS* 191 (1965), 37-49, finally alerted the scholarly world to the poetic and imaginative quality of the exilic poems, both regarding style and in the manner in which style reveals emotion. Kenney's seminal article opened up a new direction. By the 1980s it was possible to write seriously of the value of the exilic poems without eliciting disapproving frowns from colleagues.

By the beginning of this century it has become a matter of mainstream scholarship to consider the exilic poems as poetry without having to apologise. My own efforts over the past twenty years seem to have become increasingly acceptable to specialist colleagues. I no longer seem unusual in my identification of irreverence and iconoclasm in these poems, that have come into their own in an irreverent and questioning era. We have long ceased to view empire in the rosy light that suffused Augustan studies in the nineteenth and early twentieth centuries. Reception of both Ovid and Augustus has changed. This will be more thoroughly discussed during the course of this book.

Ovid's literary popularity, even when his exilic poetry was valued only as a quarry for historical factoids, may be judged from the amount of non-literary activity elicited by his relegation to Tomis, modern Constanza, on the Black Sea, which event took place in AD 8 or 9. The *Excursus* at the end of this book discusses some of the endless historicist researches into Ovid's exile, while offering reviews of diverse recent publications. This includes an important collection of essays on Ovid's *Metamorphoses* as example of the kind of attention our poet now enjoys. Recent scholarship assumes that Ovid spent part of his exile on finally polishing his

1

carmen perpetuum; hence the inclusion of this review in a work about the exilic poetry. The continued interest of modern scholars in other aspects of the exiled poet's art and life is also briefly and selectively surveyed in that chapter.

2. Brief overview of the facts of Ovid's exile

No other contemporary sources mention Ovid's exile. We have only his own evidence, contained in five books of the *Tristia*, 'Sad songs', and four collections of *Epistolae ex Ponto*, 'Letters from the Black Sea'. There is a remarkable paucity of autobiographical, 'factual' material on the poet's life before the decree of relegation, but rather, on the emotional level, a paradoxical mixture of apparent humble contrition about and strong pride in the poet's past achievements.

Born into an aristocratic family in 43 BC, Publius Ovidius Naso grew up in the turbulent times that followed the death of Julius Caesar, but spent his adult years in the comparative stability of the Augustan era. He could afford to ignore the exigencies of a state-oriented career and devote himself to *otium*. His *Amores* did not fit in with the serious Augustan call upon Roman men of letters to write patriotic poetry. With the publication of his *Ars Amatoria*, Ovid's jocular stance as independently-minded Master of Love turned his jaunty and irreverent attitude to love and marriage (in Rome not automatic harness-mates) into an act of social sabotage, duly reported to Augustus at some time during the next ten years. By AD 8, when Augustus deemed that his granddaughter Julia Minor had absorbed too much from these racy precepts and banished her from Rome, along with her lovers, Ovid, too, was banished. In his case a second, rather mysterious, accusation – perhaps political – his *error,* accompanied the first, the accusation of subversion of public morality through his *carmen,* construed as 'immoral poetry'. The poet tells us that his *error* was not illegal: *Nec quicquam, quod lege vetor committere, feci* ('Nor did I commit anything which is forbidden by law to do', *Ex P.* 1.6.71). He vehemently defends his poetry against charges of subversion. The major part of *Tristia* 2 is devoted to showing up the hollowness of such a charge. Why an exiled poet would have resorted to the very medium and even metric form that caused his downfall is a question that should always be considered when looking at the nature of Ovid's exilic poems.

Ovid's laments from Tomis, the *Tristia* and *Epistolae ex Ponto*, together with his famous farrago of curses, the *Ibis*, constitute the exilic poetry that has undergone strong scrutiny in the last forty years. Opinion is still divided on who his intended audience was, whether the poet was serious in the recantation of all that he stood for before, and whether his ostensibly subservient appeals to the Emperor should be taken at face value or whether there is a subversive subtext.

Ovid's two reasons for his punishment, *carmen* and *error* (*Tr.* 2.207f.), have been much debated. John Thibault, *The Mystery of Ovid's Exile* (Berkeley, 1964) exhaustively discussed the possible reasons for the poet's exile, and finally (pp. 125-8) gave a chronological list of theories from Sicco Polento (1437) to Norwood (1963). Fashions in theory changed over time: at first a sexual misdemeanour was the most popular theory, then some connection with the younger Julia, either sexual or political. Early in the twentieth century Robinson Ellis suggested that the error was religious in character, the violation of the sacred mysteries of Isis. 'Field research' for the *Fasti* has been suggested as a reason for the conjectured violation of some ceremony such as the Bona Dea celebrations, famously desecrated by Cicero's opponent Clodius.

More recently a political interpretation has predominated. Peter Green in the Introduction to his Penguin translation of the love poems (1982), summing up the theoretical field to that date, gave greatest weight to political reasons. This stance Green maintained, some twelve years later, in his Introduction to his Penguin translation and commentary (*Ovid: the poems of exile,* Harmondsworth, 1994). A beguiling modern theory, which I have not encountered elsewhere, is worked out in David Wishart's novel, simply titled *Ovid* (London, 1995). The work postulates that Ovid was aware of, but did not report, the involvement of the empress Livia in the events that led to the Varian disaster. That this is patent fiction goes without saying. These theories will be dealt with in greater detail in the *Excursus* (pp. 232-4 and 250-1).

The poet's various works have in turn been suggested as both *carmen* and *error*. *Carmen* has generally, following the poet's own interpretation in, for example, *Tr.* 2.239-50, been taken to refer to the *Ars Amatoria* (perhaps also the *Remedia Amoris*) whose flippancy and generally amoral tone violated all that Augustus had envisaged with his programme of cultural and moral uplift. Augustus' programme had included laws that made adultery a civil offence, and were intended to encourage marriage and family life. Instead of advocating marriage and the advantages of a family establishment, Ovid's works, including the *Amores*, first published in about 25 BC, and later republished in a shortened edition, gave a cold-blooded, racy view of the kind of *otium* enjoyed by the Roman fashionable world. That it was possibly nearer the truth about contemporary society than Virgil's or Horace's apparently patriotic restatements of 'pristine values' (now increasingly interpreted with a degree of nuancing) probably added to its unpopularity with the emperor.

The appearance of the *Ars Amatoria* in 2 BC and *Remedia* soon after had perhaps passed unnoticed by the princeps; at some later stage it may have been brought to his attention. By AD 8, if not published in final form, the *Metamorphoses* was in general circulation: it, too, may have given offence. The first six books of the *Fasti* were perhaps in private circulation, perhaps published. Here too, depending on the reader's response and interpretation, offence may be inferred. Ronald Syme in his *The Roman Revolution* (Oxford, 1939: 486) points out that Augustus' sterner measures of repression were employed against truly 'noxious literature' such as contemporary political pamphlets. 'Trifles' such as the *Ars Amatoria* were not consigned to public bonfires. However, the poet managed, in some way or another, to give mortal offence, and during AD 8 or 9 suffered a decree of relegation to Tomis, a Greek city, originally a colony of Miletus, on the Black Sea.

The earliest allusion, other than in the exilic poetry, to Ovid's banishment and the place of banishment, is in Pliny the Elder, *Nat. Hist.* 32.152, referring to the *Halieutica*, ascribed to Ovid: ... *his adiciemus ab Ovidio posita animalia, quae apud neminem alium reperiuntur, sed fortassis in Ponto nascentia, ubi id volumen supremis suis temporibus inchoavit* ... ('To these we shall add those animals described by Ovid, which are found in the works of no other author, but which are perhaps bred in the Black Sea, [which is the area] where he started this volume toward the end of his life ...'). Pliny does not specifically name Tomis, but speaks in general terms of the Black Sea area. The problem is compounded by the fact that it is now generally accepted that the *Halieutica* was not written by Ovid. Pliny was writing more than fifty years after the poet's presumed demise. Statius, celebrating a friend's wedding in *Silvae* 1.2.254-5, is more explicit: *ambissent laudare diem, nec tristis in ipsis/ Naso Tomis* ... ('They would have sought to praise the day, and even Naso would have been glad at Tomis itself'). For Statius, the exiled poet has taken on the status of a mythological *exemplum*, even a mythical archetype.

The *Tristia* chronicle the journey into exile, the first years at Tomis, and the exile's inner turmoil. The *Epistolae ex Ponto*, as a series of personal epistles to friends in Rome, depict the last years of the exile's life. Both works are in elegiacs. The poet himself pretends that they are as sterile as his place of exile, which he portrays as a region of perpetual winter, the verifiable absurdity of which statement has sometimes been insufficiently questioned. These poems offered a form of occupational therapy to an eminently industrious poet, who consistently dealt in poetic truth, which may or may not show affinity with literal truth, but cannot be dismissed outright as 'lies'.

The poet remained a prolific writer. There are signs of a reworking of the first six books of the *Fasti* during his exile. Although Ovid avers in the *Tristia* (1.7.15-16) that he held a symbolic conflagration in which the 'unfinished' *Metamorphoses* was consigned to the pyre, the final polishing and editing of the work (which was not lost) was probably completed during the years 8 to 12. Officially, the books were banned from public libraries: actually, they all appear to have been in free circulation.

3. Problems of approach

The question of the interpretation of Ovid's poetry of exile is complex. Ovidian research has been much affected by the 'historicistic approach'. Earlier critics tended to believe even verifiably fantastic depictions of the Tomitan area as perennially snow-bound (Sir Ronald Syme is said to have carried about with him a photograph of an ice-bound Black Sea beach, taken no doubt during a very cold wintry spell). Individual critics differed in their approach to the poet's various works. Historicists tended to doubt the 'sincerity' or 'factual truth' of the *Amores*, but turned around and accepted as literal fact all that the poet chose to represent in the exilic poetry, as if 'relegation' had caused a type of 'Damascus-road conversion'. Critics with a more literary bent tended to judge the erotic and 'national' poetry by literary and generic standards, whereas the poet's protestations about and explanations of the 'poor quality' of the exilic works were accepted without ado and without application of standard literary-critical methods. Acceptance of the poet's claims of 'decadence' and poetic debility led to discovery of such 'decadence' in a variety of stylistic approaches. Chapters 2 to 4 represent my attempts to counter some of these with stylistic analyses of my own.

Concentration on Ovid's subject matter to the exclusion of his style implies that his poetry is of an inferior sort. Concentration on stylistics, and consideration of the poet's mind at work, brings us nearer both to understanding the tone and setting of the poetry and grasping the poet as historical person. The central question should be how the poet's style reflects his attitudes: the lover's stance toward his mistress, the exile's reactions to his place of banishment, his fluctuations of hope and despair. Ancient theoretical description often lagged behind ancient literary practice. A poet's intuitive system appealed to a reader on an intuitive level, whereas criticism confined itself to 'sets of rules'. For that reason the terminology and concepts employed in stylistic analysis, as we have them from the ancients, are sometimes over-precise and over-defined, and sometimes sadly lacking in precision. My analyses largely ignore traditional categories, considering in turn units of diction (vocabulary, aural effects and the tectonics of verse-making) and units of thought (that is, those stylistic ploys which are generally included under 'rhetorical devices' in discussion of both poetry and prose). General literary mechanisms such as parody, imitation and generic experimentation merit attention, whatever they are labelled.

The poet's depiction of the physical aspects of exile, when compared with archaeological evidence and literary antecedents, shows very little relation between subjective poetic information and objective, verifiable fact. Tomitan archaeology shows strong Milesian connections, a flourishing Greek community, an advanced state of Thracian culture and even indications of much larger Roman occupancy than Ovid admits to. Agricultural, geographical and meteorological evidence also diverges sharply from the picture the poet paints. To explain these discrepancies as 'understandable exaggeration' is inadequate. The erroneousness of the verifiable facts of the exile's external circumstances seems to cast a strong shadow of doubt on any autobiographical information the poet cares to divulge. The exile apparently intends to strengthen his appeal by the pathetic depiction of his circumstances. Information on the exile's own more personal circumstances is equally paradoxical and inconsistent. The poet realistically externalises inner suffering in concrete, physical terms, which has sometimes led to critics' acceptance of these externals as factual rather than metaphorical.

Hence controversy has long raged about how much of what Ovid says in his ostensibly biographical poetry can be taken as literally true or 'sincere'. Critics (particularly if lacking a sense of humour) sometimes labelled him 'shallow', or 'insincere', or 'without depth or emotional involvement', usually in a deleterious comparison with a predecessor or contemporary. Criticism has of late, as I indicated above, tended to modify this approach. It is now a commonplace of criticism that poetic reality stands somewhere between poetic fiction and historical reality. We can comfortably assume that Ovid's approach to truth is essentially Aristotelian, portraying potentiality, rather than actuality. In modern idiom, Ovid's 'sincerity' is not necessarily based on 'factual reality'. Ovid addressed himself to this same problem in *Tr.* 2.253-466 in an elaborate defence of his art as opposed to his life.

The problem of 'historic truth' versus 'poetic truth' is crucial in Ovidian studies. The search for 'facts' in poetry was countered in the middle of the last century by A.W. Allen's insistence in a seminal article (' "Sincerity" and the Roman elegists', *Classical Philology* 45, 1950, 145-60) on *poetic* rather than *factual* sincerity as a function of style. Yet 'historicism' and 'the literary approach' need not be mutually exclusive. Jasper Griffin in *Latin Poets and Roman Life* (London, 1985) rebuts Francis Cairns' concept of total distancing between life and literature in the ancient world (*Generic Composition in Greek and Roman Poetry*, Edinburgh, 1972). For Griffin, Augustan poetry was based on contemporary Roman experience, not on Hellenistic typology. Griffin's interpretation of Augustan poetry as a reflection of the realities, whether factual or emotional, of contemporary life, postulates a compromise between consideration of poetic craft and emotional content. Green's Introduction to his Penguin translation of the exilic poems (xxxi) makes a similar point. Arguments for the predominance of literary precedent over emotion with Ovid have problematically been resuscitated by Jan-Felix Gaertner in a recent collection of essays on ancient exile edited by him (2007).

A series of paradoxes precludes a final reconciliation of all the disparate aspects of the exilic oeuvre into one clear picture of 'poetic truth'. Hence an essentially paradoxical approach is needed. Problems addressed by modern Ovidian historicist criticism must be reformulated on the literary level, and a compromise attained. Historicist problems relating to the identity of 'Corinna', the reasons for Ovid's exile, the historic 'reality' of his geographical and meteorological descriptions and the discrepancy between the poetic and the historic 'Tomis' bring the reader no nearer to any understanding of the poet as a member of Roman (or Tomitan) society, or of the exile as a literary *persona*. Both Ovid's humanity and his poetry often get lost in historical research.

The modern iconoclastic mind detects, throughout Ovid's oeuvre, a sympathetic note of irony, a gleam of irreverence or glimpse of critical questioning of 'accepted' values behind the apparently bland representation of both Augustan value-judgements and of the traditional attitude of the elegiac lover. Recent criticism exhibits a greater appreciation of Ovidian tone and tonal shifts (the topic of the first half of Chapter 2). It is impossible to pin Ovid's attitude down to a single stance, whether blandly accepting or ironical. We need to ask, '*Are what the poet appears to be saying and what the poet intends to say, identical?*' Modern criticism often questions authorial intention as a concept, stressing the role of the reader in re-forming the text and in deconstructing its verbal exterior and semiotic interior. Yet research into an author's poetics, when it assumes that the author was aware of what he was doing, essentially assumes that the author had a particular idea that he wanted to express, and a particular purpose in expressing it. This will be touched upon in the first half of my sixth chapter, where Ovidian poetics will be approached through analysis of the writings of a modern counterpart. This will be followed by an analysis of the emotional content of Ovid's exilic poetry and an exploration of the degree to which this is universalised, largely in comparison with the reactions of modern writers in similar states of isolation. Put briefly, Chapter 6 compares the emotions that may be distilled from Ovid's exilic poetry with the presentation of emotion in some modern examples.

This brings us back to the question: '*What did our poet feel?*' This question is particularly important in relation to Augustus and his programme of reform. Some twentieth-century critics, at home in the classical tradition, did not respond to what they felt was Ovid's 'improper handling' of this tradition, his 'challenging of the classical sensibility'. Active anti-Augustanism versus passive a-politicality in the pre-exilic works has been the subject of hot debate. This has now reached a state of comparative truce, with the suggestion that Ovid was simply out of step with contemporary thought. Ovid would then represent what has been termed the 'counter-classical sensibility'. With regard to the *Tristia* and *Epistolae ex Ponto* the matter is crucial. Augustus' use of the Trojan myth was central not only to his cultural reforms (as embodied in the *Aeneid,* for instance), but also in his aspirations towards divinity (the *gens Julia* as descendants of Venus) and in his whole management of propagandistic statecraft (his 'new name,' the secular games, the transcendence of West over East with Aeneas as the *stirps* of Dardanus coming into his own). Chapter 1 shows Ovid in his exilic poetry bringing Augustus' programme to its logical conclusion, thereby showing up its inconsistencies.

4. Ovidian *personae* and the myth of exile

Modern criticism takes as axiomatic that in autobiographical poetry there is a difference between the poet as empirical author and the poet as conveniently-created *persona.* Taking for granted that non-compliance with the Augustan ideal lies behind most of the poet's controversial utterances, we still need to ask whether this is Ovid the man speaking, or Ovid's first-person narrator as a 'character,' and in what way what the poet depicts is 'true'. We need to deduce emotion behind frequently stylised masks. We can distinguish at least two literary *personae* or characters, each with strong emotions, a pathetic exile and a timelessly triumphant poet, as apart from the empirical or creative poet (who happened to have been exiled).

The creative poet's style may either enhance or reduce emotional appeal. That is, it may either convey a convincing impression of the exile's suffering or create a feeling of distance between the exile's avowed feelings and the poet's real feelings (if these are at all to be ascertained). Critical attention to stylistics gives an idea of the empirical poet's mind at work, which, in the end, brings us closer to grasping the poet as person (in both guises, as factually exiled and as creatively composing). While accepting Allen's concept of poetic sincerity as a function of style, we need not lose sight of Griffin's 'complementary historicism', both using biographical knowledge as an aid to textual interpretation and deriving information about the personality of an author from his manner of presentation of even traditional material. From this we may come fairly close to an appreciation of the human emotion prompting a particular poem. With Ovid, who is both prolific and complex, this appreciation can never be absolute.

Gauging intensity of emotion, whether experienced by the exiled poet as man, ascribed to the character portrayed, or deduced by the reader, is difficult. It is further tempered by the art of the poet, the circumstances of the character and the literary and emotional background of the reader. Hermann Fränkel in his famous Sather Lectures (Berkeley, 1945) coined the phrase 'wavering identity' in relation to Ovid. The object of this volume is to discover some of the endless aspects of the Ovidian 'wavering identity' in the exilic poetry, in particular Ovid as *poeta, exsul* and *vates,* three aspects which work together to coalesce into Ovid the man. On the surface, the three concepts seem totally distinct, but as there are only one artist, the poet Ovid, and one creation, the body of exilic poetry, there is, from the beginning, a primordial unity within this diversity. This unity is the (creative) man Ovid that stands behind his work, but this man chooses to present the exiled poet as steeped in Greek and Roman literary tradition, and outside of both Roman and Tomitan 'reality'. This topic is brought into perspective by Chapter 5 (a consideration of Ovid's use of myth).

The term *poeta* refers to both the pre-exilic 'carefree' Roman artist and the composer of the exilic poetry; the creative skills of his poetic craft will be examined and reference will be made to his own poetics, or sense of artistry (Chapter 3). The *poeta* is emotionally involved with his craft, positively or negatively. An important question is whether Ovid is to be believed when he says that the *poeta* has lost his skill. With this comes the question of his own generic awareness: *did Ovid realise that he was simultaneously sending Roman elegy into a new direction and ringing its death-knell?*

Exsul refers to the 'exile', whether as a 'type' of the victims of Augustan ire or the historic Ovid himself. Here emotion is of paramount importance: his relationship with wife and friends, his mental agony and experience of physical suffering, his penitence over his error and indignation about the punishment of his *carmen* and, most importantly, his religious feelings and his feelings towards Augustus (Chapter 1). To approach Ovid without a sense of humour and an awareness of the subtle unexpectedness of Ovid's wit is to make nonsense of any study of any part of his oeuvre. The last part of Chapter 2 explores one such instance.

The question which 'divine truth' Ovid as *vates* wanted to lie at the centre of his prophetic message cannot be answered merely by identifying those poetic utterances which bear the clearest stamp of 'sincerity', but rather by analysis of tone as conveyed by style and by a particular poetic diction (Chapter 4). Discounting those parts of the exilic poetry where there seems to be a slippage between emotional content (the *exile's* lament) and flippant style (the *poet's* art) should leave us with those aspects where *exile* and *poet* do converge emotionally, bringing us closer to finding 'Ovid as *vates,* the speaker of timeless truth'. That is something different from a simplistic approach to the exiled poet as a 'changed man'. A nuanced picture of Ovid's attitudes to his own past, to his place of exile, to exile as a psychological phenomenon, to his own poetry, and to the emperor Augustus, must be sought.

Throughout my discussion the three concepts coalesce into the man behind the masks. The attitude of Ovid-the-man to his own work was complex. Occasionally the poet refers to the healing power of composition, as in his famous hymn to his Muse: *Gratia, Musa, tibi: nam tu solacia praebes;/ tu curae requies, tu medicina venis*, etc. (*Tr.* 4.10.117-20, 'My thanks to you, my Muse: for you offer comfort/ you give rest from care, you come as a healing drug', etc.). This is the type of consolation always advocated in the philosophical tradition of comfort to the bereaved or to those in exile, but this is not acknowledged explicitly. At the same time Ovid frequently berates his Muse for bringing about his downfall: it is the stone against which he is again stubbing his toe, the Telegonus or Oedipus that killed its own progenitor (Chapter 3).

Ultimately, the problem is one of the credibility of the poet's portrayal of his own past, of the exile's present, of the apparently callous unresponsiveness of most of his ostensible correspondents. Which view of the relationship of the poet's art and life is the 'true' one? Is acceptance – by the rationalistic, irreverent poet of the *Metamorphoses* – of the divinity of the emperor mere lip-service, employed in order to obtain pardon? We may even doubt the intelligence of the exiled poet. Interpretation of apparent 'tactlessness' as ironical leads to doubts about the poet's intermittent claim to transcendent, prophetic knowledge.

There is a way to reconcile all these disparate problems. We need to accept that the question of whether the poet's *error* was an insult to the emperor's public legislation or to his private family life is wholly immaterial; also that all other historicist problems are irrelevant. If we accept the exilic works as stylistically the culmination of the singularly fruitful career of a talented poet, then it follows that the poet, in his particular, stylised depiction of his exile, has assumed the role of *vates*, the singer of timeless poetic truth. This 'poetic truth' lies in the transcendental sphere of an existential myth: *the myth of exile*.

Assumption of the vitality and viability of such a myth means that we cannot take one aspect of the exilic works as 'true', and discount another part as 'obvious exaggeration' or a third as 'literary convention'. It means that the myth carries with it a greater reality and a more lasting, more objective 'truth' than any subjective perception of an aspect of factual reality. The myth of exile must be accepted in its entirety as absolutely true in its depiction of the fluctuations of attitude of a suffering individual in an existential crisis, which was precipitated by the reaction of powerful totalitarianism to the former freedom of this individual's irreverent spirit. The ability of that essentially playful spirit to come to terms with oppression and sublimate suffering is the 'lasting truth' conveyed.

5. Poetic ordering: the importance of *variatio* and chronology in studying the exilic poems

The time-span of Ovid's banishment cannot be exactly reckoned as the dates of both his relegation and his death are uncertain. Yet it is worthwhile to work, as far as is possible, within the known parameters of his last years, to establish a chronological basis for any analysis of the poet's thought. It is dangerous to ignore differences between assertions made by the exile in the first year of his wanderings and in his nebulous last years. The chronological structure of the exilic corpus is important. It would have had an impact on contemporaries who imbibed Ovid's poetic protestations in an intermittent stream over the course of almost a decade.

'Structure' is a late twentieth-century incantationary term that means different things to different critics. The structural approach to a body of poetry can refer to the position of a poem within a book, division of the poem into parts, the shaping of couplets or individual verses, the positioning of words, rhythmic arrangement, variation in aural effects, or the tonal movement within a verse or even within a word. These approaches have all been applied to Ovidian studies, with varying degrees of validity. Some commentators confined 'structural analysis' to conjectures about the underlying principles of arrangement within individual books. Depending upon their conclusions about the relative importance of content, tone or addressee (known in the case of the *Epistolae ex Ponto*, conjectured about the *Tristia*), they drew up symmetrical schemes with due consideration of the principle of *variatio*; but if the placement of a particular poem did not conform to their concept of the overriding ordering principle, they proposed to move it into a better position, trying, by judging from internal evidence, to ascertain the 'original order' in which the poems had been written. Adherents of numerological conjuring did the same.

All these tended to forget two basic principles: first, the fact that we have the body of poetry traditionally received in the order in which it presumably was arranged by the poet himself, except perhaps in the case of *Ex P.* 4, which, it is now generally agreed, may have been collected posthumously. Second, an exuberant enthusiasm for 'symmetry' and 'overall arrangement' made them forget the exigencies of the ancient bookroll. Ancient volumes had to be *unrolled*, as their name implies: the unrolling of a volume dictated poem-by-poem reception of the poet's scheme of arrangement. It was far more difficult for the ancients to flip backwards and forwards through a bookroll than we can with our very convenient codices, and even more convenient computer-search facilities. Hence the effect of juxtaposition, contrast and logical flow or illogical jumps in arrangement, that is, *variatio,* was more obvious to ancient readers than 'overall symmetry'. Elaborate overall patterns that can only be discerned by means of detailed diagrams were of secondary importance. *Variatio* as ordering principle will be treated in greater depth in Chapter 2.

Sheer chronological consideration of a poet's output is important, too. We have a body of work that can be dated fairly certainly by means of internal evidence (the poet's references to his own age at his departure, to Augustus' death and to historically verifiable events) and the limit imposed by the poet's death. Furthermore, it was physically impossible to produce more than a given number of verses within any one year. Ovid was always a prodigious worker, and his output increased at about the turn of our era but declined after about AD 14. All these considerations point to the need to examine the exilic oeuvre in chronologically defined periods, that is, diachronically, rather than as an entity that sprang into being as the result of some long-term plan in the poet's mind.

This does not mean that overall structure must be ignored, or that it is wrong to try to date individual poems as accurately as possible. Although the author's intentional (finally arranged) order is more important than order of composition, phase-by-phase examination of the exilic works may indicate changes in style and attitude and tonality, ultimately bringing us nearer to finding answers to literary questions. If some light is shed in passing on historic problems, that will be an added advantage.

Dating of the decree of relegation and Ovid's departure has been much debated. We have to rely on internal evidence. Ovid's statements about his year of birth, his age at exile and the position of celestial bodies when he left cannot be perfectly reconciled. From *Ex P.* 4.4.10 we learn he was born in 43 BC and was 50 when exiled, i.e. in the year AD 8, accepted as such by Peter Green. There was a moon and Venus was in ascendance on the night of his departure (*Tr.* 1.3). He travelled in winter (*Tr.* 1.2; 1.4; 1.11). It is known that Venus was the 'evening star' in AD 8, but, by judiciously reconciling Roman ways of counting with knowledge of poetic expression and the death of Augustus, known to have been in AD 14, we arrive at the year AD 9 as the more probable date of Ovid's departure.

It is generally accepted that *Tr.* 1 was composed soon after the decree of relegation was passed, that is, early in AD 10, completed by the time of the exile's arrival at Tomis, provided with suitable prologue and epilogue, and published at Rome by a friend. Ovid's long 'speech for the defence', *Tr.* 2, was probably composed concurrently with *Tr.* 1. The next book, *Tr.* 3, has been termed 'the first year at Tomis' as it can be dated within the first full year of exile. *Tr.* 4 seems to date from about AD 11. Its final poem, *Tr.* 4.10, offers the sort of *sphragis* which frequently ends a collection. *Tr.* 5.1 has indications that the poet is immediately following with another book as an addition to the collection which he had meant to treat as concluded. These three books, *Tr.* 3 to *Tr.* 5, may have been published simultaneously, by the end of AD 12 or beginning of 13. The *Ibis* was probably also composed during this time.

It is conjectured with a fair degree of certainty that *Ex P.* 1.1 to 3.9 were written from the autumn of AD 12 through 13 and published in Rome at the end of 13. The last years, from AD 14 to 16 or 17, saw the composition of the sixteen poems of *Ex P.* 4, which may or may not have been arranged by the poet, but possibly by an editor after Ovid's death, presumably in 17. Some of these poems may have been composed earlier, but for some reason excluded from the earlier collections. Concurrently with the *Tristia*, Ovid was probably reworking or editing the *Fasti*, and finally polishing the *Metamorphoses*. The latter was, however, already well known at Rome. Some of the later poems of the *Tristia* and the earlier poems of the *Epistolae ex Ponto* could have been written concurrently, and may have simply been separated into two books by the criterion of anonymity of addressee versus address by name.

From all this, the following chronological division will serve as the basis of a diachronic approach:

Phase 1: December AD 9 to about March 10: *Tr.* 1 and 2, totalling 1280 verses.
Phase 2: March 10 to about February 12: *Tr.* 3 and 4, totalling 1466 verses.
Phase 3: March 12 to about January 13: *Tr.* 5 (plus possibly parts of *Ex P.* 4), totalling 800 verses.
Phase 4: October 12 to about December 13: *Ex P.* 1 to 3, totalling 2264 verses.
Phase 5: From January 14 to the death of the exile: *Ex P.* 4, totalling 930 verses.

Obviously, these divisions provide for a degree of overlap. The order of composition within each phase is not fixed, and, of those parts that form clear 'collections', each has a prologue and epilogue that were probably composed after the body of a particular collection: i.e. *Tr.* 1.1 and 1.11 postdate the rest of the poems of *Tr.* 1; *Tr.* 3.1 and 4.10 postdate other poems in books 3 and 4. *Tr.* 5.1 and 5.13 postdate other poems in *Tr.* 5 (and possibly some of the poems in *Ex P.* 1). *Tr.* 2 is a long poem on its own and was composed probably concurrently with parts of *Tr.* 1 and 3. *Ex P.* 1.1 and 3.9 postdate the other poems of *Ex P.* 1 and 3, and all of *Ex P.* 2.

6. A story with a beginning, a middle and end

Even with the complete *corpus* in our hands, we need to pause and ask: What was the story that Ovid's contemporaries in Rome actually gleaned from the serial appearance at Rome of these poetic missives from the ends of the earth? A chronological survey of the contents of each of my conjectured phases will help to re-create the impact made on the exile's reading public in Rome as the poems of each phase were published. In the following centuries, until general use of codices finally supplanted the era of bookrolls, the same impression of an unfolding narrative would have been gained as any one volume was unrolled.

Phase 1: published early in AD 10
The first volume starts anonymously. *Tr.* 1.1: A book must go to Rome as the child of an unnamed poet, the victim of an angry Jove. The book is

13

suitably mournful, and limps. It will look in vain in the imperial house for its brothers, the other works of this distant, unhappy poet. *Tr.* 1.2: The unnamed poet in the midst of a storm prays to the gods of sea and heaven not to subscribe to the greater god's anger. The turmoil at last shows signs of slackening: the gods of the sea clearly consider him innocent of harm to Caesar's rule or household. *Tr.* 1.3: A 'flash-back' recounts the exiled poet's last night at Rome, his tears, his wife's entreaties to allow her to join him, his friends' laments, the stillness of the small hours. He recalls what others told him of his wife's reactions after his departure. He is glad she did not die, for she can help him.

Next *seafaring* as metaphor finds prominence. *Tr.* 1.4: Still at sea, the poet is contending with a storm on the Adriatic. It is hard to have to pray for a western wind to drive him forward, rather than the East wind driving him back to Italy. The sea gods must desist from attacking him, for he is already feeling Jove's anger: in fact, he is already dead. *Tr.* 1.5: A letter addressing a bosom friend mourns the exile's desertion by so many others. His lot is worse than that of mythical figures with supportive friends, worse, too, than that of Ulysses, for *his* wanderings tended towards home: the exile must lose his home forever. *Tr.* 1.6: The exile's wife is praised, rather formally, for her fidelity and support in the midst of his 'shipwreck'. He deplores the loss of his poetic powers, for he would have liked to bring her goodness to public notice, and to the notice of posterity.

The next group of poems features *change* as *Leitmotiv*. *Tr.* 1.7: A monologue, almost a reverie, addressed to a friend who has a portrait of him, speaks sadly of the poet's 'unfinished poems on changed forms' (which he claims to have burned), as being a picture of his own condition. At last the reader learns the exiled poet's name: 'Naso' offers a new, six-verse superscription for the title page of the *Metamorphoses*. *Tr.* 1.8: The poet starts his monologue with a series of *adynata* (citing the palpably impossible as 'more possible' than the topic under discussion, here all reversals of nature) which now appear possible, for an unnamed addressee has proved unfaithful. From the tenth verse onwards this friend is directly upbraided for his casual attitude. The *topos* of 'being born on rocks or a mountain top with a tiger to nurse him' is connected in a neat pun with the 'left-hand side' of the Black Sea. Here we have the first direct allusion to Ovid's intended place of exile. *Tr.* 1.9: In a soliloquy on the loneliness of disgrace, the poet thanks a kind friend, exhorting him to continue thus: Caesar would admire fidelity, even in an enemy. The reader is now offered, for the first time, in a brief three couplets, an assertion that the exiled poet's personal life had been clear of those 'arts' that he had formerly expounded. His writings had been an elaborate game.

Prayer in stormy times then takes over. *Tr.* 1.10 implores the poet's patron goddess Minerva to safeguard his journey, offering a playful travelogue of places on the way to the Black Sea, including those the ship will visit after the exile disembarks to travel on foot. Readers must unravel cryptic references to well-known cities in a series of verbal games. *Tr.* 1.11: The exiled poet purports to be writing in the midst of a storm. His 'candid reader' must forgive the 'poor quality' of the collection as resulting from the exigencies of the journey and the terrors of arrival. This poem ends the collection on a jaunty note: the storm 'finishes' a man, but the poet prays that he and the storm may simultaneously 'finish' their individual songs (43-4).

Tr. 2: Next the reader is presented with an elaborate 'speech for the defence' of 578 verses. The poem falls easily into two apparently contradictory parts, 'confession' and 'refutation'. Easily traceable finer rhetorical divisions need not concern us here. The poet's averred intention is appeasement of the 'angry god' Augustus, for the sake of mitigation of punishment. The first half rather obliquely explicates the exile's *error*: what he had seen ruined his family and himself. A disarmingly humble tone predominates at first, but after verse 207 the poet's indignation waxes rampant. Tactless allusions, to both the imperial family and the imperial military policy, may, so soon after both the Varian disaster and the banishment of Julia Minor, have struck a Roman reader as gratuitously unsympathetic to Augustus' dynastic and imperial problems. The picture of the lonely exile, uniquely confined to the ends of the earth, could have served to evoke memories of other exiles nearer at hand. Descriptions of the precariousness of the *pax Augusta* within the Pontic region suggest poetic *Schadenfreude*.

The author defends his poetry in a catalogue of poets and their topics, all, so the indignant Naso claims, 'treating of love': Homer (371-80) no less than the composers of Milesian ballads (409-18), Virgil (531-8) no less than the authors of mime (497-520). Here readers familiar with Augustus' predilections and favourite pastimes may have read defiant tactlessness; so, too, in allusions to gaming as a 'waste of time' (470-84). Suetonius (*Aug.* 71) tells us that Augustus was particularly fond of games of chance. This comes after the poet's bland reference to the emperor's 'lack of time' for affairs other than statesmanship (213-38). Ovid's elaborate defence breathes anything but true humility, but ends on a suitably meek note. His 'humble request' is not for recall, but for a 'safer place of exile' (575-8).

Phase 2: published early in AD 12
Phase 1 has set the tone, style and topics. Phase 2 starts with a reworking of some of the same themes, and picks up some new ones. *Tr.* 3.1 parallels *Tr.* 1.1: the book, as Ovid's child, arrives at Rome, fully personified, and 'speaking' in the first person. It portrays its 'father's' sad lot and tells of its unhappy pilgrimage in search of its 'brothers'. The

poem ends with a prayer to Caesar, but, as an afterthought, commends itself to the hands of 'common readers'. *Tr.* 3.2 starts with the word *ergo*, as if the continuation of an earlier discussion. It enumerates flatly the unpleasantness of the place of exile. On the way, fighting against the elements had given the exile something to do, but now death seems a welcome end to his exile, for which he prays. The poem breathes longing and despair.

Our poet now starts experimenting with generic play. *Tr.* 3.3: Readers get the first intimation of an elegy as a 'personal letter'. The exile explains to his wife that the 'letter' is written in a strange hand because he is ill. Although exile is 'living death', he wishes he had died sooner and could have been buried at home. The mood fluctuates between pathos, playfulness and defiance. The exile dictates his own 'epitaph', a defiant vindication of his fame as love poet. The poem ends ostensibly with a 'sigh': actually a neat pun on the root meaning of *valere*. *Tr.* 3.4 is more of a 'public address' than a 'private letter'. The exile advises a good friend in Epicurean terms to seek obscurity, hinting darkly that, had he avoided 'great names', he need never have left Rome. He praises his friend's fidelity. This poem has sometimes been read as two (a: 1-46 and b: 47-78). The latter half (4b) evokes other absent friends, whom the poet sees in his 'mind's eye' and addresses 'in his heart', where they lie, safely obscure. Links within the two parts, such as the advocacy of obscurity from 26 repeated at 77, underscore the essential unity of the poem.

Next, *Tr.* 3.5 celebrates a former acquaintance who has become a true friend, asking him to remind the emperor of the virtue of clemency, reiterating that the exile's 'crime' was a mistake. The poem starts as one half of a conversation. There is no salutation, but verse 17 addresses the new friend as 'dear chap', *care*, possibly a pun on the name of Ovid's friend Carus (cf. *Ex P.* 4.4.13). The first verse of *Tr.* 3.6 addresses another (or the same) as 'very dear chap', *carissime*. This friend's advice could have saved the exile, had he told him of his mistake. Again, his misdeed was so embarrassing it should be kept hidden, but it was the result of stupidity and not a crime. *Praeteritio* essentially underscores the embarrassment to the emperor.

In *Tr.* 3.7 we have the name of a correspondent: 'Perilla', a young poetess, perhaps Ovid's stepdaughter. The poem offers a nostalgic evocation of happier days, ending with a strongly defiant vindication of poetry and the poet's talent (*Tr.* 3.7.47-8):

> *ingenio tamen ipse meo comitorque fruorque*
> *Caesar in hoc potuit iuris habere nihil.*

> I keep company with and enjoy my own talent, anyway:
> Caesar could have no jurisdiction at all over that!

The last poems of *Tr.* 3 portray in series 'the exile's first full year at Tomis'. Its progress is impressionistic rather than chronological. *Tr.* 3.8 begins with autumn. The poem, an ostensible soliloquy, reads as an oblique appeal to Augustus for a better place of exile. *Tr.* 3.9 is again an example of a letter as *sermo absentis*, with Ovid's readers privileged only to hear his half of the implied conversation: Roman readers are entertained with the etymology of the name of Tomis as deriving from the Greek *temnô*, 'I cut', a reference to the Medea myth: Medea 'cut up' her brother Absyrtus in order to delay her father in his pursuit as she fled with Jason. *Tr.* 3.10 is an 'open letter' to all who remember Naso. The exile's experience of winter should touch the hardest heart: besides frozen wine, ice and 'everlasting snow' on the ground, there is intense danger from marauding hordes surging over the frozen Danube. The local natives are no less fearsome. Ovid's depiction of the *pax Romana* is not flattering. Pathos centres, however, on a description of the Tomitans' suffering rather than on the exile's defiant reaction to his lot. *Tr.* 3.11 harks back to the poet's Roman past, hurling defiance at an enemy who has harmed him. Endless suffering has numbed him. Wishes that this enemy could also experience the emperor's cruel wrath bring his imprecations to a climax.

Next *Tr.* 3.12 continues the seasonal portrayal of the exile's first year. Spring has dawned after a protracted winter. In Italy spring is beautiful. Evocative pictures of burgeoning plant life in Ovid's native land alternate with nostalgia for the social life of Rome. At Tomis spring merely means a thaw, the arrival of ships with news – also of the German campaign. The exile invites a sailor to his 'house', a pivotal concept: he still hopes that this abode will remain only a 'lodging' and not become a permanent 'home'. *Tr.* 3.13: The seasonal reference here is to the poet's birthday (19 March). None of the usual birthday celebrations is suitable here. The poet's birthday is personified as a 'friend', who should rather do what other friends have done: desert the exile. The conceit reflects a progressive lowering of its initial bantering tone and the poem ends on a cry of despair.

Now poetry becomes the topic. *Tr.* 3.14 closes the book with reference to the poet's changed state and consequently altered poetics. It is a letter addressed to the friend (Brutus, named in *Ex P.* 1.1, 3.9 and 4.6, perhaps also addressed in *Tr.* 3.9) who has published Ovid's other poems, requesting his care for this book too. The exile strikes a Virgilian pose, intimating that he left the *Metamorphoses* unfinished at the time of his 'civil death'. These poems are of a poor quality, he claims, beset as he is on all sides by danger and by the contaminating influence of foreign tongues. *Tr.* 4.1 introduces a new book, but links to the previous with a continuation of theme: poetics. The poet's reading public is informed that, poor as their quality may be, his songs relieve the exile's sorrow.

Life at Tomis is hard and the exile has, like a latter-day Priam, to take up arms at an advanced age. All the gods have sided with Caesar and there is no peace. Only his Muse aids the exiled poet. He writes with no one to read him, often burning what he has written. This exile-as-soldier contrasts sharply with the lover-as-soldier of the *Amores*. The technical perfection of this poem belies its content. Its poetic artistry here disproves the exile's claims.

The military theme is continued in the next poem. *Tr.* 4.2 (written before the triumph of 23 October AD 12) describes a projected triumph at Rome, as the exile sees it in his 'mind's eye'. Pervasive references to Caesar's family appear tactless. Allusion to Livia's *bonis nuribus* (verse 11) recalls her less than 'good' stepdaughter and granddaughter. The pathos of the poet's situation is pointed by overt sympathy with defeated Germanic chieftains who are to be paraded in the triumph. The coda stresses the importance of personal emotion over public triumph. Double-edged political allusions cannot hide the exile's patent love for Rome.

Love for family and friends predominates in the next few poems. *Tr.* 4.3 starts with a plea to the constellations of the Greater and Lesser Bear to go and see whether the exile's wife remembers him. Paradoxically, he is both indignant that she has need to mourn, and concerned that she may be inappropriately cheerful. He misses her sadly. The mood of the poem fluctuates between hope and fear, reproach and praise, longing and indignation. A catalogue of faithful wives is presented for his wife's emulation. The poem ends with the promise of lasting renown for her faithfulness. *Tr.* 4.4 addresses a friend, 'son of a very noble father' (easily identifiable as Messallinus, son of Messalla Corvinus), thanking him for kindness. Heavy-handed assurances of safety and anonymity appear purposely tactless, and aimed at underlining Caesar's persecution of the poet. The myth of Iphigenia and Orestes at Tauris (verses 63-4) illustrates the 'godforsaken' character of the Pontic area after the statue of Artemis was carried away.

The poems wax increasingly desperate, with undertones of defiance against Ovid's imperial persecutor. *Tr.* 4.5 addresses a bosom friend (identifiable as the second son of Messalla Corvinus, Cotta Maximus, later notorious in Tacitus' *Annales* 4.26 and 6.5-7 for sycophantic savagery against the enemies of Tiberius), with thanks for aid and prayers for good luck. Once again Ovid stresses the need for anonymity lest harm befall his friend.

Passage of time increasingly engages the exile's consciousness. *Tr.* 4.6 (datable to the winter of AD 11) offers a despairing soliloquy on the effects of the march of time. Time accustoms all others to their lot: the exile's pain simply increases with time; death its only cure. *Tr.* 4.7 chides a friend for not writing, even now, in Ovid's second year of exile. He would rather believe in literary monsters than that his friend monstrously deserted him. *Tr.* 4.8 raises another aspect of time: the old and grey exile should be enjoying a peaceful old age, but his error led him astray and he angered a man equal to the gods. The last word of the poem is *virum,* reminding readers that Augustus is all too human.

The collection closes on recollections of the past and prognostications about the future. *Tr.* 4.9 touches on what has become another exilic topos: an unnamed enemy has caused the exile unnamed pain. He is willing to forgive if this enemy repents but failure to do so will expose the man, both 'now', to all the world, and 'for all time', to posterity. *Tr.* 4.10 serves as a *sphragis*, aimed at the curious, the poet's 'candid reader', offering both an autobiography and an *apologia pro vita sua*. Its final, triumphantly defiant words vindicate the exile's poetic power. Yet the overall impression is of a virtual 'last will and testament', a dying artist looking back on his swiftly-ebbing life.

Phase 3: published during AD 13

In the third phase the exile's mood appears more anxious, his tone largely more conciliatory. Ovid is firmly established at Tomis now, longing hopelessly for home. Increasingly we hear a 'voice from the grave', alternating with suggestions of vicarious travel. The introductory poem, *Tr.* 5.1, semi-apologetically requests all interested parties to add this new book to their collections. It plaintively spells out the poetics of exile: what the exile writes is therapy, far removed from his former erotic works in tone and content. The coda offers a first intimation of the possibilities of vicarious travel. His works substitute for the man: his poetry can represent, even embody, the exile amongst his friends. *Tr.* 5.2 appears as 'half a dialogue': the exile questions the pallor of an anonymous friend (perhaps his wife) at receiving a missive from him. His miseries are described, largely in medical and nautical terms. His addressee must approach the emperor on his behalf. 'The god' himself is next addressed in thirty-two verses of direct supplication, as the poet begs to be allowed to come nearer home. The tone is obsequious, but the language is open to a variety of interpretations. The poem ends on a whimsical request for relegation to a place 'where he can be miserable in greater safety'.

Tr. 5.3 offers a prayer to Bacchus on his feast day (17 March), asking the god to intercede with Augustus. This is one of only a few addresses to deities other than the emperor himself (as embodied Jupiter). Notable is the poetic usage of the concepts of *fatum, numen* and *casus*, and the depiction of the poet as a servant of the patron-god of poetry. The coda requests his circle of poet-friends to compose poems under the patronage of Apollo, to keep alive Ovid's name. *Tr.* 5.4 has the poem acting as the personified ambassador of the poet, praising 'in its own voice' a kind and true friend. Third person verbs reflect the exile in an ostensibly new, 'objective' light, but with well-worn topics. *Exempla* evoking the beauties of the Italian countryside depict the poet's nostalgia.

Tr. 5.5, a potentially happy poem celebrating his wife's birthday, is heavy with the exile's personal misery. Even the smoke of his oblation tends towards Italy. All good things were born with her. His misery has made her famous. The poem ends on a prayer for long life for Caesar and for grace for the exile's wife. *Tr.* 5.6 picks up the theme of recalcitrance in a friend, exhorting him with mythical *exempla* to remain faithful. New is a suggestion that this friend may be angry with the exile.

Some editors suggest dividing *Tr.* 5.7 at the 25th verse; yet apparent divergence between the two halves of the poem may be ascribed to deliberate contrast, hence rather intricate ring-composition. The first 24 verses depict the miseries of life at Tomis. Next the poet discusses the popularity of his verses at Rome and the continued therapeutic value of composition, returning to comment on the uncivilised state of the local population, and ending with his problems of language and communication. *Tr.* 5.8 again reviles an anonymous enemy for unspecified harshness, warning him that man's fortunes can change. If the emperor becomes more lenient, the exile will be recalled. He prays for a *more serious charge* (than the 'trifling' one levelled against him) to trip up his enemy. In contrast, *Tr.* 5.9 once more celebrates a kind friend (possibly Cotta Maximus). Had this friend allowed it, all the exile's works would have been full of him. The poem ends on a death wish, turning the poem into a 'death-bed blessing'.

Time again becomes the subject. *Tr.* 5.10 commemorates the exile's third winter in Tomis. Time goes slowly. The barbaric Getae are wild, hirsute, cruel and menacing. The exile is the 'barbarian' here: no one understands him. The poem ends with a general complaint about the length of his life and the severity of his punishment. This is undercut by the coda, where, for the first time, the exile confesses to having deserved death. The next poem reflects a changed opinion and tone: *Tr.* 5.11 explains a technical point to his wife: she is not the wife of an *exsul*, but of a *relegatus*. Ovid has retained his possessions. His tone is comforting, complacent, with fulsome wishes for Caesar's health and earthly apotheosis: the gods must keep him out of heaven yet a while. Such disingenuous wishes in a poem written shortly before the death of the by now clearly ailing emperor could have struck a wrong note at Rome.

Tr. 5.12 contrasts in tone with the previous poem. The exile explains to a friend how misery prevents composition. If he writes at all, he burns his poems. He wishes he had done the same with the *Ars Amatoria*. In such an exile even Socrates would have been unable to write. Astute readers will remember that Socrates actually *wrote* nothing himself. *Tr.* 5.13, a 'real' letter, asks an anonymous friend to write. Letters are a good substitute for conversation. The exile is ill and miserable, ascribing his friend's silence to a letter having gone astray.

Tr. 5.14 ends the whole collection on a defiant but peevish note. The exile's tone is consistently more querulous in missives to his wife. Ovid's poetry is a monument to her which the world could envy. He praises her courage and fidelity, requesting her to *live*, not *die,* for him. The letter ends on an exculpatory note: she must not think he is blaming her, merely reminding her to do 'what she is doing anyway'.

Phase 4: published presumably during or after AD 14

This phase marks the greatest change in the poet's manner of keeping contact with Rome. The Pontic epistles are 'real letters' addressed to recipients by name. Friendship is celebrated in its various forms. Book 1 is redolent of penitent confession, but with a certain edge. *Ex P.* 1.1: The poet announces to his editor-friend Brutus that he is no longer hiding the names of addressees. This new set of three books must take the place of the three of the *Ars Amatoria.* The content, he says, is roughly similar to what he wrote before. A degree of acceptance of blame for his *error* is discernible, but Ovid's fulsome protestations of penitence strike a false note. The poem ends on a time-worn request: release from the Black Sea – if need be, by death.

Ex P. 1.2, to Fabius Maximus, an *amicus Caesaris,* approaches the great man with circumspection, graphically depicting the exile's misery and requesting intercession with Caesar. Hyperbolic descriptions of winter (his fourth) and warfare at Tomis alternate with assertions of the powerlessness of Rome in this barbaric area and appeals for legal aid. Protestations of innocence from earlier phases have now given way to simple confession. The exile appears both more desperate and more resigned. Flattering allusions to the emperor appear more fulsome, less ironical. *Ex P.* 1.3, to Rufinus, includes a didactic interlude on the general value of medicine for physical ailments but its impotence in healing a sick spirit. Sustained medical imagery is supported by mythical and historical *exempla*, among others the exiled Rutilius (verse 63), a victim of the Marian regime (of which the Julian family was the ideological heir). The exile remains grateful for friendship. The area remains bleak and dangerous, far worse than any exilic refuge in myth. Feeling, not fact, is of greatest importance. In contrast, *Ex P.* 1.4 offers a dispassionate description of the exile, worn out with age. Myths increasingly feature as illustration of his woes. Ovid's wife is regaled with all those aspects in which his lot differs from that of the heroic traveller Jason. Jason was *aided* by Cupid, whereas Amor *was taught* (with play on use of the double accusative with *docere*) by the poet. He imagines a longed-for reunion with his wife, now old and thin, but still beloved.

The next letters alternate between hope and despair. *Ex P.* 1.5 purports to offer (Cotta) Maximus an apology for the quality of the exile's poetry. (Both Fabius Maximus and Cotta Maximus are addressed as

21

'Maximus' but letters to Cotta are noticeably more intimate.) Reproach of his general readership for neglect predominates, the exile appearing bitterly resigned to having become a poet among the 'inhuman Getae'. *Ex P.* 1.6 sounds far more hopeful, praising Graecinus, 'whom the liberal arts have rendered sympathetic' and answering Graecinus' apparent query about Ovid's reasons for leaving Rome. Once again we have a plea of innocence: his only crime was 'wounding so great a god'. Medical imagery leads to a description of suicidal thoughts, restrained by hope, based on the ultimate goodness of the offended deity. *Ex P.* 1.7 avows friendship for Messallinus (Cotta's elder brother). This the exile is prepared to forswear, if necessary. Heavy-handed 'tact' hints darkly at the dangers of acquaintance with the unfortunate poet. The poem celebrates *amicitia* and its obligations. The exile begs that Messallinus intercede for him more intensively than strictly required by the conventions of *obligatio*, tactfully anticipating every nuance of thought that the great man may experience when reading the letter.

Ex P. 1.8, to Severus, subverts contrasting aspects of the traditional opposition between city and country. 'City' involves both Rome and Tomis, 'country', both Italy and the Dobroudja. Idyllic pastoral scene-painting is undercut by reality, in the Tibullan manner. The exile's imaginative visions of Rome and of becoming a 'local farmer' (even learning to drive his oxen in Getic) are undercut by intrusions of reality. Pathos, nostalgia, fantasy and reality shift and intermingle in this unusual poem.

Death and illness recur as binding topics in the next poems. *Ex P.* 1.9 takes up a new topic: the poet consoles Cotta Maximus on the death of their common friend, Cotta's client, Celsus, who had been very kind to the exile. The poem celebrates the duties of friendship, in particular, 'active aid to the exile': duty to the 'living' dead. *Ex P.* 1.10 tells a friend, Flaccus, about the exile's dismal state of mind and lack of bodily strength. The gloomy tone is unrelieved. Flaccus and his brother must pray for a diminution of punishment, not for recall. In an inversion of the stuff of Ovid's amorous elegies, the physical symptoms of his misery resemble the symptoms of 'being in love'.

The second volume of this collection reaches out widely to potential new helpers (particularly within the imperial family) without abandoning earlier addressees. *Ex P.* 2.1 starts with a 'public address' to Augustus' grandson Germanicus, reviewing Tiberius' triumph and prophesying great honours (following victories in Germany) for the younger general. The body of the poem consists of a graphic description of the trappings of a triumph. Its tone is generally conciliatory, and hopeful of reprieve (as expressed in the coda). *Ex P.* 2.2 differs sharply in tone: a humble but desperately defiant exile pleads with Messallinus to use his influence with the Julian family. The reader who has been following the fluctuations of Ovid's emotions over four years has the impression that the exile's friends, no less than the emperor himself, are deaf to all pleas, which each in turn appears as a 'first approach'. Here the poet poses as *praeceptor captationis*. Tactless references, with heavy emphasis on *pietas* (verses 73-4, 81-2), to the females of the imperial family (where only the two disgraced Julias actually carried the Julian name), may explain why none of the exile's prayers has prevailed.

Ex P. 2.3, again addressing the poet's *sodalis* (bosom friend) Cotta Maximus, celebrates the joys and duties of *amicitia*, with thanks for Cotta's continued loyalty and care not to 'incriminate' Ovid in the emperor's eyes. Once again the hereditary nature of obligation is stressed. *Ex P.* 2.4 continues in the same vein, thanking the exile's friend Atticus for his friendship and giving nostalgic vignettes of city life shared. *Adynata* expressing the poet's faith in his friend point the pathos of the exile's lot. *Ex P.* 2.4 continues this celebration of friendship: Salanus, formerly a mere acquaintance, has become the exile's friend through reading his poems, 'bad as they are'; Salanus trained the young prince Germanicus in the art of oratory. The coda expresses an obscure wish that Germanicus may one day succeed as 'ruler of the world', with Salanus' restraining influence to guide him – a wish that would not have endeared either to Tiberius.

Ex P. 2.6 offers the exile's friend Graecinus poetic immortality, in return for services rendered. As often, the exile, apparently afraid to offend, explains his gratuitous exhortation as 'speeding on' a fast ship or galloping horse. *Ex P.* 2.7 voices a despairing cry to his friend Atticus: the exile has suffered much. The gods and fortune are against him. Circumstances at Tomis are terrible. No one is in a worse position than he. Even the truculent Getae pity him. Some friends still aid him. Atticus must stay loyal.

The next two poems deal with the ruling elites of Rome and Thrace. *Ex P.* 2.8 thanks Maximus Cotta for the gift of 'portraits' of the imperial triad, which the exile has placed in his household shrine. (Of various interpretations I favour the idea that Cotta had sent him money: coins with Augustus on the obverse, and Livia and Tiberius on the reverse, a common mint in the last years of Augustus' life.) The whimsical poem shows the 'portraits' looking angry, but by its end softening their expressions. References to the rest of the emperor's family are tactfully vague, but a bias towards the Claudians is increasingly discernible. *Ex P.* 2.9 addresses Cotys, king of Thrace, a 'barbarian prince' civilised by the humanities: common interests make colleagues of exile and king, binding them by ties of mutual obligation. Complimentary praise of the king's achievements in the liberal arts, 'surprising in a barbarian', are blatantly tactless. Explanations of the poet's mysterious 'crime' lean toward his *Ars Amatoria,* brushing over his *error* with *praeteritio*: 'don't ask what it was'.

Next the poet returns to his friends. *Ex P.* 2.10 contrasts with the new outreach of the previous poems: Macer, a friend of his youth, is reminded nostalgically of their common interests, travels and pursuits. The exile recalls (in clear reference to Callim. *Epigr.* 2.2-3) they shortened the day with conversation on their journeys together, requesting present aid, and ending with a graceful conceit, 'hold me in your heart, for there it is warmer'. His tone is generally cheerful.

Ex P. 2.11 concludes the book. While thanking Rufus, his wife's uncle, for aid to them both, the exiled poet offers him *hoc ... opus* (verses 1-2), leading some scholars to argue that this poem should be placed at the end of Book 3, as conclusion for the whole collection. There is no reason, however, why this cannot be graceful acknowledgement of one friend within a three-volume collection entrusted to another (Brutus).

The third book frequently features geographical or anthropological aspects of the Tomitan area. Appendix II offers translations of three of its poems. *Ex P.* 3.1 begins with an apostrophe of the sea and the Tomitan landscape, explaining why Ovid wants to leave. His wife is then bitterly reproached for her apparent neglect. 'He has given her a name before all others' and she has done nothing. The poet next waxes didactic, composing an *ars precandi*. Elaborate preparation required for approach to the empress suggests oriental despotism and cruel unpredictability in the imperial household. *Ex P.* 3.2 again celebrates friendship. Cotta Maximus is told about those friends who deserted him through fear, whom the exile grandly forgives. True friends receive his thanks. Friendship is so precious that even the local barbarians appreciate it. Then follows an epitome of Euripides' *Iphigeneia in Tauris*, as 'told by an old Getic man', illustrating the friendship of Orestes and Pylades. *Ex P.* 3.3 again presents a tale within a tale: Fabius Maximus is told of a dreamlike epiphany of the god *Amor*, travelling all the way to Rome to exonerate Ovid of all moral censure and to prophesy future happiness, especially after Tiberius' projected triumph.

Tiberius' triumph features again in *Ex P.* 3.4, a *recusatio* addressed to Rufinus: begging pardon for the 'poor quality' of the triumph-poem. A dreary tone is relieved by various conceits: the elegiac metre represents a chariot limping along on oddly-sized wheels. The exile is drawing from memory, relying on his 'mind's eye'; other poets can give first-hand reports. Finally Livia is enjoined to rejoice in her son's triumph, evoked in a brief cameo. Whether this *is* the entire 'triumph'-poem, or whether a more elaborate poem has been lost, cannot be established. The reader is also left wondering what has happened to Augustus, whose name does not occur.

The third book experiments with changes of topic and tone but old friends are not forgotten. The idea of the 'mind's eye' develops into vicarious 'mental travel'. *Ex P.* 3.5 thanks Cotta Maximus for a copy of a speech, complimenting him on its style and substance, hoping for more gifts of a similar sort, and whimsically offering to serve as rhetorical *exemplum*. In a nostalgic evocation of Roman life, the exile mentally visits Rome and converses with friends. *Ex P.* 3.6: Novelty here lies in suppression of the addressee's name. A long and elaborate eulogy praises the kindness and clemency of Caesar, 'who need not be feared', while evincing touching affection toward the unnamed friend.

The next poem displays a profound change of tone, seemingly marking the nadir of the exile's hopes. *Ex P.* 3.7 purports to be an open letter, addressed to all his friends. They must be *so* tired of always hearing the same complaints. The poem breathes a new resignation, refusal to be a burden to the poet's wife and friends. The psychological stages of despair are sketched, from emotional dullness to acceptance of his destiny, alternating renewal of hope with certainty of destruction. The exile finally advocates gentle capitulation, rather than resistance, but, as an afterthought, disingenuously suggests that 'his friends have perhaps, after all, *not yet* approached Caesar on his behalf'.

Ex P. 3.8 is the accompaniment of a gift to a friend, a Scythian quiverful of arrows, the only type of reeds and 'pen-box' available at Tomis. A 'Maximus' is named in the last lines of the little 'note'. *Fabius* Maximus has been suggested as the addressee, the arrows then being poison-tipped 'vengeance' for the fate of the emperor's friend, as described by Tacitus, *Annales* 1.6. More plausibly, this poem is meant for *Cotta* Maximus, the gift, reciprocation for the gift of silver imperial portraits of *Ex P.* 2.8 or the copy of Cotta's speech from 3.5. The poem is part complimentary conceit, part subtle complaint about the harshness of the Tomitan landscape.

Ex P. 3.9 closes the collection. As in the previous poem, geography is again the theme. Ovid's editor Brutus (recipient also of *Ex P.* 1.1) is told that the harshness of the place of exile has drained the poet's powers. The poem is an *apologia pro scriptis suis*: apparent monotony of content should be ascribed to the fact that individual letters were meant for different addressees. Further, because original composition is a better palliative for his woes, the poet avoids 'taxing' revision. Finally, Brutus must forgive all flaws: the exile composed not for glory's sake, but for the sake of 'utility' and 'affection'.

Phase 5: published perhaps posthumously, covering the years AD 14 to 17

The controversy, whether this last book, the fourth of the Pontic Epistles, was arranged in the order we have it by the poet himself or whether it is a haphazard collection randomly compiled by his executor, is largely unresolved, but both the first and last poems appear functionally placed. The poems (which, where datable, are not in chronological order) are almost equally divided between address of public figures and the exile's friends, most of them fellow-poets. Most addressees are new, with emphasis on the coterie of the imperial prince, Germanicus.

The first poem, *Ex P.* 4.1, as dedicatory poem, apologises playfully and gracefully to the consul-designate Sextus Pompeius for not having addressed him before. Similarly, *Ex P.* 4.2 excuses the exile for not having addressed his friend Severus before. The poem appears as a didactic parody, replete with agricultural references: Severus, a successful poet, tills a *fertile* field; Ovid's field is *sterile and dry*. The style is as easy as ever and the tone is light. Here, famously, writing poems, without an audience to hear the poet recite them, is compared to 'dancing in the dark' (33-4).

An unnamed faithless friend is reproached in *Ex P.* 4.3 for not supporting the exile, even actively insulting him. He is reminded that Fortune can change people's lot, with the exile himself as the supreme example. *Ex P.* 4.4 is a whimsical celebration of the impending consul-ship of Sextus Pompeius, the dedicatee of the volume (an event datable to AD 14). Congratulations serve as springboard for the depiction, once more, of exile. Personification of *Fama* and the device of the 'mind's eye' frame a graphic depiction of Pompeius' impending inauguration at Rome. Next, *Ex P.* 4.5, a conceit ostensibly addressing the poet's elegiacs, again celebrates Pompeius' consulship. The poems, as the exile's emissaries, will find the hero at Rome, discharging his consular duties – one of these being the safeguarding of his 'gift', the life of the exiled poet.

Ex P. 4.6 mournfully comments to Brutus on the death of Fabius Maximus. The fact of Augustus' death (also datable to 14) receives passing mention, as having also taken place some time before. Fabius 'would have prevailed' with Augustus, the exile laments, if death had not intervened. This diffuse poem features various arguments and compliments, leading to a request that Brutus take over Fabius' mediating role, and ending with the thought that only a reversal of all nature could make the exile forget his friend. Ovid's admiration of Brutus sounds rather forced: the exile takes great pains to turn into a virtue Brutus' known caustic tongue.

Next *Ex P.* 4.7 eulogises Vestalis, prefect of the Pontic coast and son of a Ligurian client king, calling him in as eye-witness to testify that the exile's complaints are justified (for instance, about the frozen state of the sea). This poem appears elegantly wrought, aimed at impressing: Vestalis' victory over Aegisos in AD 12 is depicted in epic terms. The coda reminds the hero that Ovid's poems have testified to the great deeds of Vestalis: he expects a favour in return.

Friends influential with Germanicus are approached. *Ex P.* 4.8 is ostensibly aimed at Suillius, husband of Ovid's step-daughter. The exile's *curriculum vitae*, attached, seems aimed at Suillius' friend and patron

Germanicus, praising him as both military victor and fellow-poet. Germanicus shares Apollo's facility with 'both kinds of strings' (the lyre and the bow). This graceful, elegant poem ends whimsically with an allusion to Suillius' 'almost-father-in-law', the exiled poet. Next, *Ex P.* 4.9 addresses the influential Graecinus, celebrating his impending inauguration as consul (datable to AD 16). The exile pictures in his mind's eye his friend in office, and envisages the consulate of Graecinus' brother Flaccus, fixed for the following year. Again, Flaccus can testify about adverse conditions at Tomis. Yet, even here, the inhabitants have come to like the exile. They see how Ovid honours the Caesars: he hopes the Caesars, too, will notice this, especially the 'games' he celebrated on the birthday of the new deity.

With the next poem we are back at AD 14, the 'sixth summer' of exile. *Ex P.* 4.10 addresses a fellow-poet, Albinovanus Pedo. Ovid is worse off than Ulysses. The topos of time wearing away all else but the exile's misery leads to a discussion of winter at Tomis. Why the sea freezes is explained: it is augmented by many rivers (listed in a ten-verse catalogue), whose fresh water, being lighter than the salty sea water, forms a top stratum which easily freezes. Ovid explains that his excursion into science was aimed at entertaining himself. He next urges his poet-friend to continue composing his *Theseis*, while emulating its hero in faithfulness, with the usual rider: he is merely encouraging Pedo's proven fidelity. *Ex P.* 4.11 purports to console another poet-friend, Gallio, on the death of his wife, adapting the trappings of the consolatory tradition to Ovid's own circumstances. Gallio's grief is akin to exile. The poet refuses to trot out the trite consolatory sayings of others. The topos of time assuaging grief is tied to the 'fact' that one exchange of correspondence between Rome and Tomis takes a year. The coda (perhaps a reflection of the realities of Roman social life) seems callously jarring: by the time the letter reaches Gallio, he may even have happily remarried.

Poetics are never far from our poet's mind. In *Ex P.* 4.12 Ovid ingeniously explains to Tuticanus the difficulties of accommodating his name within the elegiac metre: neither a spondaic nor a dactylic foot works. Various 'wrong' versions are dismissed in playful *praeteritio*. Tuticanus and the exile meant much to each other, both as poets and as friends. A series of *adynata* for the first time includes 'mitigation of the exile's lot' as an 'impossibility'. The poem ends abruptly with a request that his friend must himself decide, and pray for, what is best for the exile. *Ex P.* 4.13 offers poetics of a different kind: in a discussion of recognisably individual style, the exiled poet compares himself unfavourably with his addressee Carus. He confesses to having composed in Getic, an assertion that has been variously received. His recitation of a poem in honour of the imperial family evoked wonder and sympathy in the natives. The poem ends with a request for continued support, contrasting the uselessness of Ovid's poetry with Carus' useful talent, that needs feeding by 'much imperial military activity'.

The natives' reactions are, however, not always favourable. *Ex P.* 4.14 tells Tuticanus about a new problem: the place is as terrible as ever, but now the Tomitans (miraculously able to read Latin) have taken offence at what the exile wrote about them. Once more Ovid's poetry has harmed him. He protests his innocence on all counts: he may hate the place (as have many native citizens before him) but he *loves* the Tomitans. They are kind and pleasant and have heaped honours upon him. Tomis is to him as Delphi was to Leto in her wanderings. Tomis is dear to him – if only it could be safer and warmer. This is difficult to reconcile with all that was written before. *Ex P.* 4.15 conventionally thanks Sextus Pompeius for all his kindness. Stock but suitable similes are adapted to a list of Pompeius' possessions. The exile seldom intends to ask to be moved: these requests arise of themselves, from an inner compulsion. The theme of the poem is that the exile is Pompeius' 'possession', his metaphorical slave.

The book ends on a subdued note. *Ex P.* 4.16, at first reading, seems almost flat. The collection has wavered in address between public figures and private friends. This poem addresses an unnamed enemy, purporting to be a mere versified catalogue of contemporary poets, of which the exile considers himself a not undistinguished member. Ovid is the last in the list, following his friend Cotta Maximus, 'a great poet and a great man'. The last expression of emotion at the end – of the poem, of the collection, of the book, and presumably of the exile's life – is a dull, animal cry of despair to Envy to stop torturing a body that 'has no more place for new pain'. Yet behind this despairing cry looms the same conviction that the poet trenchantly asserts at the end of the *Metamorphoses*: Envy can do its worst, Ovid's poetry has gained immortality, no matter what blows his body continues to experience.

This, then, is the unfolding narrative that Ovid's Roman readers followed as (over almost nine years) they unrolled missive after missive arriving at sporadic intervals from the Pontic area. These are the poems that survived for two millennia, triumphing in the end, and giving the desolate Roman that immortality he endlessly promised his wife and friends, if only they would help to facilitate his return. Of the fluctuations in the exiled poet's personal, emotional and intellectual life this book strives to make some sense.

1

Persons and personalities

1.1. Error and the imperial household: an angry god and the exiled Ovid's fate

Where in the past critics have tended to take at face value most of what the poet chose to write from exile, recent criticism has shown an increasing awareness of Ovid's propensity for irony, also during exile. Central to the interpretation of the *Tristia* and *Epistolae ex Ponto* lies the question of the relationship between the exile and the emperor, the *raison d'être* for the poems. The topic may be approached with reference to the past, that is, the reason for exile, the present, involving the degree of sincerity or irony in Ovid's adulatory approach to the emperor, and the future, which is frequently touched upon in the exile's requests for clemency.

The exiled poet's relationship to the imperial family is also involved. Allusions to Livia and Tiberius need to be judged on the level of 'sincerity versus irony'. Germanicus appears in the last phase of composition as the central object of appeal. None of these personages seems ever to react to the exile's almost endless appeals. Judgment of both the poet's initial *error* and his attitude to the imperial family needs to consider personages not mentioned by the exile, but apparently looming large in the consciousness of both poet and readership: the exiled members of the imperial family. Here, more than in any other aspect of the poetry, we must try to evaluate the degree of irony involved.

Stylistic considerations, the poet's use of traditional material, and Ovid's attitude to the emperor in other parts of his oeuvre can serve as pointers for the judgement of irony. I have postulated a distinction between creator-poet, suffering man, and heroic exile, while conceding that the three personalities are not always identical, or diverge to a varied extent in different parts of the exilic oeuvre. Through synthesis of these divergent elements, we may, ultimately, gain a more balanced impression of the realities of exile and of the poet's achievement. A preliminary distinction between 'exile' and 'poet' can serve as tool for disentangling a complexity of attitudes. Continued awareness of the *poet's* penchant for irreverence aids us in putting the *exile's* most abject pleas into perspective. In, for instance, *Tristia* 2, ostensibly humble pleading often shades off into either tactless gaucherie or apparently deliberate irony. A shadowy figure appears to be standing behind the exile, saying 'So, Augustus, you wanted celebration in poetry? Here is the celebration of your much-vaunted *clementia* – with a vengeance!' However, it is impossible to determine whether the exilic poems (*not* real 'letters', but literary productions) were ever read (or meant to be read) by Augustus himself.

This section attempts to determine the exile's attitude to the emperor and his family and to judge the poet's intention with its portrayal, including its possible effect on his contemporaries and on posterity. The exile's attitude to his *error* (and to the emperor) appears to change considerably over the years. It is unsafe to assume consistency in a notoriously elusive poet and even more dangerous to quote indiscriminately from poems separated by as many as eight years, when we try to build up a picture of the exile's attitude to the emperor and his family. The chronological 'phases of composition' postulated in my Introduction can serve as a guide in discerning progression in the exiled poet's thought.

It is futile to add to the mountain of conjectures about the nature of the *error* for which Ovid was exiled. Some have tried to link the banishment of Ovid and Julia Minor more explicitly than the poet himself does. Of greater interest is the manner in which the poet refers to his *error*, and the information which the exile gives. As will be shown in greater detail in Chapter 4, cursory allusions to the exile's 'fault' or 'mistake' become consistently fewer over the years of Ovid's exile. The poet's use of the words *crimen, error, culpa* and *fateor* shows a decrease in relative frequency from the first to the last phase. This may appear as only natural, the result of the passage of time, but we may assume a certain reservation on the poet's part in Ovid's apparently humble acceptance of the justness of Augustus' punishment. Perhaps, when the exile has become convinced that his pleas for recall are in vain, he simply ceases to admit to feelings of guilt that he never really experienced.

The poet has two different ways of referring to his 'error'. Cursory, passing allusions tend to show certain common elements, e.g. *lumina viderunt* ('my eyes saw'); *inscia lumina* ('unwitting eyes'); *error ... causa exsilii mei* ('a mistake ... the cause of my exile'); *non facinus ... sed ... error* ('not a misdeed but a mistake'); *qua perii culpam, scelus esse negabis* ('you will deny that the fault whereby I perished is a misdeed'); *negabis ... mali* ('you will deny ... any evil [intent]'), and so on. Longer, more extensive explanations differ most in their details. Common elements are *rogare desine* ('stop asking'), and allusions to the *vulnera* ('wounds') or *dolor* ('pain') of Augustus. The technique of *praeteritio* actually revives these painful memories every time the poet pretends not to want to do so, perhaps to titillate the curiosity of a general readership, or perhaps to amuse those friends who circulated his poems privately.

1. Persons and personalities

Over time the reader becomes no wiser as to the nature of the poet's *error* except that it was something personal affecting the emperor (or his household), that it was not illegal, and that Augustus had a possibly vindictive reason for inflicting such a heavy punishment on his hapless and inadvertent antagonist. Let us examine some late examples. The explanation of the *error* at *Ex P.* 1.6.19-26 lays most emphasis on the poet's stupidity and culpability, explaining that it is neither *breve nec tutum* ('short nor safe') to write down the origin of his *peccatum*. The exile's wounds 'fear to be touched'. The word order of the central couplet (21-2) is singularly prosaic. Its starkness bespeaks intense feeling:

> *nec breve nec tutum peccati quae sit origo*
> *scribere; tractari vulnera nostra timent.*

I can't just do it briefly, and it's not safe either, to write out what the source of my misdemeanour was, and my wounds fear to be handled.

At *Ex P.* 2.9.67-76 the exile denies having 'mixed poison' for anyone, or having committed forgery. No law was broken. The poet is criticising the sense of justice of a ruler who banished a Roman citizen for something other than a legal transgression (71-2):

> *nec quicquam, quod lege vetor committere, feci:*
> *est tamen his gravior noxa fatenda mihi*

And I didn't commit anything which I am legally forbidden to do: yet there is an even graver offence that I have to confess to.

The hint of 'something else' in the pentameter is not amplified. The two couplets that follow refer cryptically to the *Ars Amatoria*, indicating that the poem is only part of the reason for his exile: the other part does not bear close enquiry.

As Chapter 2 will show more extensively, a demonstrably ironic description of the apparition of *Amor* (*Ex P.* 3.3.67-76) has the ragged god swearing a solemn oath by his weapons, by Venus and by the head of Caesar, exonerating the *Ars* from containing any 'crime', and expressing the cryptic wish that the 'other reason' could be so easily vindicated. Culpability is imputed to the exiled poet, who is reminded that, although he might wish to hide his 'crime' under the 'mask of error', the anger of his antagonist was deserved. In the unreal context of a grotesque apparition, the accusation loses its force.

Studies of the exile's implicit attitude to Augustus tend increasingly to read his treatment by the poet as strongly critical. The tone is set at *Tr.* 1.2.1-4, where the hapless exile calls on the gods of sea and sky not to

31

subscribe to the greater god's ire. Augustus is unquestioningly treated as 'divine'. Fear of Augustus' *ira* points to an 'angry god'. Allusions to a life spared register not so much gratitude as acknowledgement of Augustus' power over life and death. Mythological *exempla* (Phaëthon, Niobe, Odysseus) indicate the persecution of a human by a god because of real or imagined transgressions (see Chapter 5).

To pre-empt another aspect of Chapter 4: the exile has a very particular way of referring to the emperor throughout exile. Words for 'gods' or a 'god', *Jupiter*, *deus* and *numen* are most often applied, not to the Roman pantheon, but to Augustus and his family. Identification is not absolute in all cases, wavering between simile and surrogate. In certain poems such allusions are extensive. In the largest proportion of the exilic poems there is at least one reference to the emperor as a divinity. Taking *Tr.* 2 (in which the divinity of the emperor is assumed throughout) as one poem, 75% of the poems of the first phase exhibit this characteristic. This proportion increases to 93% in Phase 3, dwindling to 69% in the last phase (which partly reflects the years after Augustus' death). Where the final apotheosis of the emperor is not explicitly mentioned, divinity is transferred to his successor. That this adulation is tempered by irony is likely. Negative terminology for the emperor far exceeds occurrence of positive terms. In his *Res Gestae* (34.2) Augustus lists as his especial attributes the positive terms *clementia, iustitia, iustus, moderor, pater patriae, parens, mitis, lenis*. The cult of the *clementia Augusti* formed a part of the imperial propaganda. Our poet clearly had difficulty in citing instances of the emperor's *clementia*. Some refer not so much to factual attributes as to hoped-for but never attained favours.

In context words for 'divinity/ providence/ fate' (*deus, Jupiter (Jov-) divus, numen, fortuna, fatum/ fata, fatalis*) and for 'anger' (*ira, iratus, irascor*) are grammatically closely intertwined, most often by means of nominative-genitive phrases, suggesting that Ovid's use of divine terminology implies a largely negative attitude. These decrease in frequency from first to last, with minor fluctuations. Most frequent are variations on *numinis ira, Caesaris ira, ira dei, ira laesi dei*, colouring the exile's approach to the emperor, both regarding his *error* and his own present state as the thunderstruck victim of an angry god that exacts a terrible vengeance for an unspecified wrong.

Ovid's apparently bland acceptance of Augustus' divinity reduces to absurdity the careful approach to Hellenistic flattery in other Roman authors, emphasizing the hollowness of Augustus' vaunted restoration of religion. The emperor has usurped the very position he sought to restore to the ancient gods of Rome. Every vain appeal, throughout almost a decade, adds another *tessera* to the mosaic portrait of a capriciously ruthless man-god swaying the world with his nod, all other Roman divinities swept from the board. Allusions to the divinity of the emperor almost wholly supersede allusions to the Roman (or Greek) pantheon, except by implication and with reference to the relationship of emperor and exile: an extension of the lampoon quoted by Suetonius (*Aug.* 70) which circulated after a blasphemous 'divine banquet' perpetrated in his youth by Augustus and eleven companions.

The 'gods' of the exilic works are Augustus and his family, spelled out as such in, for instance, *Ex P.* 2.8, an elaborate and possibly ironically meant poem, thanking the poet's friend Cotta Maximus for the gift of silver portraits of the imperial triad, which the exile promises to set up for daily worship in a magnificent shrine. This adulation has been interpreted as a sincere attempt by the poet to find some kind of religious fulfilment and (the imperial divinities failing him) his final recourse to adoration of a more satisfactory deity, his Muse. Yet our poet himself elsewhere states that 'poetry creates gods': the gods *need* poetry to write them into existence (*Ex P.* 4.8.55-6). Such creation would apply as much to the imperial gods of the exilic poems as to the Graeco-Roman pantheon.

Our poet's creative power presents the emperor in a rounded-out *persona*: a gloomy and terrifying figure, a relentlessly silent thunderer, who struck once, and may strike again (e.g. *Tr.* 2.179-80). This poetic creation probably has very little relation to the reality of an ageing emperor beset with imperial and dynastic problems, of which moral reform and the propagation of a national cult formed but a small part. This apparently all-powerful figure is simultaneously shown to be less powerful than he claimed to be. Consistent portrayal of the warlike aspect of Ovid's place of exile, lying outside the *pax Augusta*, negates many of the political claims of the *Res Gestae*, illustrating Augustus' powerlessness (as ineffectual saviour-god of the Roman state) to implement peace.

Our poet has not lost his sense of humour. The inconsistency of his picture of divinity on the one hand, offset, on the other, by frequent prophecies of apotheosis announced with the fervour of a *vates*, 'speaker of divine truth', indicates ridicule rather than adulation. Ovid blandly exploits the embarrassing dichotomy inherent in all Hellenistic-ruler-panegyric. As frequently noted, the imperial apotheoses of *Met.* 15 compare unfavourably with the poet's own claim to immortality. So, too, the final statement of Augustus' (re)apotheosis (*Ex P.* 4.13.23-6) is set in the ridiculous framework of an alleged *recitatio* held in their own barbaric tongue before quiver-bearing savages, who clash their arms and growl approval. The poet's statement of the immortality accorded him by his Muse (*Ex P.* 4.16) is couched as a powerful rebuttal of the power of *Livor*.

Studies of the treatment of Augustus in *Tr.* 2 suggest that both as *controversia* and as *recusatio* the poet's judgement of the emperor is negative. As a prayer for clemency the exile's approach in *Tr.* 2 appears critical, occasionally verging on irony, even satire. Here Ovid's appeal is first extended beyond the emperor to his family. *Tr.* 2.161ff. (with its possibly barbed allusions to the emperor's conjugal relationships and suggestive allusions to his dynastic and personal disappointments) strongly indicates slippage between ostensible and real meaning. As blandly ingenuous *captatio benevolentiae,* it appears both stylistically (with prominent anaphora and alliteration) and generically (as prayer) so carefully, over-elaborately contrived as to invite doubts about the exile's intentions with such adulatory hyperbole. At best, the poet's greatest fault appears to be want of tact. This passage has been read as an exaltation of Livia above her husband as the 'power behind the throne', even as the elegiac inversion of a woman to a position far above that of her lover-husband.

Ovid's portrayal of the emperor as an 'elegiac lover', simultaneously also faithfully and single-mindedly married to a *univira*, the mother of his stalwart sons, without whom he would have been doomed to celibacy, is incongruous at various levels. We need only reflect on Augustus' own various marriages, those of his sister Octavia, his daughter Julia, and his cavalier coercion of Agrippa and Tiberius into divorce and remarriage for the sake of dynastic policy, to see the hollowness, if not downright immorality, of the Augustan idea of marriage, and to read irony in *Tr.* 2.233-4:

> *Urbs quoque te et legum lassat tutela tuarum*
> *et morum, similis quos cupis esse tuis.*

> The city, too, [exhausts you] as does enforcement of your laws
> and morals, which you want to be like your own.

Whether any Roman, even Ovid himself, would have interpreted Augustan marriage policies as immoral, is open to conjecture. However, the exile's picture of his own married fidelity (as reflected in his loving outreach to his wife in various letters) emphasises the superiority of private emotion above public affairs. Hellenistic practice equated the wives of rulers with goddesses, either openly, or as allegory. Ovid's treatment of Livia as the Juno-consort of Augustus-Jupiter is fraught with innuendo.

The Julio-Claudian web of propaganda included various other goddesses beside Venus as mother of the Julian line, and Juno as the protector of the sanctity of marriage. Of these, most important were Vesta, goddess of the home, Concordia, to whom Livia dedicated a shrine (obliquely featured in *Ex P.* 4.13.29) and the Magna Mater, a syncretic conflation of various matronly goddess-figures. Tiberius, on his return from Rhodes, brought a statue of Hestia-Vesta to place in Concordia's shrine (Dio 55.9.6). *Ex P.* 1.1 has extensive allusions to the cult of Isis and the Magna Mater, appearing to endorse Livia's known favouring of this largely composite divine figure. The irreverent tone of the whole excursus undercuts any serious interpretation of the poem as honouring Livia, either as Isis or as the Magna Mater. Furthermore, the exile incongruously claims that he 'bears the Julian names like a rattle before him' (*Ex P.* 1.1.45-6). His tone is bland, but the possibility of irony cannot be discounted.

The *Fasti* serves as an interpretative model for much of the adulatory tone of such allusions to Livia. Echoes of Julio-Claudian discord in the poet's ironical treatment of Concordia (who disagrees with Juno and Hebe about the naming of the month of June, *Fas.* 6.89-100) colour our view of Livia's cultivation of these goddesses. It has been suggested that Ovid's tale, in *Fas.* 4.85, of Juno giving birth to Mars *without Jupiter's aid* as a result of jealousy of Jupiter's similar production of Minerva (Athena) is a figment of Ovidian irreverent imagination. Verses 293-300 of *Tristia* 2 list a series of mythical sons born of divine mothers. Irreverence is possible at any level. Innuendoes about Tiberius' 'looking and acting just like his father' (*Ex P.* 2.8.31-2; 4.13.27) appear as cruelly tactless allusions to Tiberius' chronologically late adoption by his stepfather into dynastic and familial succession.

Only if we deny all possibility of a consistent web of divine allusion to the imperial family can we accept adulation of these divinities at face value. 'Cross-referencing' leads to an awareness of irreverence, even if the reader finds it difficult to believe that the poet had an ironic intention. An innuendo coupling the statues of Venus Genetrix and Mars Ultor (*Tr.* 2.295-6) refers to the old Homeric tale. If the pervasive divine metaphor is logically extended, an earlier allusion to Tiberius as the martial counterpart of Augustus-Jupiter (165-78) and application of this martial role to Tiberius' position as Livia's son, makes of the joke a vicious inversion of the Homeric tale: Venus-Julia left Mars-Tiberius out in the cold, while she consorted lewdly on her father's forum. For the rest, except for one reference to Livia's godlike beauty and morals (*Veneris formam, mores Iunonis, Ex P.* 3.1.117) and *Amor*'s oath by his mother (*Ex P.* 3.3.68), the Julian Venus seems deliberately to have been avoided in the exilic poems.

Stylistic considerations seem consistently to point to the possibility that *Ex P.* 2.8 is strongly ironical. The fulsome gratitude of the exile for the gift of silver representations of the emperor and his wife and adopted son (whether statuettes, medals or coins) shifts into a prayer, addressed in turn to the members of the imperial triad. Verses 29-30 repeat the innuendoes of *Tr.* 2.161, with a ridiculous sexual *double entendre* in [*Livia*] *cui maiestas non onerosa tua est* ('Livia, for whom your majesty is not [too much of] a burden'). In a rather charming conceit the angry visages of the divine triad soften during the course of the poem, playfully displaying the familiar Ovidian sense of fun.

The most extensive treatment of Livia serves as an *'Ars precandi'* (*Ex P.* 3.1). Its preamble is longer than the body of the poem. For more than 100 verses the poet first sketches his position, querulously calling upon his wife to aid him, offering her immortality, and praising her fitness to do his bidding, offering mythological *exempla* of virtuous wives as potential inspiration. Finally, in masterly *praeteritio* (119-24) Ovid exaggeratedly 'refuses' to equate the empress with a series of seven monstrous females from myth, thereby underscoring the ostensibly negated resemblance. The approbation of *Fortuna* that Livia enjoys (125-6) is portrayed as negative, for by verse 152 the animosity of Fortune is spelled out: *hostem fortunam sit satis mihi* ('Let it be enough that Fortune is my enemy').

Elaborate directions for choosing just the right moment to approach the august lady evoke instructions to an elegiac pupil on how to approach his mistress. Assumption of an artificial role is prerequisite for approaching the Caesars: tears and prayers will prevail. Capriciousness, a playful aspect of amatory intrigue, appears as monstrously irresponsible rigidity in the *grande dame* of the state. The equation Livia-Juno is completed at verse 145. The somewhat incongruous expression *non mortales ... pedes* ('not mortal feet', 150) is in line with the terminology of Hellenistic ruler-panegyric.

Tiberius is generally more elusively designated. His ability as general features sporadically, particularly in allusions to his triumph in the first half of *Ex P.* 3. The 'prophecy' of a triumph in *Ex P.* 3.3 is, however, placed in the mouth of the sorry-looking, bedraggled Amor, who has come from Rome to Tomis to vindicate the poet's earlier works. The incongruity of the exile's bedroom as the setting for a divine epiphany and the ridiculous exchange between the erstwhile *praeceptor amoris* and his wayward divine pupil undercut the solemnity and ostensible earnestness of the 'prediction'. Such instances can be multiplied.

An explanation of Tiberius' imperial accession in *Ex P.* 4.13.27-8 appears to parallel Tacitus' version so closely that one wonders whether Tacitus perhaps had the passage in mind when he wrote *Ann.* 1.12. The exile claims to have explained to the quiver-bearing Getae (at his famous *recitatio* that drew their growling approval with a barbaric clash of arms) that Tiberius, 'who now held the reins of Empire, after having frequently been requested, and refusing, to do so', was 'equal in virtue to his father': [*docui ... Tiberium*] *esse parem virtute patri, qui frena rogatus/ saepe recusati ceperit imperii.*

The poet's appeals to Messallinus and Cotta Maximus, known to have been close associates of Tiberius, cease in the last four years of exile (except for an allusion in *Ex P.* 4.16 to Cotta as poet) and the coterie of

Germanicus takes over. Peter Green has noted that various appeals to Germanicus (*Ex P.* 2.1; 2.4; 4.8; 4.13) show warmth and liking. He guesses that Ovid's natural sympathies were always Julian, rather than Claudian. There is the common tie of poetry (*Ex P.* 4.8.67) but the exile has earlier prayed for Germanicus to succeed to imperial rule (*Ex P.* 2.5.75) – a rather dangerous prayer for the disgraced exile to utter. At *Ex P.* 4.5.25 and 4.8.23 Germanicus is allocated divine status. Suillius, the son-in-law of Ovid's wife, Germanicus' *quaestor*, is exhorted to 'prayer', in an awkward plural-singular coupling. The bare boldness of the appeal is striking: *di tibi sunt Caesar iuvenis. tua numina placa* ('The young Caesar is your gods. See to it that you please your divinities'). Germanicus clearly assumed mythical stature after his death in AD 19. It would appear that Ovid aided the process while both were still alive. However, if appeals to Augustus are to be treated as ironical, as I have sought to do, these appeals also require caution. Yet the poet neither harmed nor was harmed by Germanicus, and so their relationship was less complex.

The triumph poem *Tr.* 4.2 has sometimes been seen as a recantation of Ovid's light-hearted approach to national themes in the *Ars Amatoria* and *Amores*. It refers in passing to various members of the imperial family, including Germanicus, and Drusus, son of Tiberius, at whose expense his father had been coerced into adopting the 'Julian' Germanicus, son of the older Drusus. Allusion to the female members of the imperial household is more significant (4.2.11-12):

> *cumque bonis nuribus pro sospite Livia nato*
> *munera det meritis saepe datura deis.*

And may Livia, with her good daughters-in-law, frequently give well-deserved gifts to the gods as thanks for her son's safety.

The ornamentally elegant *hyperbaton* of the hexameter refers to Tiberius. The prominent phrase *cumque bonis nuribus*, referring presumably to Agrippina, wife of Germanicus, and Livilla, wife of the younger Drusus, carries with it, by contrast, a reminder of *nurus* that have proved not to be 'good'.

A problem of Ovidian criticism is the influence of the reader's preconceptions. We tend to assume that, as the poet 'must have been writing these poems to achieve his recall', therefore allusions to the imperial household 'could not have been other than positive'. When such allusions seem negative, we start doubting the evidence of our senses, or think that we have an incomplete grasp of the temper of the times. Why would the poet have risked his chance of recall by treating the emperor and his family in this way – why compound his *error,* so to speak? Flippancy

37

would have been grossly irresponsible, an indictment of the emperor as cruel despot, dangerous, *if Ovid had really been trying to end his exile.* We begin to distrust our own powers of observation.

Further, the bland assumption that the poet had of necessity to resort in his appeal to elegiacs, the poetic form that caused his downfall, needs qualification. The talented author of the *Metamorphoses* was adept at hexameter composition, a medium possibly more suited to earnest appeal. There was no reason why such appeals should have been couched in poetic form. To assume that the exiled poet 'could not do otherwise', or that his flippancy was an automatic, unintentional and ineradicable feature of his style, is to deny the greatness of Ovid's achievement in the rest of his oeuvre. His continuation of an essentially non-serious approach must be interpreted as deliberate, demonstrating to Augustus that the playfulness of the offending poetry was a matter of style rather than attitude.

Other conjectures may be essayed to explain the exile's irreverent, often apparently vindictive, attitude to the imperial family. First, the poet may have felt that his appeals were superficially flattering and adulatory enough for him to risk some dangerous fun, always with the possibility of retreat to the surface level, if taxed with his irreverence. Second, the poems may have been sent to Rome for private circulation, and never really intended for the emperor's perusal (as, for instance, it may be doubted whether *Ex P.* 2.9, tactlessly praising King Cotys' 'remarkably good poetry for a barbarian', was ever read by the Thracian monarch). The poet possibly knew that the emperor normally ignored lampoons, and assumed that negative or flippant aspects of these poems would be similarly treated, had Augustus become aware of them. Fourth, perhaps the exile, soon realising that his sentence would never be repealed, consoled himself with barbs only half-hidden in ostensibly guileless appeals he knew would be fruitless. After *Ex P.* 3.7 the exile no longer appeals to his wife, having long since ceased mentioning any possibility of return, appearing resigned to asking for relegation to a 'safer' area.

A recurring theory (treated more extensively in the *Excursus*, pp. 229-30), is that Ovid's exile was totally fictitious. Such a theory would neatly endorse interpretation of the poems of exile as a vigorous indictment of the emperor's policies of literary censure. It postulates the invention of physical exile for the poet, perhaps when his *books* were banned after the Julia Minor debacle of AD 8. Association of poet and poetry, as in *Tr.* 1.1 and 3.1, where the 'little books' go to Rome as the exile's ambassadors, would then mean the 'exiled poet' is speaking for his 'banned books'. However, this attractive theory does not serve to explain the palpable emotional intensity of a poem such as the poet's autobiography, *Tr.* 4.10.

More acceptable is an explanation which in a sense accommodates and extends the first four: interpretation of Ovid's exilic poems as the creation of *the myth of exile*. This topic is treated in Chapter 5, but serves as theme throughout this volume. Our heroic exile displays the propensities of all mythical heroes, standing alone in a mythical world where malevolent nature conspires with a relentlessly angry god to persecute him. The hero is comforted and sustained by an all-powerful goddess, his Muse. This is essentially a literary approach. For Ovid the poet, literature was life. In the poetry of exile, this fusion is shown at its most complete. At this level it is immaterial whether the exiled poet had resigned himself to non-recall, or whether the author of books banned through imperial moral zeal had decided to retaliate by means of his poetry. He has created the myth of exile, and with it the genre of poetic exilic autobiography.

A last consideration may be tentatively entertained: the subliminal synergetic effect of the literary activities of a truly great artist. Just as the *Metamorphoses* essentially deals in *victims*, so the exilic poetry also treats of *victimisation*. With two millennia of hindsight, we can more easily distinguish within the voice of the exile the voices of other imperial victims, from the early victims of political give-and-take on the proscription lists of the second triumvirate (Cicero is the prime example) to victims of early jealousy (the poet Gallus as Prefect of Egypt was forced into suicide in 26 BC) and early dynastic rivalry (Sextus Pompeius, termed in *RG* 25 a 'pirate'), to later victims of imperial power-struggles (Mark Antony, a 'faction' in *RG* 1.1, and possibly too his son Iullus Antonius, the 'lover' of Julia Maior), to the pitiful victims of Augustus' dynastic aspirations.

The loneliness of a Vipsania, wife of Agrippa, divorced from Tiberius so that he might marry Julia, and of Tiberius himself, fleeing from an uncongenial marriage and apparently upstart stepsons (see Dio 55.10.19 on Gaius' cavalier treatment of Tiberius at Rhodes), had never been given expression. No one had written of the earlier suffering of Scribonia, mother of Julia, put away for producing a daughter and because her political connections rendered her 'neither worthy nor useful'. Scribonia had later joined the disgraced Julia, sharing the loneliness of her daughter's exile. A Roman reader might not immediately have thought of Julia, when he read the heartfelt cry *Parce, pater* ... ('Spare me, father!' *Tr.* 2.179,181), but by hindsight we see that both Julias were as much the victims of Augustan moral legislation (perhaps also of imperial autocracy) as the poet. His appeal takes on the piquancy of *double entendre*.

The loneliness of Agrippa Postumus, exiled close to the Italian mainland, but unable to reach Rome, and finally, all the longings and heartaches of other victims of the aged despot appear to our modern perceptions to have gained a voice. The embodiment of this voice could not have endeared himself to the emperor. Even the memory of the child of Julia Minor, exposed as an infant in AD 8, may, by an effort of our imagination, be read into the poet's playful personification of his works. The mourning of a mother over the death of her child, illegitimately brought forth against laws promulgated by its great-grandfather, may be found vaguely embodied in the words of the poet mourning over his 'children' that harmed him (*Tr.* 1.7.20 *viscera nostra*, 'my innards', a term usually applied to the fruit of the womb).

Finally, if the exilic poetry is essentially about victims, also the victims of loneliness, then it shows both Ovid the exile as victim of the emperor Augustus, and the emperor (with his wife and stepson) as victims of Ovid the poet. Virgil demonstrated that Aeneas' achievement could only be reached at the cost of much personal suffering. Augustus as the 'embodiment of Aeneas' had experienced much suffering and was in his old age disappointed, possibly embittered, at having outlived those upon whom he had pinned his hopes. The loneliness of outlived hopes is perhaps no easier to bear than the loneliness of exile, and it has no voice. The loneliness of Ovid's perhaps unjust accusations, to which the ruler could give no other answer than a dignified silence, is conjectural. At the remove of two millennia we cannot judge what Augustus' feelings could have been when he read *Tristia* 2 – if he did indeed read it. We merely know that a subjective portrayal by a perceptive and talented genius has stained one of the last deeds of the emperor a questionable colour from which not one assertion of moral rectitude can cleanse it. In the end, perhaps, the emperor's *error* was greater than that of the poet.

Ovid has created a monument that celebrates the power of poetry to transcend totalitarian oppression. In the playful personae of the poet's 'little books' and in his hymn to his transcendent Muse we hear the voice of literature and a literary consciousness that would not be silenced. That topic needs further exploration. We start with the poet's identification of himself with his poetry.

1.2. Ovid's wavering identity: personification and depersonalisation

Ovid's *Metamorphoses* has, as its essential theme, the depersonalisation of human beings into other forms. It deals in impossibility, requiring a suspension of belief in the rational – in both poet and reader. The exiled poet himself frequently refers to the work as his poem on *mutatae ... formae*, in which he appears not wholly to believe. In *Tr.* 4.7.11-20 Ovid calls into question the concept of metamorphosis in an excursive *adynaton*. Here he features aspects of the *Metamorphoses*, 'which he would rather believe than ...'.

The poet takes pains to explain that he is *relegatus* not *exsul* ('banished', not 'exiled', *Tr.* 5.9.22), yet frequently refers to his loneliness and desolation as tantamount to *exsilium*. When he is required to 'believe in' his own exile, this exile displays the incredible aspect of metamorphosis. Exile is an *adynaton* that has come to pass (*Ex P.* 4.3.51-4). In his loss of opportunities to participate in Roman urban life, this most urbane poet experiences his own metamorphosis into an outcast as a form of depersonalisation, a concept inherent in the formal Roman terminology for the loss of civil status preceding exile, *capitis diminutio* (diminishing of his 'head', or authority).

The complement or reverse of depersonalisation is personification, involving another impossibility: the 'humanising' of animals or inanimate objects. Personification, like the *adynaton*, involves a blurring of limits: between man and animal, animate and inanimate, author and works, or creator and created, even between concrete and abstract. Suspension of disbelief is requisite. All personification of the non-human is essentially a type of *adynaton* that has come to pass. Like the true *adynaton*, personification seems to have its roots in a pre-literate, psychological perception inherent in humanity. It can convey either playful humour or pathos. Humorous aspects of personification are largely lacking in Ovid's exilic works. For the exiled poet, personification offers a useful means of conveying the pathos of his psychological reaction to loneliness, imbuing inanimate objects with human qualities, for lack of real human contact. Yet the poet's sense of humour did not absolutely desert him at his departure for Tomis. Ovid's sense of fun sometimes influenced his use of the device, as will emerge from discussion below.

'Pathetic fallacy' is the term for the imputation of human feeling, particularly sympathy, to either nature or inanimate objects that are not fully personalised, that is, the fallacious impression that sentient nature concurs with the subject of emotion in his grief or joy. In early Roman culture, with its animistic and numinous conception of the forces of nature, awareness of these forces as sentient was perhaps stronger and more ubiquitous than in the Greek anthropomorphic belief-system involving a clearer distinction between human and non-human, requiring a more definite transgression of these limits with personification.

Fränkel's coinage, 'wavering identity,' is an appropriate designation for Ovid's multivalent presentation of the *self* in his poetry. Fränkel tendentiously imputed to our poet an almost Christian awareness of the *other*, the *non-self*. Yet the term is a useful critical tool for pinning down, or labelling, aspects of our elusive poet's multi-faceted self-awareness. The most extensively worked-out conceit, involving such 'wavering,' in Ovid's earlier poetry, occurs in the charming and witty *Am.* 2.15, where the lover wishes that he could become his own gift, a ring, yet retain his most apposite human quality, his virility. Interchange of identities here involves personification of the ring and depersonalisation of the lover.

41

Below we shall consider Ovid's exhibition, in his exilic poetry, of a 'wavering identity,' his use of the related literary devices, personification and depersonalisation, to convey his psychological reactions to exile. We need to establish how far the exiled poet either personifies the non-human, or depersonalises himself in his self-depiction. Again chronology is important for establishing whether the passage of close on a decade of exile made any difference in the poet's use of these complementary devices. Insofar as the application of such statistics is valid, it is noteworthy that use of personification increases from the first book of the *Tristia* to the last book of the *Epistolae ex Ponto,* from an average of about 1.4 occurrences per hundred verses to something in the order of 3.5 occurrences.

There are distinct degrees in the conceptualisation of personification. As a specialised form of personification, apostrophe of the non-human is often no more than a useful means of scene-setting. The tendency to apply to non-human objects the nouns, adjectives and verbs that indicate human functions is a mere extension of metaphor, non-literal diction. Such 'personification' is purely ornamental, lending itself to vivid or pathetic depiction. It has no wider symbolic outreach. A bold application of a 'human' adjective serves as ornament, but can also add graphic point, as with *peregrinis columnis* for 'imported marble' at *Tr.* 3.1.61 in the description of the temple of Apollo on the Palatine. The phrase supports the sense of *Barbarus ... pater* (Danaus, who incited his daughters to kill their foreign bridegrooms). Such lexical transpositions to the non-human may be termed 'petrified personification', as in *Tr.* 3.12.9-10, where the poet speaks of swallows building 'cradles' (*cunas*) or *Ex P.* 2.1.36, where rocks graphically 'blush' with roses. Use of the convention is often dictated by metrics. More complete personification is involved in the conceit at *Tr.* 5.5. 35-6, where the continued enmity of the two Theban brothers is shown by the diverging smoke of their funeral pyre: even at their obsequies, their enmity continued. Such a contrived conceit, in an apparently pathetic context, tends to distance modern readers. Typically Ovidian wit here appears out of place.

The examples quoted above belong in the category of 'ornamental flourish.' Ovid's functional use of personification falls into two broad categories relating to the central themes of exile. There is, on the one hand, a consistent picture of malevolent nature conspiring in support of the human forces that oppress the exile. Here the pathetic fallacy is almost consistently negative. Elsewhere literature and the exile's own mental powers each take on an independent personality, the poet wavering between *identification with* and *consolation by* such 'independent personalities'. Personified objects act alternately as his surrogates or his companions. Where poet and poetry merge, the poet undergoes a process of depersonalisation.

1. Persons and personalities

The poetry of exile exhibits many of the typical characteristics of elegy in a new setting. Conventional *topoi* such as personifications of *dolor, ira, decor, timor*, and *cura* appear in passing. For references for these and similar concepts see Appendix I (pp. 252-3). More important and consistent are the several occurrences of *livor*, where the concept takes on the malevolent personality of a human oppressor. *Livor* is traditionally carping Envy, trying to suppress the poet's voice. Such personification serves as veiled metonymy for the poet's imperial persecutors. *Livor* may be scanned as the prosodic equivalent of both *Caesar* and *Livia*. Ovid elsewhere shows a fondness for *paronomasia* (verbal play involving two similar-sounding words). He may be deliberately echoing the first syllable of Livia's name while suggesting the emperor's name through consonantal *homoeoteleuton* (two words ending on the same letter).

Positive qualities may also be personified. *Pietas haec mihi Caesar erit* ('This faithfulness will act as a Caesar for me', *Tr.* 1.3.86), the departing exile's wife urges when she wants to accompany him. Here the process of personification is complex. 'Caesar' has been depersonalised to an abstraction, the *necessity* or *force* that is driving the exile away. The equation of *pietas* as a virtue with an impersonal force has in its turn been personified by the introduction of the emperor's name. Other personified virtues are *gloria, voluntas, facundia, gratia, voluptas, virtus*.

Youth, age, times and seasons have traditionally lent themselves to personification. The first two are conventionally depicted in the exilic oeuvre. The poet's treatment of time is, however, often strongly personified. In *Tr.* 1.3 the moon indicates both timeless serenity and the passage of time on the night of the exile's departure, time being marked by reference to a personified celestial and meteorological phenomenon. Times and seasons are part of malevolent nature conspiring against the exile. Sometimes 'personification' is limited to the employment of a 'human' verb, as at *Ex P.* 4.13.39-40 where the 'sixth winter *sees* the exile in his suffering'. At *Tr.* 3.13.3-6 the exile reproaches his birthday for having *followed him* to Tomis, in a conceit that concretely applies the pathetic fallacy. Verses 7-8 reproach Ovid's birthday for not having allowed the poet to remain in the same place where as a baby he was 'first unfamiliar' (*male cognitus*) with it, an inversion of the *topos* of 'the place where someone first was known'. Again a charming but contrived conceit serves to distance modern readers without extending their perception of pathos. Invocation of the stars and a prayer that they will spy out what the exile's wife is doing and whether she still remembers him offers stronger pathetic appeal (*Tr.* 4.3.1-10).

The poet's extensive use of the Bear constellations to place his exiled home 'directly beneath the Pole Star' offers a prime example of complex and allusive personification, with various levels of abstraction and concretisation. The constellation is personified as the unfortunate

43

maiden Callisto, whom readers remember from *Met.* 2.401-530 as one of the first of Jupiter's victims, saved from her predicament by transposition to the stars, that is, by depersonalisation. Now she is equated with the poet's oppressor, who, if the Jupiter-Augustus equation is carried to its logical conclusion, turns out to be the originator of her woes. This complex allusion gains in piquancy in the light of the tradition, recorded by Suetonius, *Aug.* 80, that Augustus had a birth-mark on his chest resembling the constellation of the Great Bear.

From the beginning, the Getic shore is depicted as inimical. The hostile impression conveyed by puns on *sinister/ Euxinus* (meaning both 'on the left' and 'inimical') is strengthened by frequent personification. At *Tr.* 1.11.31-2 the reader is told that the 'left-hand shore' of the Black Sea is 'held' by blood and war. This impression is progressively strengthened. In the first four phases, words from semantic fields pertaining to human activity indicate a certain degree of personification. In a poem from the poet's first year of exile, the *place* either *sees* or *fears* (*aut videt aut metuit*) the enemy (*Tr.* 3.10.69). Its shore is *robbed* or *bereaved* (*orba*) of harbours (*Tr.* 3.12.38). Later, it is *poor* (*inops*) in peace, and its waves are *chained* by ice (*vincta*, with a variant, more literal, reading *iuncta*, *Ex P.* 2.2.94). It *teaches* (*docet*) by its fruits how bitter it is (*Ex P.* 3.8.16), for the only gift it can send (*mittere posset*) is a quiverful of poisoned arrows (verse 2).

By the time that the exile is writing the last book of the Pontic epistles (AD 14 or later) the country with its river has become fully personalised. It is a (not wholly malevolent) sentient being. The Hister *allows* (*non negat*) Vestalis to display his courage, and the hostile city of Aegisos *felt* (*sensit*) that its natural talents were unequal to the fray (*Ex P.* 4.7.19-22). At the last, the Pontic land can even act as a *witness* (*testis*) who *knows* (*scit*) that the exile celebrates with games 'the birthday of the recent god' (*Ex P.* 4.9.113-16). Here *Pontica tellus* serves as a metonymic expression for its inhabitants. A second look at this passage brings certain doubts. Are these funeral games, or games dedicated to the god, or perhaps a metaphor for joy evinced at the death of the oppressor? Are these games a fact of exile or a fiction of *obsequium*? If the picture of the Pontic region has so far been consistently unpleasant, is the 'calling to witness' of such an unreliable source not a pointer to irony? Does the 'birthday' refer to the emperor's official day of *birth* or to the day of his *death* and presumed apotheosis? It is difficult to decide.

The exiled Ovid frequently plays with the idea of being already dead, his poetry dirge-like. The *Tristia* and *Epistolae ex Ponto* exhibit a strong affinity with the techniques and approach of funerary epigrams, particularly in use of the pathetic fallacy. Death is a prominent theme. Yet toward the end of the last book (*Ex P.* 4.10.8) comes the surprising statement: *duritia mors quoque victa mea* ('Even Death has been defeated by my hardship'). This is a far cry from the kind of resolution of pain offered by, for instance, pastoral dirges, where death is resolved by the cyclic continuation of nature. Virgilian pastoral treats of death and the problems of exile and dispossession, but in pastoral the bereaved is consoled by sympathetic nature. The harsh setting of the world of Ovidian exile is anti-pastoral in the sense that it is antipathetic. Man and nature are at terrible odds.

The active conspiracy of malevolent nature against the exile is paramount in the storm poetry of *Tr.* 1.2, 4 and 11. The tone is set at *Tr.* 1.2.1-4: sea and sky gods underwrite Caesar's wrath. These are not personal powers, but impersonal numinous forces that have gained a malevolent personality. The borders between numinous and natural waver. More directly, there is identification between exile and ship, which *groans* (*ingemit*) over his lot (*Tr.* 1.4.10) and which he in his turn pities for being *tired* (*fessa, Tr.* 1.10.20).

Here, as elsewhere, wordplay implies personification. *Syllepsis* (combination of disparate nouns as objects of the same verb) illustrates the belligerence of the storm at *Tr.* 1.11.27: *simul insidiis hominum pelagique laboro* ('I simultaneously labour against the onslaughts of men and the ocean'), and by use of 'human' verbs at verse 41, *pugnat hiems, indignaturque...* ('Winter fights against me and it is indignant...'). Knowledge (or lack of it) can be imputed to these personalised beings. At *Tr.* 1.2.26 the wave does not know (*nescit*) which ruling wind (*domino*) to obey. The powers of sea and sky know (*scitis*) that the exile is innocent (*Tr.* 1.2.97-8). Finally, feeling for him and supporting him in his innocence, they subside (107-10). The culmination of their personified characteristics is 'to set a good example' to Caesar. These beings, believing in the exile's innocence, have withdrawn their persecution; hence the 'great god' must follow suit. The exile at *Tr.* 1.4.21-2 exploits the pathetic fallacy, exhorting the wind to 'obey' the great god with him (*quaeso ... mecum ... pareat*). Personification of the winds has been a conventional topos throughout classical literature. The traditional names of the winds lend themselves to 'humanisation'. So in the last book from exile, at *Ex P.* 4.10.41-2, the poet can claim the Pontic area as the '*birthplace* of Boreas, the place whence it gains its power (*vires*)'.

Inversion of the pathetic fallacy (unsympathetic nature and dehumanised people) develops strongly from about the third year of exile. *Locus* and *homines* are consistently malevolent natural forces conspiring to oppress the exile. The adjective *inhumanus* is applied to an impersonal 'barbarity' (*barbaria*) at *Tr.* 3.9.2, but to the Getae themselves in later poems. People have been depersonalised, the place personified, in a relaxation of the normal borders between animate and inanimate, the exile's perception of reality seeming to waver. At *Tr.* 5.7.43-52 the Getae are depicted as 'scarcely human, unworthy of the name' (*vix ... homines hoc nomine digni*) and 'fiercer than wolves'.

We turn next to extension of the exile's identity, particularly in his use of personification of abstract concepts. Against four fully elaborated allegorical figures in the *Metamorphoses*, namely *Invidia*, *Fames*, *Somnus* and *Fama*, the exilic works have individual personifications of abstract qualities as part of their metaphorical fabric. Such personification, as with Ovid's allegorical figures, renders them more concrete and therefore more 'real.' Here such figures seem, for want of a better term, more intensely 'personalised', involving autobiographical self-revelation. *Fortuna* occurs fairly frequently, always with a negative connotation, as at *Tr.* 1.5.34. Elsewhere the exile's fate is a 'ghost' that haunts him (*Tr.* 3.8.35-6). The poet's *Fama* is usually identified with him, as at *Ex P.* 1.5.83-4 (where it appears as an equally pathetic victim of the decree of exile) and *Ex P.* 3.1.47 (where it complains 'in his stead'). His *Fama* becomes the exile's *alter ego*, with a distinct personality, but identified so closely with him that at times their identities merge. At *Ex P.* 2.1.1 it is depicted as having 'won its way' (*pervenit*) to the distant Pontic region. *Fama* features only once, at *Ex P.* 4.4.11-20, as a fully separate, personified abstraction, bringing news to the poet of Sextus Pompeius' consulship. It is a far more sympathetic apparition than Virgil's famous monster from *Aen.* 4, acting as a substitute for the friendly daily intercourse that the lonely exile lacks.

Extension of the exile's identity is not limited to identification with his reputation. The concept of mental travel and the mind's eye (e.g. *Tr.* 4.1.57, *Ex P.* 4.4.45) grows in importance through the exilic years, offering the exile a surrogate existence and extending his outreach towards the familiar. The frequency of words denoting mental activity, as opposed to physical anguish, is significant. Positive mental activity, visualisation of scenes removed in time and space, informs a large part of the exile's existence, lying behind frequent use of the word *imago* for what is essentially 'memory,' as in the poet's depiction of his last night in Rome (*Tr.* 1.3.1).

The concept of mental vision occurs explicitly four times in the first four chronological stages (representing the first six years of exile). It occurs as frequently again in the last stage, comprising poems from the last four years of the poet's life. The efficacy of such psychological escape from an unpleasant present may be read from the poet's evocation of Roman scenes. Urban scenes are graphically described in *Tr.* 3.1, supporting the poet's thesis that he can actually return to the city by means of his imagination. In *Ex P.* 1.8 an unrealistically idealised projection of himself as gentleman-farmer on the Getic shore contrasts with a far more convincing, graphic evocation of his friend Severus engaged in the daily round at Rome, moving from the Campus Martius to the porticoes of the city, or along the Via Appia from Umbria to his Alban estates. Projection in time as well as space also feeds the meagre resources of an exiled present, as in *Ex P*. 1.4.47-54, with the exile's realistic evocation of reunion with his wife. Such existential consolation is passionately stated at *Ex P*. 4.9.41: 'the mind alone is not an exile'.

Poetry is frequently personified. The syntactic construction consisting of the pronominal adjective *mea* and a feminine or neuter noun as the antecedent of a masculine relative pronoun introducing a verb in the first person occurs at *Tr*. 1.5.41, *causa mea est melior, qui non contraria fovi/ arma* ... ('my cause is better, [I] who did not favour enemy arms ...') and *Ex P*. 3.4.91: *nec mea verba legis, qui sum summotus ad Histrum* ('and you don't read my words, [for I] am removed to the Ister'). This fairly common poetic construction is not so much a matter of *ad sensum* syntax as of basic psychological reaction, a blurring of the distinction between the first person 'I' and his cause or his work. This is personification of a sort, involving identification of creator and creation. Ultimately the exile's consolation lies in such extensions of his personality.

The convention personifying poetic creation occurs from Pindar (*Nem*. 5.2ff.) onward. Personification of individual poems, of his books, of his talent as his Muse, and of Elegy itself (involving punning on metrical 'feet') is typically Ovidian, occurring frequently in the *Amores*. Such personification can be casual, involving use of 'human' parts of speech and parts of the body as ornamental flourish, or it can form the basis of a consistently worked-out conceit, for instance, of his book as the poet's child, as in *Tr*. 1.1, 3.1 and 5.4. This type of personification seems, by the end of the *Tristia*, so well established that it consistently informs the poetic apparatus of the *Epistolae ex Ponto*.

The establishment of the convention is progressive. *Tr*. 1.1 is a monologue. The exile instructs his book as his ambassador, child and surrogate, to go to Rome. The appearance of the book (3-8) is the opposite of an ancient luxury edition, with instructions to its publisher to keep it so. The term *incultus* (verse 3) 'unkempt', 'rough', perhaps even 'unshaven', plays on Catullus *Carm*. 1, where the little book is 'neatly polished' and trim. Verse 8 runs *candida nec nigra cornua fronte geras*. It has been suggested that *nec* should be read with *candida* rather than with *nigra*. The translation could be either: 'And you must wear black knobs on your [dingy] front' or '... horns ... not very clean forehead'. The book's general dishevelment is a sign of mourning. In Roman custom tokens of mourning were displayed both by the bereaved at funerals and by the accused and his relatives in a court of law, to evoke sympathy, even his children being displayed dressed in mourning. The book acts as a surrogate for the poet in this sense also: the dilapidated book is the poet's mournful child.

This conceit, once established, occurs in passing at *Tr*. 1.7.20 (*viscera nostra*): the poet plays with the idea of his children as having 'perished with their parent'. This is inverted from verse 35 onward, where a new prologue is proposed for the *Metamorphoses*, 'orphaned volumes, bereaved of their parent', *orba parente suo ... volumina*. Such apparently contradictory inversion is typically Ovidian, an incongruous extension of *Tr.* 1.1.111-16, where the books of the *Ars Amatoria* are depicted as 'parricides'. As always, our poet has managed to evoke a multiplicity of meanings with a single ploy. Ovidian wit delights in the conceit, regardless, or perhaps even because of, the contradictions inherent in its literal application.

The progressive identification of poet and book continues in *Tr.* 3.1, where the book itself is the speaker. With this device the poet can speak with the tactless naiveté of a child. The conceit lends itself well to both playful pathos and playful irony. Ovidian *topoi* such as 'limping' elegiac feet gain new life with reference to the long journey from Tomis (11-12). The assurance that the book does not 'teach how to love' (4) is at once an allusion to the ostensible cause of his exile and a pointer to the pathos of the apparent futility of the poet's attempts to gain sympathy. Ovid dwells lovingly on the buildings of Rome which the little book 'sees' for the first time, while it looks for a place of publication. The public libraries, gifts from Augustus to the nation, are passed by. There is pathos, but also irony, in the fact that not even the library attached to the temple of *Libertas* (Freedom) will receive it. At last the book finds a place in private homes, turning to the broad reading public. The coda (81-2) affirms the greater value the poet attaches to his general readers than to imperial patronage, rejecting the current sycophantic stance of contemporaries. This may be construed as a glancing attack on literary censorship.

The charming conceit of poems as the author's children gets a new (and insidious) twist at *Tr.* 3.14.11-14. The exile explains that, like Pallas Athena, his children (*stirps ... progeniesque*) were produced by him 'without a mother'. Such apparently playful mythological ornament has several layers of meaning. Zeus gave birth to Athena from his head, that is, she is an intellectual product. So is poetry. No woman was involved. The poet's past life that produced his erotic poetry was therefore blamelessly intellectual, with no women involved. However, Athena, like all Zeus' children, was the object of Hera's jealousy. The equation Zeus-Jupiter-Augustus would make of Livia 'Hera' and of Julia 'Athena', with the implication of stepmotherly *animus*. If this is stretching interpretation too far, there is a more obvious parallel. Zeus-Jupiter was known for his extramarital adventures. So was Augustus. Finally, Augustus had no son to follow him and had banished his daughter and lost his grandsons. He had no true *progenies*, in the basic sense of the word. Against this the poet affirms his own cyclic continuity after death, his immortality through poetry.

The degree of identification between poet and poems varies. Even considering the autobiographical nature of the exilic works, we can usefully distinguish between Ovid the creative poet and Ovid the suffering man, whose moods the poet records. Identification of a subtle nature may be discerned in *Tr.* 5.4, where the personified poem speaks, not as naive observer, but as an advocate who is fully cognizant of all facts. The ploy lends objectivity, externalising the poet's plea. The poem-*persona* describes the poet as weeping during composition (a variation on the elegiac *littera-litura* conceit). Finally, it can ask 'what he does not' (49-50), that its addressee look after the exile's interests. The conceit enables the poet to demand once again, through a mouthpiece, what in his own person may seem repetitive importunity. Behind the ploy of a surrogate lies a further psychological ploy: the ostensible reader (the addressee of a poetic, literary epistle) and the real reader (Ovid's reading public) know that the voice of the exile is speaking through his poem. The exile knows that they know. Therefore it is really still Ovid who is estab-lishing contact with his Roman readers. The identities of exile and ostensible speaker have merged fully, yet the independent personality of his poetic creation appears as 'another *persona*'.

This convention has become firmly established by the beginning of the Pontic epistles. It consistently wavers between surrogate *for* (as in *Ex P.* 1.1.5-10) and identification *with* the exile. Such identification is expressed at *Ex P.* 2.6.3 *praebet mihi littera linguam* ('my letter offers me a tongue'). With it has developed, also, the convention of Ovid's 'comforting Muse', first fully established at *Tr.* 4.10, in his grand invoca-tion to his Muse (verses 117-24), leading up to an assured statement of the poet's own immortality. This 'Muse' frequently stands, not for an externalised inspiring deity, but for both the recipient of such inspira-tion, the poet's intellect (as in *Tr.* 5.9.26 or 5.12.60) and the product of his inspiration, his poetry (*Ex P.* 3.9.49). There is a constant shift between these three meanings of the word. The circle is completed by a fourth aspect, identification of Muse and exiled poet as active creator of his works. The essential message of the verse, *pro se Musa locuta mea est* (*Ex P.* 3.4.66, 'my Muse spoke for herself') may be conveyed prosaically as, 'I defended myself and my poetry by means of poetry'. However, such a rendering destroys the poetic force of the verse, inherent in Ovid's powerful personification of poetry as an independently creative and sentient being.

During the last book of the Pontic epistles a conscious separation (or perhaps stronger differentiation) between the varying degrees of identi-fication of the poet and his works may occasionally be discerned. *Ex P.* 4.2.25 speaks of a non-personal *impetus ... sacer qui vatum pectora nutrit* ('a sacred ... force that feeds the hearts of poets'). Later in the same poem (45) the Pierides are termed *solacia frigida*, 'cold comfort'. Yet at *Ex P.* 4.3.16 the exile equates himself fully with his Muse. He reproaches an erstwhile friend, now a bitter enemy: formerly this man had admired his talent. Verse 16 occurs in a series beginning *ille ego* ('I am that he ...'), with its epitaphic (and pseudo-Virgilian) resonance, recalling their past friendship: *ille ego iudiciis unica Musa tuis.* There is no copulative but the correlation is clear. Identification is complete: 'In your judgement I was the unique Muse'. However, personified *Ex P.* 4.5, again portrayed as a separate personality, is sent as the poet's 'ambassador' to the consul at Rome. Here we have personification but non-identity, or only identity at remove. The degree of identification has wavered once more.

In a final inversion, our poet is depersonalised. Inversion of conventional personification is an inescapable concomitant of most Ovidian conceits, as in the ring-poem, quoted above (*Am.* 2.15), where personification of the ring in the end leads to identification of gift and lover, that is, depersonalisation of the lover in his desire to become an attractive object.

We have seen that no very strong pattern of arrangement obtains in *Ex P.* 4, which appears as a loose collection of poems from Ovid's last years. Yet in Ovid's use of the device of depersonalisation, this book displays a progression that is more psychological than chronological. Perhaps 'retrogression' is a better term. In the first poem of *Ex P.* 4 Ovid makes explicit exilic depersonalisation. The exile denotes himself a 'creation' of the consul Sextus Pompeius, a thing. This he illustrates by reference to a series of works of art. He begs Pompeius to look after this creation. The conceit works as a serious but contrived and elaborate compliment. It appears typical of the psychological debilitation and alienation caused by loneliness or long isolation, symptomatic of loss of a sense of identity, as Chapter 6 will show.

Fluctuations of identification between poet and poetry occur in the poems that follow, as discussed above. Total depersonalisation reappears in *Ex P.* 4.15, also addressed to Pompeius. This poem illustrates the various threads of Ovid's use of personification, yet its chief thrust focuses on depersonalisation. At verses 13-14 the exile begs the consul (known for his wealth) to place him 'amongst his possessions'. Noun-adjective *hyperbaton* in the hexameter graphically illustrates the exile's request: *inter* **opes** *et me, parvam rem, pone* **paternas**/ *pars ego sim census quantulacumque tui* ('Please place me, a little bitty thing, among your ancestral goods/ I am part, however small, of your estate'). This playful request is elaborately recast as emphatic statement in verses 15-20, leading to the further request that Pompeius remove his insignificant possession to a better location.

The poet reverts to the human mode in verses 25 to 37, with accent on the cerebral rather than the physical. Verse 37 assures Pompeius of the exile's unforgetting regard, but 38 reverts to the idea of the exile as 'a possession', a virtually inanimate 'thing'. Personality and sentience are taken over by his Muse, who, the exile hopes, will transcend malevolent nature as represented by *feros ... Getas* (39-40). Ovid's Muse finally will recognise (*norit*) Pompeius as guardian of the welfare of his possession, without reference to *libra et aere* (41-2, a scale and bronze ingot, the formal symbols of sale in Roman commercial practice, cf. Gaius *Inst.* 1.119-22). The roles of creator and creation have been reversed. Although this poem is clearly an elaborately wrought compliment, involving conventional ornament of different kinds, depersonalisation of the exile to inanimate object sounds a note of psychological urgency.

The transition from inanimate 'thing' in *Ex P.* 4.15 to 'dead body' in the last poem is slight. In *Ex P.* 4.16 the exile wavers between being dead (verse 1), to having been a name only (3), to being his own immortal Muse (45-6), to being dead (47), to having (being) nothing except sentient life (49), to being a dead body (51), to being (having) no room left for blows (52). All limits – between life and death, extinction and immortality, feeling and being, body and spirit, personification and depersonalisation – have been blurred. These shifts and contradictions, familiar to readers of the poet's earlier, witty love poetry, here combine to create a sombre conceit with powerful impact. No matter that the strong rebuttal of carping *Livor* (47-52) portrays its victim as 'dead.' Depersonalisation of the victim here, has, as final paradox, shown the creative poet Ovid as immortal and able to transcend the restrictive bounds of exile. This last poem, with its compelling cry of psychologically urgent anguish, is the living poet's final triumph over the unmoving imperial authority that sought to still his poetic voice. The metaphorical death of the exile has ensured the continued life of the poet.

Poetic *nequitia*: the constant factor

We have seen that Ovid's attitude to his own work and to the imperial family is more nuanced than he is sometimes given credit for. Further, interpretation of Ovid's poetic intention and emotional evocation in any part of his oeuvre differs widely from critic to critic, particularly with his exilic poetry. Generations of critics happily accepted at face value Ovid's own strictures on the poetry sent from the ends of the earth as desperate appeals for aid or forgiveness. Even an esteemed critic like Wilkinson was satisfied to accept the poet's claim that the exilic works were 'monotonous'. Although these approaches are no longer as fashionable as before, they need to be finally laid to rest.

Discovery of the poet's own attitude to his art is more difficult than appears at the initial cursory reading of the exilic poetry. Appearances are not always what they seem. Differentiation of *personae* and of topics and time are of value. As in *Heroides* 15 (the letter of Sappho to her lover) – whether by Ovid or not – where the creator-poet, ostensible poetess and suffering woman, although merged in one articulate voice, may be distinguished, the creator-poet of Ovid's exilic poetry and the articulate exile must be judged differently, if only as a point of departure, with the intention of their ultimate reintegration.

When dealing with this most irreverent of poets, we need to acknowledge, even with the exilic poems, the poet's humorous bent. Ovid's *nequitia* ('levity', rather than 'wickedness') is the constant factor that binds the diverse aspects of his oeuvre. This chapter starts with detailed study of fluctuations of tone within the exilic books, and continues with detailed analysis of a single poem. *Ex P.* 3.3 is a subtle example of the exiled poet's art. Its analysis will serve to indicate the thrust of much that I shall present in subsequent chapters, and it will offer a paradigm for a less serious and less literal interpretation of the exilic oeuvre as a whole.

2.1. Structure, chronology, tone and undertone: tonal variation

The issue of 'monotony' needs to be dealt with first. Was the content of the exilic poems lugubriously monotonous? As with other aspects of Ovidian self-deprecation and *recusatio*, the poet's ostensibly candid admissions that his poetry is 'not only sad but monotonous' must be studied in context. The formerly widely-held idea of the whole exilic corpus as an ocean of snivelling lachrymosity has increasingly lost ground, but the fact of our author's extreme versatility, also in exile, needs greater emphasis.

First some definitions and restrictions. The word 'monotony' refers to 'singleness of tone', not of content. By 'tone' is meant the effect upon the sensibilities of the reader of the prevailing attitude of mind of the writer. 'Content' refers to the information conveyed. Discrepancy between tone and content is often an indication of ironic intent, colouring with new insights the reader's perception of what has gone before. Reversal, inversions and shifts of tone are aspects of the general poetic principle of *variatio*. This applies both within individual poems, and within the various collections that comprise the exilic works. To appreciate this, we need to examine the structure of some poems.

The Introduction noted that the term 'poetic structure' has many different applications, involving, among others, metre, vocabulary, content, or use of poetic devices. Ancient rhetorical theory offered a battery of technical terms for the description or denotation of the various parts of an oration, involving formulaic aspects of *thought* rather than of *tone*. This type of structural analysis would work to denote the various parts (units of thought) of *Tr.* 2, or of Ovid's autobiography (*Tr.* 4.10). Generic rhetorical terminology is sometimes applied to formulaic units of thought, with a '*genre*' utilising various '*topoi*'. Mere taxonomy of units of thought or units of diction is less useful than assessment of tone by means of such taxonomy, yet synthesis of these elements can be used to pinpoint tonal shifts. Tone is closely bound to style. So, taxonomic stylistic analysis followed by synthesis leads to an appreciation of tone. Close attention to words in context, to sound and rhythm, so as to catch the shifting tones of a poem, produces a better appreciation of nuances of meaning and tone than mere formal analysis, taxonomy and *Quellenforschung*.

Micro-analytical, progressive attention to detail, can, however, obfuscate final poetic interpretation by sheer weight of words, within which the poetry is simply lost. Furthermore, such progressive analysis can be so carefully descriptive of the 'flesh' of the poem, that it loses the spirit, failing to give (or purposely avoiding) any indication of the critic's personal reaction to the poet's outreach towards his readership. Without stopping to assess emotional impact, we substitute a new petrification, the verbiage of 'structure', for the old, taxonomic destruction of a poem that we sought to supplant.

Does this mean that a critic's appreciation of the tone of a work is so elusive as to be virtually impossible to convey? Our subjective reaction to the poet's appeal can be aided by recourse to all the above means of analysis, but finally we can do no more than voice an impression of tone as conveyed by the poet through his style. With Ovid, in all his works, we need to note both tone and undertone. How these aspects are conveyed is the topic of this section.

2.1.1. Variatio *and arrangement*

'Structure' is a popular critical buzz-word, applied to the exilic poems in various ways, especially in conjectures about the underlying principles of arrangement within individual books and the 'original order' in which the poems were written, even leading to rearrangement of the received ordering of poems within a book. Better to assume that any body of poems, edited by an ancient author in his lifetime, offers these poems *in the order that the poet wanted them to be read*. Overall structure should not be ignored. Symmetry is a consideration, but numerical grouping, framing and chronology also play a part.

Variatio is perhaps the most important principle. The author's intentional arrangement of individual poems is more important than compositional order. Juxtaposition, novelty and echoes within reasonable physical distance from one another (e.g. ring-composition within a poem) would have been the most important factors in ancient readers' appreciation of texts as they unrolled the scroll on which they were written. Hence, more important than 'overall symmetry' are the effects of juxtaposition and contrast indicating logical flow of thought, or, conversely, illogical jumps in arrangement. With a complex poet like Ovid, one single principle of *variatio* should, however, never be upheld without consideration of the possibility of a multiple approach and typically Ovidian subtleties of tone.

2.1.2. Chronology

Chronological examination of the exilic works may also indicate changes in style and in attitude and tonality. As I have postulated above (Introduction §5), the overriding tone of one of the earlier books from exile may be vastly different from a work published a few years later, after exile has become a way of life for the erstwhile *lusor amorum*. The time-span as well as chronology of a poet's output is important: where about 25 years separated the first and second editions of Ovid's *Amores*, the problem of time is very complex. The exilic poetry can be dated fairly certainly by means of internal evidence and by the limit imposed by the poet's death, by which time his tempo of composition had apparently slackened. All this points to the need for examining the exilic oeuvre consecutively (that is, largely chronologically) for shifts in tone.

The conjectured order of composition of the exilic works will not be repeated here. That the poet arranged the order of *Ex P.* 4 himself cannot be proven, but the possibility cannot be excluded. There is some evidence of an ordering principle similar to the almost symmetrical ordering of the previous books according to principles of *variatio* (by both addressee and main topic as well as tone, even though our poet seems to wax increasingly lugubrious).

2.1.3. Analyses of tonal shifts in individual poems

An examination of the contents of two poems will give an indication of the kind of tonal shifts that we are looking for, and the means by which our poet achieves these shifts. I start with the shorter of the two.

Tr. 4.9, one of the poems addressed to an unknown enemy, begins with a cryptic and anonymous accusation and a mild offer of mercy to be extended to the addressee, after repentance. Verses 1-8 appear on first reading to portray Augustus Caesar as speaker, offering the exile forgiveness in lofty tones. Only at the ninth verse the reader realises that it is the exile who is addressing an enemy who has harmed him: *Sim licet extremum, sicut sum, missus in orbem* ('I may well have been sent, as I have in fact, to the ends of the earth'). Verses 9 to 14 sound a tone of assurance in the strength of the exile's civic position and certainty of pardon by Caesar: *omnia, si nescis, Caesar mihi iura reliquit* ('If you don't know it, Caesar left me all my rights'), shifting at verse 15 to reliance on a stronger power: *denique ... Pierides vires et sua tela dabunt* ('finally, the Muses will give me power and their own weapons'). Verse 21 shifts to lofty assurance of a transcendental ability to expose this enemy to the world: *ibit ad occasum quicquid dicemus ab ortu* ('whatever I say will travel from East to West'), shifting once more at verse 27 to whimsy: *iam feror in pugnas et nondum cornua sumpsi* ('I'm now being borne into battle, but I have not yet taken up the bugle!'). The vocabulary derives from the amphitheatre, rather than the battlefield. Logical extension of this metaphor involves depiction of the exile as 'gladiator' (27-8), his temporary patience with his enemy as the Roman 'winter recess' (December to April) and finally himself as an 'angry bull' (29-30).

Playful imagery has deflated the severity of the threat. From its initially elevated tone of cosmic power, the poem has moved to a rather incongruous minor key. Finally the threat is deflected (by means of a pun involving *canere*) into a rather feeble 'or else ...'. This last shift in tone reveals in retrospect that the first part of the poem was playful bombast, Ovidian *nequitia* at its most subtle (31-2):

> *hoc quoque quam volui plus est: cane, Musa, receptus*
> *dum licet huic nomen dissimulare suum.*

> This, too, is more than I wanted: sound the retreat, O Muse,
> while this man may still hide his own name!

Our longer example features earlier in the collection. *Tr.* 4.3, addressed to the exile's wife, displays subtle shifts of tone and mood. Verses 1-10 introduce a dramatic monologue with an elaborate address to the two Bear constellations. These stars, that can look on Rome, must spy on the exile's wife. The tone is pathetic, but not completely so, for an elaborately 'learned', circumlocutory style undercuts pathos. At verse 11 the tone changes. The exile reprimands himself for doubting his wife's fidelity: *quae sunt manifesta, requiro* ('I'm looking for things that are evident'), leading to ten verses overstating the obvious.

Verse 21 shifts naturally to an explanation of the reason for the exile's doubts, now addressing his wife directly. The tone is candid: at night the exile's fears increase. He does not doubt her, but he is tortured by nocturnal suffering. The tone of agony is undercut by the uncomfortable intrusion of a suspicion of sexual innuendo in verse 25 *et veniunt aestus* ('and heated passions come', or even 'lust rises'). The exile's nocturnal longing is more physical than mental. The joke, if joke it is, is furthered by the exile's likening himself to Andromache, in agony at having to watch the mutilation of Hector's body (29-30). Incongruity of physical and mental suffering is supported by the incongruous inversion of male and female points of view.

This is subtle Ovidian *nequitia* again, but the exile's tone waxes increasingly querulous, becoming the selfish grumblings of a peevish husband, concerned with his wife's feelings only in relation to himself, with little concern for her happiness. Whether she is sad or happy, he is hurt by what she feels (33-40):

> *tristis es? indignor quod sim tibi causa doloris:*
> *non es? at amisso coniuge digna fores.*

Are you sad? I deplore being the cause of your sorrow. Are you not sad? But sadness would really have been suitable for someone who had lost her husband!

From verse 31 onwards the tone is extremely pathetic, culminating at verses 39-40 in a death wish: *utinam lugenda tibi non vita, sed ... mors* ('If only you did not have to mourn over my life, but rather over my death!'). This leads to a fantasy where the exile imagines a death-bed scene, even his own funeral. For no apparent reason, verse 49 displays a violent change of tone: the exile suddenly imagines his wife as turning away from him (49-52):

> *me miserum, si tu, cum diceris exulis uxor,*
> *avertis vultus et subit ora rubor!*
> *me miserum, si turpe putas mihi nupta videri*
> *me miserum, si te iam pudet esse meam!*

2. Poetic nequitia: *the constant factor*

Poor me, if you, when you are called the wife of an exile,
  avert your face, and a blush suffuses your cheeks!
Poor me, if you think it a disgrace to appear to be married to me!
  Poor me, if you are now ashamed to be mine!

We may feel that elaborate literary devices such as *anaphora* and the deliberate echoing of *tu* (49) in *turpe* (51) are totally inconsistent with intensely felt, sincere emotion. Within the elegiac tradition such elaboration is, however, not necessarily a sign of shallowness.

The exile speaks nostalgically of the time when his wife was proud to be known as his, leading at verse 61 to a new shift, toward a tone of reassurance. His wife has new opportunities for pride. After all, she will become more famous for her fidelity than a whole series of faithful wives or friends, traditional epitomes of conjugal and amicable fidelity (see Chapter 5). The tone is matter-of-fact. The exile's situation can be exploited by his wife to achieve fame (79-84). The coda offers a reasonable, logical and sober gnomic statement resembling a forensic peroration: *quae latet inque bonis cessat non cognita rebus,/ apparet virtus arguiturque malis,* etc. (79-80, 'Virtue, which lies hidden, and in good times even hangs back without being acknowledged, appears and is vindicated during bad times', etc.). The scene has shifted from the cosmic sphere to the Roman forum, the mode from the metaphysical to the legal. An initially dramatic monologue has become a soberly persuasive speech. It takes a moment of reflection for the reader to recall both the humour and the pathos that went before.

2.1.4. Contrast in tone between consecutive poems

Hence it is safe to say that the general impression left by a poem is not the note upon which it ends, overriding what has gone before, but the result of the sum of its shifts. This final impression depends largely on the poetic force with which a particular stance is portrayed. It may, in its turn, be overridden by the tone of the next poem, if poems are read in order, as we have postulated that the poet intended. The next poem, *Tr.* 4.4, begins in an adulatory tone, an elegant eulogy of an anonymous friend (probably Messallinus, son of Messala Corvinus, the poet's patron). It clearly contrasts with the largely sober tone of the conclusion of *Tr.* 4.3, but there is an even greater contrast between the 'manly stance' of 4.4 and the peevish attitude evidenced toward the exile's wife in the larger part of the monologue comprising the previous poem. Such contrast in tone between the two poems adds to the psychological portrait of an all-too-human exile that the poet is slowly building up.

Contrast between our next pair of consecutive poems, both addressed to 'fellow-poets', is on more levels than mere tone. *Ex P.* 2.9 addresses

Cotys, king of Thrace, a 'barbarian prince', civilised, so Ovid claims, by the humanities: common interests make poetic colleagues of exile and king, binding them by ties of obligation. We have noted before that ostensibly complimentary praise of the king's achievements in the liberal arts, 'surprising in a barbarian', jars with its tactlessness. Possibly this gauche compliment was another instance of Ovid's *nequitia*, a gentle squib intended merely to entertain his Roman readers, and never sent to the king. The following poem, *Ex P.* 2.10, reminds Ovid's bosom friend, his fellow-poet Macer, of their youthful common interests, travels and pursuits. Nostalgic remembrance of things past contrasts with ostensible outreach to a new addressee in the previous poem. A distant, pleasant 'there, then' in 2.10 offers a foil to the exile's unhappy 'here, now' of 2.9.

The tone of *Ex P.* 2.10 is generally, almost consistently, cheerful, although it opens with a series of pathetic questions implying that Macer may have forgotten the exile. At verse 7 the tone becomes brisk, ostensibly accepting that any missive from Ovid must now seem extremely unfamiliar, and continuing with a reminder of their various ties (2.10.7-8):

> *sis licet oblitus pariter gemmaeque manusque,*
> *exciderit tantum ne tibi cura mei*

It's quite in order for you to have forgotten both my seal and my
                                                                      handwriting,
       as long as your concern for me won't disappear!

Verse 10, *vel mea quod coniunx non aliena tibi est* ('or perhaps because my wife is not a stranger to you') could be construed as a hint that Macer has taken over the exile's conjugal role, but there is no other indication of such a suspicion. The tone is candid rather than bland, indicating relationship rather than intrigue. Verses 15-16 follow on praise of Macer's own more successful exercise of his talents (*studiis ... sapientius usus*, 11, '[you who] used your studies more wisely'). Here the poet is deprecatory about his own harmful exercise of poetry (*Naso parum prudens*, 15, 'Naso, the not-so-wise'). Next Ovid asserts the power of the bond between fellow-poets: *sunt tamen inter se communia sacra poetis* (17, 'for poets have certain things in common that they hold sacred'). At verse 21 the exile turns nostalgically to an enumeration of the travels he and Macer shared in their youth (a conventional 'grand tour' that included Roman Asia Minor and Sicily), contrasting it rather sadly at verse 30 with the place to which he has had to travel alone: *eheu, quam dispar est locus ille Getis!* ('Oh dear, how different is that place from the Getae!'). Verses 31 to 42 recall with further nostalgia their erstwhile spiritual communion, with echoes of conventional *topoi* contrasting shortness of day and length of road in an echo of Callim. *Epigr.* 2.2-3:

2. Poetic nequitia: the constant factor

saepe dies sermone minor fuit, inque loquendum
tarda per aestivos defuit hora dies (37-8)

Often the day was too short for our conversation
and the slow summer hour was not long enough for our chat.

At verse 43 the tone changes to quiet certainty about the poet's meta-physical power to transcend space, shifting at 49 to the assertion that he has the reciprocal ability to evoke his friend at will. Macer is as much present among the Getae as Ovid is mentally present in Rome. This is a vindication of the almost magical power of the mind over the limitations of the material world. A final shift, at verse 51, to a request that his friend should employ a similar imaginative power to evoke the exile offers a logical conclusion to a graceful exposition of the various facets of their communion. The exile requests present aid, ending with a graceful conceit, 'hold me in your heart, for there it is warmer'.

2.1.5. Variatio by retrospect

The tone of each part of a poem is influenced by what has gone before, and colours what follows. This applies between poems as well. An examination of three consecutive poems will illustrate this. Contrast and shifts in tone parallel the considerable contrast in content of the second, third and fourth poems of *Ex P.* 3. In order to give readers the opportunity to develop a 'feel' for such tonal shift and cross-referencing, Appendix II (pp. 254-60) offers fairly literal prose translations of the three poems. Readers are invited to try to form their own judgement before proceeding to read my assessment of these poems.

The style of *Ex P.* 3.3, 'the midnight apparition of *Amor*', invites a less serious assessment of the poem than it is sometimes accorded. This poem will be dealt with more fully in §2.2 below: here we shall merely note its contrast with the poems preceding and following it. Its mock-solemn, clearly whimsical tone contrasts with the bland, almost conciliatory tone of *Ex P.* 3.2, informing Cotta Maximus about friends who deserted the exile (along with his good fortune) through fear. He forgives them, rather grandly, with the 'poetic plural': *ignoscimus illis,/ qui cum Fortuna terga dedere fugae* (*Ex P.* 3.2.7-8). True friends receive his thanks. Friendship is such a precious thing that even the local barbarians can appreciate it. As illustration the exile repeats the tale of the friendship of Orestes and Pylades in the land of the Taurians, as it was told by an 'old Getic man' (43-96). It is in fact a concise reprise of Euripides' version of the myth in his *Iphigeneia among the Taurians*. The barbaric Artemis celebrated in this cruel countryside is a gory, nightmare version of the ruthless 'Diana the Huntress' of *Met.* 2.401-65: here her reeking altar is sprinkled with

59

the blood of human sacrifice (53-4). That the locality is removed from Tomis by several hundred kilometres as the crow would fly, is an irrelevance that would not have troubled a Roman readership, with its less than perfect grasp of geography. Yet this fact does help us to put the fictional nature of the situation into perspective. The discursive and chatty style of the 'old Getic man' is in apparently deliberate contrast to the exile's formal address of his loyal friends.

Next, *Ex P.* 3.4 promises a triumph poem and then proceeds to give it in miniature, as will be shown below. Framed as it is between these two widely divergent poems, *Ex P.* 3.3 strikes us forcibly by its mock-solemn tone, moving into comedy and back to spurious solemnity. Internal evidence suggests that *Ex P.* 3.3 was composed around or after 23 October AD 12. It again presents a tale within a tale: the exile tells his patron and friend, Fabius Maximus (an *amicus Caesaris*), of his dreaming that a bedraggled '*Amor*' had come from Rome to exonerate him from all blame. The god's appearance is suitably mournful, as befits another victim of Augustan repression.

The incongruity of a dream-setting contrasts with and undermines the poet's solemn protestations of fealty to Augustus. The ridiculous context militates against face-value acceptance of the information conveyed. The poet, at first terrified by the apparition, recovers and rails at his 'pupil' for having caused his exile, making him swear that he (the poet) had taught nothing unlawful. Ovid plays on the fact that the Latin verb *docere* takes two accusatives, of animate pupil and inanimate topic. Hence '*Amor*' (the topic of the didactic *Ars Amatoria*, the supposed cause of Ovid's ruin) is personalised and berated by the poet as an ungrateful pupil, a non-Achilles to his non-Chiron, a non-Numa to his non-Pythagoras. This is a typically playful Ovidian conceit, wresting every possible nuance from the situation. *Amor* exonerates him from all blame in the matter of morality, prophesying future happiness, especially after Tiberius' projected triumph. This triumph is briefly described.

While purporting to serve as a further elaboration of this triumph, the apologetic tone of the fourth poem in the book contrasts with the 'dream sequence' of its predecessor. *Ex P.* 3.4 is addressed to Rufinus, apparently as the 'covering letter' for a triumph-poem. If a separate poem ever existed, it is now wholly lost, but it is possible that the last quarter of the poem (87-112) *is* the promised 'triumph poem.' The whole serves as *recusatio*, begging pardon for the 'poor quality' of a poem written on Tiberius' triumph. In the Callimachean tradition *recusatio* has as its more salient elements: the request of a dignitary for patriotic poetry, refusal by the poet on the grounds of smallness of talent and the greatness of the task, a warning god that calls him away, vindicating his choice of the humbler mode, and a defiant challenge to personified Envy to do its worst. Imagery is consistently related to water, sailing, or travel on land (as here).

2. Poetic nequitia: the constant factor

This poem wavers between humility, tearfulness and pathos, while attempting to sound ingratiating and conciliatory. A final apostrophe addresses the empress Livia, enjoining her to rejoice in her son's triumph and giving a small cameo-like evocation of a typical Roman triumph (95-112). Ovid's ostensibly admiring description of the triumph (which he has had to imagine after reportage at second-hand) is undercut by the reader's memory of the bathos, in the previous poem, of the 'prophetic' figure of 'Amor' with its bedraggled feathers, which had incongruously proclaimed that this triumph would take place. Allusions in both poems to the familial relationships of the various actors in the triumphal procession (Livia as mother of Tiberius, 3.3.87; 3.4.95-100, Tiberius as father of Germanicus and Drusus, and – by means of zeugma – of the 'Fatherland', 3.3.87-8) gain a strange colouring when read immediately after Ovid's *reductio ad absurdum* of the Caesars' claim to divine ancestry: '*Amor*' is Tiberius' great-uncle (3.3.62). The various imperial adoptions are glossed over, but are hence accentuated in readers' consciousness. Tiberius is uncomfortably aligned with his 'great-uncle's' vindication of the errant poet. More of this in §2.2.

Ovid's mock-recusationary stance in *Ex P.* 3.4 is not wholly convincing, for in various passages (notably 65-74, 93-4, 113-14) great pride in his ability as poet still shines through. Hence the greater part of the poem is more concerned with poetics, and the power of poetry against mordant Envy, than with Tiberian glory. Ovid claims to be drawing from memory, relying on his 'mind's eye', whereas other poets can report at first hand – a central passage asserts the important power of poetry to transcend space and time (65-84), even while ostensibly deploring the inadequacy of elegy to bear the triumphal burden. A tone of dull fatalism is relieved by a playful conceit: the elegiac metre represents a chariot with wheels of disparate size (a joke the poet has made before):

> *ferre etiam molles elegi tam vasta triumphi*
> *pondera disparibus non potuere rotis.* (85-6)

My gentle elegies with their wheels of unequal size were inadequate to bear the so enormous weight of a triumph.

Flattery is evident in personal address of two of the recipients of our three consecutive poems (Cotta in 3.2.3-7 and 103-10, Fabius Maximus in 3.3.95-108). It is not afforded in equal measure in *Ex P.* 3.4 to Rufinus as potential editor. Address of these great men evokes that unpleasant side to Roman *obligatio* which prompted not only daily attendance on the great by suppliant clients, but sycophancy in a poet at the mercy of the powerful. Yet playful punning on the two meanings of *salutem* ('greetings' and 'health') in *Ex P.* 3.2.1-2, and the ridiculous circumstances of the 'dream' solemnly recounted to Fabius in 3.3, with its echoes of the apparition of Corinna in *Am.* 1.5, contrasts with, and consequently tempers, the poet's apparently over-obsequious attempts to draw the families of both addressees into his constellation of worthies. The poems succeed because of the variety and intrinsic interest of their contents, not because of the conventional flattery in their concluding lines.

When the exilic poetry is critically read in order as described above, the tone of consecutive poems may often leave a general impression which is subtly different from the impression left by a single poem. The sum of these impressions gives, in the end, a different flavour to the interpretation of each individual poem. A rapid survey of consecutive individual impressions within a collection is necessarily selective as well as subjective, but the exercise would be worth pursuing, resulting in a tonally nuanced reading.

2.1.6. The last poem before Ovid's death

Having seen Ovidian *variatio* at work between consecutive poems, we arrive at the very last of the exilic poems with an expectant curiosity tempered with the awareness that critics are unsure whether *Ex P.* 4.16 is perhaps only fortuitously Ovid's last poem from exile. Book 4 represents, as we have seen, the last of our five chronological phases, published perhaps posthumously, and covering the years after the death of Augustus. The initial impression of its sixteen poems is that attitude and tone are positive, but this is soon undercut by our awareness of increasing pathos.

Addressees fall into two almost equal groups, public figures and the exile's friends, most of them fellow-poets, one (in 4.3) an erstwhile friend who had harmed the exile, and the last, an enemy. It has been suggested that the faithless friend was Messallinus, who did not react to the exile's supplications, or perhaps Hyginus, keeper of the Palatine library. Most of the addressees in this book have not been approached before. The collection seems marked by a new approach, aimed largely at the coterie of Germanicus, in whom, it seems, the poet hoped to find a new champion. It is, however, possible that some of the poems had been written earlier, and simply excluded from previous collections. Hence assessment of *variatio* in this collection must be done with caution.

Variation of tone (even if the shifts seem often to remain in essentially the same mode, moving merely from despondency to outright despair) may have been the principle applied for the ordering of individual poems. If that is so, it may be evidence of intentional arrangement, either by a posthumous editor, or by the poet himself. A case can be made out for the deliberate placement of Poem 16 at the end of Book 4. Its tone and content invite us to believe that *Ex P.* 4.16 was intended by our poet as the climax of his exilic oeuvre, and perhaps also of his total *corpus* – Ovid's *last word* in symbolic and metaphorical (as well as literal) sense. Hence it often recurs at the close of my chapters or subsections. The poem does not, at first reading, seem to offer a great emotional culmination to a collection that has wavered in address between public figures and private friends. It addresses an unnamed enemy. Its body (5-44) purports to be a mere versified catalogue of contemporary poets, many otherwise unknown. The present claim to fame of several of these poets lies only in their inclusion in this catalogue. The exiled poet is the last of this list, following his friend Cotta Maximus (the addressee of *Ex P.* 3.2), 'a great poet and a great man'.

The poem is striking for its curious play of tone. A statement of defiance (1-4) gives way, after the catalogue of poets (5-44), to pride in his poetry and the exiled poet's position as leader among a host of his contemporaries (45-6). The last part of the poem exhibits rapid shifts from this modest but obviously justified pride in his Muse, to violent challenge of *Livor* (Envy) to stop its inhuman persecution (47-8), to dull despair and utter abnegation (49-52). The contrast with Ovid's challenge at the end of the *Metamorphoses*, to *Livor edax* to do its worst, is pointed and presumably deliberate. The tone here is finally negative, bespeaking an apparently resigned hopelessness.

So, from first to last, variations of tone in *Ex P.* 4 have dwindled into a fixed focus upon a feeling of utter doom. The end of the poem, of the book, and presumably of the exile's life, is a dull, animal cry of despair (47-52):

> *ergo summotum patria proscindere, Livor*
> *desine neu cineres sparge, cruente, meos.*
> *omnia perdidimus: tantummodo vita relicta est*
> *praebeat ut sensum materiamque mali.*
> *quid iuvat extinctos ferrum demittere in artus?*
> *non habet in nobis iam nova plaga locum.*

> Therefore, remote from the fatherland, bloody Envy,
> stop tearing me apart, and do not scatter my ashes.
> I have lost all: my life alone is left to me,
> So that it can offer feeling and an object for your evil doing,
> What does it help to keep stabbing your blade into my lifeless
> limbs?
> A new blow finds no unbruised area on me.

Yet, in the silence that follows on the cessation of the poet's voice, the reader begins to remember and pick up echoes of previous tones. Behind this apparently hopeless cry a second, more forceful, impression obtrudes: the poet is certain that he has gained immortality. And so the last impression is not wholly of despair. Stronger than this despairing cry to *Livor*, the memory of Ovid's earlier hymn to his Muse remains in the reader's mind (*Tr.* 4.10.121-2):

> *tu mihi, quod rarum est, vivo sublime dedisti*
> *nomen, ab exequiis quod dare fama solet.*

You have given me while I was still alive something very rare, a sublime reputation, which Fame usually bestows on someone only after his burial.

The poet, speaking as it were from beyond the grave, is in a unique position to view his poetic career as an entity. Ovid formerly held pride of place on the slopes of Helicon, and, for all his shifts of tone and mood, he has told his readers that he knows it.

In conclusion, then, this section has tried to show that consistent attention should be paid not only to fluctuations of tone and mood within single poems, but to the order in which the poet presented the poems of exile to his readership during the course of nearly ten years. The poet's own ordering of individual books, and the discernible tonal shifts between poems, are indications of Ovid's conscious use of the principles of *variatio* to create a composite mood, in which the old Ovidian *nequitia* often features. This nuanced mood is part of a psychologically convincing picture of the fluctuations of hope and despair experienced by a sensitive soul relegated to the uttermost ends of the Roman earth. A last, negative, picture of the exile is tempered by our awareness of a gradually built up, and tonally nuanced, cumulative re-creation (by the poet) of himself as an heroic, mythical and therefore immortal figure, which Envy has been unable to vanquish.

2.2. Detailed analysis of *Ex Ponto* 3.3: *Praeceptor amoris* or *praeceptor Amoris*?

This section returns to the central poem of the three discussed above and translated in Appendix II, but should be read with reference to the original text. *Ex P.* 3.3 offers fruitful material for close analysis because it is clearly founded in unreality, and so, obviously and demonstrably, does not present a 'true', factual picture of either the exile's life at Tomis, or of his inner life as an artist. The poem, which is a palpable fantasy, offers clues for a less literal interpretation of the rest of the exilic oeuvre. No depth of analysis is needed to aid us in differentiating between poetic fantasy and emotional reality here. We need only to pinpoint those devices which enhance (and hence elsewhere may lend) an aura of fantasy, including, particularly, those devices that convey apparent irony, indicating a discrepancy between real and ostensible meaning, a consistent aspect of our poet's *nequitia*.

2. Poetic nequitia: the constant factor

In what follows a short analysis of the poet's stylistic techniques will lead to consideration of the literary components of the poems (from units of diction through technical devices and units of thought to literary devices) leading to a new synthesis. That is, to interpret what the poet presents, analysis of his style will offer the first step towards literary interpretation. This model will serve as a preliminary to more detailed analyses of Ovid's poetic techniques in the next two chapters. Appraisal of the stylistic characteristics of the poetry of exile will aid us in pinpointing those characteristics which enabled the artist's creative genius to produce a body of apparently simple poetry that actually requires great subtlety in interpretation.

2.2.1. Units of diction

The vocabulary of this particular poem offers no great problems, if some odd word choices. The word *torus* 'marriage bed' (verse 8) refers to the bed where the exile lies *alone* (as in *Met.* 6.289: *stabant .../ ante toros fratrum demisso crine sorores* ('the sisters were standing with flowing hair by the couches of their brothers'), but also in clear evocation of Ovid's own tale of 'Love in the afternoon' from *Am.* 1.5). In this context, reference to the exile's *languida membra* ('flaccid limbs/ members') lying alone on a 'marriage bed' appears to redirect a potential *double entendre* to a more innocuous sphere. Such redirection is made even more explicit when the word *toros* is repeated in a more usual context at verse 50, with *scis tamen .../ non me legitimos sollicitasse toros* ('You know that I never sought [to defile] lawful marriage beds').

The poem exhibits the usual trappings of Ovidian irreverent lip-service to a long poetic tradition, such as the incongruously applied, but clearly discernible, evocation of Vergil's description of Charon from *Aen.* 6, *horrida pendebant molles super ora capilli* (17, 'his soft hair hung down over his bristling cheeks') – an echo, too, of the poet's own 'mournful *Amor*', from *Am.* 3.9, on the death of Tibullus. A transferred epithet (the god's 'hair' should logically be 'standing on end', not *Amor*'s 'face') offers an unusual cameo of a rakish, unkempt and 'Charonesque' god. Another transferred epithet, *barbarus Hister* (26) evokes in compressed form a more complex vignette. The river is, strictly speaking, not 'barbaric' – the area around it is the home of *barbaric tribes* living far removed from Rome.

The inflated, epic style of the passage appears comical in the context of the burlesque apparition. Equally incongruous are grandiloquent circumlocutions (perhaps merely for metrical convenience) *apposui senis te duce quinque pedes* (30, 'under your guidance I attached a five-beat line to my hexameters'); '*Olympus*' (42) presumably for Zeus-Jupiter; *Memnonio ... colore* (96, 'with the colour of Memnon') for 'black' in an elaborate *adynaton*, and *lacteus umor* for 'milk' (97).

65

In 91 variant readings *templum/ numen* both appear as bland synonyms for 'the god', by implication the emperor Augustus, whom Ovid's predecessors had mostly hesitated thus unquestioningly to equate with deity. The word is qualified by *venerabile*, normally 'reverend', but here it may possibly imply 'old', in pointed differentiation between Augustus and the ever-young *Amor*.

As always with Ovid, past master of the simple statement, there is nothing particularly unusual or strained in the poet's grammatical usage: the imperfect tense is mostly employed for narrative sections (5-20: *erat, intrabat, habebat, pendebant,* etc.), perfect for the substance of the 'conversation' (23-76: *fuit, venisti, apposui, passus es, vacavit,* etc.) and future for 'prophecy' (83-4: *mitescet, veniet*), while he glides into the present tense for an effect of immediacy (85-92: *times, instat, habet, gaudet, gratatur, calet, praebet*). Compliments to Fabius Maximus are in the present tense. The only rather unusual tense form is the present of *dum canto* (35, 'while I sing') combined with *vacavit* ('has been available'), but the sense is clear. The poet is stating the continuation of the power of his genius.

We have noted (§2.1 above) Ovid's exploitation of a common grammatical usage for comic effect, his play on the double object of the verb *docere*. From teaching (how to) love as *subject* of study, the exiled poet refers to himself as having taught (the personified) Love as *pupil*. It implies a shift within the semantic field of a single objective genitive. By a subtle inversion, *Praeceptor amoris* has become *praeceptor Amoris*, an amusing example of grammatical sleight of hand. This shift is then logically extended to apply to both the verb for teaching and the noun 'pupil' (24 *quem docuisse*, 47 *te ... docemus*, 48 *te discipulo*, etc.).

2.2.2. Technical devices

The concept of *hyperbaton* (split phrasing) will be further explored in Chapters 3 and 4. The term may be taken to refer to any distortion of normally acceptable, prosaic word-order, such as *pax est ubi tempore nullo* (25, where peace at no time occurs), where inversion lends emphasis to the word *pax*. More precisely, *hyperbaton* is normally taken to refer to the splitting of the two elements of a phrase (most often noun plus adjective) by the insertion of a grammatically unrelated word or words between them. Particular, conscious separation of noun and adjective is a function of conscious artistry, a technical literary device *par excellence*. Where *hyperbaton* does not occur within an elegiac verse, this lack may simply result from a dearth of adjectives in a particular verse, or it may be deliberate, a restructuring of the verse into a 'simple' or prosaic word-order. Such verses often appear to carry a particularly heavy emphasis, conveying a richness of emotion. The presence of elaborate noun-adjective *hyperbaton* serves as a technical ploy often indicating slippage between real and apparent meaning.

Nouns and adjectives are separated by one or other kind of *hyperbaton* in all but three of the fifty-four couplets of this poem: of these, sixteen have some form of 'linked', 'chiastic' or 'double' hyperbaton. A good example of this typically Neoteric poetic device is to be found in the parody of Vergil's description of Charon cited above (*Ex P.* 3.3.17-18):

> *horrida* pendebant **molles** *super* ora **capilli**
> *et* visa *est* **oculis** *horrida* pinna **meis**.

> His soft hair hung down over his bristling cheeks,
> and my eyes noted that his feathers were all standing on end.

Two of the three exceptions noted above contain no adjectives except a relative, demonstrative or possessive. The third is the introductory couplet of *Amor's* speech. Its solemn, almost prosaic word order gives great emphasis and weight to the words of the grotesque apparition, which is further enhanced by rhetorical use of ascending *tricolon* and *anaphora* and by its rhythm. A largely dactylic hexameter is slowed down at its centre by a single spondee. Spondees in the first hemistich of the pentameter similarly slow down the verse, lending solemnity. Here almost consistent non-coincidence of *ictus* (stress on the first syllable of a foot, marked with ' after the syllable) and word accent creates a halting effect (67-8):

> *Pēr' měǎ | tē'lǎ, fǎ | cēs', ēt | pēr' měǎ | tē'lǎ, sǎ | gīt'tās,*
> *pēr' mā | trēm' iūr | ō' ‖ Caē'sǎrě | ūm'quě cǎ | pūt'...*

> By my weapons, my torches, and by my weapons, my arrows,
> by my mother I do swear, and by the head of the Caesar ...

Vowel quality enhances the solemn effect. As we have no true idea of the musical accompaniment of Latin lyric verse and the degree to which the tonality of vowels was supported by this accompaniment, we can only record the poet's alternation of vowels, and guess at the effect. A series of high pitched vowels can convey an impression of hysteria, a series of low pitched vowels gloom, or, as here, solemnity. To depict the tonal structure in this couplet I have devised an adaptation of modern musical notation. Latin verse does not have the musical tonality of Greek verse, but it *does* have pitch. As in modern Italian, gradation of Latin vowels ranges in pitch, from deepest, *u*, through *o, a* and *e,* to highest, *i.* These vowels can be written between or above (and diphthongs, *on*) the lines of a musical stave, expressing dactyls with a minim and two crotchets, spondees by two minims. Such differences of pitch are slight, and use of

the stave is a mere convenience. This device combines metric and rela-
tive phonic display, but without indication of vowel *tone*. There is no need
to differentiate between the phonic nature of a vowel that is naturally
either short or long, and of a vowel that has been lengthened or short-
ened 'by position'. Notation merely indicates length of syllable in context.

In the hexameter an almost monotone sound (alternation of *e* and *a* is
broken only once by high-pitched *i*) is incantationary; in the pentameter
there is more tonal movement, through four of the five vowels, as follows:

At verse 22, *talibus adfata est libera lingua sonis* (my tongue was loosened
and addressed him with such words), alliteration of *l* and *s* combines with
its epic diction (*talibus ... sonis*; *adfata*) to underline the impression
conveyed by the sense of *libera lingua*. The exile was at first dumb-struck
by the vision but managed at last to speak freely. The halting effect of *-li-*
is carried on into the next two verses by *exilii* and *utilius*.

The presence or absence of intentional rhyme in Latin verse is a bone
of contention among critics. Essentially, 'true rhyme' is possible only with
stressed syllables; hence the penultimate (stressed) syllables as well as
the endings, of 'rhyming' words should coincide. The term
'*homoeoteleuton*' covers the coincidence of sound of unstressed ultimate
syllables. Whether *homoeoteleuton* is considered a form of rhyme or not,
it is as much a feature of Latin verse as initial consonantal coincidence
(alliteration), or coincidence of vowels (assonance). However, the
rhyming effects of noun and agreeing adjective may often be discounted
as fortuitous, the result of hyperbated similar case endings. Other
instances of *homoeoteleuton* may betray deliberate intention. These
aspects receive attention in Chapter 3.

When *homoeoteleuton* occurs in consecutive couplets, or even within the
same couplet, not all incidences should be discounted as the result of
linguistic exigencies. With Ovid there seems to be a difference in effect
between internal rhyme and end rhyme, or the use of *homoeoteleuton*
within a single verse and that spanning successive verses. In verse 77 the
jingling effect of the acoustic coincidence of verb and participial object *ut
tamen* **aspic*erem*** *consol*arer** **iacentem** undercuts the solemn tone of
Amor's comforting words (further heightened by assonance in *-ere-...-arer-*).
The following examples (some from alternating verses) may also be cited:

2. Poetic nequitia: the constant factor

23 *magistro* ... 25 *nullo;* 27 *videres* ... 30 *pedes* ... 33 *ignes;* 35 *parentis* ... 38 *meis* ... 40 *locis* ... 41 *talis;* 50 *toros* ... 51 *pudicos;* 80 *meis* ... 82 *meis* ... 84 *tuis;* 86 *habet* ... 87 *gaudet* ... 90 *calet;* 107 *iuvandis* ... 108 *velis.* In all these cases, especially with more than two consecutive rhyming words, rhyme serves to point the words, which gain in importance, as is illustrated by the coda (107-8):

> *at tua supplicibus domus est adsueta iuvandis*
> *inque tuo numero me, precor, esse velis.*

> But your house is used to helping supplicants:
> one of that number I pray to be made.

The jingling, somewhat obtrusive rhyme *iuvandis* ... *velis* adds an extra dimension of meaning to the concept *iuvare*: the exile needs his friend to be *willing*. Again, it is difficult to gauge whether the poet's contemporaries would have interpreted the jingle similarly. In a variant reading, *in quorum* for *inque tuo* in verse 108 creates an aggressive *epanastrophe* (acoustic coincidence of the last syllable of a word and the successive initial syllable, *quorum numero*). This device, which tends to jar on modern sensibilities, was apparently considered particularly elegant by the ancients.

Anaphora (repetition) is a useful technical device serving either to emphasise, or as a striking substitute for sometimes prosaic conjunctions or other connectives. In this poem, repetition of *seu* (for instance, in 3-4), *nec me* (31, where it frames the line), *sic* (59, 61), *dum* (87, 88, 89, 91) results in balanced verse structure. Repetition of *horrida* in 17-18 lends solemn emphasis, as does the repetition of *per mea* in verse 67, discussed above. Use of variant forms of the same root (*figura etymologica*), as in 35 *tua* ... *tuae*, 47 *tibi* ... *te* and 62 *tibi* ... *tuus*, has a similar effect.

Framing creates an elegant flourish, as in verse 31 *nec me* ... *nec me*, but often it does more. In verse 55 the meaning of *summota* is visually supported by the removal of the two components of the phrase *his* ... *libellis* virtually to the two extremes of the verse. Yet the rhyming jingle created by the juxtaposition *his omnis* tends to undercut the effect:

> *an sit ab **his** omn**is** rigide summota **libellis***
> Or if each [virtuous woman] be strictly kept away from these books

Meaning is supported by word placement in various ways. Verse 86 offers another type: *cuncta* ... *plena* frame the word *laetitiae*, the abstraction of which 'everything' is 'full':

> ***cunctaque** laetitiae **plena** triumphus habet.*
> And the triumph has filled everything with joy.

69

2.2.3. Units of thought

The most consistent imagery throughout this poem is military. This ties in with both Ovid's re-inversion, in the exilic poems, of the 'make-love-not-war' theme of his erotic poetry (as spelled out in *Am.* 1.9), and the climax of *Amor's* prophecy, the triumph to be celebrated by Tiberius. Examples are 30 *te duce;* 47 *damus arma tibi;* 67 *per mea tela, faces, per mea tela, sagittas;* 82 *o castris miles amice meis.* In the context of the exilic poetry military imagery is also important for its emphasis on the exile's hard lot. Like another Priam, he takes up weapons in his old age (*Tr.* 4.1.73). Much of the *pax Augusta* in the Moesian area is extremely precarious (cf. 25 *huc ... pax est ubi tempore nullo,* to this place where there never is peace). It would not have escaped an intelligent readership that Ovid's combination of literal allusions to matters military and his consistent use of a military metaphor tie the dishevelled *Amor* and the triumphant general in an uncomfortable alliance.

The so-called *adynaton,* illustration of an argument by reference to an impossibility, is demonstrably more frequent in Ovid's exilic oeuvre than in any other part of the whole Latin poetic corpus. The poet anticipates favourable comment on the part of his friend, emphasising his trust in him (95-6):

> *si dubitem faveas quin his, o Maxime, dictis*
> *Memnonio cycnos esse colore putem.*

> If I should doubt that you would favour my words, o Maximus,
> I would be thinking that swans are the colour of Memnon.

Here present subjunctives indicate potentiality but not unreality: there is still a faint chance that both *protasis* and *apodosis* may be realised. This *faint chance* is apparently negated by the sense of the *apodosis.* That black swans actually *are* a fact of nature may or may not have been known to the poet. More of this below.

The most striking simile in the poem is Ovid's likening of the dishevelled *Amor* to a dove that has been manhandled (verses 19-20). There may be an echo here (hence including implicit criticism) of Ovid's previously likening Augustus to an eagle or vulture frightening a dove (*Tr.* 1.1 75-6). Other illustrations are (predictably with Ovid) all from myth: teachers who were treated better by their pupils than the poet as teacher was treated by his 'pupil'/topic *Amor* (41-6). These illustrations lead to a further playful paradox: the teacher-poet's almost helpless subjugation to his 'pupil'. He was led (perhaps also 'taught') by *Amor* to write elegiacs, both in his youth and in his old age, and *Amor* prevented his writing 'Homeric' verse (29-32). The only other mythical allusion involves the story of Medea, a recurring theme in the Ovidian system of reference. *Amor* explains that he has been 'here' before, at the behest of his mother (the Augustan *Venus Genetrix*, readers will remember), to transfix the 'Phasian maiden' with his arrows (79-80). That Colchis and Tomis are on the opposite shores of the Black Sea is conveniently ignored.

The poem as 'letter' has the epistolary characteristic of 'one-sided dialogue': the exile calls upon Fabius Maximus to listen to his story (1-2). Asides, interjections and parentheses add to the impression of 'conversation', as in verse 21, where after stating *hunc simul agnovi* (as soon as I recognised him) the poet explains, in a rueful aside: *neque enim mihi notior alter* (and no one else is better known to me). 'Conversational' asides form part of the stock-in-trade of a didactic author, and our poet slides almost imperceptibly from 'chatting' to 'telling' and then to 'teaching'. Assumption of common knowledge is a characteristic of both dialogue and didactic poetry and these aspects alternate: dialogue between the exile and the apparition is signalled by 28 *si nescis* ... and 72 *scis* ...; whereas 37 *nec satis hoc fuerat* works as didactic conjunction, leading to the next point to be made. Amalgamation of narrative and dialogic elements is reminiscent of our poet's frequent generic experimentation, particularly in the elegiac didactics of the *Ars Amatoria*, which frequently switches from a mock-solemn, 'teaching' tone to a disarmingly conversational stance. A didactic vocabulary sets the tone of the whole dream sequence, recalling the *Ars Amatoria* as the root-cause of the episode: 23 *magistro*; 24 *docuisse*; 46 *discipulo*; 46 *te discipulo* ... *magister*; 47 *docemus*; 69 *te didicisse magistro*.

The dialogue between exile and apparition moves from normal conversational exchange to a formal, didactic stance, signalled by rhetorical questions and exclamations (for example, verses 53-58). It then switches to conventionally prayer-like formulation, with a series of votive promises introduced by *sic ... sic ... sic ...* (59-64). The answer of the god (67-92) is formal, as befits the pronouncements of a divine epiphany, contrasting with the earlier bathetic depiction of the same divine figure, travel-stained, bedraggled and in a general state of disarray (13-20). Such constant switch in the centre of narrative focalisation lends variety and enhances the dream-like atmosphere of the tale.

2.2.4. Literary devices

Much is conveyed in this poem which is not actually *said* by Ovid, either as poet or as exile (to the degree that there is non-identity between the two). Intertextual echoes are important. Framing the exchange between exile and apparition lies the 'one-sided dialogue' addressed to Fabius Maximus, with behind it the wider implication of rhetorical outreach both to the poet's readers at Rome, and to Augustus himself. The discerning reader would have remembered that this epiphany is being related to the very (Paullus) Fabius Maximus to whom an ageing Horace many years before had referred Venus, portraying Fabius as a more suitable, young host-cum-victim, and singing 'Love, leave me alone' (*Carm.* 4.1.9-12).

Our interpretation of the *adynaton* cited above is affected by our awareness of the 'normal whiteness' of swans. The colour *purpureus* of Horace's *purpureus ales oloribus*, in verse 10 of his poem, is usually translated as 'lustrous, brilliant' to accommodate the idea of a 'white' swan. Yet if we assume that Ovid was deliberately evoking Horace and alluding to the more common meaning of *purpureus* as 'blackish, dark, Memnonian', it would imply that our poet was aware of the literal possibility of his ostensible *adynaton*. It would then follow that the poet's attitude to Fabius Maximus was not altogether guileless. This is perhaps too strong an assumption to build upon such a flimsy foundation. Yet in the atmosphere evoked by the memory of Horace's view of Fabius Maximus as gallant playboy, the *praeteritio* of verses 71-4 takes on an added piquancy: '*Amor*' claims to wish that the poet could have refuted 'the rest' of the harmful charges against him as well as he could the charge of corrupting married women. '*Amor*' then 'refuses' even to discuss the pain involved.

Such divine *praeteritio* serves to emphasise the pain it pretends to gloss over, as does the apostrophe of Augustus in verse 88: *dum gaudes, patriae magne ducisque pater* ('while you exult, o great father of the fatherland and of the general'). Readers are reminded that Augustus had only recently become the *adoptive* and not *natural* father of Tiberius. Allusion to Augustus' 'fatherhood' inevitably reminds readers of the year 2 BC, when the emperor was proclaimed 'father of his country' by the senate, but also when he finally repudiated the only person truly, biologically entitled to call him 'father,' the disgraced Julia Maior.

Our poet's propensity for reworking themes and *topoi* has often been noted. Recounting of dreams is a common literary *topos* (as in *Ex P.* 1.2.43-56, *Am.* 1.5 and 3.5). References to *carmen* and *error* have by the fifth year of the poet's exile become the *topoi* of the exilic genre, as has Ovid's plea for ultimate clemency. The epiphany of a god is a well-known *topos* in ancient literature: the reader remembers various epiphanies in the poet's own oeuvre. A mournful and almost similarly dishevelled *Amor* appears in the elegy on the death of Tibullus (*Am.* 3.9); he celebrates a triumph in *Am.* 1.2. *Amor* appeared several times, along with Elegy, to guide the poet toward amorous verse (*Am.* 1.1 and 2.18, *Rem.* 549).

Amor is here portrayed in bathetic terms (13-20): 'looking different from previously', not properly dressed, hair unkempt, unshaven, with his 'feathers standing on end', holding on to the foot of the bed with his left hand. We have noted above that the poet's references to *Amor/amor* waver between *amor* as object of didactics and '*Amor*', the personification of love, the poet's pupil. The wit in such oscillation lies further in the palinodic effect of *AMOR*, which, reversed, would be *ROMA*. The essence of Augustus' criticism of the poet was his refusal to join other poetic celebrants of the greatness of Rome. More than a refusal, Ovid's poetry depicted a reversal of all that civic Rome stood for. '*Amor*' here personifies this reversal. Solemn denial of the poet's culpability by the god serves only to remind readers of all that went before. As noted above, the irreverence inherent in use of the mythological antecedents of Augustus, depicting '*Amor*' as his youthful 'great-uncle' through the Aenean line, struck a wrong note. This *topos* Ovid has used elsewhere, with largely similar effect (at *Her.* 7.32, a wronged Dido incongruously terms Aeneas 'the brother of *Amor*'). Here it occurs within a prayer for Augustan prosperity (61-2):

> *sic regat imperium terrasque coerceat omnis,*
>   *Caesar, ab Aenea qui tibi fratre tuus.*

> May Caesar so rule his empire and control all the countries,
>   Caesar who through your brother Aeneas is kin to you.

Intertextuality serves to underscore the poet's creative *nequitia*. Early in the twentieth century W. Ganzenmüller, *Philologus* 70 (1911) 274-311, listed the occurrence in this poem of 125 different echoes of and borrowings from earlier works, including the poet's own. This he interpreted as a sign, less of a total loss of power, than of the narrowness of Ovid's poetic experience of life during his exile. These borrowings and the subtlety of their use more clearly signal talent, originality and parodic wit. For example: 5 *nox erat ... luna fenestras* combines two allusions to *Aen.* 3 (147 and 152) but also evokes *Am.* 1.5: *aestus erat ...*, leading to the 'epiphany' of Corinna, in Ovid's famous 'afternoon idyll'. More elusively, the setting evokes but distorts Ovid's earlier magical love-scene: the half-shuttered room, the figure of the poet lying alone, the sudden appearance of another figure. All is, however, out of pattern, grotesquely different: this figure, too, has flowing, unpinned tresses, but it is a figure from burlesque. The mournful divinity stands clasping the foot of the bed with its left hand (perhaps an evocation of Roman augural practice?). The apparition finally vanishes, or the dreamer wakes (93), in an evocation of *Aen.* 2.791.

2.2.5. Synthesis

Only extremely literal-minded readers, with no sense of humour, can take this irreverent poem seriously, on its first level of meaning. It is difficult to reconcile this comedic *mélange* with the supposedly 'serious'

73

promises of the god about the future lenience of Augustus, and his prediction of Tiberius' triumph. Perhaps a better term for Ovidian 'irreverence' is 'whimsy': the poem is a conceit, with different levels of intention. The element of parody, including self-parody, must not be underestimated. Hence this is parody: of the poet's own elegies, of apparitions and epiphanies in other poets' works and in other genres, of didactic poetry in general, of aspects of rhetoric: the refutation of the charges against the poet can be interpreted as either a form of *recusatio* (he *could not* write otherwise, for the god had called him to lower service) or as persuasion, but also, perhaps, as subtle invective against the author of his woes.

Yet there may be a deeper level on which the exiled poet is wholly serious. The prophecy by '*Amor*' of Augustus' future 'mildness' (83) underscores the emperor's present cruelty in punishing the exile so severely. At the conclusion of the poem its tone changes: the poet addresses his friend directly, praising Fabius' honesty and pointing his remarks with the *adynaton* discussed above, followed by a series of very involved *hyperbata*. The gist of the rather florid compliment is that Fabius Maximus is free from all envy (*livor*), because of his nobility of birth and character (99-104) and that his house always stands open to aid the helpless (107-8). The poet has from the beginning stressed that his tale is a fantasy, whether dream or apparition. Expressions of gratitude and friendship towards Fabius Maximus frame the fantasy; that is, they occur *outside* the literary borders of the fantasy, and the poem ends on a note of apparently sincere supplication.

The question remains: what must we conclude about the poet's attitude towards his friend, himself, his poetry and Augustus? The poem is a playful exercise in ingenuity, aimed at entertaining its recipient and Ovid's broader reading public at Rome. It also has something very serious to say. As demonstrated above, rhyme, word-order and some aspects of rhythm lend emphasis to the idea of the poet's innocence; other stylistic devices indicate some slippage between apparent and real meaning. The dream sequence (5-92) has many comical elements; some aspects appear as criticism of the Augustan regime. Travesty of epiphany literature, subtle intra-textual evocation and double-edged discussion of the poet's own past works, all point towards an attempt to vindicate, rather than condemn or excuse, the poet's former attitude of *nequitia*. The solemn tone of the unkempt and ridiculous-looking '*Amor*' borders on burlesque: the final prophecy of Tiberius' triumph in the mouth of this grotesque figure (85-6) is the climax of an irreverent, near-absurd build-up. Sincere civic loyalty is not normally expressed thus.

In conclusion: let us return to the phenomenon which, we have noted above, with Ovid often seems to indicate a deeper level of seriousness. Not so much the poet's employment of a certain stylistic device, but his deliberate *abstention* from a device strongly associated with his style, may be taken as a pointer to serious intent. The apparent climax of the poem is the solemn 'prophecy' of Tiberius' triumph. A series of *dum-*clauses leads up to a final injunction (91-2):

> dum <u>*faciles aditus*</u> *praebet **venerabile numen**/ **templum:***
> *sperandum est* <u>*nostras*</u> *posse valere* <u>*preces*</u>.

> While the awe-inspiring godhead/ temple offers easy access,
> one may hope that our prayers may prevail.

There is an almost complete lack of *hyperbaton* here: the only adjective separated from its noun is the colourless *nostras* (one of a special category that most easily floats free, so that its *hyperbaton* is generally insignificant in context). Absence of any other example in the poem of this typically Latin (and supremely Ovidian) device, with its corollary, the deliberate juxtaposition of nouns and agreeing adjectives, appears to indicate special emphasis. An ostensibly innocent *hyperbaton*-less time clause in the hexameter emphasises Augustus' unpredictability. The exiled poet's attitude to Augustus and the imperial establishment can at best be qualified as 'ambiguous' in this poem. If the variant reading *numen* (= godhead) in verse 91 for the emperor is the correct one, its unquestioning use may (here, as elsewhere) be laying ironic emphasis on Augustus' adrogation of divine titles. The uncomfortable corollary of 'easy access' being granted by the *venerabile numen* (or *templum* – the imperial residence) *only at a time of triumph* is that 'normal' access is difficult, that the 'god' is capricious – or the emperor despotic. In the pentameter the three final, emphatic words of the vanishing apparition express the central hope of the exile, that his prayers will be answered.

That this hope is expressed in the context of a ludicrous description of an 'unreal' scene seems to indicate that the exile, although he has not lost his sense of humour nor of self-mocking *nequitia*, has, by the fifth year of his relegation, lost much of his hope of recall. The ebullient tone of the poem is an indication of an unusual ability to make the best of a bad situation. The humorous creativity of the poet relieves the exile's suffering. Where exile and poet coalesce, Ovid the purveyor of divine truth appears. The divinity here acknowledged is in fine not the god of erotic love, nor the emperor-god, not even hope, but the sustaining power of humour throughout all vicissitudes. Ovidian *nequitia* is a consistent factor, also in those poems from exile not so obviously rooted in unreality. We need next to consider the various means whereby Ovid the poet wields his craft.

3

Ovidius poeta

After our general examination of poetic *variatio* and a detailed study of
the manner in which Ovid constructed an alternative reality, we need to
consider Ovid's poetic practice. This chapter starts with what he says
about his own work, goes on to examine his use of metre to convey
emotion, and ends with his ornamental use of devices such as assonance,
alliteration and rhyme as a means of 'sound painting'.

3.1. *Carmen* and poetics: poetry as enemy and friend.

We have seen Ovidian *nequitia* as the constant factor in his work.
Appreciation of Ovid's exilic works as poetry requires both an intuitive
emotional response to its portrayal of inner anguish and awareness of an
indefinable spark of transcendental genius, as well as recognition of his
consistently creative use of literary convention. The exile's ostensibly
negative judgement of both his past poetry, the cause of his exile, and his
present poetry, his means of obtaining relief (offering contact with the
known world), should be considered in the light of both literary conven-
tion and of the creator-poet's endlessly inventive and playful genius.
Without a conscious appreciation of the intuitive and emotional level of
poetry, we destroy what we seek to admire. Yet, even at the risk of such
an act of destruction, this section will attempt to quantify the poet's
references to his poetry.

Ovid's famous statement at *Tr.* 2.207 reads: *perdiderunt ... me duo
crimina, carmen et error* ('two accusations destroyed me, a poem and a
mistake'). *Carmen* is the poetry written before AD 8, which occasioned the
poet's exile. It can be viewed negatively as harmful, or it can be defended
and even vindicated. Equally, the exile's present work, the exilic poems,
can be judged negatively, both on the stylistic level and with respect to
tone and content, or it can be judged positively, not only as occupational
therapy (the means whereby the exile may save himself) but also as his
guarantee of gaining literary immortality. We have seen that Ovid some-
times designates both his past works and his present poems as his
'children', parricides though they may be, and sometimes as his 'Muse',
both his comfort and his evil genius.

To quote from poems composed perhaps eight years apart as if they were reflections of a single moment of emotion is to treat a notoriously elusive and multi-faceted poet as if he were a monolith of consistency. Statistical research I conducted some years ago for my doctoral dissertation showed that the poet tends on average to refer to his past work in a negative vein about once every 200 lines in the first chronological stage, and that this tendency consistently decreases over time, but that positive allusions are always less frequent and decrease even more drastically over the same period. The poet's tendency to mention his past works, either negatively or positively, simply diminishes over time.

Literary-critical comments on the exilic works as being 'poor, weak and reflecting the circumstances of exile' occur more consistently over the years, but increase in the last phase. Again this must be offset against positive references, both literary, and as recognition of the present therapeutic value of composition and appreciation of its potential to confer immortality on the exiled poet and his faithful friends. Initially such allusions are extremely rare, but a fluctuating trend shows a steep increase in the last phase, to about one such positive allusion every 140 lines. Chapter 4 (with the Vocabulary Table) features detailed word frequency counts that show the poet's judgement of his *mens, ingenium* and *Musa* becoming progressively more positive. In very broad terms one may extrapolate from all this a progressively more positive attitude in the exile to his oeuvre and to his place within the canon of poets, both living and dead, reaching its culmination in *Ex P.* 4.16, despite its apparently despairing end.

However, such statistics relate only to the literal level of ostensible meaning. Awareness of the creator-poet's use of irony and frequent slippage between ostensible and real meaning in the rest of his oeuvre compels us to examine individual poems for a possible second level of meaning. We need also to take into account the Callimachean tradition of *recusatio* and the Neoteric tradition of 'self-denigration'. This by no means implies that the above statistics, if merely reversed, will give a truer picture of the poet's 'real opinions', as opposed to the exile's ostensible stance. Our creator-poet works far more subtly.

The jury is still out on the authenticity of *Her.* 15 (Sappho) but similarities of thought between this poem and the trend of much of the exilic poetry nudge me toward acceptance of the poem as Ovidian. It can serve to illuminate one aspect of the poet's creative art. After almost 200 verses of complaint, the lovesick poetess exclaims *nunc vellem facunda forem! Dolor artibus obstat/ ingeniumque meis substitit omne malis* ('Now I wish I were eloquent! Pain blocks my artistry, and my brain is standing still from all its woes!' *Her.* 15.195-6). The next couplet deplores the 'fact' that the poetess' lyre is 'dumb with grief'. Such 'dumbness' is patently absurd. This playfully ironic approach to the way the articulate poetess (as character) expresses the emotions of the suffering woman, is similar to Ovid's claims to sterility in the exilic works, for instance, at *Tr.* 3.14.33-4, where the poet speaks of his talent as *infecunda* and *parva*, or *Tr.* 5.12.21-32, where (after producing some 3,500 verses in a little over two years) the exile proclaims pathetically that his talent 'has wasted away through disuse'.

Ovid's claim at *Ex P.* 4.2.23-7 that he can hardly compose, that he lacks the sacred spark, and that his Muse seldom can force his hands to write, may bear slightly more weight, for, although it comes some 2,400 verses after his previous claim to 'infertility', it occurs in the last phase, comprising a collection of only 930 verses, probably composed in the course of about four years. In the context of an increasingly positive evaluation of the creative power of poetry and the lasting nature of his creation, the bitterness of this poem (where the goddesses of poetry are termed *solacia frigida*, 45), is indicative of a particular mood and not of the tone of the whole of Phase 5. The evidence of stylistics (e.g. a low frequency of *hyperbata* and extremely sober diction) also points to intensity of emotion. This poem seems to mark the lowest ebb in Ovid's view of his works, after which (if we here assume conscious ordering by our poet) positive judgements predominate.

Allusions to the poet's early work as the cause of his exile recur throughout Ovid's exilic oeuvre. Sometimes the playfulness of the poetic framework (e.g. *Tr.* 1.1 and 3.1, featuring the little book as traveller) immediately counteracts this negative impression. Further, there is consistent recognition that what harmed before can also help (as in *Tr.* 5.2.15-18, the *exemplum* of Telephus, both wounded and healed by the same means). Throughout, negative and positive attitudes, both moral and aesthetic, alternate curiously. Even within one poem negative and positive views can co-exist, as in *Tr.* 3.3.73-6, where the poet's 'epitaph' may be read as a strong vindication of his amatory poetry.

Allusions to either moral harm to others or harm done to its creator by his past poetry sometimes introduce a positive evaluation of the therapeutic value to their author of the present poems (as in *Tr.* 5.1). Conversely, defence and moral vindication of his past work occasionally lead to an ostensibly negative view of the poet's present creative powers. Such denigrations of the poet's present abilities are typical of Callimachean *recusatio* (refusal to attempt epic because of ostensibly meagre ability), frequently hiding a strongly positive view. At least part of Ovid's ostensibly negative view of his present poetry as 'poor' (as opposed to its 'moral harm', which will be discussed below) is the idea that appropriate faults relate to the appropriate 'slenderness' of the elegiac genre as opposed to epic. For instance, *Tr.* 1.7.35-40, offering a new 'author's preface to the *Metamorphoses*', pretends that the poem's 'imperfections' are representative of the author and his fate. This would also explain the concept in *Tr.* 1.1.3 of Ovid's book as the 'unkempt child of an exile'.

'Blemishes' in the exilic works relate either to the choice of the type of content (i.e. 'monotony') or to 'failure to correct'. The 'monotony' of the exilic poems serves as a metaphor for the monotony of exile. A *diminutio ingenii* (lessening of talent) would of necessity have had to accompany a civic *diminutio capitis* (loss of civic rights). In the fourth phase such 'monotony' as a fault features several times (e.g. *Ex P.* 1.1.15-20, 3.4.11-16, 3.7.1-8). At *Ex P.* 3.9.5-6 and 33-6 the exile explains that if 'monotony' were the only fault of his 'bad poems', it would hardly be a fault. Analysis of stylistics will show that the poetry is neither 'weak' nor 'decadent'; hence we may deduce by analogy that this 'doctrine of the appropriate fault' forms part of the poet's recusationary pose.

The poet's elaborate *apologia* for his past works in *Tr.* 2 in the end acts as vindication of the poet's art and as subtle criticism of the emperor, both as ruler and as literary critic. Defence of the poet's past work relates to both his poetry and his lifestyle. These are, in the main, mutually exclusive. Defence of the *Ars Amatoria* (*Tr.* 2.240, 317-36, 539-64) indicates that the work was not immoral. We have seen such vindication repeated by '*Amor*' in *Ex P.* 3.3. Defence of the poet's life admits to the justness of the charge of immorality in the poem, but separates life and art, resulting in a further paradox. The exile proclaims that his 'Muse' was *iocosa* (playful, even licentious, *Tr.* 2.354) and his life pure (*Tr.* 2.9-10), thereby undercutting any potential defence of the *Ars Amatoria* as 'not immoral'. This undercuts Ovid's earlier statement (in *Tristia* 1.7) that his poems (with their 'appropriate fault') are a truer picture of him than any cameo.

In contrast, *Tr.* 1.9.59-64 also asserts the purity of the exile's former life, as apart from his art. Yet, in fine, the trend of the exilic works seems aimed at showing an intimate relationship between life and art. The poet tries to show that his past poetry was fictional, but the paradox of 'present fact' with all its inherent layers of doubt, complicates the issue. In the late nineteenth century Oscar Wilde defended a similar view of the autonomy of literature, but his reading public found it difficult to separate art from life in their judgment of the author. In judging Ovid, these paradoxes can only be resolved by pure acceptance. They are part of the product of a genius that revelled in paradox and inversion.

The exilic works appear almost consistently to offer a conscious reversal of Horatian literary standards. It has been postulated that *Tr.* 2 embodies a polemical stance against Horace's view of the ethical role of Roman poetry (*Ars Poet.* 132-8). *Tr.* 2 supports the standpoint of absolute poetic autonomy, and the irrelevance of ethical criteria in poetry, stressing the distinction between life and art, and emphasising that poetry is not an embodiment of supreme experience. In this, too, Ovid counters the Horatian view that poetry must reflect experience (*Ars Poet.* 102-3). *Ex P.* 1.5 seems to mark the first step in Ovid's renunciation of a

Roman public in favour of a Getic one, but this may be ironically meant, and may be intended to reflect the Horation view (*Ars Poet.* 372-3) that writing poor poetry is as good as writing none.

Horation *topoi* occur in Ovid's more overtly recusationary poems: for instance, the idea of *labor limae* and the difficulty of revision (cf. Hor. *Sat.* 1.10.65-73 and *Ex P.* 1.5.15-20 or 3.9.7-26). Ovid insists, in his approach to his past poetry, on the superiority of *ingenium* above *ars*, that is, of natural talent above careful polish. Whereas Horace emphasises *labor assiduus*, *limae labor* and *mora* (hard work, erasure and pausing), Ovid joyfully proclaims about his past poetry *quidquid temptabam scribere, versus erat* (*Tr.* 4.10.26, 'whatever I tried to write, was verse'). In the end, even the most Horatian aspects of *recusatio* regarding his present works seem, however, to defer to a more Ovidian 'doctrine of appropriate fault', recognisable as a literary pose, where poetics offer a metaphor for exile (*Tr.* 5.1.71-2):

> *ipse nec emendo, sed ut hic deducta legantur*
> *non sunt illa suo barbariora loco.*

> I don't correct them, but let them be read just as I spin them;
> they're not more barbarous than the place they're from.

It is difficult to reduce Ovid's own view of the classic opposition of *ingenium* and *ars* to a single precise scheme. He does, for instance, praise Accius and Ennius equally, but for antithetical merits (*Am.* 1.15.19-20; *Tr.* 2.423-4). The contradiction inherent in such impartiality towards the two concepts may be resolved by assuming that the poet implies that epic with its 'higher', divine inspiration does not need art to polish it, whereas 'lower' forms such as elegy require *ars* to polish the product of *ingenium*. This seems to be Ovid's stance in the poetry of exile, with his frequent protestations of and excuses for the 'unpolished state' of the poems.

Yet in our final assessment Ovid leads us (by his reiterated claims to having achieved immortality, and assertion of the power of his Muse) to realise that such negative judgements are a part of his means of portraying the horrors of exile, and no true self-evaluation by the poet. 'Lack of *ars*' may be a metaphor for exile, but it is also a vindication of the poet's *ingenium*, his natural talent, his Muse. We are unavoidably led to accept that the poet's most consistent attitude to his Muse is an almost mystic elevation to divinity.

'*Musa*' can be taken as personification of the poet's artistic ability, or of his past poetry, or his present oeuvre, as well as a disembodied patron deity, a personal guide and comforter, even a depersonalisation of himself. There is a wide diversity of critical opinions as to the poet's attitude to the Muses throughout the whole of his oeuvre, from 'simply a literary ornament', to 'a divinity that does not deceive', to a metonymic language, where the 'Muse' can be a musical composition, or any kind of poem – or whatever else the poet wishes. Chapter 1 showed that, for our poet, the Muses evince a 'wavering identity' (to use Fränkel's famous phrase about Ovid). The concept fits what we have deduced about the poet's multi-faceted approach to all aspects of his life and art. The term *caelestia sacra* (heavenly rites, *Tr.* 4.10.19) offers a clue to Ovid's poetic self-conscious-ness – that does not, however, scruple on occasion to liken his Muse playfully to a horse, or a dog straining at the leash (*Tr.* 5.9.27-30).

Although the exilic poetry appears to oscillate between malediction and praise of the Muses, such praise seems more intense. We should beware, however, of taking all negative references to either his past or present works as ironical and all positive allusions as 'sincere'. For instance, a statement, couched in the pompous form of a tricolon with threefold polyptoton of *deus* serves as the introduction to Ovid's cameo 'prophecy of a future triumph', addressed to Livia: *ista dei vox est, deus est in pectore nostro, / haec duce praedico vaticinorque deo* (*Ex P.* 3.4.93-4, 'That is the voice of a god, the god is in my heart/ under his divine guidance I predict and prophesy'). Such a grandiloquent claim cannot be considered as totally disinterested. It appears as a hyperbolic attempt to conform to the ideals of 'national poetry'. That there may be a certain irony involved in Ovid's exaggeration of prophetic arrogation is not wholly unlikely. So, too, an opposite stance, claiming that the poet 'has lost his inner fire', may be ascribed more to a desire to inspire pity than to a dispassionate appraisal of the poet's art. A poetic, ornamental, and neatly versified claim, in the couplets that follow, that the poet 'can scarcely force himself to compose', must be taken in the same light as the claim by the fictitious Sappho that her lyre is 'dumb' (*Ex P.* 4.2.25-6):

> *impetus ille sacer, qui vatum pectora nutrit*
> *qui prius in nobis esse solebat, abest.*

> That sacred force that feeds the hearts of prophets,
> that used to be in mine, is missing.

The couplet gives an impression of intense feeling. No doubt the exile on occasion felt that he had lost his inspiration. Most certainly, if he means what he says, the poet here evinces at very least a loss of perspective on his own creative powers, for the couplet still impresses, both technically and with its emotional power. Ovid's 'inner spark', the 'god within the poet' may perhaps be taken as an extension of the Stoic idea of the inner *logos* or *pneuma*, or even of the Roman *genius*, the divine force that presides over individual men. As such, it may be interpreted positively as the poet's playful answer to Augustus' arrogation of special divinity by the institution of rites celebrating the *numen* of his *genius*. There is, however, no discernible philosophical system or even extensive discursive pattern of this kind in the exilic works.

The poet's mystical view of the Muse as his goddess has four aspects, none of them philosophical. Two of these relate to the *utilitas* of poetry, and two are metaphysical. First, song relieves or soothes suffering. Second, the exercise of composition works as occupational therapy, offering a pleasant means of whiling away the exile's time. Next, it transcends space and time, both reaching out to the emperor and to the exile's friends and conferring immortality. Finally, as kind and consolatory goddess, it offers an antidote to persecution by the angry god Augustus. The poet's art appears to function similarly to what has been claimed about myth: it is an aid in a liminal situation, easing the exile from one set of circumstances into another, and transcending both.

The power of poetry to relieve suffering is spelt out in concrete terms at *Tr.* 4.1.5-14, with the familiar simile of song relieving the hard work of labourers, all engaged in menial tasks. The exile's playful self-view as a slave of sorts is moved to a higher plane when the poet next likens himself to an Achilles or Orpheus (15-18), and then emphatically states (19-20):

> *me quoque Musa levat Ponti loca iussa petentem:*
> *sola comes nostrae perstitit illa fugae.*

> My Muse also relieves me on my way to the Pontic area that has
> been imposed on me;
> she alone persevered as companion in my flight.

This is a creative literary adaptation of the philosophical view of *solacium in litteris* as found in Cicero's *Tusculan Disputations* and *De Officiis*, but it also reflects profound psychological insight. So, too, Ovid's *laus Musae* in *Tr.* 4.10.117-24 (reminiscent of the Lucretian *laus Veneris*, *De Rer. Nat.* 1.1-25) is a far cry from the poet's otherwise rationally ironic approach to the metaphysical. This address is a powerful, lucid, yet mystical statement of poetics that transcends the concept of the *utilitas* of poetry.

The idea that Augustus demanded 'useful' works from his poets is no longer entertained as a critical absolute, but, even in nuanced form, may here be discounted. Yet the exercise of poetry as 'occupational therapy' is implied in Ovid's expansion of his praise of his Muse: *tu curae requies* (118, 'you offer rest from all my cares'). This concept is spelled out in *Ex P.* 1.5.43-50: the exile explains that he dislikes idleness, is not interested in drinking or gaming and needs something to do to while away the time.

In his last years, Ovid's need to fill his hours is supplemented by the realisation that the effort of composition actually allows the exile to escape mentally from an intolerable present (*Ex P.* 4.10.65-70). Increasing awareness of the ability of a poetic 'mental vision' to transcend space is reflected in an increase in the occurrences of the appropriate vocabulary, as will be discussed in Chapter 4. The reality and reciprocal power of the poet's mental vision is conveyed to others through poetry. Transcendence is also achieved by the power of the 'bosom', *pectus* (often the seat of mentality, and not only of emotion, in ancient thought) as in *Tr.* 1.6.3; 3.4b.63; 5.4.23-4; *Ex P.* 2.10.47. Again, poetry is the outward and visible evidence of such inner and spiritual vicarious contact, but also the medium for 'ordinary' correspondence, by means of which 'normal' contact at remove can be achieved (as suggested in, for instance, *Tr.* 5.13.29-30 and *Ex P.* 1.7.1). The usefulness of poetry as a counter-gift in the usual intercourse of *amicitia* is implied in *Ex P.* 4.8.34: *Naso suis opibus, carmine, gratus erit* ('Naso will return thanks with his own wealth, his song'). Personification of poems (*Tr.* 1.1; 1.3; 5.4) makes surrogate travel even more 'real'.

Transcendence of time is the sphere of an even more mystical conceptualisation of poetry. The pervasive presence of the concept of exile as death turns any outreach through poetry into a form of 'immortality', conferred by his Muse. Ovid's poetry from exile is tantamount to a voice from the grave. This concept is broadened, also to embrace future ages. Ovid's confident statement of immortality in his *laus Musae* at *Tr.* 4.10.121-2 ignores the idea of the poet as 'already dead'. He has achieved fame while yet alive:

> *tu mihi, quod rarum est, vivo sublime dedisti*
> *nomen, ab exequiis quod dare fama solet.*

> You have given me while I was still alive something very rare, a sublime reputation, which Fame usually bestows on someone only after his burial.

This idea lies behind every promise to a friend to grant him immortality (or denial of the honour to an enemy, as in *Ex P.* 4.3). The poet never loses sight of his transcendentally creative ability, which in *Ex P.* 4.8.55-6 is the basis for his claim that *poets create the gods*. Ovid remains aware that he has this apotheosising or heroising power and, in the last phase, states confidently that he is bringing this power to bear upon Vestalis (*Ex P.* 4.7.53-4) and that it is an honour, albeit a doubtful one (*Ex P.* 4.12.3-4). A promise at *Ex P.* 4.15.35-40, to publicise the poet's gratitude to Sextus Pompeius, seems aimed at transcending space rather than time, but it shows a similar awareness of poetic power. The last poem, *Ex P.* 4.16, although ostensibly deeply despondent, has one clear note of certain faith ringing through it. Alive or dead, the poet and his Muse, here fused into one, have a great and immortal name.

Finally, the poet's Muse is a deity that supports, guides and comforts him. In his 'Aeneas' or 'Odysseus' roles she is the equivalent of Venus or Athene-Minerva. This Minerva-role is apparently evoked by Ovid's subsequent use of the term *duxque comesque* (first featured at *Tr.* 1.10.10, referring to the ship named after Minerva's helmet) for his Muse (*Tr.* 4.10.119). The phrase is, however, a part of the poet's formulaic elegiac diction, and is repeated elsewhere in other contexts. Of greater importance is the implicit thought that, by resorting to poetry and to the same metre as that of the work for which he was ostensibly exiled, the poet has invoked the powerful aid of his Muse in a virtual polemic against the emperor. Ostensibly, *Tr.* 2 is the poet's defence. His Muse speaks for herself, and for the poet. On the ironical level, we have noted that excessive adulation and lip-service to the emperor's ideal of national poetry combine with instances of *praeteritio* to suggest criticism.

On the emotional level, Ovid's poetic depiction of the pathos, loneliness and misery of exile, and its concomitant, the emperor's unbroken silence, emphasise the cruelty of the man who relegated an almost innocent sufferer to such a bleak place. On another level, we saw in Chapter 1 that bland acceptance of the divinity of the emperor appears as a form of *reductio ad absurdum* of imperial claims to divinity. Even if taken at face value, 'Augustus-Jupiter', the silently cruel thunderer, essentially a creation of the poet, has a formidable divine opponent, Ovid's avenging Muse. She uses every weapon in her considerable arsenal to defeat the angry god.

When this Muse 'speaks Getic', in ostensible praise of the Caesars, she evokes the reaction from the Getae that these Caesars are unfair in their treatment of their victim (*Ex P.* 4.13.37-8). Even her ostensible lack of power against the angry god is another weapon in her arsenal. The Roman audience – and posterity – are also moved by pity and anger at the dull cry *'Carmina nil prosunt'* (41, 'Songs don't help at all'). In the final count, it is Ovid's Muse that will defeat *Livor*. The mere fact that the poet's voice can still cry from 'beyond the grave', as it were, in *Ex P.* 4.16.47-52, for carping Envy to cease her onslaughts, is thanks to the power of his articulate Muse. Ovid lived for and through his poetry.

The *carmen* which brought about Ovid's ruin is the same *carmen* that has assured the exiled poet's immortality. The Muse that offended the emperor Augustus is the same Muse that has effectively and negatively coloured posterity's judgement of the emperor. That the exiled poet was aware of his immortal power is not to be doubted. In the frequently-quoted words of Gilbert Murray (*Tradition and Progress*, London, 1921), 'He was a poet utterly in love with poetry, with the real face and voice and body and clothes and accessories of poetry. He loved the actual technique of the verse'. Next we shall consider how Ovid used this technique to good effect.

3.2. Metre and emotion

For the ancients generic criteria were metrical, not dictated by content. For that reason Ovid's *Heroides, Fasti* and the exilic works were considered as much part of the Roman elegiac genre as his *Amores*. At the same time the difference of content and approach of the exilic works has in modern times given rise to problems in critical evaluation. Their apparently facile form was often associated in the minds of critics with the artificial world of dilettantism and dalliance. The criticism that these poems verge on the compulsive, if not 'automatic,' carries with it the implication that the exile's altered circumstances required a change of style, if not of genre.

We have noted above the critical confusion created by Ovid's apparent own strictures on his verse. A critic like Bertil Axelson, writing in 1958, on the occasion of Ovid's bimillennium (N.I. Herescu, ed., *Ovidiana*, Paris: 121-35), saw in the more frequent use of long words in the second half of Ovid's pentameters a sign of deterioration of style, whereas other critics of the time considered that he was reaching out toward a totally new style. Criticism of Ovid's technical proficiency may stem from a misunderstanding of such innovation. While the versatile poet continued in exile to remain aware of the infinite possibilities offered by his own brand of adept versification, we as critics must become alert to the continued presence of the controlling hand of a master-poet in the exile's apparently endless lamentations, so as to appreciate the depth of emotion expressed and the artistry whereby it is conveyed. If there is innovation in the exilic works, it appears to be very closely tied to metrics, and deserves attention as such.

This section will briefly examine Ovid's technique of versification in the exilic works in the light of various critical theories about the influence of metric variation on tone and content, that is, on emotional impact, briefly examining the idea that the exilic works are technically less perfect than the rest of the Ovidian oeuvre. Such an analysis may seem to ascribe, without completely explaining it, a wide emotional range to the exilic poetry. In the words of Jackson Knight (*Ovidiana*, 106-20), 'Poetry is what is left unexplained, when all the scholars, critics and philosophers have done their best to explain it.' I start with an elucidation of the concepts involved.

Ancient poetry was written to be *sung* or *chanted*. Emotional effect was conveyed as much aurally, by means of sound and rhythm, as it was intellectually, by semantic means. The musical accompaniment of verse was an important aspect of lyric poetry. Quintilian (1.10.2-33; 9.3.22) considered it necessary for the orator to study music, and, although he decries some lyrical poetry as 'debilitating and effeminate', he does not consider it possible that poetry can at all be read without a knowledge of music. Ovid himself might have been amazed that poetry could ever be considered divorced from its metrics. He himself refers to his earlier poems as being 'danced to' (*Tr.* 5.7.25-6), and likens writing poetry that has to be *read* (as opposed to *heard* or *sung*), to 'dancing in the dark' (*Ex P.* 4.2.33-4):

> *sive quod in tenebris numerosus ponere gestus*
> *quodque legas scribere carmen, idem est.*

Or (because) to dance in the dark and to write something people must *read* is exactly the same.

In his autobiographical poem Ovid applies the epithet *numerosus* to the metrically versatile Horace (*Tr.* 4.10.49). At *Tr.* 4.1.5-14, as we have seen, an extended simile equates the writing of poetry with the song which lightens labour and physical hardship. Time and again the poet explains that the pain of exile is alleviated by poetry (e.g. *Ex P.* 1.5.43-50; 4.10.65-70). Clearly, for Ovid, music, movement, metrics and emotion form an inextricable whole. Quintilian (11.3.60) quotes Cicero on the fact that strong emotion evokes rhythmic speech, ascribing this to an impulse of nature (apparently because rhythm partakes of the cyclic nature of life).

A set of general definitions will clarify terms which are sometimes confused. *Metre* is the abstract verse pattern of a poem. *Prosody* is the study of the relation between abstract verse patterns and the actual language (Greek and Latin poetry share metrics but their prosody differs). *Liaison* (joining) is an important factor in the general subservience of prosody to metrics. *Rhythm* is the totality of effect produced by the phonological structure of words within the verse pattern. *Caesura* is a break between words, sometimes signalling a pause in sense.

Elegiac verse, like epic, is often formulaic. Certain metric formulae occur in the exilic poems with almost epic regularity, of which *Tr.* 1.1.33, *principis ira*, is one, alternating with *Caesaris ira* and other formulaic variants, depending upon metrical exigency. Ovid's frequent intertextual echoes of predecessors do not stem so much from unoriginality as from his awareness of the possibilities (also for *nequitia*) inherent in placing well-worn formulae in new contexts. Ovid's use of formulae is one of the most useful and amusing vehicles of his humorous irony. From Catullus' Lesbia and Gallus' Lycoris onwards, the use of metric or prosodic equivalents as pseudonyms for the objects of Roman erotic poetry had been common. We have noted that *Livor* is the metrical equivalent of both *Caesar* and *Livia*, having a strong acoustic link with the latter. Ovid's apostrophe of *Livor* in *Tr.* 4.10.123 and *Ex P.* 4.16.47 may be a hidden allusion, by prosodic means, to his imperial persecutors.

At *Tr.* 5.1.53 it may be coincidental that the prosody of the name of the tyrant Phalaris is 'by position' such that it is the metrical equivalent of 'Augustus'. Whether the poet meant his friends to read it so, is uncertain. It is tempting to equate tyrant and emperor, for here the exile is explaining that even such a tyrant allowed his victim to bellow his misery through the mouth of the bronze bull. Why then, he says, 'this victim' is 'bellowing his misery' by means of his verse. We must, however, beware of taking such an extreme statement too seriously, as if the poet's intention is bitter attack. Ovid never loses his light touch. This example shows victim and persecutor both encompassed by the poet's affable *Selbstironie*.

At the risk of stating the over-obvious: an elegiac couplet consists of a hexameter verse plus a pentameter, with variant combinations of spondees and dactyls. The Ovidian couplet usually comprises a complete sentence. There is seldom run-on from couplet to couplet, often not even enjambment within a couplet. Often the pentameter does no more than restate the thought of the hexameter, with small claim on intense intellectual effort by the reader, as in the following random example (*Tr.* 1.11.25-6):

> *nam simul insidiis hominum pelagique laboro*
> *et faciunt geminos ensis et unda metus.*

> For I labour against attack by men and by the ocean,
> and sword and wave create twin fears.

There are a few exceptions in the exilic poems to this Ovidian rule. Long periodic sentences stretching over three to six couplets occur only occasionally (e.g. *Tr.* 4.3.1-10, *Ex P.* 2.7.23-30). In a rhetorical and metrical tour de force, *Tr.* 2.155-82 features a sentence extending over fourteen couplets. This example is based on a prayer formula: beginning with the *hypomnesis* (grounds for supplication), introduced by *per* (155-60), continuing with votive conditions (wishes that may come true only if the god grants the prayer) introduced by *sic* (161-76) and culminating in two couplets of true supplication (179-82). The 'prayer' is addressed to the great god Jupiter-Augustus. It is left to individual readers to decide upon the degree of irony involved. That some aspects of both *hypomnesis* and votive conditions are highly allusive, if not dangerously ironical, has frequently been noted.

In Latin elegiac poetry, both quantity and stress are factors in prosody, as the invariably long first syllable of a foot carries some stress ('beat'), termed the *ictus*. Another factor to be considered is what may be termed 'prose emphasis' or 'speech rhythm'. This involves both the prose accent of individual words, and the emphasis required by the meaning of a sentence. Critics disagree about whether, in reading Latin quantitative verse, metrical stress must predominate over speech rhythm, or whether speech rhythm should be paramount and metrical stress ignored. The essence of the problem lies in deciding how much value the ancients placed on each of these stress systems. This problem (also a factor in the appreciation of modern, formally metrical poetry) falls away when a poem is set to music, for stress beat or even 'unnatural lengthening' of a syllable does not jar the modern ear so much when the words are *sung*, not *spoken*. It is possible that the musical accompaniment of Latin poetry had a similar effect.

The coincidence of the *ictus* with the natural prose accent of a word, as is usual in the second half of a verse, is termed *homodyne*. Here the flow of the verse is smooth. When words are fitted to a metrical scheme, however, there is not always complete concord between speech rhythm and metrical pattern. This assumption has been the basis of hotly contended polemic, which will probably never finally be settled. Some critics doubt whether the term 'stress' can be considered at all to apply to the first beat of a foot in quantitive poetry. Some speak of '*ictus fictus*' and others call for 'natural reading', no matter what the metrics say. Clash of *ictus* (if we accept its reality) and accent is termed *heterodyne*. Such clash is an essential aspect of good poetry, for absolute coincidence makes the verse clumsy, undercutting poetic impact, and giving rise to so-called doggerel. A certain interplay between these stress systems is what makes Latin verse interesting.

When there is a clash, as is often the case in the first half of a verse, either the metrics or the 'natural feel' of a word needs to be strained to accommodate the other system. Strain felt on the acoustic level can be paralleled by intellectual perception of emotional strain. Awareness of strain as a concomitant of *heterodyne* can be an important criterion for assessing the emotional impact of the exilic poems. A random example from *Tr. 2* can act as illustration of the phenomenon (*Tr.* 2.343-4):

> ēi' mĭhĭ, | quīd' dĭdĭ | cī'? ‖ cūr | mē' dŏcŭ | ē'rĕ pă | rēn'tēs
> līt'tĕră | que^ēst' ŏcŭ | lōs' ‖ ūl'lă mŏ | rā'tă mĕ | ōs'?

Poor me, why did I learn? Why did my parents teach me
and why did any literature ever draw my attention?

Only in the last foot of the hexameter (*paren'tes*) and the first foot of each hemistich of the pentameter (*lit'tera, ul'la*) do we have complete concord between prosody and metrics. Monosyllables in all the remaining feet except the penultimate foot of each verse introduce a secondary, 'speech' stress into each foot. In the penultimate foot of the hexameter, coincidence of *ictus* and accent is partly overridden by the sense of the words, which require a strong prose emphasis on the *root* of the word *docuere* in the previous foot, with consequent lightening of accent on its penultimate ('naturally long') syllable. In the penultimate syllable of the pentameter, the sense emphasis of the sentence and the requirements of verbal prosody combine into a strong secondary stress on the first syllable of *meos*.

Sometimes juxtaposed prosodic variety is purposely employed by poets in the space of four verses or fewer. This tension heightens the interest of the verse. At *Ex P.* 4.9.63 the metre dictates a variation in prosody; that is, *heterodyne* appears. The first *bis* is stressed, the second unstressed; repeated *consul* changes its stress from second to first syllable:

> *sīc' tū | bīs' fŭĕ| rīs' cōn| sūl',// bīs | cōn'sŭl ĕ| t īl'lĕ.*
> So twice you were consul, and he too was consul twice.

This variation is in part also the result of another important characteristic of ancient poetry, its complementary system of binding and breaking between words. Breaks within a foot are all termed *caesurae*, but usually one is strongly supported by sense and is termed the main *caesura* (here marked with //). The *caesura* is 'weak' if it occurs before the last of the four beats of a foot, that is, between the two short syllables of a dactyl, as in *consul et*. It is 'strong' if it occurs in the middle of a foot, as in *sic tu*. Here *et*, following the repeated *consul*, overrides a weak *caesura*, creating *liaison*, so that the last two feet read *consule tille*. Such binding of words will be discussed below.

Ovid appears to be particularly fond of the weak *caesura*. A fully dactylic pentameter at *Tr.* 1.10.10 rhythmically supports the idea of the fearfulness of the exile's flight, as he describes his boat:

> *fīdă mă| nēt trĕpĭ| dāe ‖ dūxquĕ cŏ| mēsquĕ fŭ| gāe.*
> She remains a guide and companion to my fearful flight.

Three weak caesurae heighten the effect of uncertainty. This is an instance of the exploitation of the onomatopoeic possibilities of the dactylic word *trepidus*. It appears to conform to the ancients' view of an inherent relationship between a word and its meaning. In *Tr.* 4.1.76 *trepida* occupies the same position before the verse break as in the example above.

The last three words of *Tr.* 3.1.21 (*haec ubi sum furtim lingua titubante locutus*, 'when I had spoken thus hesitatingly, with stuttering tongue') make up a dactylic fourth and fifth foot, with a weak caesura in the fifth foot. The two minor *caesurae* are, however, partly overridden by *liaison*. The whole effect is of continuous trembling, further supported by alliteration of *t*. This multiple-faceted onomatopoeic device gives a playful but graphic impression of the 'fearfulness' of the little book, Ovid's ambassador, as it wends its timid way in the great city.

Coincidence of word-end and foot-end is called *diaeresis*. When all or nearly all the breaks within a verse are *diaereses*, the effect is oddly staccato. It did not often occur in Latin verse after Ennius' famous example, *spársis | hástis | lóngis | cámpus | spléndet et | hórret*. Here complete *homodyne* in a largely spondaic verse has a strangely jaunty effect. Ovidian control of *diaeresis* is far more subtle and emotionally more effective. In *Tr.* 2.343, quoted above, *diaeresis* after the first foot creates a natural pause, underlining the sense of the exclamation of the cry of despair, *Ei mihi*! *Diaeresis* after the third foot of the same verse creates a pause on the monosyllable '*cur*,' reinforcing the sense of the hapless victim's cry. The occurrence of *diaeresis* after the fourth foot, the so-called 'bucolic *diaeresis*', is frequently considered to add pathos to a verse, as it is considered to convey a sobbing effect (but this is not discernible with *bis* in *Ex P.* 4.9.63, also quoted above).

Preponderance of spondees can express slow inevitability or extreme emphasis. Judicious arrangement of linking and stops between words can convey subtle effects. In the well-known storm passage, *Tr.* 1.2.19-22, the spondaic first hemistich of the pentameters, repeated verbatim at 20 and 22, gives an impression of the slow, smooth pull of a gigantic wave. As expressed by end-rhyme on *-es*, each pentameter ends with the crash of the billow. The spondaic hexameter between these two verses continues the verbal depiction of the slow but inevitable movement of the water:

> *mē' mĭsĕ| rūm',// quān | tī' mōn | tēs' vōl | vūn'tŭr ă| quā'rūm*
> *iām' iām | tāc'tū| rōs' ‖ sī'dĕră | sūm'mă pŭ| tēs'.*
> *quān'tāe | dī'dūc| tō'// sūb| sī'dūnt | āe'quŏrĕ | vāl'lēs*
> *iām' iām | tāc'tū| rās' ‖ Tār'tără | nī'gră pŭ| tēs'.*

Poor me, how many mountains of water roll onward:
  you'd think that they are about to touch the highest stars.
How many trenches sink downwards as the water subsides:
  you'd imagine them about to touch the dark Underworld.

The dactylic first foot of verse 19 reflects the trembling of the exile. Then follows the slow rolling of the water. Variation is provided only by the dactylic second hemistich of the two pentameters and alternation of *caesura* and *diaeresis*. A bucolic *diaeresis* in verse 21 portrays not so much a sob as the pause in the tide before the next wave mounts up.

Heterodyne in the third and fourth feet of verse 19 (*montēs' vol-*) is coun-
terbalanced by a corresponding *homodyne* in verse 21 (*subsī'dunt*). This
is sure and capable technical virtuosity by a master hand.

In speech, words are bound together by means of the *elision* of vowels,
or by *liaison* of vowel and consonant. In Latin poetry binding forms the
basis of prosodic subservience to metrics, that is, of 'quantity by position.'
Elision is the most obvious binding device. It is, however, less frequent in
Ovid than, for instance, in Virgil. Elision within a foot counteracts the
break caused by the *caesura*. *Hiatus* is a sense break that overrides poten-
tial elision. *Liaison* occurs with elision of vowels, binding of closed syllable
and following open vowel, or binding of open syllable and following conso-
nant. It is often exploited by poets to override the break between individual
words, in order to counteract the halting effect of *caesura* and *diaeresis*.
With liaison, the phonemic basis for accent in individual words is lost, that
is, it allows *ictus* to supersede word stress. Where *heterodyne* predomi-
nates, and the words are bound by the various techniques of liaison, the
final effect would be of an almost 'wordless' emotional upwelling of sound.
The fusion of a verse into such a metrical unit reduces the phonological
independence of an individual word, which in its turn influences sense.

Where *homodyne* is predominant in a verse, in that verse the effect of
liaison is counteracted, that is, coincidence of *ictus* and word stress actu-
ally re-establishes the value of a word as a phonologically independent
unit. This means that the poet is using individual words as units of
thought, as in *Tr.* 3.3.18:

> *nūl'lă vě| nīt' sĭnĕ | tē' ‖ nōx' mĭhĭ, | nūl'lă dĭ ēs'*
> No night comes to me without you, no day.

Here *heterodyne* predominates. *Homodyne* lifts out and pinpoints the two
central monosyllables, *te* and *nox*, which are further clearly demarcated
by means of *diaeresis* and a strong *caesura*. By this means the words can
be made to bear a secondary level of meaning, adding to the emotional
weight of the couplet. The key word is 'you', the key mood is 'night'. This
new emphasis partly overrides the strongly antithetical placement of *nox*
and *dies* and the isolation of *sine* by means of a strong *caesura*. The
reader is left with a secondary impression, created by *heterodyne* and
binding in the rest of the verse, of a fusion of the exile, his days and 'noth-
ingness.' The whole bespeaks extreme pathos.

The smoothness of Ovid's style, both in epic and in his early elegiac
poetry, has frequently been commented upon. The hexameter of an
elegiac couplet differs from the hexameter of epic verse. Easy flow of
verse, smooth *caesurae*, fewer elisions than in Virgil, all make Ovid's
hexameters run smoothly. The verse scheme can be extraordinarily
varied to fit the exigencies of the poetic message. Lightness stems partly

from an increased usage of dactyls. Unique rhythmic effects are occasionally achieved by the onomatopoeic use of rhythm to underline sense. In other words, Ovid uses functional word music as an aurally descriptive device. Such a subtle fusion of music and sense is familiar to readers of Lucretius and Virgil.

Musical variation between dactyls for lightness and speed (more words sung more quickly) and spondees for solemnity and weight (fewer words sung slowly) alternates light-hearted joking with solemn appeal. So for instance 'fear and trembling' is conveyed by means of a preponderance of dactyls, as in the following example (*Tr.* 1.1.95):

> *Sīquĭs ĕ| rīt, quī | tē dŭbĭ| tāntem^ĕt ă| dīrĕ tĭ| mēntēm*
> If there will be anyone who [will accost] you as you hesitate and
>   fear to approach.

Such play of spondee and dactyl, hexameter and pentameter is alluded to in *Tr.* 3.1.53-6 when the 'little book' explains why it is so frightened that its 'teeth' (letters) are chattering, its 'face' (paper) is pale and its 'feet' (a pun) tremble. A fully dactylic hexameter (53) is followed by a fully dactylic pentameter (54) and then in the next couplet (55-6) the measures alternate, slowing down with spondees in the middle of each verse. It is clever and funny:

> *āspĭcĭs | ēxsān| guī chār| tām pāl| lērĕ cŏ| lōrĕ?*   55
> *āspĭcĭs | āltēr| nōs ‖ īntrĕmŭ| īssĕ pĕ| dēs?*   56

> Do you see that my paper is pale with a bloodless colour?
> Do you see that my feet tremble alternately?

The fifth foot of the hexameter has the 'pathetic' weak caesura, and the second hemistich of the pentameter has a prosodic form which appears to predominate when the poet is expressing the 'pain of exile'. Here the 'pain' is that of the little book: the exile's pain has been sublimated by the poet's play. A similar play of dactyls and spondees occurs at *Tr.* 5.8.15-16, depicting the uncertain rotation of the wheel of Fortuna.

So too, acoustic effects enhance rhythmic flow, emphasising the metrical structure of a verse. In *Tr.* 1.1.95 (quoted above) predominant assonance of tonally high *i* and *e* sounds conveys an impression of shrill fear. In verse 111 of the same poem, alternating dactyls and spondees metrically portray the hesitation and sudden quivering of the 'fearful' personified books of the *Ars Amatoria*, hiding in an obscure corner:

> *trēs prŏcŭl | ōbscū| rā/ / lătĭ| tāntēs | pārtĕ vĭ| dēbīs*
> You will see three [books] hiding far away in a dark corner.

The playful conceit charms the reader, simultaneously belying the exile's supposed fear of the emperor which it pretends to illustrate.

Two allusions to the myth of Icarus convey the effect of 'fluttering' by means of alternating dactyls and spondees. At *Tr.* 1.1.89 the alternation is regular, giving the impression of jerky flight. At *Tr.* 3.4.23, two spondees first give the impression of a steady sweep of wings, illustrating Icarus' hubris in flying majestically on high. Then two dactyls portray Daedalus' quicker, more energetic flight:

> *nēmpĕ quŏd* | *hīc āl* | *tē,//* *dē* | *mīssĭŭs* | *īllĕ vŏ* | *lābāt*
> Probably because the one was flying high, the other lower.

The joke, if joke it is, is that the play over the full spectrum of vowel pitch counterpoints the picture conveyed by the rhythm. Pitch appears to negate the meaning of the two words denoting altitude: a lower-pitched word (*alte*) refers to the higher flight of Icarus, whereas a series of high-pitched *i*-sounds, dipping down to -*e*- and even -*u*- (*demissius ille*), indicates the lower (but apparently uneven) track of Daedalus' flight. The whole is an interesting exercise in ingenuity. This alternation of pitch is best illustrated by means of modern musical notation, as explained in Chapter 2:

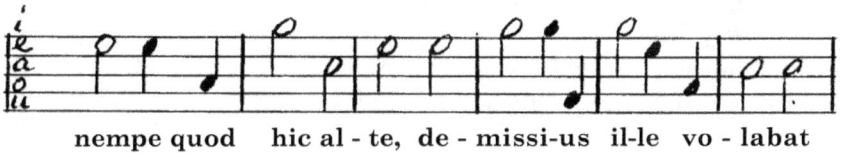

nempe quod   hic al - te,   de - missi-us   il-le   vo - labat

The arrangement of words in the pentameter is important at both the semantic and the metric level. At the intellectual level, perhaps the most important and characteristic aspect of elegiac verse construction is the distribution of nouns and their epithets over the two halves of the pentameter (*hyperbaton*). The phenomenon is central to the appreciation of both verse technique and emotional tone. The history of the development of *hyperbaton* in ancient poetry is a fascinating but contentious subject. Chapter 4 will explore it more fully. Separation of noun and adjective is only one of many variants of the technique. This type of hyperbaton appears in its most developed form in the most consciously *literary* poetry, standing as it does at the other end of the scale from early oral poetry, with its functional convention of fixed, formulaic adjective-noun phrases. The device, although used more sparingly in Latin hexameter verse, lends itself most aptly to elegiacs. It is common to all the elegists, but appears to be particularly characteristic of Ovidian verse. That such *hyperbaton* is the rule rather than the exception in elegiac versification gives symmetry and balance to the verse, also serving to override the 'splitting effect' of the metric break at the middle of the pentameter. Cases where this type of *hyperbaton* does not occur, merit special attention. The 'prosaic' word order of a couplet such as *Tr.* 1.2.57-8 seems to increase its emotional impact:

> *fingite <u>me dignum</u> **tali nece**, non <u>ego solus</u>*
>   *hic vehor: inmeritos cur **mea poena** trahit?*

> Imagine <u>me as worthy</u> of **such a death**, I'm not the <u>only traveller</u> here:
>   why does **my punishment** drag others undeservedly along?

It is unusual in elegiac verse that four epithets within a single couplet should be juxtaposed to their nouns, as here. The only variation in 'the logical order of thought' is the chiastic arrangement **NA-AN-NA-AN**, which seems to have been dictated by the logic of emotion. The important pronouns '*me*' and '*ego*' and the possessive adjective '*mea*' are placed before the words with which they agree. A strong sense break after *vehor* disturbs the smooth flow of the pentameter. The normal verse break after the first hemistich in its turn slows the run-on sense of the verse, and emphasises '*inmeritos*'. The 'awkwardness' of the couplet appears deliberate. Form supports sense in the exile's cry of distress.

Apparently there are 38 prosodic combinations possible in the second hemistich of the pentameter of a Roman elegy. The type that is fifth in frequency consists of a long monosyllable, then a four-syllabic word consisting of two short syllables followed by a long and a short, and finally, an iambic or pyrrhic word. The monosyllable in such a verse is usually an indeclinable, the four-syllabic word most frequently a verbal form, and the last word often a noun. This form occasionally sets a pattern in the first hemistich which is followed by the second, creating perfect reduplication. It seems to be a potentially effective vehicle for the expression of poignant emotion. Analysis of the poems of the earlier elegists found that this verse type has a frequency in the order of 6.77%. Ovid displays a much lower frequency, ranging from 1.2% in the *Remedia Amoris* to 2.61% in the *Fasti,* but the figure for his exilic works has been fixed at about 5.5%. There may be a relation between this apparent change in technique and Ovid's emotional experience of the pain of exile.

Elision in the second hemistich of the pentameter is usually avoided by the elegists, but occurs at *Tr.* 2.202 where it creates a four-syllabic compound word, which is preceded by a monosyllable. It is an example of such a 'painful' hemistich, stressing the fears of the exile:

3. Ovidius poeta

nē sīt | cūm pătrĭ-| ā ‖ pāx quŏque^ă-| dēmptă mĭ-| hī
Lest peace also be taken from me, along with [the loss of] my
fatherland.

A pentameter that also achieves a 'painful' effect while simultaneously
managing to convey the impression of broken-hearted stuttering, is the
dactylic pentameter *Tr.* 3.3.28 with two central monosyllables framed by
six bisyllabic words, three on either side. A stuttering or sobbing effect is
gained by the alternation of weak caesura, strong caesura, *diaeresis*,
verse break, strong caesura, *diaeresis*, weak caesura:

tēm'pŭs ă| gī' sĭnĕ | mē' ‖ nōn' nĭsĭ | trīs'tĕ tĭ| bī'
(It is clear that) spending time without me (can be) nothing other
than sad for you.

Liaison between all the words (except *non* and the second *nisi*, but where
repetition of *-n* works to counter potential *diaeresis*) partly overrides the
breaks, creating an impression of a 'wordless' cry in which only *me* and
non before and after the sense break (also stressed by means of *homo-
dyne*) stand out as individual units. The otherwise predominant
heterodyne (positional loss of stress on the first syllables of *agi, sine, nisi,
tibi*) bespeaks strong emotion. The exile projects his own longing into his
picture of his wife's solitude.

Critics sometimes object when a poet appears to have broken a
prosodic rule to which he previously adhered. Bertil Axelson (cited above)
saw the virtue of *liaison* as a vice, rejecting the concept of *heterodyne* as
a 'Chimaera' and asserting that scholars would have been spared infinite
pains had they accepted as fact that the ground for metric rules is always
and exclusively 'aesthetic.' He took as axiomatic that elegiac pentameters
should end on bisyllabic iambic words, arguing that Ovid preferably uses
'*inhaltslose*' words like *habet, erat, tibi*, etc., at the end of the pentameter,
joining these to the previous word by means of some form of *liaison*,
thereby creating a 'five-syllabic word'. He listed as 'most frequent' in this
position: *tuus, equus, amo, opus, habeo, aqua, ago, humus, iter, ovis, tibi,
mihi, meus* and forms of *sum*. This he then decried in the terms of
Quintilian's judgement (9.4.66) of an ending of five syllables as '*prae-
mollis*', that is, 'lax', but Quintilian was writing about oratory, not verse,
and expressed this judgement in an aside.

Liaison of an apparent bisyllable with the word preceding it, to create
a longer word, is a form of poetic variation and not necessarily 'techni-
cally superficial'. The bisyllabic ending is not essential to elegy, but a
later development. In Propertius there is, for instance, a progression
from 36% non-bisyllabic endings in the *Monobiblos* to, respectively,
10.5%, 2.4% and 1% in his three subsequent books. Scholars have

collected impressive statistics on the topic, but we may be content with the observation that Ovid appears first to have perfected the technique, and then to have moved consciously away from it.

Axelson's observations are, however, of value as a guide in exploring this aspect of Ovidian versification in the exilic oeuvre. A cursory count of the total occurrences of the eight most frequent of the words he has singled out will show that they are consistently employed throughout the exilic oeuvre at about once every 25 verses, except in *Tr.* 5, where they are only half as frequent. There is, however, after this no further, strong sign of movement away from use of the device, and also no reason why the poet should have wanted to discard it, as it makes for efficient versification and also enhances the ebb-and-flow effect of some types of elegiac couplet.

At the same time the exilic works are characterised by a noticeable increase in truly polysyllabic words at the end of the pentameter, with the greatest number (17) occurring in *Ex P.* 4. This characteristic appears as deliberate innovation towards the end of the poet's career. Critics taking at face value Ovid's own aspersions on his exilic poetry have occasionally seized on this innovation as an indication of a failure of technique, apparently forgetting that Quintilian was discussing endings to periodic sentences, not prescribing an absolute poetic standard. Longer words placed in this prominent position are key nominals relating to the exiled poet's circumstances, such as *adulterium, amicitia, ingenium, auxilium, officium, imperium, exsequiae, obsequium, posteritas, utilitas, barbaria, patrocinium* and (at *Tr.* 2.416, where it is emphasised by means of syntactic rhyme and *hyperbaton*) *impurae ... historiae.* Verbs are: *perlegere, aspiciant, invenies, imposuit, (non) faciet, scelus^est* (turned into one word by *liaison*) *liceat, recitent, videor, tegeret.* The innovation appears therefore as the beginning of a consciously new direction, conveying a greater intensity of thought and pointing words for special effect. Such a concentration of this innovative usage points to *Ex P.* 4 as being a collection consciously arranged by the poet, or by an editor, and not a mere posthumous residue of rather inferior poems, as has sometimes been supposed.

As noted before, in *Ex P.* 4.13 Ovid tells a fellow-poet of having become a *poeta Getes* and having held a *recitatio* of a poem on Augustus' apotheosis before an audience of 'savages', who clashed their arms and growled approval. It is very likely, given the archaeologically demonstrable advanced state of Tomitan culture at the time, that at least parts of this poem may have been less than factual. It ends with a celebration of the deeds of Germanicus. The poem may be seen as an entertaining experiment, meant to amuse Germanicus as much as to compliment him, and it comes as no surprise to find two consecutive couplets ending on such polysyllabic 'key words'. The poet's addressee is a member of the young prince's entourage (*Ex P.* 4.13.43-6):

3. Ovidius poeta

at tu, per studii communia foedera sacri,
  *per non vile tibi nomen **amicitiae***
(sic capto Latiis Germanicus hoste catenis
  *materiam vestris adferat **ingeniis** ...) etc.*

But you, by the common pacts of our holy zeal,
  and by the name of friendship so dear to you
(so may Germanicus, after he has bound the enemy with Latin chains,
  offer matter for your genius ...) etc.

In the end we remain aware of the fact that it is virtually impossible to separate the various strands of a complexity of techniques. Interesting effects created by a combination of all the above devices abound in the poems of exile. I close this section with a single example (*Tr.* 2.87-8):

ēr'go^hŏmĭ | nūm' // quāe | sī'tum^ŏdĭ | ūm' mĭhĭ- | cār'mĭnĕ- | quōs'quĕ-
dē'bŭĭt, | ēst' // vūl | tūs' ‖ tūr'bă-sĕ | cū'tă-tŭ | ōs'.

And so hatred was sought for me by my song, and,
  as it should, the crowd followed your expression.

The hexameter has no strong central *caesura* and two elisions, also binding by other means (e.g. the reduplicated consonant *-m m-* at the end and beginning of consecutive *odium mihi*), also open-syllabic liaison (marked here with hyphens). The only real break in the hexameter is the *caesura* between *hominum* and *quaesitum*, which is partly over-ridden by rhyme. Enjambment carries the sense of this 'bonded compound word' into the pentameter, where the first pause is at the *diaeresis* after the first foot, after which a *caesura* breaks up a spondaic foot (*est vul-*), giving slow emphasis. *Heterodyne* at the third and fourth feet of the hexameter (*ŏdĭ | ūm' mĭhĭ* as opposed to prose *ódium mihi*) stresses the painful allusion to 'hatred'. *Homodyne* in the last two feet separates *cār'mine* as a thought entity from this phonic agglomeration, giving it suitable emphasis. *Liaison* turns the second hemistich of the pentameter into another compound word, its unity supported by the *heterodyne* of *tuos* and the jingling alliteration of *tu- tu- ta- tu-*. What such alternating sweep-and-stop is portraying is the information given in the couplet: that all the world clung to the emperor's expression, closely following its every nuance.

In every poem of the exilic corpus we find other instances of sure and adept versification, too many and too consistent to be mere offshoots of the remnants of a degenerate mechanical ability in a debilitated poet. When analysed, these instances may be seen to heighten emotional effect, express pathos or add musical emphasis to the content of a poem. It is not unjustified to state that, far from showing signs of weakening or degeneration, Ovid's exilic poems may be judged, at the prosodic level, as the culmination of his oeuvre. That the mature poet chose at this stage of his career still to experiment and innovate within the confines of a generic form that he had helped to perfect, is the sign of fertile genius.

3.3. Ovidian *Lautmalerei*

As this last example demonstrates, also in the *sound* of his poetry Ovid's talent remained undiminished in exile. We shall next consider under various heads the aural effect of Ovid's poetry, with due awareness that he was still writing poems that were meant to be read aloud (in Rome), in spite of his claims of having no audience (at Tomis). Part of the richness of Ovidian verse, his 'logodaedaly' ('verbal artifice', the topic of Chapter 4), is his employment of a series of acoustic devices in what the Germans call *Lautmalerei*, 'sound painting'. The undisputed musicality of Ovidian versification stems not only from his metrics, but also from his use of a range of these devices.

Some of the following technical terms have occurred in passing already, but in the interests of clarity I here repeat their definitions together with some not yet discussed: *alliteration* occurs when consonants or groups of related consonants are repeated at close intervals in a verse or couplet; *assonance* means that vowels or groups of vowels are repeated in a noticeable way within a short passage of verse; *onomatopoeia* involves the support of the sense of words by their sound; *rhyme* occurs when syllables (comprising a grouping of vowels and consonants) are repeated at close intervals (or two dissimilar syllables with at least the final vowel or vowel plus consonant coinciding follow in close succession). When whole groups of syllables concur, we speak of *holorhyme*, or *rich rhyme*. *Homoeoteleuton* refers to instances where only the unstressed last syllables of words concur. *Epanastrophe* involves reduplication of the same sound or sounds at the end and beginning of consecutive words.

There seems to be little evidence for an appreciation of the aesthetic value of acoustic devices among ancient critics. Yet the devices abound in ancient poetry. It has been said that ancient critics 'defended' rather than 'recommended' alliteration and assonance. Quintilian (12.10.31) speaks of closing -*m* as sounding 'like the lowing of an ox'. For Quintilian (9.4.41) reduplication of syllables and clusters of consonants breaks continuity and impairs the rhythm of both prose and poetry. This may be a virtue in prose, but for him it is a *vitium* in poetry. Cicero, *De Oratore* 2.59.240, seemed to think that the only purpose of cumulation of consonants was for comic effect. Yet Ovid's poetry is characterised by his use of *epanastrophe* as an alternative to liaison to achieve binding. The most frequent position for this device is between the short syllables of the fifth foot of the hexameter, overriding the break caused by a weak caesura in this position. This device also binds words into longer phonic units or 'compound words'. An interesting example occurs in the last poem of the collection (*Ex P.* 4.16.3-4):

> *famaque post cineres maior venit. et mihi nomen*
> *tum quoque, cum vivis adnumerarer, erat.*

> Fame usually grows greater after death. But for me, my name
>   was already established
> Even then, while I still was counted among the living.

Here syllabic *epanastrophe*, -er, er- in the second hemistich of the pentameter is preceded by -era-, the whole virtually palindromic complex of sounds hinging symmetrically around a central -rer-. This complex arrangement picks up and amplifies -ere- from *cineres* in the third foot of the hexameter, in a subtle and deliberate echo of sounds, reemphasising in the pentameter the semantically most important word of the hexameter. Alliteration of -r- further fuses the whole of the second hemistich into a 'wordless growl.'

It is extremely difficult to generalise about sound effects: the same sounds can, in different contexts, and in slightly different combinations, convey the effect of distance and alienation, or of intimacy and emotional involvement. Discussion of the cumulative effect of particular sound groupings can do no more than speculate on the possible emotional impact of that particular grouping on an ancient audience. Modern opinions may also differ on what effect a set of sounds may have within a verse. Unsubstantiated statements such as 'alliteration of *c* and *q* adds a note of scorn' or 'the effect of chattering teeth is conveyed by *d* and *t*', are frequent in close analyses of Ovidian verse. In the latter case, reference to the effect of dentals makes sense. The following formulation has on occasion been suggested: *u* expresses sadness; *l*, pleasure and voluptuousness; *m*, despair; *p*, a variety of effects: prayer, bitterness, confession and (combined with *c* and *t*) the harshness of life at Tomis. No stylistic device can be considered in isolation: pathos is mostly conveyed by a combination of effects. Further, the experience of sound effects is subjective and would even differ in the same hearer depending upon her mood. There is no consistent 'scientific formula' by means of which we can express exactly what effect a particular set of sounds will consistently convey. Context is all.

3.3.1. Alliteration, assonance and onomatopoeia

We must beware the 'intentional fallacy'; that is, reading intentional sound effects into fortuitous groupings. Yet alliteration and rhyme often do *not* seem fortuitous in Ovid's *Metamorphoses*, occurring frequently at the beginning of verses and at major verse breaks. Alliteration can work as a binding factor, cutting across metrical divisions and setting up new connections by overriding syntactic divisions. Hexameter verses frequently end on two alliterative words, a stylistic quirk that adds to the musical effect of a verse. Such musical effects still occur in popular speech, in incantationary verse, and in the language of children.

For the gauging of musical effects it is hardly necessary to differentiate between assonance and alliteration. Initial vowels, when repeated, can be classed as alliterative. Vowels are purely assonant when preceded by a consonant. As we have no true idea of the musical accompaniment of Latin lyric verse and the degree to which the tonality of the vowels was supported by such accompaniment, we can only approximate the effect in an evaluation of assonance, as with my adaptation of modern Western musical notation to indicate pitch. Ovid frequently exploited the natural differences of pitch between the five vowels by means of contrasts in assonance. Again, interpretation of effects so created depends largely on context: sometimes our interpretation of sound effects seems to depend on our understanding of the sense, rather than that the sound actually and objectively supports the sense.

A striking case of phonic play appears consistently about once every forty verses throughout the exilic oeuvre. Because observation and analysis of the phenomenon are so very subjective, I shall not try to give any breakdown of changing frequency of occurrences from phase to phase. Most frequent is play on *s*, which appears almost twice as often as the next group of sounds, *t, p* and *m*, followed by the most striking vowel *i*, then *u* and its semivowel *v* (pronounced *wh*); then the vowel *a* and consonant *c/ qu*; then *r* (usually in syllabic combination with the vowels *a, e* or *o*); next *l*; then the vowel *o*; then assonance with *e*, and alliteration of *f*; and, least frequently, alliteration of *d* and its unvoiced equivalent *t*. The frequency of monosyllables like *nec* and *nunc* ensures a high frequency for the sounds *n* and *c*, but the letter *n* otherwise seldom features in striking alliterative groupings. Finally, combinations of sounds, particularly of the four most frequent consonants, *s, t, p, m*, with the three most common vowels, *i, u* and *a* (also *c/qu* and *r* with these vowels) offer striking effects. Chapter 4 deals with repetition of words, which necessarily also entails alliteration and assonance.

Examination of some examples will give an indication of the emotional impact of these various phonic effects, starting with play on dentals *d* and *t*. At *Tr.* 3.2.3-4 the poet reproaches his Muses and Apollo for not having helped him. The third verse has some alliteration of (frequent) *s*, with *i*, *r* and the ubiquitous *nec ... nec*, but the fourth verse has the unusual (*nec .../*) *docta sacerdoti turba tulistis opem* ('and you, learned throng, didn't bring aid to your priest'). The effect of *do – do – ti – tur – tu – tis* appears comical to the modern ear, seemingly undercutting any impression of pathos the poet may have tried to convey. Such ribaldry is further enhanced by calling the Muses a *docta ... turba*, which could be translated 'learned mob'. The poet is apparently poking fun at himself by means of so-called *Selbstironie*. At *Ex P.* 3.3.47-8 (in the dream sequence) *du – da – du – do – di – do* combining with *s* creates an effect of bluster (and of fun by the poet at the expense of the exile):

> *dum damus arma tibi, dum te, lascive, docemus,*
>   *haec te discipulo dona magister habet.*

> While I provide you with arms, while I am teaching you, wanton fellow,
>   with you as his pupil, your schoolmaster gets these gifts.

At *Tr.* 1.11.3 assonance with predominant *e* and *i* is striking. We have noted before that on a scale of 1 to 5 the tonal pitch of these two vowels would be considered highest:

> *aūt haēc | mē, gĕlĭ | dō trĕmĕ | rēm// cūm | mēnsĕ Dĕ | cēmbrī*
> *scrībēn | tēm mĕdĭ | īs ‖ Hādrĭă | vīdĭt ă | quīs*

> Or the Adriatic saw me writing this [letter], while I was shivering in mid-ocean during the freezing month of December.

The increasingly shriller pitch of vowels over the couplet combines with alternation of dactyls and spondees to indicate shivering fear ending on an hysterical note.

The same sound can create completely different effects, depending on context. The consonant *f* predominates at *Tr.* 2.412, in a scathing comment on the travesty of Achilles' manly status in Aeschylus' *Myrmidons* or Sophocles' satyr play *Achilles' Lovers*. It did not harm these poets, Ovid says, *infregisse suis fortia facta modis* ('to have denigrated heroic deeds in their poetry'). The combination of *f* with *s*, *t* and *r* seems to express the deflation of heroic bombast. At *Ex P.* 4.1.25-8 repeated *f* has a completely different effect: it frames and hence emphasises the all-important word *fiducia*, 'trust', in verse 27:

> *nunc quoque nil subitis clementia territa fatis*
>   *auxilium vitae fertque feretque meae.*
> *unde rogas forsan **fiducia** tanta futuri*
>   *sit mihi? quod fecit, quisque tuetur opus.*

Now also, not at all fazed by my sudden fate,
  your kindness brings aid for my life and will bring it for ever.
You may perhaps ask from where such unfailing **faith** in the future
  for me? Every man cares for his own artifact.

Exclamations of horror often resonate with the sound *o*. At *Tr.* 3.14.28 the exile excuses his 'bad poetry' by requesting whoever reads it, to reckon *compositum quo sit tempore quoque loco* ('at what time and in what place it was composed'). The sounds of the verse suggest the sympathetic 'ohs' that the exile hopes to elicit. In contrast, readers may possibly detect a note of irony at *Tr.* 5.2.49-50 in the adulatory tone of a hyperbolic compliment to Augustus. Predominant *o* combines with alliteration of *p* to convey an impression of fawning obsequiousness which, in combination with exaggerated flattery of the emperor, invites suspicion:

> *o decus, o patriae per te florentis imago,*
>   *o vir non ipso, quem regis, orbe minor ...*

> O ornament, o image of the fatherland that flourishes through
>   your efforts,
>   o man no smaller than the very world you rule ...

A curious combination of the liquid *l* with *r*, *s* and *-ng* occurs at *Ex P.* 1.10.3-4 where the sense of *longus* and *languor* is supported by a series of long syllables, in particular *a*:

> *longus enim curis vitiatum corpus amaris*
>   *non patitur vires languor habere suas.*

A continuous languor does not allow my body, sapped of strength by bitter cares, to maintain its vigour.

Similarly, *r* combines with different vowels for interesting effect. At *Ex P.* 3.1.19-20 vowel gradation with *r* produces a series of 'growling' reverberations:

> **rara**, *neque haec felix, in apertis eminet* **arvis**
>   **arbor**, *et in* **terra** *est altera forma* **maris**.

Rarely does a tree rise up in your bare fields, and even then it's stunted, and your landscape appears like another version of the ocean.

At *Ex P.* 4.13.1-4 the appearance of the poem purports to be an indication of the poet's place of exile. Its initial effect is positive. Verbal echoes initially emphasise the name of the addressee (*ve̱re̱*, **Ca̱re̱**, *vocaris*). Yet

3. Ovidius poeta

the continued *r*-sounds -*ari*-, -*or*, -*ro*-, -*ru*-, -*ura*- and -*ar* in the third and fourth verses grate cumulatively. Gentle alliteration of *s* in the first verse appears as cheerfully ornamental. In verse 4 predominant *s* could be taken to recreate the sibilance of a sigh, but the effect is strangely jaunty, the result of four *t*-sounds, setting up a castanet-clicking counterpoint. Our final impression is of the poet's continued playfulness in adverse circumstances:

> *O mihi non dubios inter memorande sodales,*
> *qui quod es, id vere, Care, vocaris, ave.*
> *unde salutaris, color hic tibi protinus index*
> *et structura mei carminis esse potest.*

O my bosom friend among all other indubitable friends, who are called what you truly are, dear chap, hail! This tone and the structure of my song can clearly serve as an indication to you from where you are being greeted.

Predominant assonance of *i* appears whenever the exile speaks of losing his Latin, for instance at *Tr.* 3.14.47-50 and 5.12.55-8 (verse 58 recurs at *Ex P.* 3.2.40). Repeated *i* is combined with alliteration of *c/qu*: *nam didici Getice Sarmatice loqui* ('for I have learned to chatter in Getic and Sarmatic'). It is tempting to conjecture that this is, indeed, an onomatopoeic reference to the local language of Tomis – not some conjectural Thracian dialect, but rather the local dialect of Milesian Greek (which had apparently at this time already developed considerably in the direction that modern Greek now reflects). In the second instance the noticeably deeper tones of the previous couplet, with predominant assonance of *a*, *ae*, *au*, *o* and prominent *r*, *t* and *b*, may, again, be an onomatopoeic reflection of the proto-Germanic Thracian dialect of the Getae (but probably not of the Sarmatians, who lived further north; *Ex P.* 3.2.37-8):

> *hic quoque Sauromatae iam vos novere Getaeque,*
> *et tales animos barbara turba probat.*

Here too the Sarmatians and Getae know you
and the barbaric horde approves of such an attitude.

Alliteration with *m*, both initial and final, is frequent. At *Tr.* 3.8.37-8, repeated -*um* in the hexameter gives way to triple -*im* in the pentameter. Tonal switch from *u* to *i* conveys the effect of protracted moans giving way to shrill crying: *cumque locum moresque hominum cultusque sonumque/ cernimus, et, qui sim qui fuerimque, subit ...* ('and when I regard the place and the habits of the people, their degree of civilisation and the noise, and when it strikes me who I am and who I was ...').

103

Alliteration of *t* occurs frequently. At *Ex P.* 1.2.103 the exile urges Fabius Maximus to plead for his removal: *non petito ut bene sit, sed uti male tutius, utque ...* ('I'm not asking to have it all good, but simply to have it bad in greater safety, and that ...'). Repeated *t* and *s* convey a strange urgency, the exile's teeth chattering with fear. This is partly due to the staccato effect of a preponderance of short words: four monosyllables, four bisyllables, and only two trisyllables (with alternating *i* and *u:* -*tit*- ... *tut*-). Juxtapositioning underlines the paradox of *male tutius*. Whether this picture would evoke less sympathy than amusement is a matter for speculation.

Alliteration of *p* is frequent. At *Tr.* 2.179-90 (in the exile's plea for clemency) key words over altogether ten verses all begin with *p*, originating from an allusion to Augustus' title as *pater patriae* ('father of the fatherland'). The pattern, with the usual counterpoint of other sounds, is built up as follows: 179 *parce, precor* ('spare me, I pray'), 181 *parce, pater patriae* ('spare me, father of the fatherland'), 182 *placandi spem* ('hope of placating'), 183 *precor ... petitis* ('I pray ... to petitions'), 184 *saepe dedisse deos* ('that the gods have often given'), 185 *propriusque* ('and nearer'), 186 *pars erit ex poena parva levata mea* ('a small part of my punishment would be lifted'), 187 *perpetior* ('I go on enduring'), 188 *patria* ('fatherland'), 189 *septemplicis Histri* ('of the Ister with its seven folds'), 190 *Parrhasiae gelido Virginis axe premor* ('I am oppressed under the cold pole of the Parrhasian Virgin'). The reader is tempted to remember those other exiles, the two Julias, who could have pleaded in much the same terms, *parce, pater*, but whose pleas remained equally unheard.

The longest noticeably sustained alliteration of *p* occurs at *Ex P.* 2.8.17-52 in the poem thanking Cotta for his gift of imperial portraits (conjecturally, coins bearing images of the imperial family). Starting at verse 17 (where the exile claims 'he now has everything at hand except the Palatine'), the pattern continues: 20 *patriae*, 23 *parce*, 24 *supprime*, 25 *parce, precor*, 27 *per patriae*, 28 *per*, 29 *perque ... reperta*, 31 *perque*, 32 *potest*, 33 *perque ... patre nepotes*, 34 *per tua iussa*, 35 *parte ... poenas*, 36 *procul*, 37 *proxime*, 38 *precibus*, 39 *primum pavido*, 41 *pater in Pylios*, 42 *possis*, 43 *nupta*, 44 *supplicis ... preces*, 45 *sospes ... prole nepotes*, 46 *peperere*, 47 *rapuit*, 48 *pars ... partus*, 50 *purpureus*, 52 *praesentis aliquid prosit habere deos* ('may it be a little profitable to have the gods here present'). This is the formula of prayer. Insistent, cumulative *p* invites an ironical reading, as in *Am.* 1.3.14 *nudaque simplicitas purpureusque pudor* ('naked simplicity and blushing modesty') where the apparently ingenuous, 'guileless lover' is at his most guileful.

Alliteration of the semi-vowel *v* is seldom obtrusive, but verses 13-14 of the same poem offer an exception. Again it is tempting to read irony into the exaggerated alliterative effect in such flamboyant protestations of gratitude for the gift (*Ex P.* 2.8.13-14):

> *Caesareos video vultus, velut ante videbam:*
> *vix huius voti spes fuit ulla mihi.*

> I see the visages of the Caesars, just as I saw them before:
> I scarce had any hope that this prayer would ever be granted.

This effect is enhanced by the accompanying assonance of the vowel *u*, usually associated with wailing, which spills over into the next couplet. Whether this is a display of genuine heartache at no longer seeing a beloved emperor in the flesh, or whether it is assumed to amuse the exile and his friend — and, incidentally, either to pacify or to annoy the emperor — is for the reader to decide.

In many of the verses quoted above, a secondary alliteration (of *s*) is noticeable. The sibilant is the most frequent object of reduplication, as also, for instance, at *Tr.* 3.9.21-2 where a sinister note is struck as the fugitive Medea wonders what she should do: *dum versat in omnia vultus/ ad fratrem casu lumina flexa tulit* ('while turning her face in all directions, she by chance directed her wavering gaze at her brother'). The sibilants enhance the ominous atmosphere created by the 'clicking' rhyme of (mostly alternating) verses 18, 20, 22, 23, 24, which all end on *-it*. In the next poem alliteration of *s* is onomatopoeic, conveying the sound of creaking wagon wheels: *Tr.* 3.10.59-60 *ruris opes parvae, pecus et stridentia plaustra/ et quas divitias ...* ('the small riches of a rural home, flocks and creaking wagons/ and whatever wealth ...').

Readers may, however, interpret these sounds differently, and we can only guess at the interpretation of Ovid's original audience.

3.3.2. Homoeoteleuton

Alliteration and assonance often work as a binding factor in the last words of consecutive or closely aligned verses. *Homoeoteleuton* (similar, but unstressed, word-endings) is a special case. The final word, especially in the hexameter, is of great significance, frequently marked by *homoeoteleuton* in consecutive verse-ends. It may be argued that there is a limited number of sounds upon which Latin inflected words can end, making *homoeoteleuton* inevitable, but a consistent series of similar endings to verses, as in *Tr.* 1.2.5-13, does not appear wholly fortuitous. If we mark a dissimilar hexameter-ending as *0H* and dissimilar pentameter as *0P*, the series here reads: *Apollo – 0P – Turno – 0P – 0H – suo – 0H – deo – perdo*. A similar series, on *i*, occurs in the same poem at verses 101 to 109, thus: *illi – mihi – 0H – dedi – divi – 0P – 0H – 0P – vocati*.

Groups of two words with *homoeoteleuton* may be fortuitous. Patterns of alternating sounds can hardly be so. One such pattern occurs at *Tr.* 1.8.27-40, with alternating *i* and *s*. Only verses 29 and 32 end differently, but here the final word of 29, *essem*, repeats the alliterative *-sse-* of verses 31 and 33: *-iuncti – sui – essem – tibi – nosses – 0P – esses – loci – ventos – aquis – Quirini – mihi – sinistri – iugis.* On occasion a set of verses with *homoeoteleuton* seems purposely to display degrees of vowel *Ablaut,* that is, vowel gradation. *Tr.* 3.7.10-20 displays the full five-vowel range combined with final *-s*, thus: *pedes – inhaeres – canis – pudicos – 0P – undas – 0P – annis – 0P – 0H – opus.*

This phenomenon recurs at intervals throughout. *Homoeoteleuton* sometimes appears to emphasise phonically the message of a poem, but often it is merely ornamental, setting up reverberations that afford musicality to a verse. Let us consider the ornamental play with *-s*, *-m*, and *-t* through the endings of almost the whole of the last poem in the collection, *Ex P.* 4.16, as follows: *0H – dies – 0H – erat – oris – 0P – Carus – foret – Severus – 0P – aequis – habes – 0H – 0P – dierum – opus – Largus – senem – Troiam – habet – posses – deos – dixit – genus – 0H – Lupus – 0H – 0P – coturnis – levis – tyrannis – 0P – herbas – daret – amatas – modis – 0H – habet – est – adest – 0H – 0P – paternos – dedit – 0H – erat – 0H – meos – est – 0P – artus – locum.* More striking in this poem however, are the 16 verse-endings which do *not* conform to the pattern of *homoeoteleuton*. These are: 1 *rapti*, 3 *nomen*, 6 *Pedo*, 10 *Numa*, 13 *Ulixen*, 14 *mari*, 25 *auctor*, 27 *una/ une*, 28 *lyrae*, 32 *iter*, 37 *referre*, 41 *silere*, 42 *fori*, 45 *Musa*, 47 *Livor*, 50 *mali*. Whether (or why) the poet wished these words to stand out by their very difference to the norm, is uncertain: that *Musa* and *Livor* are not part of any jingling pattern is sure. That the poet wished to point these two words, at least, by non-conformity to a set pattern, seems likely.

3.3.3. Rhyme

Rhyme, a specialised type of *homoeoteleuton*, occurs when the same syllable, or the vowel plus final consonant of two different syllables, or a bisyllabic combination of the two, recurs in close succession, most often at the end of consecutive or alternating verses, but also within a verse. The question of whether or not the ancients observed rhyme schemes has not yet been finally decided. It can be shown fairly conclusively that internal rhyme occurs in Ovidian verse at major verse breaks, and that much of this rhyme is not due to syntactical agreement, but often comprises similar-sounding endings without grammatical parallelism, but also metathesis (as with *Ex P.* 1.2.37 *amaro*, 38 *mora*). As with *homoeoteleuton*, end rhyme occurs in greater or lesser degree throughout the exilic works. Unless a rhyme is bisyllabic, with stressed penultimate syllables (as at *Tr.* 2.262 *Venus*, 264 *genus*), it is not very obtrusive in Latin, which never stresses the final syllable of a word. Even such rhyme may be discounted as fortuitous, but when it occurs in an extended series, authorial intention may be suspected. This observation also applies to parallel assonance, as at *Tr.* 2.234 *onus*, 236 *opus* and to combinations of assonance and rhyme (such as *Ex P.* 1.2 .121 *velox*, 122 *ferox*).

Favourite positions for rhyming words are at the end of alternate hexameters, as a binding factor in a chiastic arrangement between two couplets, at the end of a pentameter and the following hexameter (hence binding two couplets), or simply at the verse-ends within a couplet, very often the coda of a poem. End rhyme often seems to stress key concepts within a poem. Certain key words seem to attract rhyme, of which the most noticeable appears to be *malis* (as in *Ex P.* 1.2.21 *sagittis*, 25 *sagittis*, 27 *illis*, 30 *malis*, 35 *nostris*).

Often there is a combination of alliteration, assonance, *homoeoteleuton* and true rhyme. The whole adds to the musical effect of a poem. A few examples will suffice: In *Tr.* 3.4 these effects occur in pairs or groups: 1 *duro*, 3 *amico*; 18 *humo*, 19 *alto*, 20 *suo*; 21 *alas*, 22 *aquas*, 24 *suas*; 32 *tui*, 34 *frui*, 36 *mihi*; 37 *gementem*, 39 *cadentes*; 40 *bibi*. A variety of principles of connection forms a chain: first *homoeoteleuton* (-o in the first two couplets and again some fifteen verses on), next initial alliteration combined with rhyme, *alas – aquas*; then true rhyme, *tui – frui*, changing to *homoeoteleuton – mihi*, next compound alliteration, -ente- – -ente-, and finally a return to an assonant double *i* in *bibi*.

In some poems recurring *homoeoteleuton* and rhyming end words (often in a rhyming chain) are so widely spaced that their endings may be fortuitous; yet any repetition may indicate conscious ring composition. At *Tr.* 1.3.89-96 four couplets are bound in various ways, as follows: *ferri – comis – obortis – domo – turpi – humo – 0H – viri*. A closely connected series occurs in *Tr.* 1.8.24-40: *die – 0H – vale – iuncti – sui – essem – tibi – nosses – 0P – esses – loci – 0H – aquis – Quirini – mihi – sinistri – iugis*. Often there is a secondary sound effect supporting the rhyme, as, for instance, the assonance of *i* in the last five words of this series.

Different sound patterns occur. At least one poem has a series of initial alliteration of the final words of its verses, which turns into other kinds of sound-play: *Tr.* 5.12: 6 *procellas*, 7 *potest*, 8 *plaudat;* 12 *reo*, 13 *ruinae;* 18 *queat*, 19 *quietum;* 20 *locus*, 21 *laesum;* 22 *ante*, 23 *antro*, 24 *ager* etc.; 34 *pedes*, 37 *vires*, 43 *suades*, 45 *sorores*; 51 *retemptem*, 53 *aurem*; 55 *ferinae;* 56 *soni*, 57 *Latine*, 58 *loqui*; 59 *teneri*, 62 *mei*. A similarly linked pattern of changing acoustic principles again appears at *Ex P.* 2.3.51ff.: 51 *resistis*, 53 *hostis*; 55 *ducis*, 58 *ratis*, 60 *tuis*; 64 *tuum*, 66 *meis*; 68 *deum*; 71 *amicus*, 74 *onus*; 75 *linguae*, 77 *famae*; 79 *cultus*, 81 *unus*; 82 *fores*, 83 *cadentes*; 84 *genis*, 88 *notas*, 90 *genas*; 95 *precor*, 96 *precabor*; 97 *parens*, 98 *pinguia ture*. From first to last, the variety is infinite, musical and deliberately euphonious, often serving to link couplets or to carry a significant burden of meaning.

A couplet with apparently intentionally pointed, elaborate internal and end rhyme plus assonance on *-sse* occurs at *Tr.* 2.445-6. The exile cites Gallus as the first elegist to fall victim to Augustus' anger.

> *Non fuit <u>opprobrio</u> celebra**sse** Lycorida <u>Gallo</u>,*
> *sed linguam <u>nimio</u> non tenui**sse** <u>mero</u>.*

> Nor was it held against Gallus to have celebrated Lycoris in song,
> but rather not holding his tongue after too much heady wine.

Rhyming stresses 'wine', suggesting that Gallus as erstwhile *amicus Augusti* died much as the Macedonian king's friend Cleitus had died at the hand of a drunken Alexander the Great. Augustus apparently liked to associate himself with Alexander. He is said by Suetonius (*Aug.* 18) to have visited Alexander's mausoleum at Alexandria when he was in Egypt after Actium and to have crowned the Macedonian's mummy with a golden diadem. Internal rhyme works to underscore an uncomfortable similarity.

3.3.4. Internal rhyme: a special case?

Internal rhyme is frequent as the function of typically elegiac split phrasing or *hyperbaton*, that is, the separation of noun and agreeing epithet (see Chapter 4). The relegation of rhyming words to the two halves of a verse often serves to give balance to the verse and to stress the words involved. Also, polysyndetic linkage of verbs or nouns by double *-que*, *-ve* or *et* is typical of an elevated style. Not all words thus linked rhyme, but many do, largely because similarity of grammatical function often involves similarity of form. An example occurs at *Tr.* 1.3.27 *iamque quiescebant voces hominumque canumque* ('and already the voices of men and dogs had grown quiet'). Play with *-ve* occurs at *Tr.* 1.2.31 *fugiatve petatve* ('[the helmsman is uncertain] whether to flee or to follow [the wind]'). Often such rhyming words are separated by one or more words, in which case, the rhyme may appear less apparent. At 1.2.53 *suo* separates linked alliterative rhyming words but adds to the overall acoustic pattern: *fatoque suo ferroque* ('whether [you die] by the sword or at your appointed time').

Internal rhyme of syntactically disparate parts of a verse can also occur, with varying effects. Internal rhyming of words not arranged in some form of parallel construction, as in the above instances, occurs rarely but fairly consistently throughout the exilic oeuvre. Mostly the ornamental effect is pleasing, but sometimes such internal rhyme can jar on modern sensibilities. The jingling effect of the rhyme often appears unsuitably jaunty, undercutting apparently serious discourse and serving to alienate apparent from real meaning. At *Tr.* 1.1.23 a jarring *protinus admonitus ... lector* ('immediately a reader, so reminded ...') underscores a postulated audacity in the incorrigible reader, who will, the couplet goes on to say, remember the charges against the poet, and, by implication, will want to criticise the emperor.

At *Tr.* 1.6.17 a jingle in the hexameter *ergo ... misero ... vero* is followed in the pentameter by what may perhaps be construed as an erotic pun, hinging on the two meanings of *testis* (see Chapter 4). The couplet seems to be deliberately bathetic. Three cases of apparently unsuitably jaunty internal rhyme occur in *Tr.* 3.11, with varying effects. At 17 *ut mala nulla feram nisi nudam Caesaris iram* ('although I should bear no other ills than Caesar's naked anger') the jingle is further pointed by means of other alliterative effects (-*la ... -la ...*; *nu- ... nu- ...*; -*si ...-is ir-*). At verse 72 internal rhyme underlines the accusation of unfairness implicit in the verse: *omne trahit secum Caesaris ira malum* (Caesar's anger drags every ill along with it). Earlier, at verse 33, there is a series of five words ending on -*a*, of which the central word has a stressed, long *ā*: *omnia vera putā mea crimina* ('just imagine that all the counts against me are true'). We sense an alienation between ostensible and real meaning. Similar play between short and long vowels also varies the apparent internal rhyme which serves to ornament a gnomic saying at *Tr.* 4.8.21: *miles ubi emeritis non est satis utilis annis* ('when a soldier is no longer of use after he has performed years of service [he deposits his arms at his family's shrine]'). At *Tr.* 5.1.45 apparently random internal rhyme adds point to the poet's appeal:

> *quod probet ipse, canam, poenae modo parte levata*
> *barbariam rigidos effugiamque Getas.*

> I'll sing something that he would himself approve, if only part of
> my pain could be relieved
> and I could get away from this barbarous place and these
> unbending Getae.

In the next poem a jingling rhyme seems to indicate irony: *si fas est homini cum Iove posse loqui* (*Tr.* 5.2.46, 'if it's not sacrilege for a man to be able to talk to Jupiter'). A similar suspicion of ironic rhyming arises at *Ex P.* 2.8.63, in the poem about the silver images of the imperial family. The exile again asks to be removed from Tomis, stressing that 'these portraits will remain with him indefinitely', and so both he and they 'need to be moved to safety', lest these 'celestial beings' of silver suffer hardship. The conceit is ornamented with a curious bisyllabic rhyme in a verse made up largely of mono- and bisyllables, framed by two trisyllables: ***denique*** *quae mecum est et erit* ***sine fine*** *cavete* ('finally, take care that these [images] which are here with me and will be so without end [are not endangered]'). Combination of internal rhyme (*-ine -ine*) with metathesis (*-eni-*) and assonance of *e* in a staccato rhythm alienates rather than persuading. Such play contributes to the joke that turns coins (or medals) into gods.

From these examples we may safely conclude that, granting that consideration of context is important in judging the tone induced by rhyme, in many cases internal rhyme tends toward comical or ironic effects. These devices form only one facet of Ovid's brilliant sound play. We next turn to other aspects of his play with words.

4

Ovidian logodaedaly

From general attention to Ovid's poetic practice we now focus on his use of vocabulary, looking at both choice and arrangement of words. Ovid's artistry with words has been called 'logodaedaly', creative word-magic. His artistry with words when in exile offers continued pleasure. Words were of paramount importance for an exiled poet who was reaching out to his friends and to the enemy who exiled him. In the process he created a word-portrait of himself as suppliant. Ovid's readership in Rome would have been familiar with the whole of his earlier oeuvre as context for a particular lexis. In the context of his exile, the poet's choice of words and the uses to which he put his vocabulary were a powerful means of influencing public thought. Augustus, as a very particular member of Ovid's more general readership, had to be persuaded of the innocuousness of his previous works, if ever the exile were to be allowed to return. The poet seems simultaneously to have sought a means of criticising his antagonist without further eliciting his ire. Ovid's 'painting with words' lies on many levels, from choice of vocabulary, to word play and sound play (as we saw in Chapter 3), also in a controlled use of synonyms. For example, the exilic poetry has about ten different terms for the sea: *mare, fluctus, fretum, aquae, undae, aequora, montes aquarum, Oceanus, pontus, pelagus*. The poet's originality in creating new words has been much commented upon. This chapter will explore various aspects of Ovidian word-magic.

4.1. The vocabulary of exile

Betty Rose Nagle in her ground-breaking monograph, *The Poetics of Exile: program and polemic in the Tristia and Epistulae Ex Ponto of Ovid* (Brussels, 1980), showed that a large part of the 'specialised vocabulary' of Ovid's exilic works is really an erotic elegiac vocabulary adapted to the exiled poet's circumstances; that is, she stressed the intertextual relationship between the poet's early and late works. The reason for this she ascribed (p. 70) to his search for an appropriate medium to express exile as poetic death, and when 'he realized the similarity of the *poeta relegatus* and the *exclusus amator*, ... he hit upon erotic elegy as providing the closest approximation to his new situation' (my underlining). Hence, for Nagle, Ovid's adoption of erotic themes and vocabulary. Her argument intrigued me, inviting further exploration of Ovid's apparently deliberate choice. Of possible importance is the original provenance of the traditional 'erotic' vocabulary. Many of these words are not essentially related to aspects of love, but come from different spheres, notably politics, friendship and the law. In the hands of both Ovid and his predecessors, these had been moved into the erotic sphere. Perhaps, I conjectured, the exilic context offered our poet a chance to realign the semantic implications of these words, thereby perhaps also influencing his readers' perception of their previous 'erotic' use. It has frequently been shown that Ovidian love poetry deconstructs the premises of elegy. I sought to discover how the exilic works reconstruct the common elegiac vocabulary.

The phenomenon of intertextuality relates a work of art with others. It is a reciprocal process, whereby an earlier text provides the reader with the means of interpreting a later text, and *vice versa*. Ovid's re-use of vocabulary from the erotic sphere redirects the reader's interpretation of its earlier usage. Again with full awareness that 'authorial intention' is difficult to establish, I nevertheless allowed myself to speculate about possible deliberate reinterpretation of words by our author in order retrospectively to influence his readers' reception of his earlier works. Obviously, attention to the functioning of a poet's words in context is the only way to deal with his poetry; that is, *what* the poet says can only be read from *how* he says it. Equally so, while only attentive reading of the poems – in order – will discover shifts in the exile's attitude and thought, I have postulated above that this process can sometimes be aided by quantification, if only to delineate patterns in the poet's selection of topics and the tools he employs when dealing with them.

So, context is needed to illuminate usage, but awareness of a general trend in the usage of a particular word will sometimes guide the reader towards a particular reading within that context. This is of specific use in judging possible irony or slippage between what is said and what is implied. It has increasingly been noted that covert criticism of a powerful political figure in any totalitarian regime may be deemed safe as long as an innocent meaning can *also* be read into the words. Where Ovid's poetic transgression had been given a political colour by Augustus, he may have felt the need to give new stress to the innocence of the vocabulary he had formerly employed in erotic contexts – but he may perhaps also have enjoyed continuing with his dangerous fun.

This chapter will therefore begin by examining sets of semantically related words employed by Ovid in his exilic poetry, including re-use, in a different setting, of words made familiar in a previously erotic context by both our poet and other authors. Predominant semantic sets in Ovid's exilic works will be identified, and the chronological occurrence of the most prominent words from each set will be briefly explored in order to map shifts in the exile's use of vocabulary over his years of exile. This will have three functions: first, it can serve as a reference tool to aid any reader's critical judgement of particular occurrences by awareness of the trend of the exile's thought; second, it can be used to judge either change or consistency in importance over time of particular topics or themes (as represented by these words); finally, frequency of use of certain words from earlier works in a changed context may indicate the degree of revision of the value readers should place on the poet's earlier use of such words. That means that, within such patterning, a conscious reworking or redirection of these tools may become discernible.

4.1.1. Overview of premises and method

Choice of vocabulary: The assumption that most of the 'specialised' vocabulary of the exilic works was adapted from erotic elegy is only partly true. Many words common to the exilic works and the erotic elegiac genre originally derive from other semantic spheres and were adapted to specialised elegiac use by Ovid's predecessors. Ovid is adept at using familiar words in new settings, particularly in an erotic context, where *double entendre* and various levels of meaning are often discernible, but he is never obscene. The most common 'doublets' in his amatory works are: *membrum, testis, nervus, latus, coire, miscere, surgere, cadere, iacere.* In the exilic works a seemingly conscious system of 'de-punning' both evokes earlier elegiac usages and restores words to their original semantic sets, thereby inverting the elegiac tradition (itself an inversion of 'real life').

Chronology: Again the chronological structure of the exilic *corpus* is important: we need to distinguish between the tone of poems from the first year of Ovid's wanderings and those from the nebulous last years of his exile. We have already seen that chronological examination of the exilic works shows changes in style, attitude and tonality.

Method: The distribution over our five phases of key terms will be discussed, and relative frequency will be established by statistical means, that is, the number of occurrences per hundred lines of verse will be used as a comparative tool. The Vocabulary Table (pp. 261-4) summarises frequencies of key words in the *Tristia* and *Epistolae Ex Ponto*, offering a statistical interpretation of relative increase or decrease of occurrences within the course of the poet's years of exile.

Semantics: What moderns would consider as 'false etymology' represented for the ancients a valid connection between disparate words. For the Epicureans, there was an inherent relationship between a thing and the word for it. Dissimilar objects with similar-sounding names therefore had some intrinsic relationship. Such sound-play is important in the interpretation of word-play with Ovid and other poets, but such similarity involves more than homophones and homonyms. For the ancients, commonality of the elements of two words could imply an intrinsic relationship, as with Lucretian 'verbal atomism' in word groups like *lignis – ignis; mater – materies.*

Where possible, therefore, attention will be paid to the often fanciful ancient etymologies of words as collected by Robert Maltby in his *Lexicon of Ancient Latin Etymologies* (Leeds, 1991) in order to ascertain what weight certain words would have carried for our author and his contemporary readers. With those etymologies that post-date Ovid, particular circumspection is required, but it is not unjustifiable to postulate an etymological tradition, or to guess that Ovid would have subscribed to popular interpretations, even if these were recorded only much later.

4.1.2. The interpretative process

Awareness of frequency and trend of usage may influence the contextual reading of a particular word. For example, *turba* is a favourite Ovidian word, taking colour from its often ambiguous context. Its primary sense in Lewis and Short is negative: *turmoil, hubbub, uproar, disorder, tumult, commotion, disturbance of a crowd of people,* and only the secondary meaning is more neutral: *crowd, throng, multitude, mob,* etc. A German lexicographer offers as first meaning *ungeordenete Menge, Haufe, Schwarm, Schar,* as secondary meaning *Getümmel, Gewühl.* In political terms *turba* has been termed a 'political group, following'. The word occurs altogether 34 times in the exilic poems. Of these 18 have an apparently positive or neutral connotation, 'following', 'large group', usually in a civic sense; but 13 are negative with the connotation of unruly mob, and in three cases the value of the word is unclear. There is no particular variation through time; the word is, however, always negative when applied to the inhabitants of the Euxine area, or, metaphorically, to the exile's ills, whereas allusions to civic activities in Rome are positive. Awareness of its use in negative contexts, then, influences interpretation of apparently positive instances.

At *Tr.* 2.88 the exile reproaches the emperor: *est vultus turba secuta tuos.* The emperor was angry with the exiled poet. The meaning of this line may simply be 'your followers watched your expression', but awareness that the majority of the occurrences of *turba* in the exilic works is negative gives the reader pause. The line may also mean 'that mob followed your [angry] expression [and reviled me too]'. Even more uncertain is the emotional 'feel' of *turba* in *Tr.* 3.1.77-8 *di precor, atque adeo (neque enim mihi turba roganda est!)/ Caesar, ades voto, maxime dive, meo* ('o gods, and above all – for there is no need for me to pray to the whole crowd – Caesar, greatest deity, accede to my prayer'). This is perhaps an echo of Cicero *Nat. Deor.* 1.39 *turbam ignotorum deorum* ('a mass of unknown gods'), which Ovid has echoed before: *deorum/ cuncta Iovi cessit turba* (*Fasti* 2.668, 'the whole crowd of gods yielded to Jupiter'). The question is how much irony is to be read into the couplet from *Tr.* 3. The exile prays directly to Augustus, adding in an aside, 'for I don't have to apply to a whole mob of gods'. The observation may be read as a compliment: 'you, Augustus, are paramount among your following of (minor) gods'. However, at the same time the line suggests the extent to which Augustus has superseded the gods in Roman civic and religious life. Similarly, *turba* in *Tr.* 4.1.54 *namque deorum/ cetera cum magno Caesare turba facit* invites a negative interpretation, if only in the sense that it again stresses the degree to which the emperor has arrogated deity: 'for the rest of the mob of gods makes common cause with great Caesar'.

4.1.3. Specialised vocabulary

The following words are listed by Nagle (pp. 63-4, and n. 112) as examples of 'erotic diction' from the exilic works: *miser, me miserum, tristis, infelix, maestus, sollicitus, curae, mala, labores, dolores, amarus, lacrimae, fletus, metus, luctus, taedia, desiderium, cupido, carere, spes, improbus, crudelis, durus, saevus, mitis, lenis, ira laesi dei, crimen, scelus, culpa, error, poena, deus, numen, supplex, preces, vota, auxilium, solacia, levare, fides, memor, immemor, utilitas.* To these we should add *amor, amica* and *amicitia.* Any Ovidian glossary will confirm that these words appear frequently in both the erotic poems and in the exilic oeuvre. Still useful as control is the century-old compendium by René Pichon of the vocabulary of erotic elegy (Paris, 1902), which lists words in different categories, under their original semantic provenance, showing that military, political, medical, literary, legal, religious, nautical, hunting and fishing terms had been adapted to erotic use. Beside words unique to Ovid, Pichon lists some words which in Propertius had a negative meaning, but with Ovid have a positive connotation.

Pichon's erotically adapted words are far more specifically 'erotic' than the words (many denoting *suffering*) quoted above, and may be compared with the Roman political terminology collected by Joseph Hellegouarc'h some sixty years later (Paris, 1963). Words connected with the exile's misdeed have a legal provenance. Words from the political sphere relate particularly to the merging of the language of statesmanship with the language of friendship, and to specialised rhetorical and didactic uses. Some words from these various sets appear so consistently within the exilic context, that they may be called the 'specialised vocabulary of exile', and, of these, some (particularly words denoting misery and longing or expressing distance) may by their nature be termed 'inherently exilic'.

'Political' words

'Political' words the poet employs are *turba, clementia, iustitia, moderatus, nobilitas, pater patriae, princeps, prohibere, vetare, imperium, salus, triumphus, pax, hostis, infestus, eques.* Cognates and derivatives can usually be considered with these key words.

Some of these words are clearly positive, and are frequent enough to warrant phase-by-phase comparison. Hellegouarc'h lists *clementia, iustitia* and *moderatio* as characteristics of the Roman political man, his *clipeus virtutis*, in Cicero's phrase. In *RG* 34.2 Augustus connects these terms, together with his *virtus* and *pietas*, when recounting the celebration of his assumption of his new name in 27 BC by the award of a civic crown and the setting of a golden shield in the Curia Julia. The exile dutifully applies the words to Augustus, but also to others, including his friends.

CLEMENTIA, 'mercy', the characteristic Augustus took particular pride in, may be termed 'kindness', mercy beyond deserts. It (and cognate *clemens/ clementissimus*) occur only once each elsewhere in Ovid's works, in both cases in the *Metamorphoses*, and only ten times in the exilic poetry: once in Phase 1, four times in Phase 2, once in Phase 3, three times in Phase 4, and once only in Phase 5. The relative infrequency of a term one might have expected the exile to use often in pleas for recall is perhaps significant. Allusion to the emperor's *clementia* (e.g. *Tr.* 4.4.53, *quantaque in Augusto clementia*, 'and so great is Augustus' mercy') may indicate wishful induction by the poet, as with Seneca's *De Clementia*, aimed at the young Nero. The last occurrence is applied to the exile's patron Sextus Pompeius, dedicatee of the last book (*Ex P.* 4.1.25).

IUSTITIA, 'justice', another of Augustus' vaunted characteristics, is rare; its cognate IUSTUS very frequent in the Ovidian oeuvre as a whole (some 71 occurrences in all). Often the word *iustus* has a neutral sense, 'justifiable', 'good', but its context may relate to either a negative or a positive judgement by the exile. In the first phase *iustus* has a positive context at *Tr.* 1.3.62, *utraque iusta mora est* ('each is a good reason to delay'). At *Tr.* 2.29 *illa quidem iusta est* refers to the emperor's anger, conceding that there was some reason for this emotion. Of four occurrences in Phases 2 and 3, only one refers to the emperor. The others can be discounted. In Phase 4 five occurences out of eight acknowledge the 'justness' of the emperor's attitude, and then the topic is dropped. In Phase 5 *iusta* refers to complaints, by the poet or his friends, as being 'justified'.

The next characteristic of a good ruler, *moderatio*, the setting of a measure, is precluded by its prosody from use in elegiacs. MODERATUS is infrequent, occurring once in each of the first three phases (twice relating to the emperor). The fourth phase has *moderatus* twice (and MODEROR, as applied to the emperor, once): *principe nec nostro deus est moderatior ullus/ Iustitia vires temperat ille suas* (*Ex P.* 3.6.23-4, 'No god is more moderate than our princeps: he tempers his strength with justice'). Flattering appeal appears to acknowledge guilt.

We have noted Augustus' pride in his new title, PATER PATRIAE, conferred in 2 BC (as noted in *RG* 35), twice acknowledged in apostrophe during the course of *Tr.* 2 (181 and 574, *parce, pater patriae ...*, 'spare me, o father of the fatherland'). A third occurrence acknowledges him as *patriae rector ... paterque* (*Tr.* 2.39, 'guide and father of the fatherland'). Significantly, Augustus is reminded at *Tr.* 4.4.13-14 that as *pater patriae* he had suffered himself 'to be read' (*legi*) in Ovid's song. *Pater patriae* and the semantically related PARENS occur altogether eleven times throughout the exilic works. No virtues, other than 'saving the state' or physical parenthood, are ascribed to Augustus as *pater*. In the fourth phase two occurrences allude elliptically to Augustus' 'double parentage': of both the state and of Tiberius. Irony may be read here. Tiberius was clearly Augustus' last resort, when all other candidates for adoption had fallen away. At *Ex P.* 2.8.31-2 and 4.13.27 the poet's bland acceptance of the physical and moral resemblance between 'father' and 'son' accentuates by omission the fact of his adoption. *Parens* appears once as the equivalent of 'father of the state' (*Tr.* 2.157, *per patriam, quae te tuta et secura parente est*, 'by the father-land, which is safe and secure with you as its parent'). Isidorus' (correct) etymology (*orig.* 9.5.4, *parentes quasi parientes*, 'parents as if they are bringing forth'), if known to Ovid, would have enhanced the flattery here involved, which emphasises the emperor's having produced a reborn state. Yet generally Ovid stresses natural or adoptive relationships in the impe-rial family far more often than the political meaning with which Augustus had worked hard to imbue these terms.

IMPERIUM, a word infrequent in elegy, is almost as frequent in the exilic poems (17) as in the rest of Ovid's oeuvre together (21, of which 11 in the *Fasti*), but only in Phase 1 (6) and Phase 4 (4) does the word relate to Augustus. Varro *Ling.* 5.87 derives *īmpĕrātōr* ('general'), notoriously a metrical impossibility in dactylic verse, from *imperio populi qui eos, qui id attemptassent, oppressisset hostis* ('from the command of the populace because he suppressed those enemies who tried to do this'). Augustus appears by the time of Ovid's exile to have virtually annexed terminology deriving from the word *imperium* for the exclusive use of himself and his immediate family. Ovid often seems to be redirecting the domain of this semantic set to a sphere wider than the Caesarian house, back to Varro's *populus*. Some occurrences, in the fifth phase, are either religious or connected with the various consulships of addressees, with only two exceptions, both in *Ex P.* 4.13 (28 and 33), referring to Tiberius' rule. We have noted before that the first resembles Tacitus' depiction of Tiberius' reluctant accession: ... *qui frena rogatus/ saepe recusati ceperit imperii* (*Ex P.* 4.13.28, '... who, when asked to do so, took up the reins of government which he had often rejected').

The Vocabulary Table shows an increase through the first four stages and then a decline in relative frequency of other words from the semantic set relating to imperial rule, PAX and HOSTIS. *Pax* is most common in a negative context, as something the exile has lost. Its non-existence in the Pontic region, a major argument for Ovid's request for recall, implies negation of the *pax Augusta*. Occasionally the word has a different context, or puns on the expression *pace tua*. The marked decrease in frequency of its use in a political context by the last phase indicates the inefficacy of the exile's appeal rather than newly discovered virtue in the local populace. This is borne out by the changing usage of HOSTIS. In Phase 1, five of the first six occurrences are in *sententiae*, gnomic statements about human behaviour, while three refer to the exile's location among 'enemies'. Only one refers to a personal enemy. The exile appears largely oblivious to any personal hostility evinced by individuals other than the emperor. In Phase 2, nine allusions are to the exile's situation, one a gnomic expression. Phase 3 has three gnomic statements, four allusions to Ovid's situation. Phase 4 heightens its appeal with eighteen references to danger from local enemies, four gnomic sayings, and one allusion to the 'personal enemies' of Fabius Maximus, who, as we know, was one of the first victims of Tiberius' new regime (Tac. *Ann.* 1.4): *Ex P.* 3.8.20 reads: *hoste, precor, fiant illa cruenta tuo* ('may [my gift of arrows] become red with the blood of your enemy').

Hostis as the poet's private 'enemy' in Rome occurs only thrice. In *Tr.* 2.77 the word refers to the person who first brought Ovid's erotic works to the emperor's attention. Its use here casts a dubious light on Augustus, who, by association, is also an 'enemy'. In *Tr.* 5.1.56 whoever tries to prevent the exile's tears is *durior hoste* ('harsher than an enemy'). In *Ex P.* 3.1.151-2 Ovid attempts to disarm an enemy by ascribing the role of *hostis* to *Fortuna* alone. The poet's own (unnamed) enemy is never 'INIMICUS'. Of four occurrences of this word, three are linked with *non* in the context of a double negative, the fourth in a 'triple negative': *vix tunc ipse mihi non inimicus eram* (*Tr.* 2.82, 'Then I myself was hardly not also angry with myself') – all therefore creating strong positives. The word seems to lend itself to circumlocution.

Politics shading off into friendship

Words prominent within the overlapping semantic fields of politics and private friendship are: *amicitia/ amicus, officium, meritum, studium, favere, foedus/ fides/ fidus/ fidelis, velle, cupere, amare, deligere.*

4. Ovidian logodaedaly

In the Roman context *amicitia* was often a political concept, it has been argued. Catullus exploited this relationship by transferring the idea of Lesbia as his *amica* ('girl friend') to the sphere of (political) *amicitia* and relating to it concepts such as *foedus* and *obligatio*. Although *amicitia* should have been durable between Roman politicians, as theoretically they shared the same moral and political principles, in practice *amicitia* sometimes was a mere matter of courtesy, even the civilised cover for enmity or resentment. Augustus used the concept freely. *Amicus principis* became an almost political title. Of Ovid's correspondents, the most famous *amicus principis* was Fabius Maximus. Loss of imperial *amicitia* at the death of Augustus probably led Fabius, like Cornelius Gallus long before him, to commit suicide.

AMICITIA and AMICUS are very frequent, occurring about ten times as often in the exilic poems as in the rest of the Ovidian oeuvre. Not surprisingly, the set triples in frequency in the fourth phase (where friends are personally named, and appeals often are cast in the guise of advice on the duties of friendship), dwindling again in the last. The poet proposes to his editor Brutus in the prologue to *Ex P.* 1-3 that Brutus should replace the offending three books of the *Ars Amatoria* with this new collection (*Ex P.* 1.1.12-14). So *Ex P.* 1 to 3 becomes an 'Ars Amicitiae'. Ovidian *amicitia* is, however, seldom political. It is predominantly private and personal, with *amicus* frequently in the vocative case. Political undertones are discernible in *Tr.* 2.81, *esse sed irato quis te mihi posset amicus?* ('but who could be a friend to me while you are angry with me?') and *Tr.* 5.9.21, *di tibi se tribuant cum Caesare semper amicos* ('may the gods, together with Caesar, show themselves always friendly to you'). Yet AMOR as the relationship between friends is still less frequent than the erotic sense of the word, even in the exilic poems (nine instances out of 32 in the *Tristia* and five out of 20 in *Ex Ponto*). Occurrences of *amor* listed in the table relate only to non-erotic use of the word, as referring to the relationship between friends or in connection with Rome (*Tr.* 1.3.49; 2.160; *Ex P.* 1.3.29), death (*Tr.* 1.5.6; 3.8.39), praise (*Ex P.* 4.7.40) and in other equally neutral contexts.

Ancient sources, from Cicero *Laelius* 26 onwards, adequately derived *amicitia* from *amor*, but *amicus* was later fancifully connected with *animi aequus* (equal of mind, Cassiodorus *In Psalm.* 37.121, 238A.), *animi custos* (guardian of (my) mind, Gregorius M *In Evang.* 27.4) and even *ab hamo, id est, a catena caritatis* ('from a hook, that is, from a chain of affection', Isidorus *Orig.* 10.4). Such etymologies would not have displeased Ovid, had he been aware of them, but there is another factor. Underlying every solemn reference to *Roma* there may be lurking reminiscences of the poet's earlier works, where the punning potential of its palinode *amor* was often exploited, as in *AA* 1.55, *tot tibi tamque dabit formosas Roma puellas* ('so many and such pretty girls Rome will offer you'). In the didactic poem it was not *amor*, but *Roma*, that supplied the apprentice lover with girls. In the exilic works Ovid appears consciously to reverse any such punning allusions by the straightforward use of both *amor* and *Roma*, but, in the context of his earlier works, an echo reverberates in *Tr.* 2.321, *nec mihi materiam bellatrix Roma negabat* ('and warlike Rome offered me matter to write about'). His readers in Rome would know that, far from his having sung of warlike Rome, it was '*bellator Amor*' that had formerly been the poet's main theme.

PIETAS and its cognate PIUS, with all their Virgilian undertones, are frequent in Ovid, particularly in the *Metamorphoses* and *Fasti*. The words may sometimes carry an edge, as in *Tr.* 1.3.86, where the exile's wife demands to accompany him, driven as he is by Caesar: ... *pietas haec mihi Caesar erit!* ('this duty will be a Caesar to me [and drive me forth]'). The word gains in resonance when we remember that *pietas* is another of the salient characteristics vaunted by Augustus in *RG* 34. Allusions to the imperial family invite an ironical interpretation, as in *Ex P.* 2.2.73, where we have noted before that *nurum neptesque pias natosque nepotum* ('your daughter-in-law and dutiful granddaughters and the children of your grandsons') highlight by omission Livia's '*impiae*' (step)daughter-in-law and granddaughter. The poem is addressed to Messalinus, elder son of that Messala Corvinus who brought the *pater patriae* proposal before the senate in 2 BC. The whole poem lends itself to revised (and less favourable) interpretations, in the spirit of what has been termed 'the art of safe criticism'. Examples are: verses 27-9 and 99-100, on the dangers of evoking the emperor-god's wrath by seeking sanctuary with him, or even by helping the exile; reference in 42 to Augustus as the 'Tarpeian thunderer', evoking both an implication of arrogation of deity and of primitive, peremptory justice; and, most damningly, 115-19, depiction of Augustus as kind *parens*, whose dire punishment of others (by implication his children) 'hurts himself equally'. It is not difficult to read here another allusion to Augustus' harsh treatment of his daughter and granddaughter, which, whether justified or not, caused him much grief.

FIDES was considered by the ancients to derive from *fit quod dicitur* (cf. Cic. *Fam.* 16.10.2). From Catullus (*Carm.* 76.3) onward, readers would be accustomed to the adaptation of the words FIDES (FIDELIS) and FOEDUS to erotic contexts. This set occupies six columns in an Ovidian concordance, 240 occurrences in all. Their relative distribution in the exilic works somewhat surprisingly contrasts with the distribution of the 'friendship' words, being most frequent in the first and last phases, lowest in the second. Ovid most commonly implies a sense of 'faithfulness, faithful obligation' in relation to a friend, sometimes in gnomic statements, e.g. *Tr.* 1.5.39, *saepe fidem adversis etiam laudavit in armis* ('he often applauded loyalty, even in his armed opponents'). FOEDUS (also from the root *fid-, recognised as such by Cicero, so Servius on *Aen.* 8.641) occurs only seven times, once in connection with the exile's relationship to his wife. The Catullan echo is clear: *Ex P.* 3.1.73, *exigit hoc socialis amor foedusque maritum* ('this our shared love and our marriage pact demands'). Here, as elsewhere (e.g. *Tr.* 1.3 *passim, Tr.* 3.3.15-24), in the way the exiled poet spells out his love for his wife, Ovid seems to be rewriting his reputation as a *lusor amorum*.

Frequency figures for the complete set, *amic-, non-erotic *amor, pius* and *pietas* and the *fid-words, fluctuate between a low in Phase 2 (fewer than 25 per 1,000 verses), to almost 36 per 1,000 in the fourth phase, thanks there to the high frequency of *amicus* and *amicitia*.

Political *amicitia* involved obligatory duties. An OFFICIOSUS friend would perform an OFFICIUM, a service. The words derive from *opus facere*, to do a job (so Lewis and Short) but for the ancients, with scant distortion, from *efficere*, 'to achieve, carry out' (Maltby 1991, q.v.). The terms are frequent in Ovid's other works (59 instances, of which 27 in the erotic elegies, 16 each in *Met.* and *Fasti*). In the exilic works they recur with increasing frequency, culminating in what we have called Ovid's 'Ars Amicitiae' (Phase 4: 16 instances). Eleven occurrences in the last phase indicate a continued trust in friendship. In Ovid's exile the words often relate to the writing of poetry, as in *Tr.* 4.7.3-4 *cur non tua dextera versus/ quamlibet in paucos officiosa fuit?* ('why did your hand not do its duty [and write] even a few lines?') and *Ex P.* 1.1.20, *Musaque ad invitos officiosa venit* ('and my dutiful Muse visits [even] unwilling friends'). The semantically related UTILITAS implies efficacy, especially of poetry. *Utilitas* occurs nine times in the exilic corpus, often in a negative context, as *Tr.* 4.1.38 *sed quiddam furor hic utilitatis habet* ('but this madness [i.e. composition of poetry] has a certain usefulness'), or *Ex P.* 2.3.8, *vulgus amicitias utilitate probat* ('the common herd tests friendship by its usefulness').

STUDIUM has, as basic meaning, 'a busying one's self about, or application to, a thing'. In the context of political *amicitia* it is used for 'interest in', as in *Ex P.* 2.5.60 *et servat studii foedera quisque sui* ('and each honours the agreements relating to his interests'). In the exilic works its political connotation is secondary and the word refers predominantly to 'studies', 'scholarship', the traditional solace of those exiled, as in *Tr.* 2.9, *deme mihi studium* ('take away my studies') or *Tr* .5.12.51, *si demens studium fatale retemptem* ('if like a madman I once again attempt my fatal studies'). In either sense, it is most frequent in Phase 4 (15 occurrences). FAVERE and FAVOR together display a similar distributive pattern, with 16 occurrences in the fourth phase. With Ovid the semantic field of the highly frequent root *fav- in the context of *amicitia* usually involves condescension from a greater to a lesser personage. A possible exception is *Tr.* 1.2.101 *domui si favimus illi*, where the active agent is the exile, pleading on the ground of past merit, 'if ever I favoured the house [of the emperor]'.

The complete set is relatively more frequent in the exilic works than in the rest of Ovid's corpus (118 examples here, representing 43% of all occurrences of these words). COLERE as a political act is relatively infrequent in the exilic poetry: of about 40 instances throughout, its political or social meaning predominates in Phases 2 and 5, but the word is largely restricted to the religious domain, including cultivation of his Muse by the poet as *vates*. Its cognate *cultor* is almost exclusively religious.

Legal vocabulary

The condemned exile predictably resorts to legal vocabulary in his appeals to his judge. This semantic set includes *arguere, fateor, poena, crimen, culpa, error, exsul, relegatus*. Of these, some do not reflect the pains of exile. These words do not spring to mind as essentially erotic, but are often listed as such in the context of Roman elegy. Where on occasion the poet has formerly so employed them, here they are apparently consciously restored to their original provenance, thereby perhaps offering the exile a way of 'sanitising' their earlier erotic use. Some appear as merely neutral.

FATEOR, 'I confess', is frequent, but often in parentheses, as a verse filler, seldom in a legal connotation. The exile confesses to 'fearing', to having 'lied', to having done 'nothing more than make a mistake', to 'not having feared', but *never* to a crime. Apparently the exile's sense of contrition (or the poet's need for verse fillers) fluctuated considerably. The word is relatively most frequent in the first and last phases, least frequent in the second. The nearest to a confession of guilt is *Ex P.* 2.2.19, *esse quidem fateor meritam post Caesaris iram* ('I confess that this [comes] after Caesar's justified anger'). Again, as ever, the guilt is left unspecified.

ARGUO, 'I am accused', the semantic complement of *fateri*, first occurs in *Tr.* 2, Ovid's 'speech for the defence', at 212, *arguor obsceni doctor adulterii* ('I am accused of being the teacher of obscene adultery') and 327, *arguor inmerito!* ('I am undeservedly accused!'). Other occurrences of the word are unrelated to accusations against the exile. The substantive common with *arguo*, CRIMEN, has a wavering semantic field: from 'accusation' to what in English is termed 'crime'. It is a common Ovidian word: its 55 occurrences in the exilic works represent only 26% of total occurrences throughout his oeuvre. Both senses feature here, most often in denials of guilt: the word is most frequent in the first phase, which includes *Tr.* 2: 23 occurrences, or 18 per 1,000 verses. The second phase has 17 occurrences, the other three phases together as many again. Paranomastic play on *carmen-crimen* is first coined at *Tr.* 2.207, *perdiderunt me duo crimina, carmen et error* ('two accusations ruined me, a poem and a mistake'), firmly connecting Ovid's poetry with his 'crime'.

Distribution of CARMEN through the five phases is 40, 24, 18, 34, 33. Relative frequency is highest in the first and last phases, lowest in the second and fourth. Ancient sources on *carmen* and *crimen* indicate fanciful etymology that relates both words (with *Camenae*) to various roots containing the combinations *car-/ *cas-*. Common derivation from *carere* (to lack) in a late source (Isid. *Orig.*) acknowledges the traditional link: a crime *lacks a 'name'* (5.26.1) and a singer-poet *lacks a 'mind'* (1.39.4). Once established in Ovid's poems from exile, this relationship echoes throughout, and can be evoked at each of the subsequent 134 repetitions of the word *carmen/ carmina*. At the last, *Ex P.* 4.14.42, the relationship is firmly restated: *inque novum crimen carmina nostra vocat.* Here the first meaning suggested above is involved: Ovid needs to defend himself against a new accusation, for his poetic complaints about the harshness of his place of exile have so incensed the local populace that he is now obliged to deflect their ire with praise for their kindness (43-56).

Crimen is part of a semantic set referring to 'guilt'. With Ovid three degrees or shades of culpability are reflected ('mistake'/ *error/ atychêma* – 'fault'/ *culpa/ hamartia* – 'crime'/ *crimen/ adikêma*). Of these he admits to only the least serious, ERROR ('a mistake'), and rejects all CULPA ('blame, fault'). Varro *Ling.* 6.96 (correctly) relates *error* to the (IE) root *er-*, 'to wander'. *Culpa* is related to Skr. *skhal-* 'to fall' and may be virtually equated with *errare*. Here the further sense of 'a state worthy of blame, arising from a wrong judgement', may be deduced, which is all Ovid will ever admit to. Of importance is what we can fathom (from Ovid's use of the two words) about his attitude to his punishable deed. Changing frequency indicates a significant shift of emphasis. Figures of relative frequency give a clear picture: *error* is relatively most frequent in Phase 2, disappears in Phase 3, and is infrequent in Phase 4 (but not all instances relate to the poet's misdeed). *Culpa* occurs 14 times in the fourth phase (within the series 8, 6, 7, 14, 2). It is relatively most frequent in the third phase, but drops to the same low frequency as *error* in Phase 4, with further diminution in the last phase. Only once *culpa* is tempered by the adjective *imprudens* (*Tr.* 2.104). In the first years the exile appears ready to admit to some blame, but by the fourth phase he only once admits to a 'fault' (*Ex P.* 1.1.64, *culpa perennis erit*, 'my mistake lasts forever'). It is clear that over time the exile changes his tack: no amount of self-inculpation will move his imperial reader, and he drops the ploy. In the last phase blamelessness is twice attested: at *Ex P.* 4.6.15 in the context of the death of Ovid's patron Fabius Maximus, when Augustus 'had begun to forgive his fault', and, finally, *nulla est mea culpa* (*Ex P.* 4.14.23, 'there is nothing to blame me for') – but this is in exculpation of the accusation of ingratitude brought against him by the Tomitans, referred to above. From first to last, the exile will not admit to any serious culpability in his past or present.

While making the most of the pathos of exile, and stressing his longing for his native soil, if only to be buried in it (*Tr.* 3.3.70), the poet twice (in Phases 1 and 3) distinguishes between 'exile' and 'relegation'. Ovid was not exiled, merely relegated ('sent away'), which meant he retained his possessions. A Roman citizen settling permanently in another locality would, however, lose his citizenship; hence, although he was technically not exiled by imperial decree, Ovid's permanent relegation implied loss of civic rights, and he frequently stresses his diminished status. EXUL is postulated by Lewis and Short to derive from the root **sal-*, 'to go', as in *salire*, 'to leap'. It was commonly written EXSUL, for, on the evidence of Quintilian *Decl.* 366 p. 400.13, Caper *Gramm.* VII 95.16, Scaurus *Gramm.* VII 22.14, 28.16 and others, the word was considered to relate to *solum* (probably '*ex solo*'). This etymologising appears to have been derived from the Roman term for change of domicile, *solum vertere* (change of home ground). Loss of civic status was immediate only in cases of *solum vertere exilii causa* (involving escape from capital condemnation) or if the sentence imposed was *interdictio aqua et igni* (denial of – literally, interdiction *from* – water and fire; that is, basic human rights). Of ten occurrences of the word *solum* in the exilic oeuvre, only one features in a request for a 'change of soil' (*Ex P.* 2.2.66).

The semantic set *exsul* and its cognate verb EXSULARE (with EXSILIUM and RELEGARE) is relatively sparse throughout Ovid's oeuvre. The set does not occur in the erotic poems; there are five occurrences in the *Heroides*, ten in the *Fasti*, and thirteen in the *Metamorphoses*. In the exilic poetry the words virtually disappear toward the end, after fairly consistent use throughout the first four phases (once in about every hundred verses). In the last phase the strictly legal aspect of being a *relegatus* is touched on twice, but allusions to 'exile' hardly feature. Ovid seems to have resigned himself to his lot, but perhaps he has realised the inefficacy of this particular pathetic ploy in appeals to Rome.

Religious vocabulary

The languages of religion and politics frequently overlap in Roman poetry: *pietas* as discussed above has some religious undertones. For Ovid, writing poetry is a divine calling, and he sees himself as a member of a divinely-inspired fraternity. SODALIS (with *sodalicium*, *sodalitas*) most often occurs in politico-religious contexts. The word is probably cognate with Sanskrit *svadha*, 'will, power', but its origin was ascribed by the ancients to the act of 'sitting down to a common meal' (from *sedere*, so Sextus Pompeius Festus 297, etc.). In Ovid it often appears as synonymous with *amicus*, but its religious undertones cannot be ignored, and the implications of its contemporary etymology are exploited in the poet's celebration of his *sodales* as his boon companions, former table-mates, but also fellow-poets and fellow-worshippers of the Muse.

Consequently, the poet sees himself as VATES, singer of divine truth, a designation that increases with time. From a rather impersonal use once in the first phase, the poet progresses to five allusions to 'poets as *vates*' in the second phase (*Tr.* 4.10.42 equates vatic poets with 'gods'), to designating himself as *vates* four times in Phase 3. The word does not feature in the first book of Phase 4, but thereafter the poet increasingly ascribes the term to himself. Three of eight occurrences in Phase 4 refer directly to himself, as e.g. *Ex P.* 2.9.65 *ad vatem vates orantia bracchia tendo* ('as poet I extend supplicant hands to a fellow-poet'). Here Ovid is addressing the poet-king Cotys of Thrace, where heavy-handed praise of the 'barbarian bard's' poetic effusions (51-4) may be taken as either humorously-intended insults or ill-concealed irony. Whatever the poet's intention, he depicts himself and the king as 'fellow-singers'. In the last phase the word occurs in the gnomic context of the Muse-inspired vatic duty of poets to utter divine truth. In the context of Ovidian worship of his Muse, *carmen* also takes on religious dress, and may be considered as part of this set. The table shows consistent increase of positive allusions to both *carmen* and *Musa*.

Imperial deity

The greatest number of words from the religious semantic set centres around Augustus, his deeds and the exile's reaction to emotions exhibited by, or fancifully ascribed to, him: *Jupiter, deus, divus, numen, fata, fortuna, ira, mitis, lenis, tonans, sinister, cultor, preces, orans*.

The frequency of occurrence of the four words *Jupiter, deus, divus, numen* over the five chronological phases shows a declining arc. About one third of these occurrences refer to other, 'real' deities, such as the weather gods, and the rest relate to the imperial family. A high frequency in Phase 1 (where the emperor is often approached or referred to as a god) is followed first by a decline, and then by a marked increase in the fourth phase (*deus* 57 and *numen* 28 times, in absolute count), after which ascription of divinity to the imperial household lapses. Whether these allusions are adulatory or ironically meant, needs further examination. Here, too, our awareness of the pervasive possibility of two levels of meaning in any praise of the Roman imperial family and the general drift of similar allusions in the poet's other works elicits the suspicion that the exile's bland acceptance of imperial divinity is not all it seems. The Olympian gods receive scant mention. Ovid's exilic oeuvre (whatever his original intention) has been considered by some as contributing to the process of deification of Roman emperors. From the first storm in *Tr.* 1.2, where minor gods underwrite the great god's ire, to Ovid's final address of the apotheosised emperor in *Ex P.* 4.9.127-34, 'Augustus as god' predominates, accentuating the emptiness of Augustus' much-vaunted religious reforms.

Substitution of the name of Jupiter for Augustus is significant. JUPITER/ JOV- is frequent throughout. Whereas in the *Metamorphoses* 'Jupiter' is the Olympian Zeus, here most often the name is synonymous with 'Augustus' or 'Caesar'. Ovid, although a master of words, apparently never thought to play on the (erroneous) derivation of the name from *iuvare* (as quoted from Ennius by Varro *Ling.* 5.65 and in Cicero *Nat. Deor.* 2.64), nor on the (etymologically sound) source for *deus* in a common root with *dies* (postulated by Varro *Ling.* 5.66) meaning 'light' or 'gleam'. To Ovid, 'a god is a god', and nuancing reflects only the equation of the imperial family with the divine. DEUS (172 instances) and NUMEN (64) are frequent, both culminating in the fourth phase, with about one instance in every 25 verses. Ovid has, for his poetic purposes, unquestioningly equated Augustus with *deus* and its less frequent adjectival cognate, *divus* (five instances), as in *Tr.* 3.1.78, *Caesar, ades voto, maxime dive, meo!* ('Caesar, favour my prayer, greatest of gods!'). Ovid appears unquestioningly to accept the process whereby a comparatively humble *C. Julius C. f. Caesar* had finally been apotheosised as *Imp. Caesar Divi f. Augustus.* Ovid's less frequent plural *di* refers to 'other gods', usually unnamed, such as *di caeli et maris* ('gods of sky and the ocean') in *Tr.* 1.2.1.

NUMEN (from the root **nu-*, 'nod', so understood also by Varro, *Ling.* 7.85) has a wide semantic spread, apparently reflecting its early, animistic adaptation, from 'authority' or 'divine authority', to 'protective genius', 'vaguely divine power', 'impersonal god', and a later adaptation to 'personal god'. With Ovid in exile the word ranges from 'impersonal *deus*' to an indiscriminate substitute for the names of members of the imperial family. Scholars generally differentiate between worship of Augustus (and Rome) in the East, and of Augustus' *genius* in the West, citing archaeological evidence to show that the *genius* or *numen* was usually considered to be a separate entity, a 'guiding power'. With Ovid, a tenuous semantic difference has been reduced to its logical conclusion.

There are ten direct references to Augustus as *numen* in the *Tristia*, about as many in *Ex Ponto*, seven of which are concentrated in *Ex P.* 2.8, the poem that celebrates a gift of 'silver portraits' of the imperial triad. Here the exile claims to worship the 'present deities' daily at a magnificent shrine in his humble hut, while exhorting them to remove themselves and their pious adherent to safer shores. Toward the end, his pleas appear to prevail and the *numina* soften towards the suppliant. Significantly, they are seen to 'nod' their acquiescence to his words:

visaque sunt dictis adnuere ora meis (74). I tend both to doubt the exile's claim to new-found religious fervour and to read a continued sense of fun from both the ramifications of his argument and his apparently conscious etymological play.

In my statistical count I chose to interpret repeated use of the word in this outrageous passage as a single occurrence. Equally, a triple designation of Germanicus as the plural *numina* in the course of *Ex P.* 4.8 can be taken as essentially a single reference. The word is decreasingly applied to the imperial family, its use in the imperial context dwindling noticeably from first to last, either a sign of final despair by the exile about the usefulness of such a ploy, or a further indication of a change in the poet's interests and choice of topics.

A more sinister equation is reflected in the substitution of the terms FATUM and FORTUNA (roughly equivalent to the Greek '*Moira*') for 'Caesar', often with a strongly negative connotation. *Fatum* (from root *fa-, 'to utter, appear', so recognised by Varro *Ling.* 6.52) has many related shifts of meaning, from 'fixed lot, what has been spoken or decreed' (even as an equivalent of *vita* 'life'), to passive 'what will happen' or 'has happened', to 'instrument of doom', to 'death' (equivalent to *mors*). Its plural *fata*, 'fates' or PARCAE, combined the ancient Greek idea of 'the rulers over the thread of life' with 'verbal prophecy', 'what has been decreed'. FATALIS as adjective takes on related meanings. Often *fata* as active agent virtually equals the emperor, as in *Tr.* 3.6.15 *sed mea me in poenam nimirum fata trahebant* ('but my doom undoubtedly dragged me toward punishment'); *Ex P.* 4.9.36 *mitia ius urbis si modo fata darent* ('if only a kinder fate would give me the right to the City'). In both cases the exile's lot and the person who decreed it appear interchangeable, with implicit covert criticism of the powerful imperial personage. The poet was exiled *because the emperor spoke the decree*, not because he had in any way transgressed.

Fortuna, 'chance' (from *fero*, 'to bring', but related by the ancients merely to its cognate *forte*, Aug. *Civ.* 4.18 p. 161.6D; Isid. *Orig.* 8.9.94) is in Roman thought most often the incalculable factor bringing victory or defeat (the Greek *tychê*), but it is often used, as in English today, as the equivalent of 'possessions', 'what has been brought by chance'. The word occurs 75 times in the exilic works, against only 40 occurrences in the rest of Ovid's oeuvre. *Fata* is seen by some scholars as an Homeric concept, *Fortuna* as Hellenistic. In the exilic works the concepts merge, being both the 'agents shaping events', and the 'outcome of these events'. Here, too, Augustus as agent, 'shaping events', appears as their shadowy equivalent. SORS (from *sero*, 'sow', Varro *Ling.* 6.65) 'a lot, throw of chance' usually implied the 'impersonal decision of fate'. For Ovid it most frequently implies 'lot in life', the result of the decrees of fate (or of the emperor), as when he rebuts a suggestion that he should console himself with the usual occupations of an exile, namely literature: he cannot, he says, for *sorte nec ulla mea tristior esse potest* (*Tr.* 5.12.6, 'no lot can be more wretched than mine'). That the very rebuttal is an example of such an exercise shows the poet's old sense of fun still at work.

The combined semantic set *fortuna, fata, fatalis, Parcae, (dirae) sorores* and *sors* is typical of Ovid throughout his oeuvre (539 instances, of which 27% in the exilic works). The set has its highest frequency in the third phase where the exile often complains about the hardness and inevitability of his lot.

The synonyms MITIS and LENIS, 'kind', words elsewhere often associated with divinity, are with almost formulaic regularity applied to words denoting the emperor. Thence *fata* can plausibly be equated with 'Augustus' in *mitia ... fata* (*Ex P.* 4.9.36) quoted above. *Mitis* occasionally applies to the exile's wife and friends, but more often to the emperor, in combination with requests for a better place of exile. Of seven occurrences of *mitis* in Phase 5, four refer to the emperor (e.g. *Ex P.* 4.5.32 *a miti Caesare*) and three to friends (e.g. *Ex P.* 4.15.32 *mitis amice*). *Mitis* and *lenis* sometimes paradoxically combine with IRA, a typically divine attribute. Its root is cognate to the Greek *eris* 'strife' (with the implication of the involvement of both protagonist and antagonist), but ancient etymologists associated it with 'departing, taking leave (of oneself)', implying unilateral action by the antagonist, so Donatus *Ter. Phorm.* 794. With Ovid this subjective implication predominates, and *ira* means 'wrath', often with the implication that his antagonist has exceeded just bounds, a concept that accords with the ancient etymology of the word. The exile felt the *ira* of the god, of Caesar, of the *princeps*, of the *numen* and of 'that man'. Use of *ira* (with its cognates IRATUS and IRASCOR) decreases from Phases 1 to 3, again perhaps an indication that the exile was turning his attention elsewhere. Yet Phase 4 shows a marked increase, deriving from the exile's increased outreach to potential mediators between him and the being he has angered. During the last phase significantly less concern about the emperor's anger may be ascribed to the death of Augustus in AD 14.

Prayers for remission of sentence are expressed by means of the verbs PRECOR and ORO and the less frequent noun PRECES. Words involving the root **prec-* (cognate to Skr. **pracch-/*prast-*, Ger. *fragen*, Eng. 'pray'), 'to ask' (but not necessarily of a divinity), predominate. *Oro* is predictably less frequent, deriving as it does from *os, oris*, 'mouth'. One of the exile's chief complaints was that exile offered him no chance for personal communication. He could *write* to Rome, but there was no one to *speak* to. Combined statistics for *precor* and *oro* show a strong appeal during the first two phases, which virtually ceases in the third phase, arising anew in the fourth phase, when friends are addressed on the subject of *amicitia* and its obligations. The exile's appeals, beside supplication of the purportedly divine imperial family, predictably reach out into the sphere of private and political friendship. Again the words are not specifically 'elegiac' or 'erotic', but may be said to have reverted to their original provenance.

The specialised vocabulary of exile

Now to the specialised vocabulary of exile, mostly words for longing and desolation (largely pathological and psychological terms – these may be seen as continuing the 'elegiac' mode) and a vocabulary of defiance and endurance. Ovid's vocabulary of pathos derives largely from precedents set in the *Heroides*. The words are also extremely frequent in the *Metamorphoses*, where change often involves pain. The most important are *queror, querulus, fleo, flebilis, lacrima, litura, miser, vereor, timor, metus, stupor, torpor, attonitus, solus, sollicitus, tristis, infelix, pudet, procul, longe, extremus, ultimus, abesse* and *deesse, desero, desiderium, diversus, peregrinus, profugus, vulnus, cura, morbo*. Many of these, although not intrinsically 'erotic', also occur in amorous elegy, especially in the context of exclusion from the beloved.

Ovid's heroines were frequently 'tearful'; the exile more often exhibits other signs of a growing unhappiness. In the *Heroides*, the words *queror/ querulus, fleo/ flebilis/ fletus, lacrima, litura, plango(r)* occur 170 times, of which *lacrima* (51) and **quer-* (39) are most frequent, as against 62 occurrences of the whole set in the exilic works (where *plangor* does not feature at all). The pattern of occurrence of *lacrima, fleo, flebilis* and *fletus*, taken as a unit, through the exilic phases, is erratic: 10, 18, 8, 23, 4. Some occurrences are retrospective in context: some poems from Phase 2 recall the exile's departure (which belongs in the first phase), and in Phase 4 the exile weeps for lost friends. Other words in this set increase in frequency from first to last, indicating no remission of misery.

The semantic set *attonitus, infelix, miser, sollicitus, tristis, pudet* (all reflections of the subject's inner life) is represented by 85 occurrences in the *Heroides*, by 158 in the exilic oeuvre. Their distribution here is suggestive. By Phase 4 the exile has, perhaps not surprisingly, ceased to be ATTONITUS ('lightning-struck with unpleasant surprise') or SOLLICITUS ('worried') but he continues unhappy, MISER (69 occurrences in all). TRISTIS is most frequent in the second and fourth phases. The second-century Festus (351) derived *sollicitus* from *solo citare*: [*i.e.*] *ex suo loco ac sententia* ('to call up from the ground, that is, from its own place or opinion'). This zeugmatic derivation is most apposite to the circumstances of an exiled poet, as pointed out in the context of *exsul* (*solum vertere exili causa*) above. About *miser* Isidorus *Orig.* 10.173 quotes Cicero *Tusc.* 1.9 on the dead as *miseros ... propter quod iam amiserunt vitam* ('miserable because they now have lost their lives'). Such a fanciful etymology could have represented reality for the exile, who

129

frequently depicts removal from Rome as 'living death', loss of all life that he held dear.

MALUS and MALA (the latter as substantive for 'ills') are emotionally related to the above semantic set: the words reflect the exile's inner perception of outer reality. Their relative frequency displays a decreasing arc (12.5 – 25.9 – 21.2 – 14.5 – 9.6 per 1,000 verses). The poet appears over time to be moving away from depiction of outer ills toward stronger concentration on his inner life.

The semantic set comprising words of destitution or desolation is represented by 72 occurrences in the *Heroides*, 143 in the *Tristia* and *Epistolae Ex Ponto*. The words are: *desero, desiderium, diversus, extremus, ultimus, procul, longe, peregrinus, profugus.* Perhaps surprisingly, the fourth phase does not display a proportionate increase of expressions denoting 'longing' as the exile attempts to gain sympathy from his friends. More prominent here are words denoting 'distance': PROCUL (9) ULTIMUS plus EXTREMUS (11), PROFUGUS (6), LONGE (5). With Ovid *ultimus* sometimes has a temporal connotation, 'last in time' as in the 'last deed of his life that brought about his downfall' (*Tr.* 2.99 *ultima me perdunt*), and his 'last (third) wife [who] bore being married to an exile' (*Tr.* 4.10.73, *ultima ... sustinuit coniunx exulis esse viri*), but generally the focus is on the vast distance between the exile and home. Ten out of fourteen words of desolation in the last phase come from this subset; the others all derive from DESERO (all but one applied to the exile). This word and its cognate *deserta* relate to *sero*, 'to join', implying disjunction, but were by the ancients derived (as antonyms) from its homonym, which means 'to sow' (Isidorus *Orig.* 14.8.31, etc.). Ovid makes much of the bareness of his place of exile and its lack of agriculture (e.g. *Tr.* 3.12.14 and 16). The paranomastic possibilities of like-sounding *desiderium* (of uncertain etymology, so Lewis and Short) could have prompted Ovid's continued frequent use of the word in the exilic poems, as elsewhere in his oeuvre, which often deals with loss and longing. Ancient etymologists ascribed the origin of the word to 'a change of stars' ('*de + sidera*', Paulus Diaconus *Epit. Festi* 75), which, again, in the context of Ovid's exile, opens interesting possibilities. He consistently depicts himself as living 'under a distant star', even 'the Polar star' (*Tr.* 1.5.61; 3.4.47-8; 4.4.62, *Ex P.* 4.10.39-40).

An important part of Ovid's very specialised exilic vocabulary deals with his inner resilience. Here one word with a widely divergent semantic field and widely differing emotional appeal stands out: the IMAGO, the surrogate vision, a unique exilic concept. It has a fluctuating semantic field, depending on the presence or absence of symbolism or degree of abstraction. In the Platonic view an idealised concept is more 'real' than a transitory object. In that sense an *imago*, a mental vision, can be more 'real' than the concrete object it represents. A reflection in a mirror is also an *imago*, transitory in a different way; so too a picture on a wall, a concrete representation of either another concrete object, or of a concept, a creation of the imagination. Paulus Diaconus, following Festus, proposed the derivation of *imago* from *imitatio*. This is semantically close to its probable origin as a cognate of *aemulatio*, from root **im-*. This appears to have been the significance *imago* held for Ovid, for whom its basic import was 'representation of reality'. Context helps the reader to distinguish between the meanings of *imago* in *Tr.* 1.3.1, *cum subit illius tristissima noctis imago* ('when my memory of my last night in Rome rises up within me'), and (about the son of Messallinus), *Tr.* 4.4.3; *cuius inest animo patrii candoris imago* ('in whose mind is a mirroring of your father's brilliance'). To the poet his poems are, almost in the Platonic sense, a truer representation of himself (*maior imago*) than his own person can be (*Tr.* 1.7.11-12).

The frequency of occurrences of IMAGO is of interest here: in Phases 1 to 4, the word occurs with the frequency: 4, 3, 2, 8. In the last phase, *imago* has been replaced by the semantically related OCULI MENTIS, 'the mind's eye'. The concept occurs four times in each of the last two phases, after a first appearance in the second phase, at *Tr.* 4.2.57, *haec ego summotus, qua possum, mente videbo* ('far removed as I am, I shall see these things in my imagination – with which I can'). The future VIDEBO (with *absens/ animo/ mente*) gains a similar meaning in the context of the exile's inner life. The impression is not so much of an increase in visionary activity, as of the poet's development of a novel way of expressing such activity. The concept occurs only six times in the rest of Ovid's oeuvre: five in the *Metamorphoses*, one in the *Heroides*.

MENS is more frequent in the context of expression of the exile's emotional anguish. Such use of the word implies remembrance of a happier past. Isidorus *Orig.* 11.1.12 offers (as second variant origin) for *mens* an etymological link to words for 'memory', and gives a list of 25 postulated cognates, with wide-ranging paranomastic play, some of which appear only faintly to adumbrate a reminiscence of the root **men-* ('thought'). Ovid's opposition of mental activity to corporeal suffering is significant. Frequent references to the exile's anguish picture a sensitive thinker for whom Platonic reality is paramount, corporeal reality almost negligible (only eleven references in all to his own body; all other instances of **corp-* in the exilic works have a different context). This contrasts with the physically sensual approach of the erotic oeuvre and the central position of bodily change in the *Metamorphoses*. In these works *corpus*, in all semantic contexts, is extremely frequent, with over 400 occurrences (almost double that of *mens* and *ingenium* combined).The poet's frequent use of INGENIUM ('inborn talent', so Varro *Ling.* 8.15, Cic. *Fin.* 5.36 etc.) attests to this same attitude. Many of Ovid's references to *ingenium* are either nega-

131

tive (he has lost it) or unfavourable (it harmed him), but the combined relative frequency of *ingenium* and *mens* (on average once every 50 verses throughout) compared with CORPUS as applied to the exile himself (relatively scarce in the first phases, dwindling further toward the last) underscores the superiority in the poet's consciousness of the exile's mental activities and woes over matters corporeal or physical. The exile's unhappiness has been depicted differently from phase to phase, with decreasing concern about 'distance from home'. The final impression is predominantly of resignation, fewer desires, and more pain. The exile relies increasingly upon the powers of his mind and his poetic imagination.

The poet's 'Muse' features prominently throughout the exilic oeuvre, sometimes in the sense of 'patron deity', but more often as a synonym for *carmen*, referring to his poetry, even his talent. His Muse is twice designated *antistes*, thrice *solacium*. The *Pierides*, the daughters of Pieros (with variants *Pieridas* and *Pieriae deae*), feature in fourteen instances as synonyms for the Muses. Only in *Met.* 5.302ff. are the daughters of Pieros rivals of the Muses, elsewhere (*Am.* 1.1.6; *AA* 3.548; *Fasti* 2.269 etc.) they are synonymous with 'Muses', often no more than an ornamental poetic flourish, as in *Tr.* 3.7.4, where *Pieridas ... suas* is a metaphor for 'studies'. As Chapter 3 showed, the poet's attitude to his Muse fluctuates from strongly negative to wholly positive. It is important to weigh negative references against positive. The most negative allusion occurs at *Ex P.* 4.2.45, *qui nisi Pierides, solacia frigida, restant?* ('what is left, beside the Muses, a cold comfort?'). Yet cold comfort is comfort still. After the second phase, where positive references (5) outweigh negative (3), negatives cease. Positive allusions continue, reaching a vindicatory climax in the very last poem: *Ex P.* 4.16.45, *dicere si fas est, claro mea nomine Musa/ ... erat* ('if I am allowed to say so, my Muse had an illustrious name'). The final judgement of the *vates* about his goddess is positive, underlining the exile's increasing reliance on his own poetic powers for comfort and support. His confidence in his prowess as a poet is restored, and even overtures to a new imperial patron, Germanicus, are couched in terms of virtual equality; the poet's tone in *Ex P.* 4.8.65-82, Ovid's appeal to the prince through Suillius, although pessimistic, is one of 'We poets, my dear Germanicus ...'.

The most well-known word of defiance in the whole of the Ovidian oeuvre is LIVOR, which editors obligingly grace with an upper case L when they suspect personification. Of 17 occurrences in the complete Ovidian corpus seven are usually printed thus. The other instances are clearly impersonal. The most violent outburst against personified 'Envy' occurs at *Rem.* 389, *rumpere, Livor edax!* ('burst, biting Envy!'). At *Tr.* 4.10.123 defiance is equally strong:

4. Ovidian logodaedaly

nec, qui detractat praesentia, Livor iniquo
ullum de nostris dente momordit opus.

Nor has Envy, which pulls down everything in the present, ever gnawed with its mean fang on any work of mine.

Address of a personified Envy has its antecedents in the Callimachean tradition of *recusatio*, related by some to the (perhaps dubious) 'Battle of the Books', an early literary enmity postulated between Callimachus and Apollonius Rhodius, now largely discounted. We have noted before that personified Envy can serve as a metrical or paranomastic euphemism for *Caesar* or *Livia*. According to Quintilian (9.2.67), delicately disguised criticism of 'tyrants' was safe. A 'tyrant', although offended, could not react to it, as long as an innocent meaning could also be attached to the author's words. Multiple levels of meaning are so often discernible in Ovid, that this possibility cannot be rejected out of hand as 'potentially dangerous and therefore outrageous'. Ovid, toward the end of his life as an exile, was perhaps recklessly discarding the circumspection regarding mention of the empress displayed by most of his contemporaries. The name *Livia* occurs altogether eight times in the whole of Ovid's oeuvre: twice each in the *Fasti* and *Tristia*, four times in *Ex Ponto*.

The exile's final address to *Livor* smacks of pathetic desperation: *Ex P.* 4.16.47, *ergo summotum patria proscindere, Livor, desine* ('hence, Envy, desist from tearing to shreds someone so far removed from his homeland'). The poet here depicts himself as defunct, yet alive to the pain inflicted by his imperial persecutors, as depersonalised in the mysterious *Liv-*. The exile has suffered much at the hands of the imperial family. So the last poem of the oeuvre ends on a sombre note, but the exile's vindication of his place among living poets (3-44) leaves us with an impression of the superiority of mental achievement over matters corporeal, and of the creative and visionary power of the mind to transcend time and space.

Conclusions about the exile's attitude to Augustus and his appreciation of the emperor's *iustitia* and *clementia* cannot be drawn absolutely by reference to series of figures. The degree of irony versus surface credibility ('sincerity') needs to be gauged in connection with each allusion. Yet from a tentative interpretation of the trend of the figures in the table we may conclude that at first the exile was more defiant, less prepared to concede that he was to blame, less concerned for clemency than for justice, but that this attitude changed over time. At the last a general movement away from both protestations of innocence and cries for mercy leads to an increasing claim on the emotional support of friends, and insistence on the reciprocity of obligation, culminating in the prolific fourth phase, which offers a surrogate for the *Ars Amatoria*, an *Ars Amicitiae*. The drastic diminution of terms relating to imperial matters in the fifth phase points to a final renunciation of externals in favour of the inner life, fed by literary contact with distant friends. Admittedly the thrust of Ovid's appeal at this stage is directed, through his literary coterie, at a potential new imperial patron, Germanicus, but there are few signs of success. In the end only his Muse offers the exile any solace.

In sum: Ovid's exilic vocabulary achieves both more and less than would be implied by Nagle's designation as essentially 'erotic'. Ovid has sent these words in new directions, yes, but these directions tend towards home; he has rewritten their context, thereby giving earlier use of the words a new innocence. He has further established a language of imperial criticism and of poetic vindication which could not be faulted by his antagonist, but which could be read at different levels by a readership sensitive to contemporary meanings attached to these words. Next we turn to the means whereby Ovid achieved this.

4.2. *Exsul ludens*: punning and word play

Gilbert Highet once remarked of Ovid that he had the ability 'to say the most outrageous things in words as pure as sunlight'. We have noted before Gilbert Murray's description of the poet as someone 'utterly in love with words'. Ovid's exilic works reflect new directions for his undiminished ingenuity. This section examines some aspects of Ovidian word-play, with particular attention to punning and *double entendre*, highlighting the endless nuances in our poet's sense of play, even in most dire circumstances. The multivalence of Ovid's art is paramount: each layer of humour may actually be covering another. Ovid continually challenges his readers to rethink their reactions to what he says.

Where we have above explored Ovid's exilic vocabulary, here we consider the degree to which Ovid's words should be taken at face value in his ostensibly 'serious' attempts to gain recall from exile. The question to ask is whether Ovid's exilic vocabulary is consistently disingenuous: whether at least some of his exilic words carry a secondary load or hidden meaning. Is Ovid deliberately misleading his readership, perhaps by punning?

This question may further be rephrased in terms of reception: did Ovid's contemporaries have a similarly ambivalent reaction to his words from exile as do many modern readers? Although open to question, the concept of 'authorial intention' offers the only means of exploring the interesting phenomenon that Ovid's words often seem to mean either more or less than can be read into them at first glance. The question then becomes: 'What did the exiled Ovid want his readership to make of his particular use of words?' I have suggested above that much of the exilic

134

poetry may be palinodic, in the sense that it draws attention to the poet's earlier elegies, and redraws the alignment of some of the sentiments there expressed, particularly by the new directions in which familiar words are sent.

First some general observations. A tendency to punning appears intrinsic to the psychology of language. Puns treat both homonyms and homophones as synonyms. A clever poet would exploit similarities in sound between words, continuing a practice popular and current in colloquial speech. The basic concept is ambiguity. *Figura etymologica* and *polyptoton* both involve variations of the same root or stem. Each occurrence evokes a reminiscence of the previous context, thereby subtly altering its present meaning. *Double entendre* is a phrase or clause which says two things at the same time. Understanding of Ovid's verbal play is essential to appreciation of his art. Punning word-play is not essentially 'funny'. 'Humour' lies in the eye of the beholder: that is, the reader's recognition of a clever verbal trick evokes amusement in the modern mind. To the ancients, punning was often a serious matter. The Epicureans regarded verbal similarities as stemming from substantial likeness. A key element in the Epicurean approach was the equation of individual letters with 'atomic elements'. For Lucretius, any two words with even a few such elements in common were essentially related. Hence, intentional word-play may be read into poets' use of any two words with common elements. We have already noted Ovid's play on *carmen – crimen*.

In the exilic works Ovid sometimes takes over extant word-play, often in an apparently sombre mood. The Greek play on the name of the Black Sea, *Axenos* versus *Euxenos*, was a literary commonplace: 'unfavourable' versus 'favourable to strangers'. This apotropaic euphemism was reasonably established by Ovid's time. It was probably originally derived from false etymology, based on an erroneous interpretation of the old Avestan name for the Black Sea, *ackshaéna*, meaning 'dark, of a dark colour'. Ovid refers to this play in *Tr.* 5.10.13, *Euxini mendax cognomine/ ... vere terra sinistra* ('the Black Sea with its lying nickname/ a truly *sinister* land'). Ovid takes the play further: the Latin *sinister*, his equivalent for *Axenos*, meant both 'unfavourable' and, more literally, 'on the left hand', and as substantive, 'the left'. To ships travelling northwards to Tomis, the Euxine coast is to the west, that is, on the left hand, and so play on the name of the area is extended from *sinister* (*Tr.* 2.197; 4.8.42) to *laevus* (*Tr.* 1.2.83; *Tr.* 1.10.17). Further, in Roman augury the left was favourable only when the augur faced south. In common speech, Neo-Pythagorean influence had reinterpreted the left as largely unfavourable, a precedent followed by our poet. Exceptionally, *Tr.* 1.9.49 applies Romano-Etruscan lore to indicate *tonitrus ... sinistri* ('thunder on the left') as favourable.

So much for Pythagorean influence in the exilic works. What of other philosophical *topoi*? An ingenious and complicated series of puns may be read in *Ex P.* 3.6.35-6:

> *adde quod exstinctos vel aqua vel Marte vel igni*
> *nulla potest iterum restituisse dies.*

Add the fact that no day can ever again be able to (have) restore(d) those who have been extinguished by water or war or fire.

Restituere is a medical term ('restore', 'heal'), but also the technical term for the restoration of civic rights: loss of civic rights was imposed *interdictione aqua et igni*. Ovid's relegation meant for him denial of water and fire. This has been interpreted as an oblique allusion to the recurrent Stoic dogma of extinction through fire or water, which would tie Ovid's denial of cosmic restitution to negation of the idea of Augustan renewal after the ravages of war. If his banishment were to be undone, restitution for Ovid from his 'living death' would mean restoration to life, to Rome and, according to this interpretation, a recantation of his former denial (in the *Metamorphoses*) of the possibility of cosmic restoration. This theory does not accommodate the fact that all restitution (of whatever kind) is explicitly denied, nor does it attempt to explain the inclusion of the word *Marte* within the putatively Stoic phrase. It could plausibly be taken as a passing allusion to the dangers of the place of exile, but the consistent connection of Augustus with *Mars Ultor* and his great temple to that deity would fit the pattern more happily. The implication may rather be that the exile's doom has been sealed because of the intervention of a martial Augustus.

Even if the above fanciful interpretation is discounted, a pun may be read at the level of the *adynaton*: 'no day can restore the exile to his full civic rights'. This then anticipates and negates the following lines (37-50) in which Caesar's clemency is celebrated. The poem ostensibly celebrates Augustus' institution of a cult and shrine of *Iustitia Augusta* (January, AD 13), but the total effect is heavily negative. The emperor is negatively depicted – by means of strenuous denial of such a possibility – as a 'Busiris' or 'Phalaris', the prototypical cruel despots of myth, and the addressee's 'fears to be directly named' underline what the exile pretends to deny: that it is dangerous to be associated with a despot's victim. Ovid's apparently grovelling appeal may here conceal stringent indictment.

Yet much of Ovid's more pervasive punning is consistently playful, even in exile. So, at *Ex P.* 2.7.3-4, to his friend Atticus, *quid agis?* is taken both formulaically and literally, as both 'How are you doing?' and 'What are you doing?' – with the implication that Atticus should be acting on the exile's behalf. Punning at this level is obvious, and typical of Ovid's elegant wit. As in *Heroides* 11.1, formulaic epistolary greetings offer opportunities for playfulness: more than once *salutem dare* is adapted to show the exile giving 'what he has lost' (*Tr.* 5.13.1-2; *Ex P.* 1.10.1-2). *Salus* represents three ideas: 'greetings', 'good health' and, in a political context, 'full civic rights'. So too, the exile plays on the meaning of *valere* 'fare well!' and 'feeling well' in *Tr.* 3.3.88:

> *accipe, supremo dictum mihi forsitan ore,*
> *quod tibi qui mittit non habet ipse, vale.*

> Accept what is perhaps the last word uttered by my mouth:
> something that the one who sends it to you himself lacks, good
> health!

Covert criticism may be read from some examples of word-play. At *Tr.* 3.14.5 an ostensible compliment to Ovid's editor friend (probably Hyginus, keeper of the Palatine library) is considered by Peter Green (1994 ad loc.) as possibly hidden criticism: *conficis ... mea carmina*. *Conficere* could mean either 'record, compose, collect' or 'chop up, defeat, ruin'. In the light of some recent conjectures (now most often discounted) that Hyginus could have been the mysterious enemy attacked with endless ingenuity in the *Ibis*, such an interpretation is attractive, but the role of an editor is so clearly implied in the poem that it is probably better to accept the word at its face value in the context of a 'letter to an editor'.

The poet's friends Carus, Fabius Maximus and Cotta Maximus have names that lend themselves to witty, gracefully complimentary punning. In *Tr.* 1.5.3, 4.7.19 and 5.7.5 the exile's use of the vocative, *carissime*, combines, with particularly subtle play, formulaic address to any friend with address of Ovid's particular friend Carus (as in *Tr.* 3.4.1, *o mihi care quidem semper*, 'O you who are always equally dear to me', also in *Tr.* 3.5.17-18). Written in the script of Ovid's day, 'care' and 'Care' are indistinguishable, except perhaps to the *docti*, i.e. the poet and his friend: CARE .../ SCIS CARUM VERI NOMINIS ESSE LOCO, 'dear Carus .../ you know that "dear chap" is in the place of your real name'. On the face of it, the name 'Carus' is explicitly excluded, but to readers aware of our poet's sense of play, his most explicit negations often become inverted jokes and negation serves to emphasise what it pretends to deny. The pun is spelled out in *Ex P.* 4.13.2 *qui, quod es id vere, <u>care</u> vocaris* ('you, who are called exactly what you are, "dear friend" ').

At *Ex P.* 1.2.1-2 the poet plays on the name of Paullus Fabius Maximus:

Maxime, qui tanti mensuram nominis inples
et geminas animi nobilitate genus.

Maximus, you who are big enough to fill the measure of such a
great name,
and duplicate your ancestral line with the nobility of your
mind.

The implication of the first verse appears to be that Maximus was fat, but
the second imputes magnanimity to the great man, rather than *avoirdu-
pois*. The verses that follow make explicit who the addressee is, with a
reference to the famous ambush against three hundred members of the
gens Fabia by the people of Veii (Liv. 2.48-50; Ov. *Fasti* 2.195ff.). Ovid is
having a little fun with his friend and patron, a relative of his wife's –
and *amicus Caesaris*.

There often appears to be a deeper reason for punning than the poet's
mere sense of etymological play or a love of riddles. Puns serve to point
to aspects of his exile that the poet wishes to emphasise. As we know, the
major difference between the *Tristia* and *Epistolae Ex Ponto* is that in the
latter friends and addressees are named. Probably no great harm would
have come from such naming. Ovid's elaborate pretence of retaining his
addressees' anonymity in the *Tristia* is one way of underlining (in subtle
praeteritio) the despotism of the offended emperor. Elaborate circum-
spection shows up Augustus' vindictiveness.

Similarly, we may sometimes read more into ostensibly innocent
protestations about the emperor's actions. Some passages defy precise
circumscription. The elusiveness of individual words sometimes lends
itself to irony, its degree being open to interpretation. Such elusiveness
is protective: the poet can hide behind one connotation, or deny that he
ever recognised a different connotation when employing a particular
word. Such protection applies equally to punning, *double entendre* and
general verbal play. Some allusions appear dangerous in their contem-
porary context. The formulaic *pace tua* in *Ex P.* 3.1.7-10, which normally
means no more than 'with your permission', has sometimes been inter-
preted as an ironic reference to the *Pax Augusta*. This phrase occurs in a
poem (increasingly seen as problematic) instructing the exile's wife on
the way to approach the empress Livia, who – again by strenuous denial
of the very possibility – is portrayed as despotically vindictive.

Some of Ovid's word-games are familiar from his earlier works.
Metrics and the rules of elegiac verse produce playful allusions to alter-
nating six- and five-footed verse, as first employed at *Am.* 1.1.4, *risisse
Cupido/ dicitur atque unum surripuisse pedem* ('they say that Cupid
laughed and slyly took away a foot'). Elegy personified appeared to the
poet, with one foot 'longer than the other' (*Am.* 3.1.8). The exiled poet

sends his book (*liber*), which is 'free' (*liber*) to travel, to Rome as his surrogate: *contingam certe, quo licet, illa pede* (*Tr.* 1.1.16, 'let me reach her with that kind of foot which is allowed'). And the tired little book travels to Rome to tell its own sad story: *longinquo referam lassus ab orbe pedem* (*Tr.* 3.1.26, 'I go on foot, all worn out, from the ends of the earth'). The book is 'nervous' and wants its readers to notice how its feet tremble: *alternos intremuisse pedes* (*Tr.* 3.1.56, '[see] that my feet trembled alternately'). As Chapter 3 showed, extensive dactylic metre, with its uneven pace, reinforces the sense of the verse.

The idea of this pun is extended at *Ex P.* 3.4.85-7, to include 'wheels' of uneven size, here gracefully incorporating a reference to customary triumphal trappings, which included carts carrying tableaux:

> *ferre etiam molles elegi tam vasta triumphi*
> *pondera disparibus non potuere rotis.*
> *quo pede nunc utar, dubia est sententia nobis.*

> My weak elegies couldn't bear the enormous triumphal
> weight on their uneven little wheels.
> I can't decide what foot I should employ now.

The setup here offers grounds for reading criticism of imperial policy into Ovid's ostensibly laudatory words. The exile is importuning his friend Rufinus to foster his 'triumph poem' (apparently written after the death of Augustus, and celebrating Tiberius' Pannonian triumph). As Chapter 2 showed, this mysterious 'triumph poem' was either lost, is non-existent or forms part (87-115) of the very poem (*Ex P.* 3.4) in which it is touted as a celebration of the great deeds of Tiberius. In the end, the poem is about *Ovid's own* triumph, whatever he may have meant by it. Such ambiguity is consistent with our poet's wit. Noticeably, unlike *Ex P.* 2.1, this poem carefully steers clear of references to Germanicus – perhaps wisely, in the light of what we know about the relations between the reluctant new emperor and his heir-apparent. More importantly, however, it draws attention to Ovid's earlier prophecy of a triumph for Gaius Caesar (*AA* 1.177-216), both by its context and tone and by its very glossing over of references to imperial heirs, both living and deceased. Against what was prophesied by the *praeceptor amorum*, Gaius did not triumph, but died. Ovid's claim to vatic and oracular authority has already proved false when he makes it (*inrita votorum non sunt praesagia vatum*, *Ex P.* 3.4.89, 'the presagings of divine prophets are never in vain', repeating the thought of *Ex P.* 2.1.55, *quod precor, eveniet: sunt quiddam oracula vatum*, 'what I pray, will come to pass: the prophecies of soothsayers are real'). Now, when the *exsul* predicts a triumph for Tiberius, at best there has in the past been a discrepancy between what he promises and what Fate delivers; at worst, such a prediction may appear as a literary 'kiss of death', presaging doom for the would-be *triumphator*. In either case, of course, it is to be taken as little seriously as any of the more overt flatteries of later emperors by a poet such as Martial. So, on a deep level, we may read a disparity between what the poet says and what he is implying.

Beside claims to vatic veracity, other aspects of the poet's craft receive mention. Poetics are a frequent topic, both references to the poetry that harmed the exile, and to his present work. Play on the word *ars* in some cases suggests both the exile's poetic talent and the *Ars Amatoria*, as in *sic ego do poenas artibus ipse meis* (*Tr.* 5.12.48, 'so I myself am punished for my skills/ Arts [of Love]'); *ingenii .../ artibus exceptis saepe probator eras* (*Ex P.* 2.2.103-4, 'you often approved of my talent, except of course for my Art [of Love]'); and (to his friend Macer) *nulla factus es Arte nocens* (*Ex P.* 2.10.12, 'you were not made guilty by any Art [of Love]').

Assurance of the greatness of his art alternates with despondency about the harm it did him, but here, too, Ovid's tone is often playful, in spite of signs of gathering gloom, even in his verbal play. The idea of exile as death may lie behind *Tr.* 5.1.19, where Gallus, Propertius and Tibullus are listed as Ovid's great elegiac predecessors. He then exclaims *utinam non nos essemus in isto!* – 'I wish that I weren't one of them!' The joke gains a new twist when we remember that, beside being love poets, all three are *dead*. The exile has no desire to be a dead poet, but exile is tantamount to death. In time this mood changes. At *Ex P.* 3.7.20 *extremum* can either mean 'at the ends of the earth' or 'at my death'. The exile is now resigned to ending life far from Rome.

We have above noted Ovid's frequent play on *carmen – crimen*. The connection is first coined at *Tr.* 2.207, *perdiderunt ... me duo crimina, carmen et error* ('two accusations ruined me, a poem and a mistake'). The reminiscence of *crimen* at each use of *carmen* works as 'acoustic punning', the suggestion of a different word by means of the sounds within a word, specifically by inversion or metathesis of its elements. The effect of such association of two words is that, whenever one of the words is used, the other flickers into the reader's consciousness. Intertextual allusion presupposes the reader's consciousness of an earlier text (which helps to interpret a later) when reading the later text. This is of particular importance in Ovid's use of palindromes or quasi-palindromes. We have noted before that the prime palindromic example of 'one word, two ideas' is epitomised throughout in Ovid's approach to the Augustan literary ideal, where instead of ROMA, he sang of AMOR.

The exiled poet insists, in his proposed autobiographical epitaph, on the essentially amorous content of his works, calling himself *tenerorum lusor amorum* (*Tr.* 3.3.73, 4.10.1, 'playboy of tender loves'). This is a complicated pun, suggesting gentle dalliance with 'loves' in the plural, rather than a single Catullus-like burning obsession, but also stressing the playfulness of Ovid's art. Intertextual connotations load the phrase with significance. Echoes of the poet's own past works re-colour those works by hindsight. At *Am.* 3.15.1 the *vates* of the goddess Venus had implored her, as *tenerorum mater amorum*, to exploit a new votary and leave this poor lover alone; now the remembered verse is evoked in a lighter context, that of play. *Ludere* implies performance on a musical instrument, even song. So the poet sang his *'Amores'*, the title of his songs – but it was all just play, and the 'mother of all loves' is almost forgotten.

There is another factor: an element of 'acoustic punning'. The assonance, alliteration and rhyme of the phrase *tenerorum lusor amorum* continue a derisive and repetitive echo of *Roma*, familiar, too, from a phrase in *Am.* 1.3.15: *non mihi mille placent, non sum desultor amoris* ('I am not charmed by a thousand girls, I'm not a circus rider of love'). This has been read as subtle contrast of 'circus-rider' with 'knight', involving allusion to Augustus' own youthful amours, and Ovid's ancient lineage. The sound play recurs by implication in *Ex P.* 3.3.38 when the poet vaunts himself as former *praeceptor amoris* 'who did not want Love to be unsophisticated'. Extensive word-play of a particular kind occurs in this poem. Chapter 2 discussed the sorry and bedraggled personified *Amor*, worn out from his long journey to Tomis, confessing to having harmed his former teacher, and expressing regret while exonerating the exile from blame. We noted there that Latin verbal synonyms *doceo* and *praecipio*, and, by extension, their respective nouns of agency, take a double accusative, of impersonal 'matter taught' and personal 'recipient of instruction'. So the matter taught, the abstraction *amor*, becomes, by Ovid's sleight of pen, the person *Amor*, no longer object, but recipient, of instruction by the *praeceptor amorum*.

The subtleties imputed to this phrase suggest a crucial problem. We have seen that the poet can, with punning, take refuge in the surface meaning of words. If offence is taken, he can stand upon the first level of meaning and deny any double intent. In some cases I may, as reader, perhaps be ascribing more levels to a word than the poet intended to convey. For instance, in the catalogue *Pannonia, Illyris, Raetica, Thracia, Armenius, Parthus, Germania*, all bowing before the Caesars, in a form of *synecdoche* singular *Armenius* represents *Armenia*. I suspect (against much criticism by colleagues) that Ovid may, under the guise of imperial panegyric, be hinting at the ineffectuality of the Roman legions against the German *Arminius: Nunc petit Armenius pacem* ('Now the Armenian/ Arminius seeks peace', *Tr.* 2.227). This, in a poem appearing, at the latest, in March AD 10, soon after the Varian disaster, appears dangerously tactless if the poem is meant as *captatio benevolentiae*, yet the acoustic relationship obtrudes. Such a reminder of the Varian disaster, if reminder it is, seems deliberately crude. The tone of *Tr.* 2 is ostensibly ingratiating, but few modern critics now would insist that it be taken wholly at face value. Slippage between ostensible and real meaning may safely be postulated. The whole poem serves as a vindication of the poet's life and art, and as an accusation against the despot who attempted to regulate both literature and morality, the one by means of the other.

In other cases there seem to be attempts at 'un-punning'. We have seen how various words from the elegiac tradition recur in Ovid's exilic works. Perhaps Ovid intentionally continued in essentially the same genre that had earlier proved dangerous, in part at least to enable himself to influence interpretation of what he had written before. For example, *perire* has been removed from the erotic sphere to form part of the consistent metaphor of exile as death. As discussed above, the vocabulary of erotic elegy was drawn from many spheres of life. Ovid's reuse during his exile of ambiguous words from erotic poetry often appears as an attempt to redirect their implication. Catullus' erotic vocabulary (in particular words from the political sphere) seems to have informed much of his successor's work. We have noted that *fides* is lifted from the erotic sphere and restored to the sphere of friendship, even when applied to the exile's wife. It still lends itself to graceful play and ornamental flourish, as in *Tr.* 4.3.14, with a play on 'faithfulness' versus 'trust': *deque fide certa sit tibi certa fides* ('and may my explicit trust in your absolute faithfulness continue'), where a chiastic arrangement adds elegance and emphasis. The word has clearly been divested of any erotic content.

More problematically, it has been conjectured by a seeker after the (incalculable) reason for Ovid's exile that repeated references to his *error* as the reason for the exile's banishment form an erotic pun, basing his argument on Virgil *Ecl.* 4.2, where *malus error* may be translated as 'a fatal passion'. *Error* is not generally considered as an 'erotic' term. Ovid's explanations of his *error* are always cryptic, but there is never any glimpse of an erotic context. Even if we concede that the Virgilian phrase in that context may be associated with love-making, Ovid's usage in the exilic poems would then be another example of restoration of a word to a single meaning.

So much for single words evoking second thoughts. Often phrases or whole passages seem to invite rereading at a second level. *Double entendre* is common in erotic elegy. Such a semantic set then carries heavy sexual innuendo. Such words, taken singly, are by and large 'lexically inoffensive': Highet's 'words as pure as sunlight'. In the exilic poems some loaded terms recur (e.g. *membra, surgo, pars virilis*) in such contexts as to suggest sexual *double entendre*, but it is never certain that the author intended a second meaning to be read into the words. The poet may consciously be restricting these words to a single semantic context, and thereby inviting a single reading of the same expressions also in his earlier poetry. The expression *pro parte virili* at *Tr.* 5.11.23 and *Ex P.* 2.1.17 in both instances refers to vicarious salutation of Caesar, apparently a conscious restoration of a potentially erotic phrase to a non-erotic context, where *double entendre* can scarcely be read. Stephen Heyworth (*Proceedings of the Cambridge Philological Society* 41, 1995 ad loc.) comments about the second instance: 'an extraordinary locution from the man banished for his composition of the *Ars Amatoria*'. But that, I think, is the very point: formerly ambiguous words are consciously stripped of any double meaning, thereby lending an aura of innocence to their original use. Such sanitising is as much a playful ploy as Ovid's first, ambiguous use of a phrase.

The ambiguity of *Am.* 3.3.19 *sine pondere testes* is clear in context. Yet an almost identical expression, involving the same nouns, at *Ex P.* 3.9.49-50 carries no second meaning:

> *Musa mea est index nimium quoque vera malorum*
> *atque incorrupti pondera testis habet.*

> My Muse is an all too true indicator of my ills
> and has the weight of an honest witness.

The Muse is his 'honest witness': a pun would be inappropriate. Here an ambiguous phrase has been firmly redirected, serving to underscore its innocence in its previous context. Yet ambiguous play also continues. So, for instance, at *Ex P.* 1.10.27-8 a discussion of the exile's debilitated state may offer a simple description of illness, a subtle erotic pun or a conscious restoration of ambiguous words to a single, non-erotic context:

> *parvus in exiles sucus mihi pervenit artus*
> *membraque sunt cera pallidiora nova.*

> A meagre juice reaches my emaciated joints
> and my limbs (or: member[s]) are paler than new wax.

Exilis, 'thin', may evoke a false etymological connection with *exsul*, but the description is more reminiscent of the appearance of an unhappy lover. The equation of the symptoms of exile with the symptoms of love may be traced back to the origins of both, physical illness, but it is not impossible to read sexual innuendo into the pentameter. Five lines down Ovid takes pains to state (33-4) that his debilitation was not caused by excessive veneration of the goddess of love, thereby emphatically turning his reader's attention away from (or underscoring?) such an interpretation. This poem was addressed to L. Pomponius Flaccus. Its general tone serves to show the physical effects of his place of exile on the exiled poet.

Green (1994: 314) discusses the relationship of this poem to the portrait of Flaccus drawn by Suetonius (*Tib.* 42.1) as a sexual athlete and boon companion of Tiberius in vice, coming to the conclusion that the 'abjuration of erotic activity recalls ... [that the writer is] ... the quondam "instructor in passion" '.

So, also, had he been lying at death's door, 'if someone should announce that she had come' (*nuntiet huc aliquis dominam venisse*), the exile assures his wife, *resurgam/ spesque tui nobis causa vigoris erit* (*Tr.* 3.3.23-4, 'I shall rise up and hope of [embracing] you will be the cause of [new-found] vigour'). This may indicate a private and intimate conjugal joke. Reference to his wife as the *domina* (commonly 'mistress' of both a Roman house and the Roman elegiac lover's heart) may again be a subtle pun-on-a-pun, restoration of the elegiac word to its original social meaning, thereby attaching the rest of the statement to its innocuous surface meaning. On the other hand, it may be a further subtle pointer to an erotic joke. With Ovid we can never be sure. Other elements serve to direct our suspicions. The possibility of *double entendre* is flagged by the bathetic rhyme *dominam ... resurgam*, by the internal rhyming *aliquis ... nobis ... vigoris* within the couplet (which frames the more obvious rhyme of the hexameter), perhaps even by the alliterative sibilants of the pentameter.

A much more certain use of erotic *double entendre* occurs at *Tr.* 4.1.71-2, reminiscent of *Am.* 2.10.23-4:

> *aspera militiae iuvenis certamina fugi*
> *nec nisi lusura movimus arma manu.*

> As a young man I shunned harsh military battles
> and never handled arms except to play.

All the key terms (*certamina, lusus, movere arma*) occur in Pichon's list as examples of erotic punning. In his youth, the poet says, he took part in love matches only, and that in play. Now he is another ancient Priam, taking up arms to defend himself against marauding hordes. Punning here offers opportunities for contrast. Restoration of the terminology to its 'correct sphere', the military, is not so much retraction of what has gone before, as an exploration of a new direction for the poet's ingenuity. Intertextual reminiscences serve to add a note of playful pathos. The memory of Ovid's earlier pervasive use of the paranomastic contrast of *arma – amor*, as epitomised in his ingenious poem on the similarities between love and war (*Am.* 1.9), points the contrast. Youthful amatory drill in no way equipped him to become a real soldier at an advanced age.

These examples again confirm what Nagle has more extensively shown, namely that the exiled poet has used the language of elegy for his appeals. But he has done more; some of these words have been consciously restored to their more common non-erotic contexts. Such restoration works by mutual intertextuality to recolour by hindsight the elegists' use of a particular word. By redirecting an erotically-tinged vocabulary, Ovid is signalling to his readership in Rome (including Augustus) that his original works were not as 'naughty' as the emperor claimed. His power as poet stands undiminished, and the *crimen* imputed to his earlier oeuvre has been refuted. Ovid's formerly 'erotic' vocabulary emerges from the exilic poems sanitised and newly innocent. At the same time he may be sharing a quiet smile with whomsoever of his readers as chooses not to be fooled. Such knowledgeable readers would have been those of his friends who still kept in their personal collections the *carmina* of the banished *lusor amorum*.

4.3. Word-order and placement as a key to meaning

Next we need to examine Ovid's placement of words within his verse, as another means of conveying meaning (and sometimes concealing a secondary set of meanings, as with punning). We shall consider, in turn, verbal repetition, play with word order, juxtapositioning and contrast of words.

4.3.1. Repetition of words: figura etymologica *and* anaphora

There is a profound difference between punning and verbal repetition. The economical use of a single word offers both poet and reader cerebral satisfaction: punning is 'clever'. Repetition of words initially adds to the musical effect of a verse, impacting on readers' thoughts (perhaps also their emotions) only by retrospect.

There are two distinct kinds of repetition: anaphora (and related concepts *conduplicatio, reduplicatio, epanalepsis, epiphora*) and *figura etymologica* (or *polyptoton*). The basic difference is that anaphora involves the simple repetition of the same word, often at the beginning of a verse or at a verse break, whereas *polyptoton* involves variations on a root or stem, whether in different inflections, or in etymologically related words. Further, where there is an acoustic correspondence between etymologically unrelated words, the ancients usually accepted that there was an intrinsic relationship, so that repetition of similar-sounding words should also be considered as *figura etymologica*, as we have seen above with Ovid's play on *carmen – crimen*. Such false etymology amounts to a complex form of alliteration and assonance. All these are aspects of *paranomasia*, which Quintilian defines as a figure that 'depends on some resemblance in a word that has gone before' (9.3.66, transl. J.S. Watson, London 1907).

Of these two forms of repetition, etymological repetition lies closer to punning in its impact on the thought of the reader or hearer. We need both to consider the words involved and to 'think out' their connection. Its primary impact is, however, aural. This impact can differ from repetition to repetition. Chapter 3 analysed the effect of such aural impact (involving both alliteration and assonance) on hearers. Here we shall consider the secondary effects of *mental and emotional impact* by means of repetition of words.

Recognition of the stylistic value and typical use of a figure such as *polyptoton* is important for textual criticism. Failure in a textual critic to recognise an instance of anaphora or *polyptoton*, or, indeed, without due cognisance of its literary opposite, the principle of *variatio*, may lead to erroneous emendation of an uncertain text. It has been said that Ovid uses etymological repetition when he wishes to imply a close (often reciprocal) connection or a contrast between two things, such as: *Tr.* 1.1.128 *a terra terra remota mea* ('a land far removed from my land') or *Tr.* 4.6.43 *corpore sed mens est aegro magis aegra* ('my mind is far more sick than my sickly body'). The reader will find many more examples.

In *Ex P.* 1.2.125 *multa metu poenae, poena qui pauca coercet* ('he controls more things through the fear of punishment [than] the few [that he controls] with punishment'), etymological play is enhanced by a chiastic arrangement, alliteration of *p, m*, and *c* and the contrast *multa … pauca*. Clearly etymological repetition is seldom the only ornamentation of a couplet. It combines with other devices, such as semantic contrast, oxymoron, and, inevitably, assonance and alliteration, to add point, particularly to gnomic statements of 'commonly-held truth' as in the paradoxical *Ex P.* 1.5.53-4:

> *cum bene quaesieris quid agam, magis utile **nil** est*
> *artibus his, quae **nil** utilitatis habent.*

> When you seek carefully what (or: how) I am doing, there is
> > nothing more useful
> than this art of mine, which has no use.

Etymological repetition of personal pronouns often emphasises intimate reciprocity, giving a conversational tone to Ovid's exilic monologues. A multiple example occurs in *Ex P.* 3.1. 9-17, *tua … tu … tu … tu … tu … tibi … tu … tibi*. In the same poem, verse 65 *tu praesta* ('do me a favour') is spatially close enough to 71 *ego praestarem* ('I'd do you a favour') for a strong echo to be noted in the interplay of *tu … ego*. Similarly, *Ex P.* 4.15.13-20 has *… me … ego … tui … tua … tua … tibi … tuus … ego … te.*

Some cases of etymological repetition are particularly sonorous, combining with rhyme and other, non-etymologically related grammatical correlatives to produce a particularly pleasing, almost rocking rhythm. In *Tr.* 2.153-6 sound strengthens the poet's assertion of fluctuations of hope and despair:

> sic *abeunt redeunt* mei variantque timores
>   et spem placandi *dantque* negantque tui.
> per superos igitur, qui *dant* tibi longa *dabuntque* (with variant *dent*)
>   tempora ...

> So my fears go away and return and always change
>   and in turn give and deny hope of placating you.
> By the gods above, then, who (or: and may they) give and will go
>   on giving you a long
>   life ...

The influence of *polyptoton* on the tone of a verse differs from poem to poem. In *Ex P.* 4.8.33-56 six variations on *carmen* serve to emphasise the power of poetry. At *Ex P.* 4.12.43 triple *polyptoton* (*peream ... periit ... perire*) underlines a savage joke ('may I die ... that is, of course, if anyone who has died, *can* still die'). Exile is a living death and oaths involving ordinary mortal imprecation have become obsolete. Repetition of the stem **de-* at *Ex P.* 3.4.93-4 supports a tricolon offering an ostensibly powerful statement of the poet's right and ability to utter divine truth:

> ista *dei* vox est, *deus* est in pectore nostro,
>   haec duce praedico vaticinorque *deo*.

> That is the voice of a god, there is a god within my bosom,
>   with this god as my guide I predict and utter divine truths.

We have noted before the ambiguity of the context of Ovid's assertion here. Yet, in general, etymological repetition heightens emotional intensity. The figure is very common in the exilic oeuvre, occurring roughly once in every sixty verses during the first two phases, and about once in every forty verses in the last three phases.

A final example (of triple *polyptoton* in one verse of seven words) illustrates the levels of appeal of this figure: *laeta fere laetus* **cecini, cano** *tristia tristis* (*Ex P.* 3.9.35, 'I almost always sang happy songs when I was happy; now that I am sad, I sing sad songs'). The inevitable alliteration caused by repetition of the same three roots charms the ear: **lae-* sounds have a soothing lilt; *tr-* and *-s-* are 'rough', sound supporting sense; c-c-c binds the two central words. Both contrast and compression have a strong emotional impact. In seven words the pathos of the exile's position has been spelled out as clearly as the facts of the poet's life. This is poetry of a high order.

147

Whereas *polyptoton* involves changes in stem or inflection, anaphora involves unchanged repetition of the same word or group of words. Some form of anaphora, in all its various functions, is frequent within the exilic works, appearing on an average about once in every 28 verses, often in conjunction with etymological repetition. Any such repetition near enough to be noticeable counts as anaphora, even if not within the same verse, couplet or series of couplets. At *Ex P.* 1.6.29-39, *haec dea* (29, 'this goddess') is picked up by 31, *haec facit* ('she causes'), repeated at 33, *haec facit* and restored at verse 39 to *haec dea*. Repetition of words at the beginning and at the end of a poem, or 'ring composition', is an allusive binding device. It may sometimes be more or less fortuitous, unless it concerns the repetition of a key term, as in *Tr.* 1.10, which begins and ends with references to Minerva (verses 1 and 43). In the 'first epilogue' within *Tr.* 2, verses 155 to 205, the closing thought of the previous section, *spem placandi* (154, 'hope of placating') is repeated chiastically, near the close of this section, as *placandi spem* (182).

The musical effect of anaphora is largely similar to that of etymological repetition. It most often occurs within a separate syntactic grouping, i.e. the two or more words that are repeated are seldom syntactically dependent. Almost a hundred years ago Ludovic Otto in a Marburg dissertation analysed occurrences of anaphora in *Tr.* 2, listing fifteen 'nominals' (nouns, pronouns, adjectives), four verbs and nine 'particles' (e.g. *per, cur, ne, in, huc, o*) that lend themselves most easily to repetition. Anaphora often serves to give connective force to other 'particles,' such as adverbs (particularly of time, but also others), conjunctions such as *si*, prepositions, interrogatives and exclamations. The force of the anaphora differs with so-called words with greater weight, that is, emotive rather than neutral words. Anaphora has greater impact as a contrasting agent, than merely as a cumulative copulative. Our first example is in a tricolon from the first poem of the collection, addressed to the poet's book (*Tr.* 1.1.93-4):

> *si poteris vacuo tradi, si cuncta videbis*
> *mitia, si vires fregerit ira suas ...*

If you could be handed to him when he is at leisure, if everything seems favourable to you, if he has tempered the sharpness of his anger ...

The second and third *si* act as alternatives for the connective *aut*. Metrically *aut* would fit, but rhetorical emphasis would be lost by its substitution. Anaphora often eliminates clumsy and unpoetic connectives. At *Tr.* 5.9.7 anaphora of *te* substitutes for the prosaic *non solum ... sed etiam* . The sense is antithetic: *te praesens mitem nosset, te serior aetas* ('not only would the present age know you as kind, but so would a later age'). The position within a verse of the repeated word has given rise to a whole series of specialised terms, which we shall ignore, in favour of examining the emotional effect of such repetition. A word or words may be repeated at the beginning or end of subsequent verses or couplets, as for example *Tr.* 4.3.49-55, with its whole complex of repetitions:

> *me miserum,* **si** *tu, cum diceris exsulis uxor*
>   *avertis vultus et subit ora rubor!*
> *me miserum,* **si** *turpe putas mihi nupta videri!*
>   *me miserum,* **si** *iam te pudet esse meam!*
> *tempus ubi est illud,* **quo** *te iactare solebas*
>   *coniuge, nec nomen dissimulare viri?*
> *tempus ubi est,* **quo** *te (nisi non vis illa referri)*
>   *et dici, memini, iuvit et esse meam?*

Poor me, if you, when you are called the wife of an exile, turn away your face and blush! Poor me, if you consider it disgraceful to be seen as married to me! Poor me, if you're now sorry that you're mine! Where is that time when you used to boast about your husband, and never used to hide his name? Where is the time when you enjoyed, as I recall – unless you don't want that brought up – to be called (and to be) mine?

Here the emotive impact of the anaphora is paramount, its copulative function secondary. The repeated phrases seem formulaic. So too, *ille ego sum*, repeated at *Ex P.* 1.2.33-4 and at *Ex P.* 4.3.11; 13; 15; 16; 17, gains in impact with each repetition, echoing the *ille ego lusor tenerorum amorum* ('I am tender loves' playboy') of *Tr.* 4.10.1, itself a curious echo of the spurious *incipit* of the *Aeneid*.

Yet anaphora can, through repetition, remove power from a word and relocate emphasis on another, as for instance in *vereorque locum vereorque potentem* (*Tr.* 3.1.53, 'I fear the place and I fear my powerful opponent'). Repetition of a whole verse in epic formulaic fashion can act as a refrain, serving, as in modern ballads, to emphasise the pathos of the situation, e.g. *Tr.* 3.12.13-16. The exile is describing spring in his native land. Here words *not* repeated, and singulars for plurals, stand out with particular emphasis:

> *quoque loco est vitis, de palmite gemma movetur*
>   *(nam procul a Getico litore vitis abest);*
> *quoque loco est arbor, turgescit in arbore ramus*
>   *(nam procul a Geticis finibus arbor abest).*

And in that place there are vines, buds sprout from the branches
  (for vines are far away from the Getic shore);
and in that place there are trees, twigs are swelling with blossoms
                                        on the trees
  (for trees are far away from the Getic territory).

4.3.2. Hyperbaton, tmesis *and inversion of word-order*

Next we need to consider how Ovid arranges his rich vocabulary and to what effect. The Anglo-Saxon's confident assumption that the 'natural' and 'proper' order for words is the English word-order is illustrated by the introductory remarks by 'NB, a teacher of the Latin tongue' to his *Clavis Ovidiana, a numerical key to Ovid de tristibus* (1715): 'Those that are acquainted with the Latin tongue know, that there is so great and various a Transposition of the Words from their natural order (especially in the Poetry) that it is very difficult ...' etc. The worthy teacher's labours comprised numbers, assigned in series, verse by verse, indicating the order in which Ovid's words should be read to make 'English' sense.

About word order Quintilian says: 'speech would often become rough and harsh, lax and nerveless (*praemollis*), if words should be ranged exactly in their original order, and if, as each presents itself, it should be placed side by side of the preceding, though it cannot be fairly attached to it' (8.6.62, transl. Watson 1907). Quintilian goes on to advocate treating words like 'structures of unhewn stones', that must be placed in a position that 'will suit their nature'. The possibilities of an inflected language to achieve various effects by means of a free word-order are endless: in poetry the order is limited only by the exigencies of metre and prosody. *Tmesis* involves the separation, by interpolation of one or more words, of parts of a compound word.

The term *hyperbaton* (German: *Sperrung*), the spread over a verse or colon of words that are grammatically linked, need not be confined to the separation of a noun and its epithet (including a genitive). As a basic characteristic of most Latin poetry, it refers to all inversion of expected word-order. In Homeric verse, epithets are attached to their nouns, a natural result of formulaic composition, where fixed phrases are fitted into a set metrical pattern. The early Roman poets Lucilius and Ennius seldom separated epithets and nouns. An ornamental style, loaded with nouns, each with its own attribute, is typically neoteric. Weight is given to these attributes by separation from their nouns. This elegant device is much favoured by Ovid. The careful elegance of four interwoven *hyperbata* at *Tr.* 1.7.29-30 belies the claim of the exile that his work is unpolished:

> <u>ablatum</u> **mediis** <u>opus</u> est **incudibus** <u>illud</u>
> defuit et **scriptis** <u>ultima lima</u> **meis.**

> That work of mine was snatched from me while it was still on the
> anvil,
> and my writings lacked a final polish.

Hyperbaton of noun and adjective, in either hexameter or pentameter, is frequent. The components of a split phrase can occupy various positions within a verse. Mostly the epithet is placed first, with the substantive following in a metrically suitable position in the second hemistich. Chapter 3 showed that these words often form a syntactically rhyming unit, which, in the pentameter, binds the two halves, undercutting the dividing effect of its metric structure. Often, as above, two or even three nouns and their epithets occur within a verse, or spread over a couplet, in various interlocking (often chiastic) arrangements. The 'ideal' arrangement, the so-called 'golden line', consists of a verse with epithets and nouns in corresponding order, with a verb in the middle, so: a b V A B. *Hyperbaton* may be spread over the couplet, often in 'vertical agreement': two grammatically related words appearing in similar positions in two consecutive verses.

Elegiac poetry lends itself particularly to double *hyperbaton*. In the first half of a verse 'clues' are given by two epithets, and the suspense is solved at the end of the verse, or over the couplet, by information provided by two (often chiastically placed) nouns. In *Tr.* 1.1.110 there is no discernible sense pause as hyperbatic linkage overrides any potential break: *et sua **detecta** nomina **fronte** gerit* ('and each carries its own name openly on its cover'). In *Tr.* 1.2.32 a chiastic arrangement has a similar (but 'framing') effect: *ambiguis **ars** stupet **ipsa** malis* ('his very skill is numb from the baffling dangers').

Excessive *hyperbaton* often has a comical effect, adding to the fun of Ovid's poetry. So, too, the corollary applies: where the poet appears most serious, epithets are more frequently placed next to their nouns. In Ovid's later works the frequency of separation of substantives and their modifiers is considerably reduced, except for those adjectives syntactically most closely allied to (and hence more easily removable from) their nouns: adjectival pronouns, numerals, words denoting quantity and size. These adjectives generally carry little emotional weight. 'Ordinary' adjectives which are less consistently separated from their substantives include emotionally significant, typically exilic words such as *miser, tristis, desertus* etc. We have noted before that Ovid's decreasing use in his exilic poetry of *hyperbaton* (so much a part of the genius of Latin poetry) may be a significant indicator of a conscious move toward a new style.

Examination of an example will illustrate this thesis. *Ex Ponto* 3.7 seems to indicate experimentation with a new style. Its 40 verses display a noticeable dearth of *hyperbata*. There are still over 20 examples of single *hyperbaton*, but only three double *hyperbata*, all three in the pentameter, where the metre more easily lends itself to symmetry. Of these 20 or so epithets, a number are emotionally neutral adjectives, participles or geographical terms, for instance: 5 *nostra*, 6 *meis*, 18 *ulla*,

20 *mea*, 23 *proximus*, 25 *maiora*, 29 *Scythicis*, 32 *mea*, 37 *magna*, 40 *Euxinis*. Epithets with greater emotional weight are: 2 *vanas ... (preces)*, ('vain prayers'), 12 *(quam) proba (tam) timida* ('as chaste as she is fearful'), 16 *duro ... (iugo)* ('[under] a hard yoke'), 24 *vera ... (fide)*, ('[with] true faithfulness'), 27 *subita ... (unda)*, ('sudden breaker'), 28 *tumidis ... (aquis)*, ('turbulent waters'), 34 *(exsilium) ... triste* ('sad exile'). These all are arranged hyperbatically with their substantives, except in verse 12, where the words form part of the predicate of the relative clause.

The poem, addressed to the exile's friends, is laden with emotion, ranging from polite apology, to pathetic resignation, to bitter despair.

> *Verba mihi desunt eadem tam saepe roganti,*
> *iamque pudet, vanas fine carere preces.* (1-2)
> * * * * * *
>
> *venimus in Geticos fines: moriamur in illis*
> *Parcaque ad extremum qua mea coepit eat ...* (19-20)
> * * * * * *
>
> *cur ego concepi Scythicis me posse carere*
> *finibus et terra prosperiore frui?* (29-30)

I haven't any words left after asking the same things so often, and I am ashamed that my vain prayers never end ... I have come to the Getic regions: let me die here; let my Fate run out to the furthest end where it began ... Why did I think that I could get away from the Scythian regions and enjoy a happier land?

This extremely bitter poem manages to convey its feeling with the minimum of emotionally laden adjectives and very little *hyperbaton*. It would seem that a reduction in *hyperbaton* lends itself to intensity of expression. Similarly, *Tr.* 2.207-316, Ovid's defence against the accusation of having corrupted married women, displays an extremely low frequency of *hyperbaton*, with only ten instances of double *hyperbaton* in over 100 verses.

Analysis of the occurrence of *hyperbaton* within the whole exilic oeuvre has produced some interesting figures. The total of epithets separated from their substantives has a frequency over the five phases of 78, 72, 84, 60, 79 per 100 verses. It would appear that the fourth phase has the lowest incidence of *hyperbaton*. Further breakdown of these figures would be otiose, but a general trend is noticeable: there are consistently about three times as many single *hyperbata* as double (either chiastic or in a framing arrangement of nouns and epithets). Many pentameters and even more hexameters are without any *hyperbata*, but fully *hyperbaton*-free couplets are rare. The average frequency of couplets with no kind of *hyperbaton* is consistent at about 16% through all but one of the phases: there is a much higher incidence of such couplets in Phase 4, where almost one quarter of the total number of couplets does not show the device. Some poems display many more instances of *hyperbaton* than others, their words being so elaborately intertwined that they affect the averages for a whole phase. The frequency of *hyperbaton*-free couplets ranges from 44% in *Tr.* 5.4 to none at all in the next poem, with the mode at between 10% and 15%. Consideration of other passages with little or no *hyperbaton* may show whether a more sober tone, as evidenced by 'straight word-order', may be used as a consistent criterion for gauging intensity of feeling, as in *Ex P.* 3.7, discussed above.

A passage of three couplets (*Tr.* 1.3.57-62) has only a participle (*discedens*) separated from the subject contained within the verb (*dedi*) and the possessive adjective *meis* separated from its noun. It portrays the pathos of the exile's departure:

> saepe 'vale' dicto rursus sum multa locutus,
>   et quasi discedens **oscula summa** dedi.
> saepe <u>eadem mandata</u> dedi **meque ipse** fefelli,
>   respiciens <u>oculis</u> **pignora cara** <u>meis</u>.
> denique 'quid propero? Scythia est quo mittimur,' inquam
>   '<u>Roma relinquenda</u> est. **utraque iusta mora** est.

Often, when I had said 'farewell,' I spoke many (more) words, and gave the 'last' kiss as if I was going. I kept on giving the same instructions and deceived myself, looking back with my eyes at my dear ones. At last, 'Why hurry?' I said. 'I'm being sent off to Scythia, I have to leave Rome. Each of these is a good reason for hanging back.'

Variant readings (*nostro/ nostri*) provide or remove *hyperbaton* from the exile's statement of the separation of his life and art in *Tr.* 2.353-4. Either reading has merit: in fact **nostr-* should apply to both *mores* and *carmine*. In the context of Ovid's emphatic defence of his art, I am inclined to prefer *nostro*:

> crede mihi, distant <u>mores</u> a **carmine nostro/** <u>nostri</u>
>   **vita verecunda** est, <u>musa iocosa</u> mihi.

Believe me, (my) morals are far different from (my) poetry;
  my life is pure, only my Muse is playful.

This forceful statement is central to the exiled poet's argument. Parallelism, as in the pentameter (where each noun is followed by its adjective), is often a feature of non-hyperbatic couplets.

We have seen before that lack of *hyperbaton* frequently conveys either emphasis or pathos. *Ex P.* 2.3.7-14 has a series of *sententiae* running over four couplets, deploring the venality of most pretence of friendship. Only two substantives are separated from their epithets. The whole bespeaks great bitterness:

> *Turpe* quidem *dictu*, sed, si modo vera fatemur,
>   vulgus amicitias utilitate probat.
> Cura, quid expediat, prius est, quam quid sit honestum,
>   et cum fortuna statque caditque fides.
> nec facile invenias **multis** in **milibus** unum,
>   *virtutem pretium* qui putet esse sui.
> ipse decor, recte **facti** si **praemia** desint,
>   non movet, et gratis paenitet esse probum.

It is certainly disgraceful to say so, but, if we were only to confess the truth, the common herd tests friendship by its usefulness. The concern is rather what would be useful than what is decent, and their loyalty stands and falls with your fortune. And you would not easily find one man in many thousands who thinks that virtue is its own reward. If a righteous deed does not carry a reward, its excellence does not move them, and they resent acting honourably for nothing.

At *Ex P.* 2.7.19-20 the exile bitterly complains that the gods vigilantly prevent anything good from happening to him, and that Fortune cannot be fooled. The couplet is bare of epithets:

> ... observare deos, ne quid mihi cedat amice,
>   verbaque Fortunae vix puto posse dari.

> [It is clear that] the gods are on the lookout to see that nothing
>   favourable comes my way,
>   and I think that it is scarcely possible for me to cheat Fortune.

Emphasis seems to be the motive of the 'plain' word-order in the exile's instructions to his wife in *Ex P.* 3.1.163-4:

> e quibus ante omnis Augustum numen adora
>   progeniemque piam participemque tori.

> And of these [gods] before all, worship Augustus as god,
>   and both his offspring and the loyal consort of his couch.

There may be some hidden irony here: we have noted that simplistic equation of Augustus with the paramount deity is often suspicious. Reference to Tiberius (adopted comparatively recently) as Augustus' *progeniem* reminds readers of Augustus' earlier dynastic efforts and frustrations. Our awareness of Augustus' notorious incursions into even his friends' bedrooms obtrudes with every reference to the legitimate sharer of his conjugal bed.

At *Ex P.* 4.8.51-56 a strong statement of the power of poetry to transcend time has no *hyperbaton*. Allusion to the ability of poetry to 'create gods' points to Ovid's frequent equation of Augustus with Jupiter:

> *scripta ferunt annos. scriptis Agamemnona nosti,*
> *et quisquis contra vel simul arma tulit.*
> *quis Thebas **septemque duces** sine carmine nosset,*
> *et quicquid post haec, quicquid et ante fuit?*
> *di quoque carminibus, si fas est dicere, fiunt,*
> <u>*tantaque maiestas*</u> ***ore canentis*** *eget.*

> Writings bear [the passing of] years. Through writings you know Agamemnon and whoever else bore arms with or against him. Who would have known of Thebes and the seven leaders, and whatever happened after that, and even all that went before, without poetry? Gods, too, are created by poetry, if it is lawful to say that, and such greatness requires a poet's voice.

In contrast, the next several couplets display virtual chains of *hyperbaton*. One example will suffice. Verses 57-8 refer to Lucretius' *De rerum natura*. The inter-linked word-order underscores the idea of chaotic confusion:

> sic **chaos** ex <u>illa</u> *naturae* <u>mole</u> *prioris*
> **digestum** <u>*partes*</u> scimus habere <u>*suas*</u> ...

> So we know that chaos, severed from that mass of [its] earlier nature, has its own elements ...

These two examples most clearly illustrate my contention that when the poet is at his most playful, separation of nouns and epithets predominates, but when he is at his most serious, or wishes particularly to emphasise a particular statement, there are fewer epithets and these are most often juxtaposed to their nouns.

4.3.3. Cumulative effects of separation, framing and juxtapositioning of words

Against what we have observed above, separation of closely allied words adds another dimension to poetic presentation. One instance of *hyperbaton* within a series of otherwise 'bare couplets' can serve to emphasise a particular phrase. The final, pathetic cry of the worn-out exile has only one case of *hyperbaton* over two couplets. Here separation of *extinctos ... artus* (and significant intrusion of *ferrum ...* between noun and epithet) within an otherwise 'simple word-order' adds emphasis by its singularity (*Ex P.* 4.16.49-52):

> *omnia perdidimus: tantummodo <u>vita relicta</u> est,*
> *praebeat ut <u>sensum materiamque mali</u>.*
> *quid iuvat* **extinctos** *ferrum demittere in* **artus?**
> *non habet in nobis iam <u>nova plaga</u> locum.*

> I have lost all: only life remains,
>   so that it may offer both sensation and material for pain.
> What use is it to thrust your knife into my dead limbs?
>   There is no space left in me for new blows.

Similarly, distance is frequently expressed by separation of important words to the extremes of a colon, verse or couplet, as in *<u>a patria</u> fugi victus et exsul <u>ego</u>* (*Tr.* 1.5.66, 'I was beaten into fleeing from my father-land as an exile'). Similarly, separation of prepositions or genitives from the nouns they govern underlines the sense of a verse, as in *Tr.* 4.9.23-4:

> *<u>trans</u> ego <u>tellurem</u>,* **trans altas** *audiar* **undas,**
> *et* **gemitus** <u>*vox*</u> *est <u>magna futura</u>* **mei.**

> I shall be heard across the world, across the deep oceans,
>   and the sound (lit. *voice*) of my lamentation will grow great.

At *Tr.* 5.8.25 tremendous *hyperbaton* separates *ingens ... orbis*, illustrating the vastness of the globe:

> *vel quia nil* **ingens** *ad finem solis ab ortu*
> *illo, cui paret, mitius* **orbis** *habet ...*

> Whether because the wide world, from sunrise to sunset, has nothing more merciful than [the man] it obeys ... [there is hope of forgiveness].

Juxtaposition of syntactically unrelated *mitius* and *orbis* presents the words visually as closely allied, setting up a counterpoint of new semantic relationships and new reverberations of meaning. Such counterpoint is sometimes ironical: at *Tr.* 4.4.52 the exile hopes for a better place of exile, *quique sit a* **saevo** *longius* **hoste** *locus* ('a place that may be further away from my savage enemy'). Juxtaposition of grammatically unrelated *hoste* and *locus* underlines the proximity of hostile hordes to his present place of exile. At *Ex P.* 4.14.14 the last three words, juxtaposed but syntactically unallied (if read without the context of the first three-quarters of the couplet), epitomise the pathos of the exile's situation:

4. Ovidian logodaedaly

gramina cultus ager, frigus minus odit hirundo
   *proxima Marticolis quam **loca Naso Getis***

A tilled field hates the planting of grain less, a swallow the cold,
   than Naso hates these places close to the martial Getae.

Evocative counterpoint appears in *Tr.* 4.10.87-8, where *hyperbaton* and parenthesis combine to create allusive juxtapositions: *fama – parentales, vos – mea, contigit – umbrae*, culminating in the embracing effect of *in Stygio ... foro*, which illustrates its sense:

   <u>*fama*</u>, ***parentales***, *si vos* <u>*mea*</u> *contigit*, ***umbrae***,
    *et sunt in **Stygio** crimina nostra **foro** ...*

   If my fame, o shades of my parents, has reached you,
    and if the accusations against me still stand in the Stygian
                        court ...

Framing and alternation result from use of, respectively, single and double *hyperbaton*. These devices illustrate graphically the last embraces of friends at the exile's departure, for instance *Tr.* 1.3.15 <u>*maestos*</u> *abiturus* <u>*amicos*</u> ('before my departure [I address] my mournful friends') and 17: <u>*uxor amans*</u> ***flentem*** <u>*flens*</u> *acrius* <u>*ipsa*</u> *tenebat* where four nominatives 'embrace' the 'weeping' accusative. In verse 70, the departing exile 'embraces' his nearest and dearest 'with his mind': *complectens* <u>*animo*</u> ***proxima quaeque*** <u>*meo*</u>. Ten lines on, we have the nominatives *coniunx ... inhaerens* visually 'embracing' the departing husband, her 'sad words' literally 'mixed' with 'my tears':

   *tum vero **coniunx** umeris abeuntis **inhaerens***
    *miscuit **haec** <u>lacrimis</u> **tristia verba** <u>meis</u>*

So framing often serves as a visually graphic device. Words denoting 'full of', 'containing' or 'holding' are so placed that the verse illustrates what it conveys, as at *Tr.* 2.422: ***Romanus*** *habet* <u>*multa iocosa*</u> ***liber*** ('the Roman book contains much that is playful'). Similarly, as shown in Chapter 1, at *Ex P.* 4.15.13 the poet playfully accedes to his own request, placing himself as 'little thing', 'among' his new patron's 'ancestral goods': *inter **opes** et <u>me, parvam rem</u>, pone **paternas***.

The opposite effect is achieved in *Ex P.* 3.2.12. The exile is complaining of desertion by friends in his adversity. Separation to the extremities of the verse of *sollicito ... metu* visually portrays erstwhile friends fleeing in different directions, leaving a void (*vacuus ... locus*) in the middle:

sollicito **vacuus** *fit* **locus** *ille* <u>metu</u> ('That place becomes empty because of their fearful terror').

4.3.4. Contrast and balance

Interpretation of the visual images evoked by verbal play is, however, extremely subjective. Perception of the phenomenon may differ radically from critic to critic. The principle of symmetry is central to Ovidian technique, and balance or contrast is achieved by various means. The metrical form of the pentameter lends itself to parallelism or contrast, but we have seen our poet frequently employing these devices in his hexameters, with *hyperbaton* often overriding the division of a verse by the semantic binding of two sets of nominals in agreement. Other symmetrical arrangements work for division of verses, achieving highly ornamental contrast and balance. In *Tr.* 1.2.5-6, contrasts are so strong that the couplet appears almost as a quatrain with four very short verses:

> *Mulciber in Troiam, pro Troia stabat Apollo:*
> *aequa Venus Teucris, Pallas iniqua fuit.*

> Vulcan was against Troy, for Troy stood Apollo:
> Venus was fair to the Trojans, Pallas unfair.

Contrast and balance within a verse may be variously achieved. Parallelism, expressing two aspects of a single thought, takes different forms: apposition, extensions around the verb, functional parallelism, that is, balanced clauses or phrases, formal and (often rhyming) etymological repetition, contrasts and counter-examples. Antithesis indicates opposition of thoughts. 'Completion' occurs when the first colon has been heavily accentuated but lacks an essential word to complete its meaning, often a verb, which is provided in the second hemistich. As always with Ovid, balance is fluid, and can become contrast. At *Tr.* 2.147-8 an apparent parallel between hexameter and pentameter is pointed by means of repetition of *spes mihi ... cum ...*, and the so-called *atallage* (implied presence of a suppressed verb) of *respicio*, but in the second hemistich of the pentameter parallel becomes antithesis. Contrast of *te* and *mea facta* is finally pointed by the rhyming antithesis of *subit* and *cadit*:

> *spes mihi magna* **subit**, *cum* <u>te</u>, *mitissime princeps,*
> *spes mihi, respicio cum* <u>mea facta</u>, **cadit**.

> Great hope arises within me when I look at you, kindest of
> princes;
> my hope is dashed when I look at what I have done.

Excessive use of these ornamental devices can be indicative of playfulness; a reduction in their use may perhaps indicate intensity of feeling. Balance of alternatives and fluctuations between hope and fear are, however, so basic to intense psychological suffering that most often the device appears to emphasise pathos. The antithetical expression *non solum ... sed etiam* is prosaic. Our poet explores other ways of creating balance: *nunc ... modo, modo ... modo, sive ... seu, atque ... atque, nec ... nec, sed, tot ... quot*, also verbal parallels of different kinds, opposition of contrasting words such as day – night, near – far, even paratactic statements. Contrasting elements differ from single words to the balanced halves of verses, to verses, to couplets. Balanced pairing of contrasts is visually and intellectually pleasing.

Contrast may be comical, as in Ovid's description of Tomitan social life: *nec hausta meri, sed data frusta bibunt* (*Tr.* 3.10.24, 'They don't drink wine that is poured, but chunks handed to them'). In the same poem the pathos of local inhabitants attacked by Transdanuvian marauders is depicted in two couplets exhibiting an interplay of parallel and contrast between their hexameters, but with non-symmetrical, 'informative' statements in the pentameters: verse 62 is descriptive; 64 is explanatory (*Tr.* 3.10.61-4):

> *pars **agitur** <u>vinctis</u> post tergum **capta** <u>lacertis</u>*
>   *respiciens frustra rura Laremque suum;*
> *<u>pars</u> **cadit** <u>hamatis</u> misere **confixa** <u>sagittis</u>,*
>   *nam volucri ferro tinctile virus inest.*

> Some are driven along into captivity, arms tied behind their backs,
>   each looking back in vain to his country home;
> some fall miserably transfixed by hooked arrows,
>   for the fleet iron tips have been dipped in poison.

These victims look back longingly to their homes. They are as much the victims of *Heimweh* as the exile himself. The hexameters display parallel and contrast on both the visual and the syntactic level. Each verse consists of: nominative, verb, *hyperbaton* of ablatives, adverbial phrase or adverb, perfect participle completing the nominative *hyperbaton*, completion of ablative *hyperbaton*. An apparently perfect parallel alternates ablative of 'attendant circumstance' (61) with 'instrument' (63); adverbial phrase of 'place' modifies a preceding perfect participle *vinctis*, whereas the adverb *misere* modifies a subsequent perfect participle *confixa*. This is virtuoso composition.

The subtlety inherent in Ovid's choice and arrangement of words is a continued source of pleasure to his readers. These examples illustrate only some of the endless aspects of Ovidian logodaedaly. We next turn to Ovid's use of myth in the exilic works.

5

Myth metamorphosed: Ovid's use and re-use of mythology

5.1. Ovid, myth and intertextual allusion

Since the *Metamorphoses*, the name of Ovid has almost been synonymous with myth, but it would appear that the poet came to mythography late, and differs from, for instance, Propertius in his use of myth as Alexandrian-type ornament. From Homer onward there have been two systems whereby myth is employed in literature: as subject, or as ornament. Obviously, this ornament can be stereotyped, equating petrified metaphor, as in personified names for the winds, such as Boreas, Aquilo, Notus and Zephyr. Next, it can be both topical and functional, as in Lucretian references to Venus as symbol of procreation. Finally, it can derive from a highly original adaptation of a particular myth by a particular author in a specific context. The name of a mythical figure, then, can represent a particular characteristic that requires emphasis, but it can also encapsulate a separate story which is carried into the new literary situation. The value of such myth lies partly in the substratum of additional meaning which it introduces into the topic (and the counterpoint of contrast that it supplies), and partly in its elevation of the particular to the universal.

It was Ovidian poetic practice to adopt and adapt the conventional, and then to continue the theme with an endless variety of self-repetition. As with turns of phrase, so too with myth. Such repetition is not merely formulaic, but frequently lends itself to further adaptation and reversal. By definition, there is no single, canonical version of myth. As soon as myth was made literate, the tendency arose to think of 'right' and 'wrong' versions, but such is the nature of myth that each version has an equal claim to validity, even comical or parodic versions. These adaptations are carried into the next retelling of a myth, as part of its intertextual 'counterpoint of meaning'. The freedom of the poet-narrator (as the creator of whatever mythical reality he wishes to portray) lies centrally to the narration of a myth, so that no author may be accused of 'subverting the true version' in any re-telling of a particular tale.

Ovid's exilic poems contain several catalogues illustrating one or the other aspect of the poet's argument. Casual or ornamental allusions to mythical figures account, however, for a much larger proportion of mythological usage. This chapter examines Ovidian usage of mythological figures in the exilic poems, their frequency and their distribution throughout these works, as well as their intertextual web of reference to Ovid's other works. Finally, it considers what the author makes of these figures in the exilic context.

With Ovid, his rich intertextual tapestry is seldom confined to himself as source. Intertextual allusions to predecessors are of equal importance in considering the implications of any one mythical figure, but we shall gloss over that aspect, concentrating rather on links between the exilic works and the *Metamorphoses, Heroides* and *Fasti*. Kenney, in his Introduction to Melville's translation of the *Tristia* (Oxford, 1992), points out that intertextual exploitation of his earlier poetry is an essential element of Ovid's poetic strategy. Such an intertextual dialogue reprises, but can also reverse, what went before, also serving to carry a (sometimes subversive) secondary meaning into the apparently blandly innocent re-use of a particular image. Of greater interest, then, than originality of source material is consideration of Ovid's adaptation in his exilic poetry of familiar mythical material, that is, self-referential allusion to his own earlier works.

Extensive *Quellenforschung* in the traditional sense is unnecessary, although its assumption underlies all recognition of intertextuality. Ovid's sources of myth is a wide subject. His frequent use of patronymics and other circumlocution indicates some recourse to genealogical catalogues. We may further assume use of collections of *topoi, exempla* and categorical catalogues, the two best known being those of Parthenius, Ovid's early contemporary, and Hyginus. The question of whether Ovid employed Hyginus' *Fabulae* as we have them, or whether the *Fabulae* is a later excerption, can be shelved with reference to the commonly accepted theory that the *Fabulae* is a second-century epitome of an earlier work. It is not improbable that Ovid had recourse to the original, possibly compiled by the curator of the Palatine Museum, the best known of a series of about twelve different authors bearing the name *Hyginus*: Junius Hyginus, Ovid's friend. Curiously, none of the poems from exile is addressed to this friend, which has led to the conjecture that Hyginus may have been the original for 'Ibis', the poet's enemy.

Recent scholarship increasingly stresses the 'exilic' status of both the *Metamorphoses* and the *Fasti*, tying both in with authorial revision (or continued composition) during Ovid's earlier years of exile. In an article on the *Fasti* (*Antichthon* 29, 1995), Elaine Fantham writes of Ovid 'ambidextrously' working simultaneously with epic and elegiac metres. Similarly, the *Heroides* by their nature are now seen as closely linked with Ovid's letters from exile. His mythical world forms a coherent whole. It is my contention that, when Ovid creates the myth of exile, he, as central protagonist, is drawn into this coherent world, where Augustus takes the place accorded the king of the gods in Ovid's other works. That topic will be more extensively treated in the second half of this chapter.

Both the *Heroides* and the *Metamorphoses* offer subjectivised myth. In the case of the latter, this mythical material, like the aetiological material of the *Fasti,* is frequently ironised. Recent scholarship tends more and more to view large parts of these works as exhibiting degrees of irony, ranging from irreverence to burlesque. At best the *Fasti* are now considered as highly ambivalent, what Fantham on occasion termed 'polyphonic'. Intertextual self-reference carries the burden of thought. Much criticism may be left unsaid in a particular context, when the poet relies on his readers' knowledge of his previous version of a particular myth for ironical undertones.

Ovid shows his awareness in the *Metamorphoses* and *Heroides* of the cyclic aspects of myth. Certain basic patterns repeat themselves. The concept of 'structure' rather than individualised story, as postulated by Levi-Strauss and others, can very well be applied to, for instance, the *Heroides*, where the pattern of complaint and the range of apparently similar emotions of the 'deserted women' of individual poems have on occasion given rise to complaints of 'monotony'. Similar comments have often damned Ovid's exilic poetry with faint praise.

5.2. Scholars' time and poet's themes

Ovid's exilic letters, alternating or combined with other types of elegiac lament, flowed to Rome from Tomis in a constant stream, exhibiting (as Chapter 2 showed) changes of tone and content over the years, despite their author's frequently protested excuses for their 'monotony'. Here also, chronology should play a role in consideration of the poet's presentation of material. The *Ibis* was probably written within the first three years of exile and its publication may be dated to around AD 12 or 13, at a time when the five books of the *Tristia* had already been sent to Rome, and while the poet was working on his second, more overtly epistolary, collection. Ovid's final editing of the *Metamorphoses* and *Fasti* is now also dated to the exilic years.

In *Tr.* 2.317-20 the exiled poet pretends to deplore the fact that formerly he did not stick to well-worn themes. Why did he not once more harass Troy, he asks, or reprise the story of the Theban gates and the fratricidal brothers? This is deliberate *recusatio*, refusal to treat of epic themes, defence of elegiacs as a lesser genre, but perhaps also criticism of Augustus' taste for the predictable. The fact is that our poet *did* treat extensively of Troy in a series of his *Heroides*, including *Her.* 3 (Briseis to

Achilles), and the double-letter exchange between Helen and Paris (*Her.* 16 and 17). Yet he never featured the tale of the seven against Thebes in any of his works. Even the name of the most famous Theban of them all, Oedipus, occurs only once, in *Met.* 15.429, in a dismissively odious comparison between Thebes and Rome. There are certain well-known themes, then, that the poet did not treat of before. The question is, does he now in exile resort to these, or does he keep to familiar material?

This chapter examines the exiled poet's consecutive use of mythical figures, both ornamental and functional. It will largely leave aside the idio-syncratic *Ibis*, for literary-critical reasons and for the sake of restricting the chapter to a manageable length: only those figures designated by name in *Ibis* that also occur in the other exilic poems are included. For the moment the very few occurrences of the names of gods other than Jupiter will also be ignored. The chapter explores which mythic topics or themes predominated in Ovid's creative consciousness at any one stage – whether, in other words, his editorial activities during exile influenced his creative propensities in any discernible way. Conversely, it will also consider whether, as time passed, other interests superseded myth as the exiled poet's central metaphorical medium. This implies comparison of his use of myths in the exilic works with his use of the same myths or mythic themes in the *Metamorphoses*, *Heroides* and *Fasti*. Individual attention to *all* the exiled poet's allusions to mythical figures and to their self-referential provenance would make the chapter unmanageably long. These have therefore been organised into tables (see Myth Tables on pp. 265-83), leaving it to individual readers to pursue at greater length those lines that are not picked up. The tables list individual occurrences of names, taken from word counts, as well as certain periphrastic or other designations for figures. Certain patterns may emerge.

My concern, then, is with the poet's mythographic preoccupations during the time that he was probably still engaged in revision of the *Metamorphoses* and *Fasti* and whether these preoccupations changed over time. Of particular interest is Ovid's introduction in his exilic oeuvre of figures not featured in these works nor in the *Heroides* (nor even else-where in his earlier works). The particular resonances of at least some of these myths need identification: does their use in the exilic works carry a greater burden of significance than mere ornament? Such figures may form some sort of exilic pattern. Some attention to *Quellenforschung* in the latter case may illuminate the kind of source material Ovid had at his disposal during exile, a question that has consistently intrigued histori-cist researchers.

So far five chronological phases have served as my analytical frame-work for the examination of possible changes of style and tone over the years of Ovid's exile. Here I have divided the exilic oeuvre merely into an 'earlier' and a 'later' stage, represented, respectively, by the two distinct collections, the *Tristia* and the *Epistolae ex Ponto*. Discounting for the moment allusions to the poet's Muse and also the names of the gods, it would appear that some mythical figures occur only in the earlier stage, others only in the later. That is, some early themes seem to be discarded during the second stage, others are picked up only then, and some seem to form a consistent web of imagery.

5.3. Myths featured in *Tristia* only

The figures listed in Table 1 occur in the early stage only. Most references appear to be purely ornamental, functional in their immediate context; some seem more laden with significance than others. Of these, the most significant are Absyrtus, whose murder by Medea gave Tomis its aetiological name (*Tr.* 3.9.6), and Capaneus and Semele, as examples of humans who felt Jove's thunderbolt. Capaneus was struck down for blasphemy, but Semele was innocent of any crime, and was duped by Juno into evoking Jupiter's scorching wrath (*Met.* 3.256-315). Similarly, Actaeon, turned into a stag and torn to pieces by his own hounds, was the innocent victim of the anger of Diana whom he surprised while bathing. Exile is experienced as dismemberment by the poet. The Actaeon-myth displayed shifts of plot in its various retellings, of which Ovid's version in *Met.* 3.131-255 stresses the protagonist's essential innocence. In Roman law, being *inscius* (applied at *Tr.* 2.105 to Actaeon) was deemed to exonerate an accused from all blame. Ovid's application of the myth to himself (seemingly pointing strongly to the exiled poet's having 'seen something') feeds into the debate and historicist theorising about our poet's *error,* even evoking the grotesque suggestion that Ovid had 'seen the lady Livia in her bath'. The metaphorical implications of the myth are, however, paramount. Encasement and consequent speechlessness ensured Actaeon's initial silence, which was finally sealed by his fragmentation. The question of the justice of Actaeon's punishment mirrors the similar problem relating to the poet's exile.

Althaea, the mother who caused the death of her son Meleager when she threw into the fire the faggot that represented his life, serves to represent Ovid in *Tr.* 1.7.17-18 as 'father-poet' who placed on the pyre the *Metamorphoses* as his own literary 'child'. This, then, inverts the *topos* of the exile's little book as an Oedipus or Telegonus (*Tr.* 1.1.114), prototypical parricides.

Other figures featured in passing perhaps display the poet's preoccupations at the time of writing, but are similarly apt in their context. Leander, 'writer' of the sensuous *Heroides* 18, epitomises rash youth, but also, as we know, the suffering experienced by Hero, who lost her lover by drowning. The ill-fated lover was (in Ovid's version) spurred on to cross the dangerous strait by a 'reply' from Hero (*Her.* 19), explicitly offering him the sexual pleasures that before he had only dreamt of. The Leander evoked at *Tr.* 3.10.41-2 is, however, not so dramatically portrayed. At Tomis Leander 'could have *run* across the solid ice' of the frozen strait, and 'it would have been impossible for him to drown'. Such a bathetic allusion deconstructs by hindsight most of the dramatic tension evoked in the letter-pair from the *Heroides*.

The Scylla who betrayed her father Nisus for love of Minos occurs once only, in the catalogue of ill-fated lovers in *Tristia* 2. Yet Ovid's 'Scylla' is a strangely composite figure, partaking of the characteristics of both this betrayer and of the monstrous creature that was one of many threats to the long-suffering Odysseus. As the monster, Scylla represents the horrors of distant travel.

Other monstrous figures are infrequent, or even *hapax legomena* in Ovidian context. *Tr.* 4.7 celebrates a second winter in Tomis with a bitter complaint that its addressee has neglected the exile. Ovid pretends that he would sooner believe in a series of impossible, mythical monsters than that he would credit that his friend had forgotten him: the snake-locks of the Medusa, the monstrous Scylla, the hybrid Chimaera, Centaurs, and multi-bodied or many-headed creatures (such as Gyas and Cerberus). Soundplay, juxtaposition and the ponderous effect of a series of 'portmanteau' words call to mind the elder Seneca's tale about the poet's favourite line (*Tr.* 4.7.15-18):

> *Quadrupedesque hominis cum pectore pectora iunctos,*
>   *Tergeminumque virum tergeminumque canem,*
> *Sphingaque et Harpyias serpentipedesque Gigantas,*
>   *Centimanumque Gyan semibovemque virum ...*

> [I would sooner believe in] four-legged creatures attached to men
>   and breasts stuck to breasts,
>   a triple-bodied man and a triple-headed dog,
> the Sphinx and Harpies and gigantic dragons,
>   Gyas with his hundred hands and a half-man-half-bull ...

The scepticism Ovid assumes here as the norm undercuts all suspension of disbelief inherent in much of Greek and Latin literature, not least in the mythological framework and conceptual underpinnings of his own *Metamorphoses*. This may be set against the earlier *Tr.* 3.8.1-6, where the possibility of entering into the mythical world of dragon-wagons, winged horses, and waxen wings is fondly imagined as a means of escape for the exile. This must not be construed as 'progression in thought'. Our poet has not in Book 4 redrawn the lines of credulity that Book 3 set for his readership, for the very next passage takes the exile short with (*Tr.* 3.8.11-12):

Stulte, quid haec frustra votis puerilibus optas,
   Quae non ulla tibi fertque feretque dies?

Fool, why do you in vain hope, with puerile yearnings,
   for these things that no day brings or will ever bring you?

5.4. *Tristia* 2 and the catalogue of myths

The largest concentration of mythical figures occurs in *Tristia* 2, the poet's *apologia pro vita arteque sua*. Some of these allusions are particularly irreverent. The peccadilloes of the gods are rapidly reviewed in verses 287-300 to show up the dangerous opportunities for liaison offered by visits to temples. A deliberate pun on the emperor's name points the irreverence: *quis locus est templis augustior?* (287, 'what place is more august than temples?').

Verses 358-468 and 533-50 offer a virtually complete overview of both Greek and Latin literature in which mythical love-themes predominate. The poet argues that all other writers treat of love as their theme; he alone was punished for it. Predictably, Ovid's catalogue of those mythical heroes treated in individual literary works (371-411) starts with Helen of Troy, designated merely as *adultera, de qua/ inter amatorem pugna virumque fuit* (371-2, 'the adulteress about whom there was a fight between her lovers'), to be followed by the *flamma Briseidos* (373, 'the passion for Briseis'). The *Odyssey* is casually reduced to a 'tale about a woman sought by many lovers while her husband was away', with the addition of one other detail – the story of the adulterous love of Venus and Mars (377-8). This last reinforces an irreverent allusion, some eighty lines earlier, to Augustus' awkward arrangement of statues in the great temple of *Mars Ultor*, where the mother of the Julian line is very properly given equal honour within, her statue conjoined to that of the Avenger (296, *stat Venus Vltori iuncta*), while her husband Vulcan stands humbly outdoors (*vir ante fores*).

The poet musters a formidable array of bizarre examples, culled not only from the whole of Greek literature, but also, for the most part, from his own Latin reworkings of these themes. As may be seen from Tables 1 to 3, there is a handful of names that Ovid has never used before. In the passage in question we have: Aerope (2.391), Haemon (2.402), and, perhaps surprisingly, Clytemnestra (designated *Tyndaridos* at 2.396). Among them, these figures represent mythical cycles otherwise neglected by Ovid. Antigone features (anonymously) in *Tr.* 3.3.67-8 only; the 'Antigone' of *Met.* 6.93 is the daughter of Laomedon.

The Mycenean cycle features prominently. In *Tristia* 2 the complete traditional tale is rapidly reviewed with reference to the names, patronymics, or other distinguishing features of the protagonists, but these characters appear interlaced with other well-known mythical tales that had received extensive treatment elsewhere in Ovid's oeuvre (e.g. Atalanta, 399; Danae, 401). Here Ovid starts with the origins of the blood curse on the house of Atreus. Aerope was the daughter of Catreus, the son of Minos and Pasiphae. To evade a prophecy that he would be killed by his own progeny, Catreus sent her with her sister into exile to Argos. Variant narratives had her consecutively married to Pleisthenes and Atreus, to one of whom she bore Agamemnon and Menelaus. Her seduction by Thyestes gave rise to Atreus' terrible revenge, the cannibalistic meal that caused horror in heaven. For Ovid, here, the story gives the occasion for casuistic argument: had the 'evil brother' (*sceleratus frater*) not loved this woman, the story of the Sun recoiling in his course could not have been told (391-2). Ovid has treated only one part of the Mycenean tale before. *Heroides* 8 is a letter from Menelaus' daughter Hermione, appealing to the matricide Orestes to save her from Pyrrhus-Neoptolemus, son of Achilles.

Orestes is particularly significant. His name features with that of Pylades from *Tr.* 1.9.27 onward as one of the prototypical wanderers in the Pontic area (see Tables 3 and 6). In this catalogue Euripides' portrayal of his demented state in *Iphigeneia among the Taurians* is clearly evoked with the designation *egentem mentis Oresten* ('Orestes, bereft of his senses', 395, reprised at *Ex P.* 2.3.45 as *insano ... Orestae*, 'to the insane Orestes').

This catalogue in *Tristia* 2, then, and, in particular, figures that are relatively unfamiliar from the rest of the poet's oeuvre, may be said to set the tone for the poet's use of myth in his exilic works. It now remains to ascertain which figures will recur, and which are discarded after this single appearance in the first year of their creator's exile.

5.5. More frequent figures

Table 2 shows names that occur twice or more often in the early stage, and are then discarded. These figures derive from the whole mythological spectrum. At *Tr.* 3.4.21-2 a reference to Icarus' flight illustrates the exile's new adherence to the precept *lathe biosas* – Icarus flew too high and fell to his doom. Elsewhere Icarus (so, too Dulichium – relating to Odysseus' Ithacan kingdom – and Helle) is of importance largely for topographical reasons. Euryalus and Nisus represent one of the pairs of faithful friends which the exile holds up as *exempla* before his own friends, apparently consciously evoking Vergil. Turnus, always designated 'Rutulus', as victim evokes Vergil's ambivalent Aeneas at his most *impius* moment, with his slaying of Turnus, but the strain is discontinued after *Tristia* 1. Priam ('Dardanius' at *Tr.* 3.5.38) features as the example par excellence of spiritual suffering by an elderly victim of the wrath of others (*Tr.* 5.1.55, 5.4.11, 5.12.7).

Callisto seems to be a very special case. In the *Tristia* she serves as astronomical pointer. The 'Seven Stars', the Pleiades, occur three times in the Pontic epistles as geographical pointers, but do not refer to the same myth. Ovid uses an ingenious variety of epithets for the mythical maiden, one of the first victims of Jupiter's lust in the *Metamorphoses*. Callisto is never named in *Met.* 2, but features as the ablative *virgine Nonacrina* (2.409) and as *Parrhasis* (2.460). She is recognisable only after the naming of her son Arcas and father Lycaon. In the *Tristia* she features in the genitive: *Atlantidos ursae* (1.11.15), *Erymanthidos ursae* (1.4.1; 3.4.47), *Parrhasiae virginis* (2.190); and as *Parrhasis Arctos* (1.3.48), *Maenalis ursa* (3.11.8). Both the omission of her name and the speechlessness inherent in her metamorphosis into a bear signify the dehumanising connotations of rape. Callisto fades from the scene after *Tr.* 3.11.8.

In all the different versions of the story the young mother becomes the constellation of Ursa Maior, and her son by Jupiter, the lesser Bear (the constellation that includes the Pole star). Although Tomis is on about the same latitude as Florence or Bologna in Italy, with a night sky not much different from that of Rome, the poet lays great emphasis on having been sent to an area 'directly below the North Star', which 'burdens the axis of the earth' just below it. Frequent references to Ursa Maior, which revolves around the Pole star and therefore never 'sets' into the sea, appears to be only partly cosmographically intended. The exile seems to like to think of himself as just such another victim of Jupiter. That a 'sexual victim' is the prime signifier of the exile's misery offers an example of Ovid's continued *nequitia*. Bland equation of Jupiter-Augustus would leave the mortal ruler feeling a little uncomfortable at reminders of a common youthful propensity for extra-marital dalliance, so much at odds with both the Roman legislator's official stance and the god's purposely refurbished, transcendent Roman rule. Chapter 1 cited Suetonius (*Aug.* 80) on Augustus having a birthmark resembling the constellation of Ursa Maior: both victim and persecutor share in the characteristics of the oppressed maiden.

Significant as their allusive use may be, most of the above figures then disappear from the Pontic stage (or from the exile's poetic consciousness), their places to be taken by others, either recurrent or new. We need to explore the self-referential aspects of these recurrent figures and decide whether they have more than ornamental significance within the exilic context.

Figures that occur more than once in the earlier stage and merit continued mention at least once are the prototypes of faithful wives. Alcestis is the exemplary wife who crossed into the underworld for the sake of her husband Admetus. Ovid takes pains to cite her action as example, not precept. Penelope is the exiled poet's chief source of admonitory *exempla*. The list of faithful wives in Hyg. *Fab.* 256 is arranged in the order most frequent in the exilic works: Penelope, Evadne, Laodamia. Let us start with the last two: ostensibly innocent allusions may carry a heavier intertextual burden of meaning than appears at first sight. Evadne, as narrated from Homer onward, threw herself on the flames as her impious husband Capaneus lay burning after Jove's thunderbolt had struck him down for blasphemy. Assurances by the exile that he will make his wife famous for her faithfulness by his poetry acquire a strange colour in the light of the poet's own treatment of Laodamia in the *Heroides*. Her husband Protesilaus was the first to fall at Troy. In *Her.* 13 Laodamia, oblivious of the prophecy of Protesilaus' death, urges him to hasten on to Troy, so that he can return more quickly. Ovid shows her as already making an image of Protesilaus, before she had news of his death; she took it to bed with her, pathologically lavishing affection on it. The full story includes an interlude where Protesilaus was allowed a 'home visit' of three hours, before returning to the Underworld. After this 'second death' Laodamia's father, thinking that she had taken a lover, burst into her chamber and subsequently bade her burn the statue, whereupon she immolated herself (Hyg. *Fab.* 103-4). If the parallel is closely drawn, we must either call into question the mental health of the exile's wife, or conclude that the kind of playful 'self-irony' which includes the poet's conjugal partner as an aspect of 'self' sometimes verged on the malicious. The poet could expect a discerning reader to be aware of the discrepancy between apparent and real meaning. This may be a form of 'private joke' between marriage partners or it may be an aspect of the deliberate picture of a 'tactless fool who deserved exile' that Ovid enjoys presenting for the amusement of the *cognoscenti* (hopefully also the poet's wife).

The prototypical faithful wife is of course Penelope, from Ovid's first address to his wife (*Tr.* 1.6) onward. Stephen Hinds has argued that the poet's claim (19-22) to the ability to accord his wife a fame second to no Homeric wife refers obliquely also to his own treatment of Penelope as an abandoned female in *Her.* 1. In the *Tristia* his wife is 'first', as she would have been in the *Heroides,* if he had sung of her there. More of her below, in my discussion of the exile as an 'Odysseus'.

Niobe is a prototype of suffering humanity, but also a victim of the god Apollo, Augustus' patron deity since Actium. Her fault lay in taunting another female, Latona, mother of the omnipotent god and his equally powerful sister – in Ovidian context, the Roman Diana, but also the Greek Artemis. For Ovid, his poetry in exile is like Niobe's tears after she had been metamorphosed into stone: an indication of the continuation of sentient life. The exile finds a bloodthirsty Artemis waiting for him as one of the only divine figures of the Pontic region (at *Ex P.* 1.2.78 and 3.2.47-64). Since Euripides, Iphigenia has been portrayed as the victim *par excellence* of impious religious practices, and as a daughter sacrificed to her father's aspiration to supreme power. Chapter 2 discussed Ovid's reprisal of Euripides' *Iphigenia among the Taurians* (*Ex P.* 3.2.43-96). Ovid held up the tale to his correspondents at Rome as an example of the faithfulness of friendship. The Tauric Artemis is a sinister figure, suitably served by the bloodthirsty denizens of the area. Continued reference to Thoas, king of the Tauric Chersonese, may appear as idle ornament, working as a means of topographical placement, but Euripides' drama had established the king as the prototypical 'ignoble savage', the major adherent of this cruel deity, instigator of blood sacrifices, and the one who would have prevented Orestes from carrying his sister home. Thoas represents the horrors of the Pontic shores.

Other recurring figures have other webs of significance. Erichthonius (at *Tr.* 2.294) offers an irreverent example of illegitimacy in high heaven. He is the 'virgin Athena's son'. In a second allusion (*Ex P.* 2.9.19-20) he merely features as an ancestor of Cotys, king of Thrace – for Ovid the prototypical 'noble savage'. Telephus offers the example of 'wounding' and 'healing' coming from the same source. Again it is a bizarre story. According to Hyginus, *Fab.* 99-101, the hero was born of rape by Hercules, exposed by his mother Auge, suckled by a doe and, as an adult, he tripped over Dionysus' vine root and fell upon (and was wounded by) Achilles' spear. Achilles was at length persuaded to allow rust from the spear to be applied to the wound, because of a prophecy that Troy could not be taken without the aid of Telephus, who subsequently guided the Greeks to the place. Stephen Hinds has suggested that the original connotation of the name '*Oidi-pos*' (as denoting a deformity of the feet) offers a clever pun on the 'deformity' of the elegiac pentameter when set against the defining hexameter of epic, whereas '*Tele-gonus*' implies 'driven afar', an apt name for an exilic work. Similarly, the name Telephus (although traditionally a compound derived from the Greek for 'dug' and 'doe', '*Têl(ê)-éphus,* so Apollodorus 2.7.4.) could, in Roman context (and ignoring vowel brevity in favour of syllabic length), be taken as paranomastic play implying poetry that 'shines from afar', '*Têle-phôs',* its brilliance reaching Rome from afar.

Casual mythical ornament increasingly sets an ominous scene. We have seen Scylla and Artemis as signifying the horrors of the place of exile. The Medusa is a similar figure. Only Castor and his brother Polydeuces (Pollux), the patron gods of travellers, represent a more positive view of travel. Other reasonably positive figures gain a negative connotation in the exilic context. The poet's portrayal of Numa in *Metamorphoses* 15 is much contested, but critical consensus is moving toward interpretation of this figure as, at best, ambivalent, with strong undertones of irreverence, if not outright criticism of the Augustan regime. Hercules is one of the cult-figures with whom Augustus liked to associate himself, but he too was the victim of the unremitting wrath of Juno, queen of Heaven. Allusions to the *Gigantomachia* tie in with the poet's vision of his relationship with Augustus. Recollections of irreverent use of the *topos* in the poet's previous recusations will, however, give new direction to the reader's perception of an ostensibly bland and humble deprecation at *Tr.* 2.333-4 of the poet's powers 'to undertake so great a theme'.

Figures that occur only once in the early stage but gain in frequency in the later stage are increasingly symbolic of wandering or exile: Cadmus the erstwhile wanderer, founder of a great city, who ended his life in new exile, Aeneas the prototypical wanderer, Penelope, another wanderer's prototypically faithful wife, and Orpheus, the Thracian singer, doomed to wander after the loss of his wife to the Underworld. His music had transcendental power. Orpheus was a native of Thrace, the very same barren earth to which our poet has been exiled, and he suffered an undeserved death on his lonely travels. He is the paramount example of the prophet-poet upon whom the exile can project himself. Conversely, Pirithous, the fortunate friend of Theseus, is successfully helped by the latter to fetch his wife from the Underworld.

5.6. A pattern emerges

Casual use of myth for the sake of ornament diminishes considerably within the course of the second stage. Table 5 lists names that occur casually, once each, in the Pontic epistles. These illuminate their immediate context. Several are new to, or infrequent, in Ovid. Bistonius is a Thracian king. Cassander serves as a geographical pointer. Diomedes of Thrace, owner of the famous man-eating horses, again signifies the horrors of exile. Croesus, king of Lydia, he of the unfortunate end, and Dionysius, tyrant of Syracuse, are historical figures respectively featured by Herodotus and Diodorus, but strongly mythologised. This catalogue is significantly shorter than that of Table 1 (casual allusions in the earlier stage).

Two references each to Eumolpus (mythical Thracian founder of the Eleusinian Mysteries), Antiphates (king of the cannibal Laestrygones), Alcinous, and the Cyclops Polyphemus either relate the exile to the Pontic area or serve as reminders of the travails of Odysseus. Some, at least, of the other figures seem to carry a greater degree of intertextual significance. Clustering of mythical figures gives greater impact; that is, literary context serves to heighten the significance of each figure within a group. We have seen repeated use of catalogues of doomed heroes, faithful wives and constant friends. A complex example occurs at *Ex P.* 3.1.51-8, in a poem urging the exile's apparently dilatory wife to new efforts on his behalf. In rapid succession are listed Capaneus, Amphiaraus, Odysseus (as *Ulixes*), Philoctetes and Bittis. None would have gained great fame if they had not also suffered greatly, the poet's argument goes. We have discussed the fate of Capaneus above. Amphiaraus was the hero who was forced by his wife to join the expedition against Thebes, where he was similarly blasted by Zeus-Jupiter during the assault (cf. Hyg. *Fab.* 68-73, 128, 245 and 250). Philoctetes had a festering, malodorous wound. The close association of such unfortunates with the exiled poet and the power of all poetry to accord fame is followed by new exhortations to Ovid's wife to emulate Bittis, the woman made famous by the love-poetry of the Greek Philetas (*Ex P.* 3.1.57-68), giving these exhortations a strange (and sickly) colour. We still have here, it seems, the gauche *persona* of the 'master of love' of the *Ars Amatoria*, whose most persuasive use of myth frequently exposed him as either naïve or utterly cynical. For example, at *AA* 1.509-12 young men are urged not to resort to finery – their natural appearance is alluring enough to women. The love stories of the narrator's three *exempla*, Theseus and Ariadne, Hippolytus and Phaedra, Venus and Adonis, all ended disastrously.

Clustering of monstrous figures has a different thrust. The poem cited above (*Ex P.* 3.1) lists (119-24) a series of horrible females that the poet protests are *unlike* the empress, to whom he urges his wife to appeal. Livia is no murderous Procne, Medea, or daughter of Danaus, nor a Clytemnestra. Neither is she Scylla, nor the 'mother of Telegonus' (Circe, whose son by Odysseus in the end caused his father's death). She is no Medusa, with snake-coiled hair, but *femina princeps,* second in fame only to Caesar himself. *Praeteritio* is a common rhetorical device. Accentuation by negation draws at best an ambiguous portrait of the august lady. The ploy reprises a similar negative portrayal-by-denial of the emperor himself at *Ex P.* 1.2.119-20 as a 'non-Theromedon', with no wild lions to feed, a 'non-Atreus' who would not serve up a cannibal's meal, and a 'non-Diomedes', unwilling to feed the flesh of his victims to man-eating horses.

The tone of each mythical reference depends on its context. Playfulness may mask a serious accusation. An apparently serious allusion may offer hidden ironies. Nestor of Pylos appears simply as a symbol of longevity, but irreverence may be read from the elaborate circumlocution of a wish that the empress Livia 'may live as long as the Sibyl of Cumae' (*Ex P.* 2.8.41). This wish occurs in the poem thanking Cotta Maximus for a gift of coins or medallions portraying the imperial triad, Augustus-Livia-Tiberius. The unfortunate Sibyl's oversight in not specifying eternal youth is not mentioned, but may be remembered by readers who suspect irony.

5.7. A new system of ornament?

Yet all these instances are still merely transitory ornament. The difference in length between Tables 1 and 5 seems to indicate that the poet is moving away from this type of device. The question to ask is whether he is developing a new, more complex system to take the place of myth as simple ornament (or as self-referential reminder of the poet's editorial activities at the time).

A distinct pattern of mythological usage is emerging. From the many names and different mythic cycles considered above, some repeated structures present either paragons of virtue or paradigms of cruelty, but a stronger referential nexus may be discerned. We have seen in earlier chapters that the poet weaves a consistent web of imagery throughout the exilic works. Some mythical allusions seem to tie in with certain of the central metaphors of exile. Imagery and myth merge to carry a greater message. Allusions to Iphigeneia, Orestes and Pylades and their brush with the Tauric Artemis are fraught with the more bloodthirsty and disturbing aspects of primitive myth, tying in with the atmosphere of sinister doom that the poet has chosen as metaphor for his place of exile; so, too, the horrific ramifications of rape, incest, mutilation and cannibalism within the story of Tereus (king of Thrace) Procne and Philomela. The influence of their barbaric surroundings eventually moves the two Athenian sisters to parallel Tereus' cruelty to his inno-cent sister-in-law with their murder of Itys. In the narrative of *Met.* 6, what has been termed a 'hellish equilibrium' is underscored by Ovid's stylistic parallels between the two episodes. This is not the place to discuss the problem of what our attitude should be to the pornographic aspects of Ovid's more violent narratives, but we may safely assume that the poet himself saw his relegation to an area even beyond Thrace as the ultimate obscenity. Hence his continued engagement with these horrific figures.

Other figures seem to represent aspects of the exile's longing for home. For instance, Pegasus, the fantastic winged horse, is a transcendental symbol, signifying the kind of mental travel in which the exile increas-ingly indulges. Asclepius and his son Machaon, prototypical healers, appear in the context of 'wounding' and of the medical imagery that dominates the later poems from exile. Philoctetes, finally healed from his long-festering wound, represents both suffering and restitution. He is therefore a symbol for what the exile hopes will be his own rehabilitation. What originally caused his wound was also the means of his salvation – Ovid's *carmina* may have caused his 'stinking sore', but they also bring his ultimate relief.

5.8. Dominant themes and mythical identifications

Most important are consistent references to certain figures or groups of figures that are dominant throughout the exilic oeuvre. These are listed in Table 6. From the Trojan cycle we have: Achilles, Patroclus, Philoctetes; from the story of the house of Atreus: Orestes and Pylades, but also Agamemnon and Clytemnestra, sometimes denoted by means of patronymics. Allusions to Orestes and Pylades can, however, be dismissed, along with references to Theseus and Pirithous, as universalised *exempla* of the *officium* of *amicitia*. Hyginus (*Fab.* 257) lists as those *qui inter se amicitia iunctissimi fuerant* ('those tied together most closely by friendship'), the pairs Pylades and Orestes, Pirithous and Theseus, Achilles and Patroclus. The figure of Achilles is problematic, and more frequently symbolises inexorable wrath than prototypical friendship. Hence Patroclus merits only four references in the exilic works, as against eleven occurrences of the name of Achilles.

From the most topical, 'Pontic' myth, the poet uses Medea and Jason. Ovid's virtual obsession with the Medea-myth has often been remarked. The appropriateness of Tomis as a place of exile is almost 'too good to be true'. *Tr.* 3.9.33-4 shows that its very name symbolises bloodshed. An appealingly appropriate English derivative is found by Green (1994: 55) to convey the concept of Tomis as deriving from the Greek *temnô*, 'I cut': 'Hence the name Tomis, because (they say) the sister/ *anatomised* her brother's body here'.

At *Ex P.* 1.4.23-46 the exile compares his lot with that of Jason. He stops before reaching the uncomfortable corollary of both a Hypsipile and a Medea consecutively deserted for more strategically or diplomatically useful loves, and resorts to a realistic fantasy of reunion with his wife, a wife grown emaciated and old 'with longing' (not because of the passage of time). The passage is important for the insight that it gives into our poet's interest in the story. In his view, Jason had a far better time of it. Ovid enjoys none of the advantages that the hero experienced when visiting the Pontic shores. This dismal fact is spelt out in a detailed comparison. Eight lines will serve to show the balanced structure that gives a stylistic underpinning to what the exile is trying to convey (1.4.27-34):

> *Ille est in Pontum Pelia mittente profectus,*
> *Qui vix Thessaliae fine timendus erat.*
> *Caesaris ira mihi nocuit, quem solis ab ortu*
> *Solis ad occasus utraque terra tremit.*
> *Iunctior Haemonia est Ponto, quam Roma, Sinistro,*
> *Et brevius, quam nos, ille peregit iter.*
> *Ille habuit comites primos telluris Achivae*
> *At nostram cuncti destituere fugam.*

He travelled to Pontus, sent by Pelias, who scarcely was dreaded in Thessaly alone. The wrath of Caesar harmed me, at whose name each end of the earth, from sunrise to sunset, trembles. Thessaly is closer to the Pontus than Rome is to this sinister shore, and so he completed a shorter journey than I. He had as companions the outstanding heroes of Greece, but all men deserted me in my flight.

The catalogue continues thus for another twelve lines, with repetition of *ille* and its variant cases balanced against *me, nos,* and their grammatical variants. The discerning reader may remember another such catalogue of weal and woe: *Fasti* 2.133-44 elaborately praises Augustus as the 'refounder of Rome' in a series of odious comparisons with Romulus as founding father. The stylistic intertextuality of the patterning of this passage makes of Augustus an uncomfortable *tertium quid.* On Augustus more below.

The image of a wife awaiting the return of a persecuted wanderer is a clear pointer that the poet has cast the exile into composite roles. From the various tales of exile, wandering and return, Ovid draws himself as an Aeneas, but also, and pre-eminently, as an Odysseus-Ulysses, a composite figure. Although mentioned by name only nine times throughout the exilic oeuvre, Odysseus, or rather the Ovidian Ulysses, is the most important recurrent symbol for the storm-tossed exile. Implicit or explicit comparison with Ulysses predominates, not only in *Tristia* 1, the Ovidian 'travelogue', but throughout the exile's travails until his final apparent resignation to his lot. The long-suffering Homeric victim of the wrath of Poseidon-Neptune, a lesser god than the great Augustus-Jupiter, tends at last towards home and the virtuous paragon, sharer of his connubial bed. On his wife's birthday the exile fondly imagines, in very much the spirit of the Penelope of *Heroides* 1, that Odysseus would once similarly have celebrated Penelope's remembrance day (*Tr.* 5.5.3-4):

> *Sic quondam festum Laertius egerat heros*
> *Forsan in extremo coniugis orbe diem.*

So, perhaps, once, the son of Laertes celebrated his wife's festive day at the uttermost ends of the earth.

The exile is only too conscious of contrasts. His sufferings may make his wife famous (as he repeatedly assures her), but his wanderings do not bring him nearer home. This is first made explicit in a comparison of his travails with those of Odysseus (*Tr.* 1.5.59-6):

> *Ille brevi spatio multis erravit in annis*
> *Inter Dulichias Iliacasque domos:*
> *Nos freta sideribus totis distantia mensos*
> *Sors tulit in Geticos Sarmaticosque sinus.*

He travelled in a small area for many years between Troy and his Ithacan home. Destiny brought me through distant seas after months of travel under whole constellations and thrust me into the bosoms (or bays) of the Getae and Sarmatians.

This paradigmatic comparison is later imitated, for example, in the verses from *Ex P.* 1.4 quoted above. The fact that Odysseus, like Jason, was not alone, while Ovid was deserted by all, is stressed. The crowning feature of the exile's greater sorrows is the fact that he was leaving Rome, 'the seat of both empire and the gods' (70). It is left to the reader to decide which gods. Comparison serves repeatedly to underline his heavier lot. Even the storms that he experiences are worse, just as the ire of Caesar is more extreme (*Ex P.* 2.7.55-6; 59-60):

> *Quis non horruerit tacitam quoque Caesaris iram?*
> *Addita sunt poenis aspera verba meis.*
> * * * * * *
> *Saepe solent hiemem placidam sentire carinae:*
> *non Ithacae puppi saevior unda fuit.*

> Who would not draw back from Caesar's anger even when it is
> silent?
> Harsh words were added to my punishment ...
> * * * * * *
> Small ships often find smooth seas in winter,
> but no tsunami was rougher on Odysseus' boat [than the
> storms I experienced].

Ex P. 4.10 celebrates the exile's 'sixth summer on the Cimmerian shore' in clear allusion to the time spent by Odysseus in virtual slavery to the fair Calypso – no hardship, so Ovid exclaims: *an grave sex annis pulchram fovisse Calypso/ aequoreaeque fuit concubuisse deae?* (13-14, 'or was it hard to have cuddled the beautiful Calypso for six years, and to have shared a bed with a sea nymph?'). An extended passage (9-28) compares the exile's mood and circumstances with those of *patientis Vlixes* (9), making light of the Homeric hero's woes.

Ruefully ironic self-awareness allows the poet to depict the exile in a multiplicity of roles. With Ovid (not only in the *Metamorphoses*), characters tend to transmute and shift their identities. The exile is not only an Aeneas-Jason-Ulysses. In his role as writer of laments Ovid has also become a 'male Herois', a composite of all the desolate maidens of myth – and (possibly) of the poetess Sappho. Augustus appears as a composite figure. A whole series of divine parallels may be traced. Augustus is at one and the same time not only thundering Jupiter, but also Juno, persecuting an Aeneas figure, Neptune persecuting Ulysses, Juno once more, persecuting Hercules and, finally, Diana-Artemis attacking an *inscius* Actaeon. The Callisto-metaphor makes of Augustus both the ravisher Jupiter and the aggrieved punisher Diana, wreaking the ultimate vengeance on a 'pregnant Callisto', as we have seen above. This makes something else again of the exile. The poet does not spell out this extreme reversal of gender roles, but at *Ex P.* 4.14.57 he does liken himself to a 'pregnant Latona seeking refuge at Delos' (also a victim of two gods, both Jupiter and a vindictive Juno) in his appeal to the incensed Tomitans, who feel insulted by his mournful complaints. In *Met.* 6.313-81, Latona in her wanderings after the birth of the heavenly twins is attacked by peasants, who, as punishment, are turned into frogs. In contrast, Ovid is treated well by the Tomitans, who remain human, 'non-frogs'. As always with Ovid, no metaphor should be pressed too hard, but the comparison is suggestively complex. Comedic excess often complicates the poet's congenital inability to 'leave well enough alone', as first postulated by Seneca, *Contr.* 2.2.12.

So, playful self-irony may be discerned in the posturing of the long-suffering exile, not least when we remember that Ulysses-Odysseus, victim of a great god's wrath, was known for the sharpness of his intellect, and the superiority of his wit over even that of the king of men, Agamemnon. It is not difficult to read a feeling of intellectual superiority in the poet's attitude in his Ulysses-role toward the emperor as latter-day Agamemnon. Ovidian artistic creation can, in a sense, be equated with Odyssean pragmatic deception. In his poetic ability to transmute fiction (i.e. 'lies') into a higher truth, Ovid resembles the liar Odysseus. Similarly, comparison of the poet's Muse with Thersites, the Homeric demagogue, also famous for his ugliness, reminds the thoughtful reader of the verbal attack of an underling on the monarch whose arbitrary decisions ruled his life.

Chapter 1 suggested reading implicit criticism from various possibly double-edged allusions to the emperor throughout the exilic poetry. My tables have deliberately excluded listings of the Roman name of the 'king of gods and men', for such a listing would double the length of this chapter. Throughout the poet's oeuvre the name of Jupiter features hugely, as much in the exilic poems as in the *Metamorphoses*. Ovid's depiction of Jupiter in his other works is consistently irreverent. Whilst we elsewhere may suspect that the identities of Jupiter and Augustus have been merged, here they are virtually indistinguishable. Augustus *is* Jupiter, but not always, or not completely, so that the exiled poet experiences the double thrust of both imperial and divine wrath, keeping him enthralled on the Scythian shores, in contrast to the lot of his most consistent heroic prototype.

This returns us to the vexed question of the 'wavering identity' of Augustus-Jupiter in Ovid's exilic works, a topic treated more fully in Chapter 1; hence only a brief review here. At times the equation is complete (e.g. *Tr.* 1.5.78); Livia, by association, is Juno. At other times Augustus is said to 'act like' Jupiter, and at other times there is a complete separation of the two identities. The emperor oscillates between the human and the divine. He is cast, by negative allusion, into the roles of various human tyrants: Phalaris of Agrigentum, the owner of the brazen bull whose victims were immolated alive and made to bellow their pain (a grotesque metaphor for the act of poetic composition); Busiris, king of Egypt, an example of cruelty (where the pointed denial of any similarity can still be read as uncomfortably showing up Augustus as a tyrant); and especially, by implication, Pelias, the wicked uncle of Jason, who stole his victim's birthright and exposed him to the perils of the Pontic region.

The apotheosis of the princeps here is fleeting, sometimes presented as a *fait accompli*, long since accepted as such, and then again it is celebrated (*Ex P.* 4.6.17-18) as 'something new' after the death of Augustus. Awareness of Ovid's less than respectful, 'counter-Vergilian' attitude to apotheosis in the *Metamorphoses* arouses our suspicions of the elaborate description of the apotheosis of Augustus in *Ex P.* 4.13.23-38. Reference to the *novitas* (24, 'revolutionary nature', rather than 'newness') of his godship underscores (perhaps criticises) the strangeness of a man 'becoming a god'. We have noted before ridiculous aspects of the *recitatio* in the Tomitan market-place, attended by skin-clad Getae, to whom the exile sang *in their own tongue* of the wondrous translation to heaven of the new god, its mortal husk having been cast aside, the assumption of power by an unwilling 'son', 'true image of his father', equalled only by his paragon mother and fine helper-sons. To the growling approval of the assembled barbarian host one savage suggests that Caesar's panegyrist deserves pardon. To this the exile, however, adds ruefully (40) that 'the sixth winter sees him still relegated under the cold axis of heaven', commenting dismally (*Ex P.* 4.13.41-2):

> *Carmina nil prosunt. Nocuerunt carmina quondam,*
> *Primaque tam miserae causa fuere fugae.*

> Poetry is useless. Long ago poetry harmed me
> and it was the prime cause of my so miserable flight.

From first to last, the poet's experience has remained the same – poetry harmed him; it still does not help him. Yet the very next poem (*Ex P.* 4.14) again shows how his Muse sustains the weary exile. Ovid explains to his friend Tuticanus that the metrics of his name had kept him from writing a poem to him before (a reprise of *Ex P.* 4.12.10,11), asserting that any of the mythical horrors that he had sung of before would be preferable to Tomis, where the inhabitants (now mysteriously able to read Latin) are angry at him for having slandered them in his verse. This is mere fun, not serious history, as hypothetical as the exile's claim that he should prefer to visit the Underworld (*Ex P.* 4.14.11-12):

Styx quoque, si quid ea est, bene commutabitur Histro,
  Siquid et inferius quam Styga mundus habet.

The Styx, too, if ever there be such, could well be exchanged for
                                                    the Danube,
  and whatever the world holds lower than the Styx.

We have noted before that the last poem of the entire collection features
a long catalogue of fellow authors and their topics or works (some other-
wise unknown). Ovid plays with his contemporaries' poetic propensities,
and their exposition of various mythical cycles. He is aware of his supe-
riority, even where he deplores his total debilitation (*Ex P.* 4.16.3-8):

Famaque post cineres maior venit. Et mihi nomen
  Tum quoque, cum vivis adnumerarer, erat.
Cumque foret Marsus magnique Rabirius oris
  Iliacusque Macer sidereusque Pedo;
Et, qui Iunonem laesisset in Hercule, Carus,
  Iunonis si iam non gener ille foret ...

And fame grows after death. I already had a great name,
  then when I was counted among the living.
That was when Marsus was alive, and loud-mouthed Rabirius,
  and Macer the boffin on Troy, and Pedo, writer on astronomical
                                                    matters,
and Carus, who would have got Juno angry with Hercules,
  if he had not already by then become Juno's son-in-law (i.e.
                                        married to Hebe on Olympus) ...

In this company Ovid's own star shines brightly. The exiled poet has
created his own myth and he lives within that world. With him live both
an angry god and a divine helper.

5.9. The great omission

What is, however, most puzzling about Ovid's exilic oeuvre, is not the
mythology that it contains, but what is excluded. Archaeological sources
show a lively cult of a rain god, *Zeus Ombrinos*, in the Pontic area, also
Apollo and the Nymphs, Athena and Demeter – and, by assimilation,
syncretism and Romanisation – *Jupiter Optimus Maximus, Juno Regina,
Heracles Invictus*, Fortuna, and *Ceres Frugifera*, also Diana, Pan and
Priapus. Local syncretism combined Dionysus with the 'Thracian
horseman', Bacchus, *Liber pater* and Sabazius. Neptune was known, Mars
very popular. Apollo was worshipped at Tomis as a protector of travellers.
The Dioscuri (often confused with the Cabires, gods of Samothrace), were

venerated as protectors of seamen. Also in the Tomitan area archaeologists have found signs of the worship of Trivia and the Quadriviae (*genii* of carriageways), as well as of some deities imported from other cultures, such as Epona (a Romano-Celtic goddess) and, at burials, the Roman *Dii Manes* and unspecified *genii* as tutelary spirits.

We have seen the Roman Diana (as Tauric Artemis) featuring as symbol of Pontic blood-lust. The good ship *Helmet of Minerva* carries the exile to the Pontic shores, and there it leaves him (*Tr.* 1.10). Except for almost negligible references to Apollo, Juno, Ceres and Vesta, and one poem celebrating Bacchus as Liber, patron of poetry (*Tr.* 5.3), the Graeco-Roman pantheon simply does not feature in the poems of exile. The whole of the exile's religious perceptions is taken up with a view of a single, almost monotheistically powerful and angry god, the great god Augustus, to the exclusion of all the religious practices the emperor had taken pains to propagate. This stance denies the Augustan religious revival by totally ignoring it, bringing to its logical conclusion the institution of a divine imperial cult.

We have noted that adulatory appeals to Augustus and his household as divine beings often appear as vindictive *Schadenfreude* over disgraces in the emperor's family. The bland surface of adulatory meaning could frequently have offered a safe cover for irony. The non-responsive, angry god proved his divine omniscience by not responding to the often patent irony of ostensibly abject appeals. Yet, paradoxically, we can never be wholly sure that the poet is not depicting the exile's true feelings.

5.10. The singular myth

There is only one sympathetic divine figure, the poet's Muse, spoken of in either the singular or the plural (also as the *Pierides*). Initially Ovid's Muse is blamed for his downfall, as we saw in Chapter 2, but gradually he speaks more and more favourably of her. This kind goddess fills the gaps left by religion, family and friends, even failure of life itself. She offers comfort and solace and the promise of immortality. She takes the place accorded to Venus by Lucretius. This Muse is more than a *topos*, a mythical concept, dwelling since the days of Hesiod on the slopes of Helicon. The boy-poet may have deserted her at his father's behest (*Tr.* 4.10.23), but she accompanied the mature poet to the eternally frozen regions of a cosmic exile. Although he does not always view her with equal favour, the exile is aware of her ability to transcend the material world and defeat the aggressor. Ovid's address to his Muse at *Tr.* 4.10.117-28, normally viewed as a prayer or hymn of praise, is couched in the terms of a lover towards his mistress. Poetry fills the exile's life. The Muse is the exiled poet's *domina* and *dea*, his *solacium* and *antistes*, his transcendental reality.

180

Concomitant with this transcendental goddess appears another myth-ical figure, the exiled poet himself, the superhuman survivor of the supernatural onslaughts of both a vindictive god and malevolent nature. A largely fictional poet-hero is similarly presented in the *Amores*, but at Tomis this hero is tragic. The discrepancy between poetic depiction and geographical and meteorological facts about the Pontic area is explained in *Ex P.* 4.14.11-12, quoted above, spelling out the connection between Tomis and the Styx, hinted at throughout in the poet's use of the imagery of exile as death. The Pontic area represents the netherworld. Its cold-ness and bareness are a concrete representation of the Greek view of the afterlife, as depicted in *Aen.* 6. Tomis as the insupportably cold, perpetu-ally frozen home of the North winds (*Ex P.* 4.10.41-4) is central to this picture. Since *Met.* 8.788-91, the Ovidian stereotype for Scythia was couched in terms of a frozen underworld, the Ovidian equivalent of Vergil's Stygian home of *Fames*. This image would have been carried into the first reference to the area, at *Tr.* 1.3.61: *Scythia est, quo mittimur* ('It is Scythia, where I'm being sent'), and lies behind the unusual initial word of *Tr.* 3.2.1: *ergo erat in fatis Scythiam quoque visere nostris* ('and so it was fixed in my book of life that I should also visit Scythia').

The myth of exile partakes of the fleeting character of all myth. Its details shift with every retelling. Its hero exists alone within a zone of silence, persecuted by an angry god, and consoled by a transcendental goddess. The myth consists of a series of paradoxes, mutually exclusive but all equally valid, all part of a world where everything is possible and only one thing impossible: the cessation of blows and the end of exile. It is a world where emotion is paramount and externals parallel the inner wasteland of the hero's suffering. All nature conspires with the silently relentless god to hound the hero, who stands alone, aided only by the very goddess who originally brought about his ruin.

The hero is simultaneously dead, in a frozen and sterile underworld, and alive and sentient. He is alone and celibate. He is emaciated and ill. He forgets his Latin, and protests that he has done so in a flow of elegant Latin verse. He speaks Getic and Sarmatian, although he cowers away from the native speakers, those savage monsters who are part of conspir-atorial and hostile nature. He reaches out to these Getae, and he reaches out to Rome. To the Getae he speaks of Rome and the Caesars; to the Romans, of the Getae. He is living in a Greek city, but his savage neigh-bours wear barbarous clothing and shake their quivers when he reads poetry to them. He fights, as a Roman should, with sword and shield, against enemies who cross the frozen wastes to attack the walled city with bow and arrows.

The hero lives in a hut, and talks to sailors. He adores only his wife and indulges in erotic fantasies about her, which he tells the world. He is a poet and prophet, but so bowed down with countless miseries that he

181

cannot write. He burns what he writes. He never writes. He loves his friends. He is, and has always been, a loyal citizen, active in city life and in the daily obligations and salutations of *amicitia*. He is fervently religious and adores the god he has angered. His humble hut houses a magnificent shrine, complete with silver statues of the greatest gods, where he worships daily, with all the Pontic land to witness his unswerving piety.

He is alone, deserted even by the gods. The angry god never replies to his appeals but the threat of his continued anger hangs heavily over the hero. This hero sometimes reaches out to other heroic figures, who, having penetrated the Pontic world of myth, share in its heroic characteristics: King Cotys, Flaccus, Vitellius. His friends at Rome are in the real world, where time passes and they do not care enough. On the Getic shore, time has ceased. As brooding as the angry god, the cold Northern constellations look down on the hero, oppressing him under the weight of the Polar axis.

This hero has inner strength. Although present time stands still, his comforting Muse enables him to evoke past and future at will. His spirit roams into the real world where his body cannot follow, sometimes drawing reality back to the Pontic shore. He is dead, but at the same time eternally alive – alive to suffering, but also immortal in a transcendental 'now'. The hero of the myth of exile is silent, but verbose. He is *poeta Getes* but *vates Romanus*. As *exsul* he is the victim of the angry god, but in the end, the angry god is the poet's victim. Ovid has not only succeeded in immortalising both persecuted and persecutor, but has given us his perception of the temper of his times. The poetry of exile conveys a damning portrait of Augustus in his last years as an essentially paradoxical figure, a mortal god, an unjust ruler, a cruel father and an Envy that tries unsuccessfully to destroy the prophetic voice of poetry.

The very last poem seems to show Envy in transcendence and the final defeat of the martyr. Like the flayed Marsyas (*Met.* 6.385), he is 'all wound', with no more room for blows. Yet this information comes, as we have seen, within a poem that places him as the greatest in a long catalogue of living poets. What has survived at Tomis is a mere husk. Both the poet and his poetry have been metamorphosed into a divinity greater than any of his mythic prototypes. Apotheosis lifts the sentient sufferer out of his suffering mortal frame and onto an eternal plain. In this the exile supersedes those mythical figures that the poet culled from his own works and elsewhere for portrayal of his sufferings.

Our hero survives in the place of death. He is greater than Orpheus, whose dislocated tongue could only babble for a while as it floated down the Hebrus (his head torn from his body by the vengeful Ciconian women, *Met.* 11.53), more loyal than Jason who dared the Pontic main but deserted his faithful supernatural helper Medea. He endures more than

Odysseus, whose wanderings tended toward home, suffering more than Hercules or Theseus who both braved the Underworld and lived to tell the tale. Greater even than Aeneas, father of the Roman race, this emaciated near-wraith stood up to and defeated the envious onslaughts of the greatest god yet devised in the mind of man – and survived beyond death to create a picture of endless suffering but resilient renewal.

5.11. Statistical play

My series of tables calls for statistical counts and other manipulations, a dangerous game, fraught with pitfalls. Ornamental use of the figure of Aurora for the dawn, frequent use throughout a love-poet's oeuvre of the names Amor and Cupido, use of periphrasis rather than naming, repetition of one name within the narration of a tale, frequent allusion throughout, say, the *Ars,* to a favourite stock figure like Hercules: all these factors would skew any statistics based on absolute frequency of occurrence of mythical figures. Yet the tables offer great opportunities for play and support the notion that Ovid's contemporaneous editing influenced his choice of mythical illustrations in the exilic works.

The 55 figures of Table 1 occur once only in the early phase of the poet's exile, and are then discarded. These are relatively infrequent in the *Metamorphoses* and *Fasti* together (the works probably edited at Tomis), and even more infrequent in Ovid's love poetry. If each occurrence is accorded the symbolic numeric value of 1 in the *Tristia,* concomitant values are 1.1 in the edited works, 0.5 in the *Heroides* and 0.8 in the love poetry. Nine figures are totally new to Ovid. Of those that occur in his *carmen perpetuum,* more than twice as many each (18 and 18) derive from the first and second pentads (*Met.* 1-5, 6-10) than from the third pentad, *Met.* 11-15 (8). This tendency is reversed for the 16 figures in Table 2 that recur in the *Tristia* (4 – 11 – 13). The symbolic value of occurrence of these figures, as compared with the figures from Table 1, is doubled for the edited works (2.44) and increases for both the *Heroides* (0.9) and the love poems (1.18).

Twenty-eight figures from the *Tristia* recur once each in the later exilic works (Table 3). The symbolic numeric value of these figures, as judged against each one occurrence in the exilic poems, is relatively low for the edited works and *Heroides* (both 1.2) but has risen sharply in relation to the love poems (2.3). This is partly explicable with reference to the occurrence of both *Cupido* and *Amor* within this group. Six of these figures are new to Ovid. The largest number (12) derives from the central pentad of the *Metamorphoses.* Most telling perhaps are the symbolic values to be attached to the 18 figures in Table 4. Their occurrences elsewhere, relative to each one occurrence in the exilic works, are 3.2 for the edited works, 0.6 for the *Heroides* and 2.6 for the love poems. None is new to Ovid, but more than three times as many (20) allusions to these figures occur in Books 11 to 15 of the *Metamorphoses* as in the first pentad (6), while eleven derive from the central pentad. These would, for the most part, be the figures that were dominant in the poet's consciousness throughout his working life. Yet the shift from Table 1 to Table 4 of predominance of figures from the second half of the *Metamorphoses* suggests that the poet's consecutive editorial activities may over time have influenced his consciousness of the suitability or illustrative value of certain figures.

The statistics for Table 5 (ten figures occurring in *Ex Ponto* only) are skewed by the frequency of the figure of Aurora throughout the poet's works, but, importantly, the symbolic value attached to occurrences of these figures in the *Heroides,* relative to any one occurrence in *Ex Ponto,* has risen steeply to 1.6. It is tempting to postulate a growing affinity between the desolate poet and his deserted heroines. This conjecture is strengthened by an almost equal symbolic value of occurrences in the *Heroides* (1.5) of the figures identified in Table 6 as thematically the most strongly linked to the poet's exile.

Table 6, then, represents what I have identified as dominant figures, taken from the other tables. These twelve figures or integral pairs occur on an average 5.5 times each in the exilic poems. Their symbolic numeric value in the edited works for each one occurrence in the exilic works is relatively low (1.4) as opposed to the numeric value symbolising frequency in the love poetry (2.3). It would seem that, for expressing the essence of exile, the poet resorted most often to figures that had loomed in his poetic consciousness from the beginning of his creative life. Some, however, are totally new, adopted, it would seem, for the sake of their topicality.

One hundred and twenty-seven figures or groups of figures have been identified. These occur 171 times in the *Tristia*, only 87 times in the *Epistolae ex Ponto*. Thirty-eight recur in the *Ibis*. Their ramifications in this work call for exploration, but that will be a new project for others to undertake.

6

Ad nostra tempora: Ovid today

We have seen that Ovid's 'myth of exile' is essentially a literary creation. The exile's inner life is displayed through continual shifts and progress in tone, attitude and mood. A consistent web of imagery (storms and shipwreck in the *Tristia* and medical references in the *Epistolae ex Ponto*) is enhanced by the use of myth as both ornament and exemplar, but also as part of the fabric of the poetry. A wide range of literary, geographical and anthropological allusions portrays the frozen horrors of the Pontic area, which appears to be based partly on Vergil's Scythia from *Georgics* 3.349-83, partly on his depiction of the Underworld from *Aeneid* 6, partly on Ovid's own 'Home of Famine' from *Metamorphoses* 8.788-91, and partly on popular Roman preconceptions about distant areas.

Throughout the originality with which traditional literary material is manipulated points to poetic ability of a high order. This is something else than saying that Ovid's exile is fictitious. He has converted the real exile of a Roman aristocrat, to a Graeco-Roman city during the closing years of Augustus' regime, into an heroic state within a corpus of intensely personal yet highly literary poetry. What he has created is essentially Roman, with no Hellenistic precedent. Hellenistic exilic literature is philosophical in thrust, tending toward setting into perspective the woes of the exile against a larger awareness of the essential unity of the cosmos. Ovid's picture of the emotional sufferings of the persecuted hero transcends genre and presents us with what is essentially an 'elegiac epic'.

His poetry, the reason for Ovid's exile, was also his salvation, bridging the gap from Tomis to Rome. It enabled him to politicise his 'unpoliticality', answering in verse to obscure accusations of malfeasance levelled against him by the emperor. His poetry conveys the tone and setting of personal experience, giving a new dimension to our understanding of the *pax Augusta,* yet it speaks to the sufferings of any exiles, anywhere.

In this Ovid has tapped into a vein of feeling that underlies far more than the political sufferings of victims of power play of his own time. He seems to have sensed (and has managed to convey) the essential elements of loneliness and alienation as experienced by all those cut off from friends and fatherland through the machinations of the powerful. We may question the degree of Ovid's own awareness of what he was doing, not only politically, but generically. His poetics must be culled from his poetry – Ovid is seldom explicit. Comparison with modern exilic literature can help to clarify certain Ovidian issues. I shall attempt to pin down Ovid's exilic poetics through extrapolation from explicit statements on his poetics by a single modern exiled poet, with due recognition of salient differences of temper and times. The South African poet Breyten Breytenbach developed from youthful, self-imposed traveller (newly exploring the delights of Europe) to banished writer (for having transgressed his country's strange marriage laws), to political activist (imprisoned as a 'terrorist'), to expatriate (sent out of South Africa on a one-way exit visa), to naturalised French citizen, to occasional visitor to the New South Africa and long-distance loyal critic of its new regime. Many other South African authors experienced isolation, either imprisonment or exile, during the years of political struggle before 1994. Their writings most nearly reflect the total isolation that Ovid portrays himself as experiencing at Tomis. §6.2 will compare their emotional reactions to isolation with those of Ovid.

6.1. *Mutatis mutandis:* the poetry and poetics of isolation in Ovid and Breytenbach

While in exile, Breytenbach on several occasions proposed that a 'monument to the unknown poet' should be erected in Rotterdam (a city he had found congenial after his release from a South African prison) explaining 'The body/ corpse of a poet is his/ her poetry ... a poem is a black skeleton of the poet ... Poets form no ideological group ... we try to make ... [even] "poetry of poetry" ... The poet is just a human without his skin.' His project would comprise a sepulchre for the Unknown Poet, '... anonymous ... somewhere on the windblown polders like that of an Ovid.' This monument would reflect as its mirror-image an atomic reactor, and the 'eternal flame [would be] periodically rekindled to burn or sublimate poems'. It would be inscribed: *Here lies a body/ Eaten by words/ From such earth/ Springs poetry!* Poets 'known and unknown' would contribute to this body and '... all died happily ever after' (*Mouroir,* 1984: 190-5, echoed in *End Papers* – see below).

This startling proposal points to the possibility of a fruitful comparison, *mutatis mutandis,* between the works and motives of Breytenbach and his Roman predecessor, concentrating on both authors' awareness of the value of literary creativity in isolation for the preservation of his individuality and sanity. Ovid's unconscious poetics (those aspects of his writing about writing which appear instinctive rather than cerebral) can be more clearly delineated by comparison with Breytenbach's poetics. Both poets suffered isolation at the hands of a repressive intervention by the state into private morality, and both articulated their suffering in extensive metaphors (isolation as death or sickness, the value of the imagination to transcend time and space, isolation as the most cruel metamorphosis). Both seemed to acknowledge the 'truth' of the accusations against them while articulating a higher morality in their verse, and using writing to keep themselves alive and in contact with others.

Breytenbach's oeuvre is as varied and complex as Ovid's own, ranging from dense (and 'subversive') lyrical poetry in Afrikaans, to sometimes obscure 'magically realistic' – often savage – prose in various post-modern writings embodying his prison life and exilic experiences, to his own translations into English of these two genres (or similar original productions in English), to extremely lucid prose or compelling interviews reported by others, spelling out his poetics and his views on 'life, the universe and everything', all tempered by an avowed adherence to Zen Buddhism and an overwhelming love-hate relationship with his native country.

The list of Breytenbach's publications is long and varied. For this chapter the following works were consulted: Lyrical poetry: *Die Ysterkoei Moet Sweet* (Johannesburg, 1964); *Die Huis van die Dowe* (Cape Town, 1967); *Voetskrif* (Johannesburg, 1976); *Eklips: Die Derde Bundel van Die Ongedanste Dans* (Emmarentia, 1983); *('yk')*[*sic*, lower case title in parentheses]: *Die Vierde Bundel van Die Ongedanste Dans* (Emmarentia, 1983); *Judas Eye and Self-Portrait/ Deathwatch* (London, 1988). Prose (either post-modern novels or quasi-autobiography, with views on poetics, life and art): *'n Seisoen in die Paradys* (Johannesburg, 1976); *Mouroir: Mirrornotes of a Novel* (London, 1984); *End Papers* (New York, 1984); *The True Confessions of an Albino Terrorist* (Johannesburg, 1984); *All One Horse: Fictions and Images* (Johannesburg, 1989); *Memory of Snow and of Dust* (Johannesburg, 1989); *The Memory of Birds in Times of Revolution* (Cape Town, 1996). These works are below referred to by abbreviated titles.

Breytenbach's prison works can be better understood by comparison with the factual narratives of those imprisoned and exiled South African journalists who feature in Section 6.2 below. All report on feelings of despair and isolation, yet the dawn of a feeling of camaraderie when they became aware of fellow prisoners. Although some were imprisoned up to a decade before Breytenbach, their reportage of the reasons for their arrest, the circumstances, methods, even the names of some of their tormentors, coincide to such a degree that a strong factual background for Breytenbach's elliptic evocations of scenes and sounds may be read from them.

6.1.1. Biographies and autobiographies

The details of Ovid's life have been recounted in my Introduction, and need not be repeated here. Of concern are rather the literary questions we have been considering throughout. The major issue is his level of consciousness: was Ovid politically aware or a total *naïf*, was he serious in his protestations of loyalty to Augustus and disparagement of his own works, and, above all, was he poetically aware of what he was doing?

Breyten Breytenbach's history offers on the superficial level almost uncanny parallels with the Roman poet's life story. As a young man he abandoned university studies in favour of overseas travel. His first anthology of poems (*Die Ysterkoei Moet Sweet* – 'The Iron Cow Must Sweat') burst upon the Afrikaans literary scene in 1964, astonishing and impressing the Afrikaner establishment with its poetic verve but questioning, subversive stance, which sometimes ridiculed accepted values with dense and brilliant word-play, imagery and innuendo. Its often daring eroticism was for his critics tempered by the brilliance of his verbal dexterity. It was considered stylistically like, but ideologically unlike, the works of the so-called 'sestigers' (the Afrikaans poetic movement of the sixties) in its equation of the act of writing with all other bodily functions. Its anti-establishment implications could be swallowed by the Afrikaans literary establishment only by recourse to the, for them, then newly fashionable 'New Criticism' (already almost passé in English literary circles) which firmly separates an author from his works. However, the personal intensity of Breytenbach's poetry as mouthpiece for the man (proclaiming the unity of poem and poet) made this approach difficult to maintain.

In Paris Breytenbach had met and married a young Vietnamese woman, who would not have been allowed to share his home, or bed, had they been living in the bizarre atmosphere of South African extreme social engineering, which, just like Augustus' marriage laws, brought public sanction to bear upon the regulation of marriage, that most private of social institutions. Their marriage contravened two South African laws regulating marriage, turning an 'interracial marriage' into 'illegal miscegenation'. When in 1965 he sought to bring his bride to meet his family, she was refused a visa. Exclusion of the wife turned the husband, as voluntary wanderer, into an enforced exile. For the poet this was a sobering and radicalising event. The literary establishment was now faced with an uncomfortable dichotomy: the genius of the young poet was unmistakable and he was virtually canonised as author, but his deviant role as persistent and loquacious critic of the government of the time was increasingly decried.

As attitudes and political stresses waxed and waned, in time the couple were allowed *ex gratia* concessions to visit the country together. Breytenbach's fame as poet was growing. Battles within the Afrikaans literary establishment were furiously waged over his place within the canon. The continued safety of New Criticism enabled conservatives to praise the poetry while condemning the poet, as 'not a rebel but a revolutionary', his politics an aberration that 'did not truly touch his poetic soul'. By the early seventies reason would have dictated that he be given the highest Afrikaans literary award, the 'Herzog Prize', but in 1971 it went to another expatriate, Elizabeth Eybers, in self-imposed cultural exile in Holland. This clearly political move tore the Afrikaans literary world into two camps. Conservative critics either denied Breytenbach's importance as poet or the importance of his political stance – putting him in a double bind, making him representative of an Afrikaans culture with which he could not associate.

Such stresses and strains further estranged the poet from the Afrikaans establishment. By now he was firmly associating himself with the struggle of South African Blacks for political recognition. Much more than Ovid, who apparently fell into a political situation almost by chance, Breytenbach became firmly committed to action, slipping into the country in disguise in order to establish a 'literary resistance wing' for the broader struggle. His arrest and trial in 1975 were the sensation of the day, *literati* once again ranging themselves for and against the now apparently abjectly contrite young Afrikaner, who seemed ready to confess his sins and return to the fold, after due punishment had been exacted.

Breytenbach was convicted and sent to gaol for seven years. Two years later he was on trial again, this time for 'plotting from within the prison'. It now emerged that, unlike his Roman predecessor, he had been promised leniency and a minimum sentence on condition that he recanted – hence his abject attitude at the first trial, and his subsequent dedication of a volume of prison-writings to his captor. Of the promised leniency nothing had come. Breytenbach had, it emerged, been subjected to two years of solitary confinement; a warder, acting as *agent provocateur,* had spurred him on to plot escape. At his release in 1982, he left South Africa, taking French citizenship, at first publishing in English and French only. In time he published his Afrikaans-language prison effusions, serially confiscated as they were produced but later returned by the authorities.

Four anthologies of prison poems together comprise *'Die Ongedanste Dans'* (the undanced dance), an indication of the cessation of life within his prison walls. This is reminiscent of Ovid's assertion that writing poetry that has no audience is like dancing in the dark, *Ex P.* 4.2.33-4. Excerpts from the prison anthologies were translated by the poet himself, and published, together with an explicit statement of his view of his craft, in the anthology titled *Judas Eye and Selfportrait/ Deathwatch.* Then followed, in English, the novel-length post-modern-style *True Confessions of an Albino Terrorist.* It blends fact and fantasy, stark reality and tender longing in an evocative volume that conveys the horror of isolation as graphically as does Ovid's fantasies from Tomis, the sober journalistic narratives of other South African political prisoners or the prose-and-verse productions of Breytenbach's fellow-poet Jeremy Cronin (see §6.2 below). Breytenbach's lucid exposé of his methods and aims in his collections of English-language essays in *End Papers,* the latter half of *Judas Eye* and *The Memory of Birds in Times of Revolution* reads in stark contrast to his poems and to other post-prison publications such as the surreal sequences of *Mouroir* (a pun evocative of the French words for *death* and *mirror*) and the novel *Memory of Snow and of Dust.* Of these, *Memory of Snow* rewrites Breytenbach's attempts at political subversion and his prison life as a powerful post-modern novel. He seems aware of the 'monotony' of his themes: an introductory poem to *Memory* confesses that the poet is aware of endlessly reiterating his experiences: 'The biog-raphy/ I am repeatedly in the process of/ writing is always the same one/ ... [a] book of myself as the essential/ apocryphal memory'. *Mouroir,* composed piece-meal in prison, draws on the sickened imagination of a wounded and battered soul to portray the horror of imprisonment as a nightmare without end, logic or sense, with virtually no contact with the world outside. The mood of the work is evocative of troubled dreams, those endless searches for something or somebody that dissolves or evap-orates, to be supplanted by new faces and new horrors, a waking dream as vivid as any reality, in a sense comparable to Ovid's nightmarish *Ibis,* albeit in a totally different idiom.

Significantly, *Mouroir* ends with a morbid third-person narrative of the fates of various characters that had appeared and disappeared in the novel. The author is another of these evanescent characters: 'Breytenbach came to a sticky end' (254); 'In due time Braytenbach (*sic* – a deliberate pun) died the death, in the end claiming and maybe believing that he had been a poet, and innocent, his deathwords (*sic*) "Not guilty, your Honour" ... .' This character was by then in Panama, where he had befriended a woman he called 'Mooityd' ('Beautiful time'), who subsequently corre-sponded with the authorities in 'Niemandsland' (Breytenbach's term, together with its English equivalent *Nomansland,* for South Africa). She was sent information on a 'Bre(a)thenbach' (*sic*) who '... was eventually obliterated while still serving his time, by general debility, and the rot of said time' (255). As with Ovid, time seems to cease to exist. It serves no purpose for us here to try to sort out fact and fiction. As in Ovid's fantastic depiction of Tomis as perpetually snow-bound (*Tr.* 3.2.8; 3.10 9-50) and of himself as both ashes and a living corpse (*Ex P.* 4.16.47-52), the emotional state of the author is the true reality that his words convey.

6.1.2. A basis for comparison

Any critic attempting to draw comparisons between two authors whose circumstances were only superficially alike, but whose poetry exhibits vast differences – of genre, type, tone, apparent intent, as well as prosodic and metrical differences in the languages that shaped their art – must hedge herself very carefully. Ovid and Breytenbach share some literary characteristics, even granting that the former was composing in a strict metrical form and in a language that conveys grammatical relationships through invariable inflection, the only freedom allowed being etymological play, whereas the latter writes in any form that suits his purpose. Yet overriding the salient differences between the two poets is a psychological similarity, relating not only to the circumstances of his isolation, but also to the personalities which informed the art of each in happier times. Both poets may be described as having an ironic attitude to the accepted wisdom of his time; yet in each a certain romanticism tempers his cynicism.

Both poets are masters at word play and *double entendre*. Ovid is perhaps the more subtle. The nature of the Latin language and its linguistic conventions lend themselves to *paronomasia*, punning and etymological play, while the linguistic integrity of individual words is maintained. Breytenbach plays more freely, the genius of the Afrikaans language being such that coining of neologisms is an accepted poetic practice adding to the richness of his verse. Many of these (also in his English writings) consist of the conflation of two known words that together create a portmanteau-word carrying overtones of both, such as the title of a poem '*Autobiotrophy*', reminiscent of *autobiography* and *atrophy*. '*Moanologue*' reflects *moan* and *monologue*. 'The *wormwomb* land of Poetry' indicates both the bitterness of the poet's lot and the comforting power of poetry, but also warns of its imminent decay in a triple-conflation: *wormwood* (absinthe), *womb* and *worm*. One of the dream-sequence essays in *All One Horse* refers to a prisoner as 'the man Wormfood' or 'Bird-dream'. Breytenbach can vary prose and verse and subvert the meanings of words through acoustic play, slight semantic shifts, neologisms and the exploitation of a characteristic that Afrikaans shares with Greek (but not Latin), that allows change of the function of words – from infinitive verbs into nouns, and *vice versa* – by the mere addition or removal of an article. A random example from the poem 'Mahala' on p. 8 of the collection *('yk')* describes the process of writing poetry in prison: '*die hand/ aan die arm op die papier/ wat woordmak woordmaak frase/ kluise gedig gedagte beeld skuifel/ in die papier skuifel*' (literally: 'the hand/ attached to the arm on the paper,/ that word-tame word-makes a phrase/ safe-chaste poem thought image shuffles/ shuffles in the paper'). This is so dense in both mental and visual images, and both grammatical and semantic shifts, that it is almost impossible to render into intelligible English. For example, *kluise* is the plural noun 'safes/ vaults' but in context it evokes the sound, and thus the thought, of *kuise*, the adjective 'chaste', while the consonants of *gedig*, 'poem', are repeated and amplified in *gedagte*, 'thought', leading naturally into the idea that a 'thought' evokes an 'image', *beeld*.

191

Often such play contributes to the poet's ironical stance. Previous chapters have consistently argued for reading a divergence, or slippage, between what Ovid says and what he means in much of his exilic poetry. With Breytenbach, degrees of irony are more easily discerned because the counterpoint of his prose writings sets in perspective his most abject protestations of admiration for his persecutors. Much of his poetry is overtly politically subversive. It does not need elucidation by the author for us to read disgust with the South African political system, and yet sympathy for its perpetrators as fellow-victims, from verses such as the last stanza of 'Die toelig van metafore' ('Illustrating metaphors') in *('yk')*, 47:

> *Kyk het ek gekyk in die Bees se gelyk –*
> *sy ole [sic: for 'oë'] was ondergronds agter 'n sonbril,*
> *Sy porseleingryns getooi deur die staatsmoestas*
> *en hy is ook maar Mens …*

> Look I have looked on the equal (or 'corpse') of the Beast –
> his (l)eyes (= 'lies') were underground under dark glasses
> his porcelain-grin garnished with a State moustache
> and he too is only Human …

Much of Breytenbach's poetry is very difficult, highly allusive and elliptic. Here, perhaps, beside the more obvious aspects of generic and circumstantial differences, is a major contrast with the clarity and apparently guileless exposition of both Ovid's elegiacs and his epic narrative. Yet Ovid is equally elusive, as we have found when reflecting on the endless array of shifts of attitude toward Augustus that are displayed in his exilic works. Much of Ovid's pre-exilic work, in particular the narratives of fluid change that make up the bulk of the *Metamorphoses*, convey the impression of a dream-world in which unreality is the greater reality. In sum, the almost 'post-modern' fluidity of Ovid's narrative style in the *Metamorphoses* is approached by the urgently surreal, dreamlike (rather, nightmarish) fluidity of Breytenbach's prose works.

Metamorphosis looms large in both poets' consciousness. We have noted that Ovid's major work was probably completed in exile. His relegation to Tomis is for Ovid the ultimate, ghastly metamorphosis; its horror has made any other improbability now only too possible (*Tr.* 1.1.117-22; 1.7.11-14). Metamorphosis also lies central to Breytenbach's awareness of his own art. The chameleon is an important image, and the need for being like a chameleon recurs in several poems. It is also a frequent motif in Breytenbach's drawings and paintings. For example on p. 53 of *All One Horse* a chameleon is pictured clutching the three letters of the Afrikaans word for a moth, 'mot'. The centrality of the chameleon in Breytenbach's thinking may be read from his repeated use of the charming parable of the chameleon being sent to deliver a divine message: 'When people are old they will die but be resuscitated'. Only half of the message is delivered, and the chameleon is thereafter earth-bound, but receives the colours of the rainbow as compensation (*Voetskrif* 95, *All One Horse* 299-300). The chameleon implies a willingness to change, but only in order to blend in with its background, becoming part of the whole, and resisting individuality where individuality can work to harm the imprisoned poet. Yet its watchfulness must be emulated: 'It is not necessarily shameful to be living at the table of the political lord or the patron of the arts ... but one should do so as the chameleon ... rotating the eyes in different directions simultaneously' (*Self-portrait/ Deathwatch,* in one volume with *Judas Eye,* 131).

6.1.3. Art and life

The central difference between our two poets always must be respected in examining their attitudes to art and life: that is, the difference between first-century versus twentieth-century concepts of self, with Breytenbach's complicated by his adherence to Zen-Buddhism (where the self is seen both to disappear into and to manifest itself in all around it). This ensures a basic difference in the manner in which each poet associates his life with his art. In an interview reported in *Current Writing* 8.1 (1996), Breytenbach calls writing and reading poetry 'the oldest forms of imaginative creativity ... formal dreaming ... creating yourself'. He acknowledges the re-creative role of the reader in the reception of poetry, the 'creation of self in love ... an expression of the need to transform yourself'. To him 'prophecy is not important'; what is important is 'that it came out as poetry'. This seems both to negate and confirm the vatic principle, but above all it affirms the need for the self to express itself extra-rationally. It is difficult to imagine the cerebral Ovid consciously subscribing to this thesis, yet his fierce defence of his art essentially subsumes these principles. Ovid's poetic creativity *is his real self*; what he *says* is often play. Hence at the deepest, instinctual level, there are similarities in our poets' awareness of the role of art to sustain troubled life.

Ovid protests in *Tr.* 2.354 that his poetry, as reason for his banishment, was the mere product of his art. His life had been pure, although his Muse had been wanton (an excusable fault, so *Tr.* 1.9.59-64). Yet throughout his exilic poetry Ovid stresses that his poetry is 'bad because his circumstances are bad', as in the final elegy of *Tr.* 3, and the opening and twelfth elegies of *Tr.* 5; for example: *Non haec ingenio, non haec componimus arte/ materia est propriis ingeniosa malis,* (*Tr.* 5.1.27-8, 'I didn't compose this from inspiration, nor with my art, but the material has sprung from its own ills'). We have seen that the central paradox to Ovid's exilic poetry as a statement of his *bona fides* is that, if we accept what he says about the former separation of his life and art, we must assume that this separation still holds, undercutting whatever he says in exile about himself and his attitude to the emperor.

Like Breytenbach at his first trial, Ovid is unstinted in his apparently abject submission to the authority of his tormentor. In Ovid's exile the emperor is the supreme, just god of the Roman pantheon, on whom Ovid unquestioningly lavishes fearful worship. We know from later events that Breytenbach's initial submissiveness was meant merely to gain mitigation of sentence. With Ovid, we can only surmise that this, too, was the case, while we read subversive irony between the adulatory lines. Yet the Roman poet's submissiveness was equally unsuccessful in achieving his recall. Augustus was not taken in by Ovid's protestations in the way that the Afrikaner literary establishment was, from 1975 until 1977, prepared to accept Breytenbach's apparent recantation, until the second trial showed up both his 'repentance' and the authorities who cynically manipulated him into submission without carrying out their half of the bargain. Breytenbach later wrote , 'I was numbed. All I wanted was to please. And in my cell I was alone in the house of dying' (*True Confessions*, 49). Of enforced compliance, Breytenbach explained: 'It is possible to falsify for some time the thrust of one's words by inserting them in an environment controlled by the enemy ... but eventually ... it will become evident and be rectified (even if it is true only in its absence of truth)' (ibid., 139).

We should not, *mutatis mutandis*, assume that similar manipulations and betrayals were in force in Ovid's case, but the Breytenbach experience does illuminate the forces that play upon a poet when politics lead him out of his depth (even at Rome, where politicians regularly committed poetic *nugae* to their writing tablets in moments of relaxation). It is safer to assert, of both Ovid and Breytenbach, that the poet remained true to his Muse, both regarding the exterior trappings of his poetry, his stylistics, and the interior impetus that fuelled it – his attitude to life and art. With Breytenbach we have explicit statements after his release; with Ovid we must reconstruct his interior attitude from the exterior evidence of his poetry.

We have seen that the last poem of Ovid's exilic collections, seemingly a cry to mordant envy to let go of his nearly-extinct carcass, actually celebrates the fame the poet knows he has earned while alive (*Ex P.* 4.16.47-52). This cry asserts Ovid's pre-eminence above his poetic contemporaries. Writing thus once more separates art and life – the 'extinct carcass' belongs to a poet still very much alive and aware of his own worth. The inverse conceit occurs in *Memory of Snow and of Dust* (257): Breytenbach's fictionalised *alter ego* states, 'It is quite possible to die while nominally still alive'. In this work (217-20) the name of the protagonist Mano alternates with 'Noma' and 'Anom'. All three ring the changes on *anonymity*, the state brought about by incarceration, perhaps *obliteration*, if Mano may be equated with 'No-man'. The allusion is made explicit when the character is given the well-known Afrikaans surname 'Niemand' (259, 'Nobody'). The classical undertone is never made explicit, but a memory of the Odyssean pseudonym invites response.

6.1.4. Multiple personalities

We have noted that one of Ovid's autobiographical effusions from Tomis (*Ex P.* 1.2.33-4) speaks in terms reminiscent of the perhaps spurious opening lines of the Aeneid, *ille ego sum* ('I am that he who ...'). In spite of its lugubrious tone and sad contents, bewailing the dreary circumstances that limit the exercise of his talent, this poem yet presents Ovid (as does his autobiography, *Tr.* 4.10) as a confident poet, divinely chosen for his craft, both victim and major exponent of his creative Muse. In his self-revelations the poet deliberately creates a whole series of *personae*, from poet who is an exile to exile that can compose poetry, from greatest living poet to dead body, from victim to avenger, from deserted friend to implacable enemy, from erstwhile *desultor amorum* to devoted husband. Behind these multiple personalities stands a sure creator-poet that knows his craft and knows what he is doing when he exercises it.

We have also seen that Ovid's poetry is both his comfort and his bane, both the cause of his banishment and his only solace, his inspirational goddess and his Nemesis, the creative force that sustains him and the product of his genius – his child, but an Oedipus or Telegonus that caused his death. He can no longer write, he complains in poem after fruitful poem; his talent is gone and all that remains is a mere husk of his formerly prolific self. Breytenbach's love-hate relationship with his art lies within the sphere of the language itself. He is equally driven, the victim of a remorseless *anankê*. Afrikaans is his heart's tongue, but his Afrikaans background rejected him and his before he rejected it. He intends to write in English or French only, but his heart's tongue will speak, and it speaks in Afrikaans. For Breytenbach, release from prison did not end his isolation, for, living in Paris, not as 'an exile, [but] ... an émigré ... the only Afrikaans-writing French poet', he was cut off from 'intimate communication with his own people', finding it 'terrible for a wordsmith to be deprived of language enrichment' (*End Papers,* 207-11 *passim*). This must be taken as emotionally, not factually, true, for the poet's richness of expression continues unabated. Ovid at Tomis similarly protested, in mellifluous Latin verse, the loss of his Latin.

Breytenbach's verbal play is endlessly ingenious. In spite of his Zen awareness of being part of the great Nothingness, he creates multiple names for himself: both he and his persecutor are 'Mr I' (also 'Mr Eye', 'Mr Interrogator', 'Mr Interstigator', 'the Investerrogator'), the *ego-persona*, but he has half-a-dozen or more other names for himself. Play on his initials produces Buffalo Bill and B. Bird (a pun on 'jailbird'), also Burnt Bird, Bangai Bird, and Juan T. Bird. Beside Breathenbach, and Braytenbach, we have Beda Breyten and Barnum, even Billiard Ball (after shaving his head). Some names are playful, others reflect his bitterness. His most persistent *alter ego* is his mirror image, Don Espeglio ('Mr Mirror'), the face of the 'thin man in the green sweater' that he sees before him. Nothing is fixed, but in true Zen-fashion, everything becomes part of everything else, and so he is part of what he writes. In prison Breytenbach *is* what he writes. His being, as he sets it down on paper, is his true reality, and that is daily taken away from him by prison authorities as he completes each page. He explains that he needed to write in order to survive, but that it was a bizarre, one-way exercise, the 'enemy reading over [his] shoulder [while he was] laying bare [his] most personal and intimate nerves'. Worst was not being able to edit or revise: 'You cannot remember what you wrote before and whether you are writing in circles' (*True Confessions,* 140).

So, too, Ovid condenses all his *personae* into one: his poetry as the true reflection of himself, his true *imago*, more 'real' than his pain-wracked body: *sed carmina maior imago/ sunt mea, quae mando qualiacumque legas* (*Tr.* 1.7.11-12, 'but my songs are a greater image of me, and I entrust them to you to read, whatever they may be like'). Although his portrayal of a desolate and frozen external reality seems to reflect his inner desolation, Ovid paradoxically depicts his inner resilience as vanquishing external hardship. His imagination sustains him, travelling at will to Rome, where he sees in his mind's eye the life he can no longer share.

6.1.5. Love, isolation and death

A major metaphor in Ovid's exilic poetry is the concept of 'having died' when he was banished. Breytenbach describes survival in isolation as coming 'at the price of feeding small morsels of oneself to death' (*Memory of Birds,* 161). Central themes in Breytenbach's prison oeuvre are death, his wife, a cage, and play on various aspects of '*kreng*' – from a rotten carcass or a bad man to a 'ring', in the sense of circular composition.

The themes of love and death are interwoven in both poets. First, on *love*: a flouting of the sexual mores of his time features in the works of both poets, yet each, when in dire straits, exhibits a single-minded affection for his spouse. Where the roots of Breytenbach's troubles with the State sprang from a non-State-sanctioned marriage, we can expect that longing for his wife should be central to his prison poetry. Love for his wife shines like a clear beacon in the murk of his sequestered life and the gloom of his writings. Everything else is questioned. The third stanza of a poem (translated by the poet himself), entitled 'oh my love, my darling, I hunger ...' (reminiscent of the title of a popular 1950s love song, which continues: '... for your touch'), runs thus (*Judas Eye,* 89):

> for too long have I forgotten
> the deft tips of fondling
> the flower fingering of dalliance
> woven in arabesque in hiprock and tapis.

This, although tone and temper are entirely different, may be compared with Ovid's evocation of a reunion with the 'old and grey' Penelope-like figure of his wife, who will be emaciated through care, but still desirable, and vulnerable (*Ex P.* 1.4.47-52):

> *Te quoque, quam iuvenem discedens urbe reliqui*
>   *credibile est nostris insenuisse malis.*
> *O, ego di faciant talem te cernere possim*
>   *caraque mutatis oscula ferre comis,*
> *amplectique meis corpus non pingue lacertis*
>   *et 'gracile hoc fecit' dicere 'cura mei'.*

> You too, whom I left as a young woman when I left the city,
>   perhaps you have grown old through my ills.
> Oh, may the gods grant that I might see you like that
>   and enjoy kissing your silvering locks,
> and hug your slender body in my arms
>   and say, 'It's my worries that made you so thin!'

The concept of exile as death serves as a consistent metaphor from *Tr.* 1.2.65-6 onward; but play is inconsistent, death alternately featuring as final threat or final release for the suffering exile. That these tropes are mutually exclusive is acknowledged at *Tr.* 1.4.28 with the rider *Si modo, qui periit, non periisse potest,* varied at *Ex P.* 4.12.44 to: *... ille perire potest* ('That is, of course, if someone who has died can not have died/ can actually die'). As we noted in Chapter 2, *Tr.* 3.3 features an imaginary deathbed scene, where the poet 'watches' the 'dying' exile. The separation of *personae* is clearly evident. An 'epitaph' (*Tr.* 3.3.73-6) follows, vindicating Ovid as love poet, who died 'at his own hand' or, rather, through his own art:

> *HIC • EGO • QUI • IACEO • TENERORUM • LUSOR • AMORUM*
>   *INGENIO • PERII • NASO • POETA • MEO*
> *AT • TIBI • QUI • TRANSIS • NE • SIT • GRAVE • QUISQUIS • AMASTI*
>   *DICERE • .NASONIS • MOLLITER • OSSA • CUBENT*

> I who lie here, playboy in the tender games of love,
>   Naso the poet, I perished by my own talent.
> But to you who pass by, may it not be so hard, if ever you've loved
>   To say 'May the bones of dear Naso rest in peace'.

Yet even within the poet's words the game continues. The exile's 'death' acts as a metaphor for his isolation, both as poet and as Roman citizen. Against this Breytenbach's similar claim of having died sounds a grimmer note, as in the first lines of the Afrikaans original of the poem quoted above:

> *mon amour*
> *hierdie ek is dood*
> *met die groen van brommers om oë en mond*
> *maar uit die hara van hierdie stil plek*
> *deur gegrendelde poorte en getraliede vensters*
> ....
> *sien ek jou/ praat ek jou*
>   *mon amour*
>
> Voetskrif ('Footnote'), 8

> *mon amour*
> this 'I' is dead
> with green of blowflies at eyes and mouth
> but from the *hara* of this silent tumulus
> through bolted gates and barred apertures
> ....
> I see you/ I talk you
>   *mon amour*
>   translated by Breytenbach himself, *Judas Eye*, 94.

The poet goes on to reminisce about his wife in 'the golden city of Rome/ in that gilded cemetery …', referring no doubt to Rome's Christian architectural legacy. This cannot be taken as the poet's acknowledgement of a spiritual affinity with his Roman predecessor. More importantly, the irony of a 'dead' husband with sightless eyes and silent tongue both 'seeing' and 'talking' his wife into existence is close to the Ovidian trope of simultaneous death and sentient, suffering life, as in the last verses of *Ex P.* 4.16. Breytenbach's poem ends with a reaffirmation of his continued existence, yet with an awareness of how prison has changed him (ibid., 95):

> the man you're waiting for
> will no longer be this I
> but older, like winter snow in the cracks

old like a wounded wind from the interior
and he will carry me back with him
will you wait for us?
....
ah mon amour
look, I'll return
and until then all
over this horizonless page
I write sightless write tongueblind towards you.

Ovid, as we have seen, like Breytenbach, admits that time and isolation have changed him (*Ex P*. 1.4.1-2). He fantasises about ultimate return as an 'old and grey' Odysseus-figure, reunited with an equally ancient wife. In an earlier poem Ovid complains because, although his essence has altered, he can in no way lose feeling: *Ille ego sum, lignum qui non admittar in ullum:/ ille ego sum, frustra qui lapis esse velim* (*Ex P*. 1.2.33-4, 'I am that man who am not allowed to turn into wood/ I am that he who wishes in vain to be a stone'). Here, too, repetition of the key phrase '*ille ego*' ties the poet to the possibly spurious *incipit* of the *Aeneid,* not as a statement of poetic autonomy and the promise of future excellence, but as sad palinode of all that he has ever vaunted himself to be. In this poem Ovid both calls for death and fears it, but still cannot resist intricate etymological play (*Ex P*.1.2.57-8):

> saepe <u>precor</u> mortem, mortem quoque <u>deprecor</u> idem,
> Ne mea Sarmaticum contegat ossa solum.

> I often pray for death, and also pray that death may stay away
> Lest Sarmatian soil should cover my bones.

One of the psychological spin-offs of isolation is a fluctuation in both poets between awareness of having 'died' and awareness that isolation has not killed them off but has irrevocably changed them. Isolation and non-communication equal 'non-being'. Death in all its facets typifies the bleak existence of each. The illusion of being dead seems central to the consciousness of most prisoners, as witnessed, for instance, by the title of Wole Soyinka's prison book, '*The Man Died*', or Wilde's aphorism: 'all sentences are sentences of death'.

Even after Breytenbach's release, death remains the central metaphor for his horrific experience. One of his retrospective collections of prison poems is aptly entitled *Lewendood* ('Living death'). In *True Confessions* (108) he tells of being 'aware of being buried,' adding 'That you entertain the fancy of still being alive is of no consequence. There is no death. You are buried to what you know as normal life outside ... This death-world is filled with sounds you never imagined.' Yet in prison the urge to commu-

199

nicate with the outside world persisted. He needed 'to shout "I'm here! I'm dead but I'm here – be sure not to forget it!" ' (239). On suicide by prisoners he says (208): 'You kill yourself because they are killing you.' His own thoughts of suicide had been exorcised by his inner life, an 'intimate questioning' of his persecutors (235). The last passage in this work is a poem entitled '13 TO LIVE IS TO BURN (*Andrei Voznesenski*)' (*sic*). Its last couplet reads: 'Burn, burn with me love – to hell with decay/ To live is to live, and while alive to die anyway!' (356). Both Ovid the love poet and Ovid the lonely exile could *mutatis mutandis* have expressed a similar sentiment.

When he is asked how he survived, twice Breytenbach answers 'I did not survive'. Soon after the second denial he writes in an (unsent) letter to his wife, 'You gave me your strength and I survived. I died and you were there waiting. I was in my grave, and you wrote to me ... The husk of hurt and alienation will be shucked' (*True Confessions*, 292). Earlier (113) he had explained the effects of isolation: 'Parts of you are destroyed ... all objectivity is taken away from you ... you watch yourself changing ... without ever being able to ascertain the extent of these deviations.' In *Mouroir* (90) Breytenbach is even more explicit: 'The difference between life and death is that there is no difference'. Elsewhere he explains what imprisonment does: 'Absence and distance kill the soul' (par. 6.6 of 'Random Remarks on Freedom and Exile' in *End Papers*, 75). In the same volume (240) he expatiates upon exile in similar terms: 'Exile – isolation (exile is too melodramatic) is a method of maiming. It implies that you are turned in upon yourself ... without finding a natural outlet in a shared culture of language for your worries and your reflections ... Isolation is arrested growth ... the I can only develop as a living part of the us.'

Here Breytenbach refers to 'maiming'. Elsewhere he refers to 'exiles with unhealed wounds in their minds' (*Memory of Snow*, 104). 'Wounding' and 'illness' as precursors to dying are closely linked to the metaphor of isolation as death in both poets. In Ovid 'wounds' are of two kinds: those inflicted upon him by the emperor, and the emperor's 'wound'. Ovid calls attention to his mysterious *error* with frequent refusals to 'lacerate the emperor's wounds afresh', as in *Tr.* 2.209; 4.4.41-2 and *Ex P.* 2.2.57-8. His own miseries as 'wounds' recur frequently from *Tr.* 1.1.99 onward. The aid of family and friends is 'healing'. His melancholia is so graphically portrayed that several articles have appeared discussing Ovid's poetry as symptomatic of severe depression. Breytenbach recounts bouts of depression in similar terms: 'I was sick of myself and sick of others through isolation' (*True Confessions*, 113).

6.1.6. Singing death

The South African writer of ironic short stories, Herman Charles Bosman, was in his youth (during the late 1930s) condemned to death for murder, long before the wholesale imprisonment of political activists became a South African reality. This sentence was later commuted to a prison term. In his prison reminiscences he tells of his envy of those prisoners who were treated with contempt and hardship by unsympathetic wardens: that was an acknowledgement that they were *alive*. In contrast, those in the condemned cells were treated almost kindly, with grudging respect, *as if already dead*. Laughter and joking helped Bosman and a fellow inmate of the condemned cells to assert their continued existence, but every day was imbued with the foreboding of his imminent execution.

Laughter became, then, Bosman's means of clinging on to life. Later, imprisoned journalists all relate soberly what Breytenbach portrays luridly in *True Confessions* (194-5). The last night that condemned black prisoners, political or otherwise, would spend on earth, was whiled away by the singing of their fellows. A black man, they tell, was *carried to his death by a wave of song* that the white prisoners in their separate quarters could share only vicariously. All tell of fear and pity filling the whole prison with gloom. One refers to Bosman, commenting that in forty years 'little had changed': the rest of the prisoners were kept sleepless on the night before hangings were to take place. Hence song also worked to break through the isolation of single cells. Yet the dirge-like hymns of the condemned prisoners accentuated the loneliness and emptiness of their isolated state. Breytenbach speaks of interruption of sleep and of being 'alone in the house of dying' and of 'the defiance of those singing their death, ... raising their voices in a rhythm of life and of sorrow so intimately intertwined that it could only be a dislocation of the very notion of the body of God' (*True Confessions*, 49, 108, 194). He speaks of awakening in the dark and writing a poem while listening to a 'lone voice singing ... this week only one is due for hanging' (ibid., 115). His poem 'For the singers' (*Judas Eye*, 45) explains, 'in the singing is the endlessness/ of dying'. In one instance song brought new solidarity, the dirges giving way to political rallying-cries.

Elsewhere Breytenbach refers to the unison, rhythmic singing of prisoners polishing corridor floors, song setting a common pace for the sweep of their brushes (*True Confessions*, 242). These are often a running commentary on prison conditions, led by a 'caller' and affirmed by the chorus of workers, e.g. '*Thefoodsafree. Ja-ja. Thesleepsafree ... Free-ja. So why-ja moan. Moan-ja. Herecomesaboss. Boss-ja. Sobigbigboss. Isbig-ja. So step aside. Ja-ja. ...*' etc. Research on the 'prisoner as victim' in the gaols of America in the 1970s showed the value of prison poetry and the prison chain-gang song as a 'necessity for survival', serving to sustain the spirits of those incarcerated or subjected to long periods of back-breaking enforced labour, helping slower workers to keep up and appropriating the hated task, hence making it more bearable. I can remember the fascination with which as a child I listened to road-makers wielding their pick-axes in unison, their voices raised in harmony. Nearly two millennia earlier, Ovid had referred to the same phenomenon. In his isolation, he says in *Tr.* 4.1.5-6, he does no more than the *fossor* 'chained to his fellow', both ditch-diggers singing to relieve their pain. The idea recurs in *Ex P.* 1.6.31-2. By implication relief of pain through song brings hope, the 'only goddess' that still keeps the *fossor* alive:

> *haec facit ut vivat fossor quoque compede vinctus*
> *liberaque a ferro crura futura putet.*

[Hope] causes the chain-gang-navvy to go on living
  and he thinks that his legs will still be freed from the irons.

For Ovid, the writing of poetry in exile is a manifestation of the same desire to relieve his loneliness and tedium that is his greatest hardship. Simultaneously he complains that, as noted above, writing poetry without an audience is 'just like dancing in the dark'. Breytenbach expresses an almost similar sentiment in *True Confessions* (136), but in his case his description of *writing in the dark* is literally factual: 'I used to be a night-bird; now only a jailbird ....' Writing in the dark was 'like launching a black ship on a dark sea'. He was doing his 'black writing with ... no-colour gloves and ... dark glasses on', trying to feel the letters he could not see. 'It makes for a very specific kind of wording ... the splashing of darkness, the twirled sense. Since one cannot re-read what you've written a certain continuity is imposed on you. You have to let go. You must follow. You allow yourself to be carried forward by the pulsation of the words as they surface on the paper. You are the paper.' He makes explicit the value but also the pain of writing poetry: 'You write on in an attempt to erase' – to erase the dark, to erase the loneliness. Later he defines poetry as 'a secret way of capturing lost time' (*All One Horse*, 72). One may read into this Ovid's equal need to write himself into the minds and hearts of those in Rome.

About the lack of an appreciative audience, Breytenbach (*True Confessions*, 142) says: 'Writing took on its own pure shape, since it had no echo, no feedback, no evaluation, and perhaps ultimately no existence' – the proverbial lone tree falling unheard in the silent woods. Ovid expresses similar frustration at 'writing to Rome but never receiving a reply', clearly poetic hyperbole, an expression of his feelings of dumb hopelessness, aimed at evoking sympathy, not literal fact.

6.1.7. Submission versus subversion

For the incarcerated Breytenbach, allowed to compose but not to keep his effusions, the act of creation was a function of life, painful but necessary, its products flushed away like excreta. A poem in *Voetskrif*, entitled '(mitemosaiek)' (*sic*: '(mosaic of myths)', lower case title in parentheses), evokes the process of defecation, concluding that 'the labyrinth gives birth to a naked pyramid'. This volume appeared in the early years, dedicated to Breytenbach's police captor and interrogator, Colonel Broodryk, in ostensible submission, the only way in which the poet could get his products to the literary market place. The police interrogator features largely in Breytenbach's post-prison writings as variant play on the initial of 'investigate', as we saw above, 'Mr Eye' or merely 'Mr I'. This last appellation indicates the degree to which the victim actually associates himself with his persecutor. The one needs the other to feed his being into existence (as in the so-called 'Stockholm syndrome'). In societies which impose the death penalty, the law apparently prefers that the condemned confess, thereby relieving the state (or even the executioner himself) of some of the onus of taking a life. Conversely, the prisoner appears to need to confess in order to assert his common humanity with his punisher. After being returned to the maximum security facility from a short stay in less secure surroundings, Breytenbach commented, in ironical apostrophe of his captor, '[I was] saved ... to confess to you, my *dead I*' (my emphasis, *True Confessions,* 231). Word-play beguiles the reader's eye with the initial 'my dea...' into expecting 'my *dear*', so that '*dead*' comes as a shock. His captor is by implication no longer a living human being, brought to feeling by his victim's address, but also, this captor is essentially himself. Similarly, Ovid's poetry brings to life, and ties himself in with, the looming figure of the all-powerful man-god who banished him from Rome. Most of Ovid's poems assume the divinity of the emperor. *Tr.* 2 explicitly addresses Augustus. Elsewhere his argument frequently shifts subtly from an ostensible addressee to the persecuting figure of the vengeful god. Almost every poem assumes the presence of an imagined major reader, the emperor as powerful arbiter of Ovid's lot. An overlay of ostensible submission and admiration elicits strong suspicions of irony, the anti-Augustan stance that is subsumed in every chapter of this volume.

The picture is not flattering, casting shadows over the most exemplary achievements that Augustus vaunts in his *Res Gestae*. The moral life of Rome that Augustus tried to restore is shown as degraded, hypocrisy its major vice. The *pater patriae* appears as a cruel and unnatural father; his adopted son 'reflects his father's visage' in its cruel and vindictive expression. The religion that Augustus tried to restore has been superseded by the lone figure of a harsh man-god, his humanity displayed only in an obsession with gaming and wenching, his divinity arbitrary and repressive.

6.1.8. Poetry made visible

Breytenbach is a celebrated painter as well as a poet, and his lucid discussion of the process of choices inherent in painting a picture (deciding where limits should be set, reducing the options open to the artist) serves as easily to describe the process whereby a wordsmith chooses words for a poem, polishing the product until all alternatives are eliminated: 'Painting ... is always a *process* of never-ending decisions ... "Completing" a work is simply a matter, step by step, of reducing the choices ... The final form, if successful, is arrived at by eliminating the has-beens and the progeny' (*End Papers*, 140). Breytenbach the painter and Breytenbach the poet work in the same way. What they describe applies equally to Ovid the wordsmith.

It is a commonplace of Ovidian criticism that Ovid wrote 'visually'. Some *ekphraseis* in his love poetry and graphic descriptions of creeping change in the *Metamorphoses* have been postulated to evoke some or other lost painting. In general the poet's words convey a visual impact. As noted in Chapter 1, one of the strangest of Ovid's poems, *Ex P.* 4.1, explicitly requests the great Sextus Pompeius, his latest patron, to consider him as a possession, comparable to a series of famous art works, a sculpted heifer by the great Myron, Apelles' *Aphrodite Anadyomene* and the two statues of Athena on the Acropolis. Peter Green's translation (1994: 174-5) of verses 29-36 gives the feel of the verses of the unusual coda:

> Just as Venus forms Apelles' labour, and glory,
>   squeezing out her sea-wet hair,
> as the warrior-goddess guarding the Acropolis, Athena
>   stands in bronze or ivory, Pheidias' work,
> as Calamis claims renown for his sculptures of horses,
>   as the truly lifelike cow reveals Myron's hand,
> so I, Sextus, am not the meanest of your possessions:
>   my safeguard, you: your gift, your creation, I.

The poet is expressing gratitude for aid. It is a word-craftsman's attempt to resort, through words, to a visual medium and to lose his personality within a product of the plastic arts. Similarly, at *Ex P.* 4.5.39-44 the exile vows that he will remain the consul's *res mancipi* (a fossilised archaic legal term for certain types of possessions relating to agriculture, Gaius *Inst.* 2.14-17).

With Breytenbach the relationship between the literary and plastic arts is even more explicit. A picture in *All One Horse* (113), published six years after his release, shows the grim scene of a man hanging in a prison cell, pen and paintbrush in hand, wearing a bib, as if about to dine. This graphically epitomises the lot of the isolated poet. The covers of other books carry illustrations by the poet himself, strange, enigmatic paintings that convey the central imagery of the poems: a chameleon, a man with a horse's head, birds, butterflies and unclothed figures whose exposed genitalia offer a metaphor for the exposure of self that the poet conveys in words. The cover of *Judas Eye* features the naked figure astride a big bird within the confines of a small cell with a strong hinge and two key-holes. The figure looks defensively at a large eye, more reminiscent of the architectural feature on the gable of a Cape Dutch house (the omniscient 'eye of God') than of the small spy-hole of a prison door (commonly termed a 'Judas-eye').

The eyes of the bald, skull-like head and face on the cover of *('yk')* are covered by a white moth, the title branded in red on his forehead. On the back cover a naturalistic self-portrait of the author has a large orange butterfly covering its eyes. Butterflies and moths feature elsewhere in his art. For Breytenbach, both are important signifiers of metamorphosis, the changes that he himself underwent, from carefree traveller, to exile, to prisoner, to haunted political refugee who had lost his South African citizenship, to French citizen. He coins a verb, 'butterflying' to depict this process (*End Papers*, 20). On the cover of *True Confessions* a grey, naked figure clutches – in fingerless hands – a big, brightly-coloured bird. The figure is kneeling, again in a small cell, here with windows on either side, from which twelve hands (brown, white and pink) reach out behind him, fingers bent, as if signalling in the language of the deaf. Bandages cover the top of the figure's head, hiding the eyes. On the back cover the same figure is pink, except for the unbandaged, bald white top of its head, the eye sockets smeared shut with white paste. The lower part of its face is flecked white and crimson, as if freshly bruised. Its fingers are stained a deep rose pink. Here the bird is bandaged, all except for its head and beak and gleaming black eye. The whole powerfully portrays the frustrations of imprisonment, alleviated only by the comforting presence of the multi-coloured bird, which perhaps represents the poet's writings, also trammelled by the prison experience.

Mirror-imaging appears as the overriding metaphor of the cover of *Eklips*, visually depicting the Afrikaans pun inherent in the title (both 'an eclipse' and 'I, lips'). An eyeless face has the labyrinthine white letters of the title, outlined in black, on its forehead, with the letters of the author's name jostling each other between red, grinning lips. The back cover has the mirror-image of the title in black letters. From its closed, turned-down mouth the mirror-image letters of the name dribble out, hanging over the lower lip. The sightless, wordless writer

205

comes into being by speaking his own name, his speech clogged and muted. The image portrays a process similar to Ovid's attempts to keep his name (and himself) alive in Rome through his stream of poems from exile.

6.1.9. Breytenbach's explicit poetics

So writing is the only way in which an isolated poet can make himself believe in his own continued existence. Ovid stresses, time and again, that writing poetry prevents his extinction, as in *praebet mihi littera linguam* (*Ex P.* 2.6.3, 'Literature provides me with a tongue'). Writing confirms his own existence to the solitary author, whether at Tomis or in Pretoria Central Prison.

In prison Breytenbach can travel in his mind's eye. He describes an imaginary visit to his mother's deathbed, where he, like the dying woman, can see their common forebears surrounding the bier: ... *glinsterend geel/ het 'n son die arkadiese toneel bestreel/ gespeel oor die halfkring gesigte van ou/ uitgestorwe ooms en voorvaders wat rustig/ aan pype sit suig om rook te kweel ...* (*Eklips* 57, '... glistening gold/ a sun soft-stroked the arcadian scene/ played over a halfcircle of faces of old/ long-dead uncles and forefathers, peacefully/ sucking pipe stems, lips smoke-enfolded ...'). We know from his prose writings (*True Confessions*, 270-3) that the poet was not allowed to leave prison for his mother's funeral, but his poems give vicarious closure. Similarly, his longing for his wife achieves a degree of sublimation by the celebration of their love, as in the examples quoted above, but also in a poem recounting the value of memory and mind-travel at dead of night: '... this unforeseen shameless joy/ that my thoughts can be with you despite all my fears/ ... in the immense clustering and death of consciousness/ oh my wife' ('In the middle of the night', *Judas Eye*, 44). Ovid does much the same in various poems to his wife and friends.

For Breytenbach, reality outside his prison has become vague, but he thinks it into new existence. That is the *raison d'être* of his composition. In *All One Horse* (31) he explains 'when writing comes into its own ... the missing is transformed into a delicious mixture of ache and ecstasy ... until the very absence becomes a presence.' The conceit of 'present absence' is frequent in Breytenbach's oeuvre. He speaks time and again of his urgent need to write. In *Mouroir* he typifies words as 'holes in which you must stick death' (53), writing 'an "anti-reality" that causes reality to exist' (62). He affirms his creative autonomy: 'I am the writer. I can do what I want!' The composition of a poem can serve as surrogate for all the usual trappings of a birthday celebration: *'n man het vir hom 'n gedig gemaak/ vir sy verjaarsdag die sestiende van die negende/ ..../ die man het geraap en geskraap en nageaap/ en die raapsels en skraapsels met asem/ aan mekaar probeer wend –/ ook in die woestyn het die tong nog 'n skadu* (*Voetskrif* 27, 'A man sat down and made up a poem/ for his birthday on the sixteenth of the ninth month/ ..../ The man scrimmaged and scraped and even aped/ trying to gum together the scrapings and scribblings/ with his own breath –/ in the desert too the tongue casts a shade'). The prisoner goes on to relate that he 'wrapped up the poem in paper against making a fair copy that evening', but when he next looked at it 'the damned paper had gobbled up the verse', leaving him with nothing to show for his birthday. As we noted, Ovid berated his birthday for following him to Tomis (*Tr.* 3.13); a later poem offers his wife surrogate greeting on her natal day while comforting the exile with a description of the familiar ritual (*Tr.* 5.5).

We have seen Ovid designating poetry as '*solacia frigida*' (*Ex P.* 4.2.45). It would appear that Breytenbach, like Ovid, experienced the futility of versification as a substitute for human contact, akin to murder of the poet's self. The anguished sound-play and word-play in the following is impossible to render adequately in English: '*want skryfboek is slagblok, bladsy is bloedbad/ woord is moord – of word, en is dit/ nie dieselfde nie?*' (*Voetskrif*, 70, 'For writing pad is butcher's block, page is bloodbath/ word is murder – or becoming, and is that/ not the same?'). A poem discussing the poetics of isolation puts it explicitly: '...'tis easier for the camelword with no oil to its sound/ to slither through the needle's mouth/ than for the heart/ to escape through that judas!' (from 'The bifid route', *Judas Eye*, 15). This is clearly evocative of the Biblical Matthew 19.24, 'It is easier for a camel to pass through the eye of a needle than for a rich man to enter the kingdom of heaven'. For Breytenbach, writing is in the end both futile and infertile.

Yet poetry seems to be the one thing that sustained both poets in their isolation. Breytenbach's lucid post-prison writings about his craft explicate what transpires in the creative process and the value that the solitary artist attached to practising his craft. Writing sustained his personality against the erosions of solitary confinement and the onslaughts of the conventional, but to write was dangerous: 'If you are a writer, watch out for the words: they are traitors' ('A Note for Azania', from a series of 'notes' at the end of *True Confessions*, 328). Similarly: 'I doubted if poetry was going to save my neck; it might well have become the very noose' (ibid., 219). Yet Breytenbach continued writing, driven by an inner need to compose. We noted above that he would write in the dark – the reason for the apparent formlessness of his poetry, its lack of punctuation. He could not reread what he had written, he felt 'a certain continuity ... imposed' on him by the dark, a smaller version of the blindness of one-way composition without revision imposed by his captors. Yet writing became for him 'a means ... a way of survival ... Writing is an extension of my senses ... but becomes an externalisation of my imprisonment ... writing ... constitutes the walls of my confinement ... [I]t is unbalancing something very deeply embedded in yourself when you in reality construct ... your own mirror ... you write ... your own face, and you don't like what you see' (ibid., 136). In his fictionalisation of his prison experiences Breytenbach's protagonist Mano exclaims: 'I need ... to exist in the reader's mind ... through my writing I create myself' (*Memory of Snow*, 65).

Breytenbach was rediscovering the personal value that poetry has for the poet, if only to disturb. Long before, he had composed an '*Arse poetica*' (*sic*), a kind of political manifesto for a poet (*Die miernes*, 111-17). He experienced an emotional surge of frustration at his inability to change the South African political situation through poetry: '*Ek weet net dat daar van soveel braaksel ontslae geraak moet word ... [E]k wil sê dat die gedig nutteloos is. Ek moet die gedig kan rig ...*' (ibid., *passim* from 114 and 116: 'I only know there is so much vomit to be voided ... I want to say that poetry is useless. I must be able to direct it'). Ovid could probably have told Breytenbach that it is not for a poet to interfere in politics, but both would agree that the inverse is equally true.

After Breytenbach's release, writing serves as a catharsis, cleansing the festering sore of his memory of suffering: 'There is no composition like decomposition ... recollecting all the hurts will allow me to put them out of my mind for ever' (*True Confessions*, 133). Publishing his prison writings was a triumph of mind over hurt: 'The word dreamt in the anonymity of prison has become sap and fibre' (*All One Horse*, 37). Writing *True Confessions* was to him like taking a strong emetic: 'It is all coming back in bits and pieces ... I am vomiting words' (*True Confessions*, 268). Its final pages are entitled 'Notes from the journal of Bangai Bird'. These begin 'I realise now the preceding document is in itself for me an interstice of freedom. I had to write it. I had to purge myself ... I am not a hero; I am not even a revolutionary ... I don't believe in trying to change the past, except to the extent that a forever changing future continually throws another light on that past' (ibid., 307). Breytenbach admits that what he has written often remains to haunt an author, who may have moved on in his thinking: 'Writing is a messy way of committing suicide' (from 'Writing the darkening mirror' 1994, published in *The Memory of Birds*, 2). He tells of an obsessive, urgent need to talk on tape, to tell the things he had to hold back during his wife's prison visits. His intention had been to produce a political text – 'if it turned out to be more "literary" than expected it can only be because I couldn't help it. It is ... the seductiveness and the *life* of the word. But ... prison accounts as a genre ... are pretty much the same the world over' (*True Confessions,* 309). He became aware of the need to transcribe his experiences for the sake of all those incarcerated every-where, and even for the sake of their oppressors, a form of recognition of their essential brotherhood. A tool for survival in prison had been 'to remain aware of the humanity of the other' (ibid., 255).

6.1.10. Application to Ovid

Breytenbach's attitude to the power-structures that interfered so drastically with his life, and the way he eluded censure for his continued subversive writings, can help us to understand what Ovid was doing in his isolation. Ovid must have realised that he was wielding a double-edged sword when ostensibly praising Augustus and the imperial family, while actually denigrating the despot that punished his *carmen* for an inadvertent *error*. Ovid's pre-exilic writing had not been cast into the required Augustan mould. Exile did not change that. Breytenbach spells out the need for resistance against totalitarian control of the arts: 'Art is ambivalent. If it were otherwise, we'd be spouting propaganda ... even mediocre work may be made important by proscribing it' (*End Papers*, 143-4). And again: 'Poetry can transmit or be used by power ... [it has] the slow but sure power to break down separators' (ibid., 153-4). Breytenbach will not 'knuckle down to oversimplification [for] ... writing [is] the expression of revolt, not the sublimation of it' (ibid., 194).

Like Ovid, Breytenbach appears both to love and hate his art, which, to him, is himself. In one of the almost lyrical, but bitter, prose passages that intersperse the narrative of *True Confessions* (216), he asserts: 'I write about South Africa – which is the quintessential No Man's Land ... I write to no one, inventing an I who may mouth words that I can neither swallow nor spew out – they are the stones of the labyrinth, with the mortar of silences.' His essential being has been silenced, but he has created a *persona* through whom to protest. Elsewhere Breytenbach admits frankly that what he writes is 'corrupt[ed by his] suffering', adding '[O]ne man's penpoint of view [is] obviously formed and deformed by personal experiences' (*End Papers*, 265). What is written must be taken as a distortion of reality (whatever that reality may be). In *Self-portrait/ Deathwatch* (123) he discusses the role of the author as creator of a projected self, explaining that the process of writing objectifies the self. Chapter 1 postulates much the same about Ovid in exile.

Breytenbach continues on the next page of the passage from *True Confessions* quoted above (217): 'You must go on, even if you lose yourself along the way'. His intimate relationship with his tormentors continues: '... always ... I've kept up my intimate questioning of you, Investigator ... I have seen you as the minotaur, which is the I, which does not exist since it is a myth ... I see you now as my dark mirror-brother. We need to talk, brother I ... I must warn you that the system ... will grind us down, *me and you*' (ibid., 235). Ovid's continued address of the emperor (directly or indirectly) may be similarly construed. Sometimes the 'Other' is simply an aspect of the 'I', as in Breytenbach's frequent addresses to 'Don Espeglio', cited above. A poem in *Judas Eye* (40-1) bears the apt title 'mirror-fresh reflection' (*sic*, in lower case). It addresses in turn a warder, the poet himself, and then Death. Here his poetry is termed 'the sorrow that I squirreled away word for word'.

An introduction – punningly termed 'Pretext' – to *End Papers* explains (31): 'Part of the *how* [of writing in isolation] was using the I as prism ... as some sort of prototype of South African sensibility ... not just any old I, but ... the ever-changing "historical" *bonhomme* ...' leading to poetry: 'I know there will always be, when least expected, an eruption of the irrational, the poetic ... We all have inside of us a subterranean and bottomless pit of ink which wells up ... strained through the brain ... emerging in weak squirts called words.' This underlying impulse leads to the creation of verse. Elsewhere Breytenbach acknowledges the value of poetry, as a 'do-it-yourself survival method ... a mechanism ... a verbally transmitted passion of words resulting in silence'. At the same time it is 'language taking a risk', even 'crippled prose' (ibid., 156). This conceit happens to be verbally reminiscent of Ovid's play on the uneven length the verses in an elegiac couplet, as at *Tr.* 3.1.11-12, where the poem itself 'limps' as the result of its long journey from Tomis. More important is the idea that emotive composition ensures the survival of a poet *in extremis*.

Although Breytenbach's poetry and prose are unconventional in form, the poet remains aware of the disciplined patterning required by verse composition. The meandering, dream-like sequences of *Mouroir* often include distinct poetics, such as (104): 'I wrap up my story in words and try to present it in patterns.' On occasion the narrative is interrupted by an excursus on poetics and the nature of his tale. Our wordsmith cannot resist word-play: 'Of course I could introduce a juggling of beauty here and yonder just for the juice of it – some lacustrine (*sic*) colours perhaps, and a breath of sentiment not too lachrymose. Nothing lacerating however, no – none of that turning inside out or bringing dark mumblings to light' (ibid., 122). Later he muses about the 'possibility offered by the title of the story'. This 'possibility' encompasses play on the French for *death* and *mirror*. Breytenbach is honest about the obscurity of his writing: 'As reader you will just have to read a little harder to interpret the signals' (ibid., 245). *End Papers* (152) spells out the reader's role: 'The poem, to exist, needs a listener, a reader, a participant.' Ovid is less explicit, leaving much to his readers' intelligence to decipher, yet his writing constitutes a similar and consistent attempt to write himself into existence within readers' perceptions.

Breytenbach defines the function of the plastic arts as '... the coming to grips with a feel of reality by way of illusion' (ibid., 146). His writing does the same. *Mouroir*, the prose evocation of the horrors of incarceration (even more than his prison poetry), exhibits characteristics of fantasy similar to those of Ovid's stylised picture of Tomis. Pages 210-11 convey a fantastic picture of Breytenbach's place of incarceration as a large two-storeyed hut, with empty cells and only two guards, 'Sergeant Roog' (inversion of the Afrikaans for 'gross') and 'Warder Softly-Softly'. The place is inhabited by the prisoner and his wife 'Meisie' ('Girl'): 'Sometimes I even thought that the prison must be a holiday camp for warders and that we were there ... just to justify the presence of the guardians ... Warders will be warders ... Often we got drunk together ...'. This is not to be taken literally. Breytenbach is exhibiting in prison the same kind of durability of spirit that prompted Ovid in exile to conjure up a magnificent shrine at which he daily worshipped silver images of Augustus, Livia and Tiberius, sending reports of his frenzied fervour, to, one would hope, a sceptical Rome (*Ex P.* 2.8).

6.1.11. 'Disturbing the silence'

A cynical poem in *Judas Eye* (102) is entitled 'What counts'. It contrasts other (dead) poets with a still-living Breytenbach and concludes that life is worth more than an ability to weave words: 'They were perhaps wise in the ways of the word/ but knew sweet bloody nothing about keeping alive.' This need not be taken as his final word on poetry. The body of works emanating from Breytenbach's incarceration and subsequent exile offer, like the works from Ovid's banishment, proof of the value of writing poetry to keep the human spirit alive. For both poets, poetry was power. Long before his incarceration Breytenbach had written that 'art independent of politics does not in reality exist', and, three years later, 'The tribe expects the Poet to be an exponent of its tribal values, not a dissenter' (*End Papers,* 45 and 57). Neither Ovid nor Breytenbach could subscribe to this. Such an inability led to their downfall. After his release Breytenbach wrote 'A poem is an expressive structure and an instrument of freedom ... Word *is* act' (ibid., 93). Six years later came: 'Writing is like plaiting a rope. And the rope is the present linking past to future' (*Memory of Snow,* 306). The fact that a comparison such as is drawn in this chapter can be made between two authors separated by two thousand years is proof of the durability of this multi-stranded rope.

Finally, an address to 'My Dear Unlikely Reader' spells out Breytenbach's view of the function of poetry in a political environment: 'The simplest way to combat totalitarianism ... is to *disturb the silence*' (*End Papers,* 126). Is this not what Ovid, too, was doing, when he penned book upon book of poems and sent them back to Rome?

6.2. 'Living in a place called exile': the universals of the alienation caused by isolation

Recourse to Breytenbach's poetics has helped us explore Ovid's literary motivation. Both Ovid and Breytenbach have clearly delineated exile as a political act with extreme emotional consequences. There are more parallels between first-century Rome and South Africa of the recent past than the fact that a single poet in each era became the object of extreme political strictures. As in Augustan Rome, exile has been a major factor in South African political life.

The South African poet Stephen Gray features Ovid in a collection of poems on diverse dislocations (*Gabriel's Exhibition,* Cape Town, 1998: 78-80), very deliberately repositioning the poet: 'To charm Caesar I must turn my local friends into savages ... their whooping cousins crossing/ the Danube, or call it the Kei, into this Colony .../ ... We represent Rome to them'. Let us take Gray's postulation further, and try to pinpoint the universals of exilic alienation effected by exile or imprisonment by comparing the writings of our Roman poet with his modern equivalents, while considering the question posed by the editor of an anthology of exiled South African poets: *'How does exile affect a poet?'*.

6.2.1. Alienation: its nature and consequences

Alienation is definable as a psychological separation from the protagonist's accepted modes of thought, usually precipitated by some sudden impetus, whether internal or external. The alienated have been described as 'those people who have been excluded, or have excluded themselves, the deeply maladjusted'. Alienation is seen as a method of coping with stress. Six categories of alienation in the face of stress are usually described: powerlessness, loss of all norms, isolation, cultural estrangement, social isolation, self-estrangement, and feelings of personal worthlessness. Temporary self-alienation may be the result of an extraordinary crisis such as death of a beloved, or exile. To the alienated, all others become an overwhelming, all-embracing threat: the alienated protagonist always has an antagonist.

Hilda Bernstein, editor of a collection of interviews with South African exiles (*The Rift: the exile experience of South Africans,* London, 1994, hereafter '*Rift*'), argues that these private agonies need to be observed in a literary way – to be interpreted, that is, 'like fiction'. This section compares aspects of the alienation experienced by exiles and its sublimation through poetry in the works of Ovid and modern exiled or imprisoned authors, including the personal narratives of certain unliterary (if not *illiterate*) political refugees. The experiences of ordinary South Africans will serve as a form of 'reality check' on the emotions reported by both

Ovid and modern authors. The source for these personal narratives is transcripts of interviews conducted by Bernstein between 1989 and 1990 (before the return of most South African exiles). Some of these were reworked and published as *The Rift*. Others are housed in an oral history collection at the University of the Western Cape. Many political activists had been given one-way exit permits, and were officially exiled, others had simply fled. South African refugees, as predominantly city dwellers, had different needs from those other Africans displaced by wars. Migrant labourers experience another, itinerant type of exile. Involuntary exiles, the children of those who had elected to leave, were particularly disadvantaged by their social displacement, needing to 'choose' a new identity. Many former activists experienced a loss of idealism, an alienation that meant distancing themselves from fellow-exiles.

Most authors on the topic of alienation emphasise the loss of power of alienated individuals, and their awareness of an inability to exercise choice. Simon Goldhill, discussing the reclamation of earlier Greek thought by Greek writers under the Roman empire (*Antike und Abendland* 46: 2000, 1-20), sees Nietzsche as the 'exemplary – even fundamental – figure for contemporary discourse on exile'. Goldhill isolates five factors: nostalgic loss as symbolic of the human condition; loss of spiritual, intellectual and moral placement; narratives of exile comparable to the alienation experienced under 'modern, gendered individualism and power'; the 'logic of appropriation' that is integral to exile; and the 'changing patterns of nationalism as implications for exile'. The interviews collected by Bernstein very largely reflect similar factors, which are also integral to Ovid's presentation of himself as an exile. Another useful source is M. Robinson's *Altogether Elsewhere: writers on exile* (Boston and London, 1994, hereafter '*Elsewhere*'), a collection of largely similar statements on the exilic experience by authors ranging in era and provenance.

6.2.2. Alienation through exile and sublimation through literature

Displacement of people is a constant phenomenon today. Exile has on occasion been epitomised as 'the inability to be able to greet others casually', implying displacement to an alien and antagonistic milieu. The concepts *home* and *exile* are essentially self-referential. Bernstein quotes South African exiles: 'home is home'; '[it is] hard in exile'; 'being in exile is being in exile'. Gemma Cronin (second wife of the poet Jeremy) felt the effects intensely: 'Exile, it's poison really. I think it's poisoned us too.' Ruth Weiss, a doubly exiled South African activist, whose parents had fled Nazi Germany, yearned for South Africa but felt 'evicted' from Germany, 'a place where I had been born but ... was not my home'. Norma Kitson, whose husband was jailed for twenty years, put it thus:

213

'... that's the tragedy of exile, ... that you can never return. There is no return from exile. There's a new life perhaps, maybe a better life, but there is never a return to the familiar.'

Further definitions (from *Elsewhere*) represent various eras: 'an exile made a decision [to leave], a refugee is helpless'; 'a refugee becomes an exile when a country grants refuge'; exile is enacted 'within law, [by] force, without law, [by] violence' (so Victor Hugo), yet it is 'absence embalmed in rosy dreams' (Breytenbach), for 'love for the fatherland begins on the frontier' (Heinrich Heine).

Many exiles use literature to bridge their individual divides from the known – for example, the writers of the modern Jewish Diaspora, the South Africans Dennis Brutus, Keorapetse Kgotsitsile, C.J. Driver and Bessie Head. Sublimation of exile through literature is not merely a modern phenomenon. Ovid as exile declares his innocence in poem after poem, describing his loneliness and isolation, and the comfort that writing poetry affords him. Posturing as the Exiled-Poet-that-Suffers, Ovid often seems to mock his own performance. A perceivable distance separates poet and exile. Thereby his alienation is sublimated into a newly integrated, powerful stance, supported by his comforting Muse. Yet the distinct characteristics of alienation are discernible in his writings. Ovid converts intensely personal, subjective suffering into an objective, quasi-fictional mode, a poetic depiction of alienation during exile comparable with modern authors' narratives and metaphors.

Sometimes authors have deliberately associated themselves with Ovid, each finding a different reason for drawing a parallel. Oscar Wilde composed *De Profundis* ('From the Depths') while in prison, depicting his woes in Ovidian terms. The South African poet N.P. Van Wyk Louw, teaching in the congenial atmosphere of Amsterdam, nevertheless produced a volume of poems entitled *Tristia*, where Africa is set against cultured Europe as the 'place of barbarity'. D.H. Lawrence was, during the First World War, made to leave Cornwall because of his German connections. He several times referred to himself as feeling 'like Ovid in Thrace', another victim of literary and political prejudice. David Malouf's novel *An Imaginary Life* (which sets Ovid in Tomis as the tamer of a traditional 'wild child') has been interpreted as an exposé of the psychological experience of the alienation from their 'European roots' felt by many Australians.

These authors all consciously identified with the persecuted Roman poet. I argue for an innate psychological relationship between all in isolation, transcending imitation and lying within the nature of human reaction to a particular kind of hardship. It is best articulated by writers who have been isolated, while experiencing (whether as political prisoners or exiles) a similar cutting-off from all that is familiar, along with feelings of repression and persecution. Ovid's presentation of exilic alienation can be verified by comparing it with the sufferings of later victims. In the words of Breytenbach, 'Exile teaches you about individual fate with universal implications' (*Elsewhere*, 182).

Poet and activist Jeremy Cronin terms political imprisonment 'exile in one's own country'. Imprisoned living authors such as Breytenbach, Cronin, the Nigerian Wole Soyinka and the Kenyan Ngugi wa Thiong'o wrote about their experiences. Each was ahead of his times, resistant to collective thinking, and averse to the political hegemonies of his era. The Greek activist George Mangakis in the early 1970s explained that writing helped him to fight the nightmarish thoughts that beset his mind while in solitary incarceration. Their writings have been termed 'confessional narrative', that is, the fictionalisation and hence universalising, of individual stories. The act of writing converts experience into 'fiction', in the basic sense of the word. Imprisoned South African journalists, objectively detailing their own emotional fluctuations during isolation, all report on feelings of despair and isolation, yet the dawn of a feeling of camaraderie when they became aware of fellow prisoners.

Loss of a sense of belonging can occur within the home country. Sensitive individuals may feel ill at ease within their own milieu. Ovid's exile may have stemmed from a single, unspecified disruptive act, but what he wrote before did not fit into the general atmosphere of the Augustan societal reform. He was culturally dispossessed within Roman politics, despite his popularity with ordinary readers. The author Christopher Hope comments: 'Exile becomes a condition, almost an affliction ... I went into exile before I left South Africa' (*Rift*, 346). Hannah Arendt reports on an unusually high rate of suicide among Jews 'put into concentration camps by our foes and internment camps by our friends' (*Elsewhere*, 110). Edward Said quotes Simone Weil on the need 'to be rooted [as] the most important but least recognised need of the human soul' (ibid., 146). For Said (139) the task of exiled poets is to 'lend dignity to people denied an identity'. This can sometimes be best realised by fictionalisation of experience.

Themes reflecting alienation in Ovid's poems appear universal, and would still be valid in situations of exile today. Verbalisation of such alienation serves to heal a wounded soul. In the words of an author discussing modern Somali displacements: 'The person whose story has been told does not die.' Such stories also 'need to be told for the sake of posterity', wrote an early chronicler of the exile to Ceylon (now Sri Lanka) of defeated South Africans after the Anglo-Boer war. Many of the dispossessed were unable to write down their experiences, let alone generalise about them. My readers may want to apply these universals to today's millions of inarticulate and disempowered refugees and exiles, and to imagine at third hand what their emotions would be. Ovid's articulate voice offers help in this process.

6.2.3. Listening to non-literary exiles and prisoners: similarities with Ovid's voice

Hilda Bernstein's *Rift* features the stories of many well-known exiles who have since returned to high positions within the South African government. For example, Kader Asmal, who went on to become South African Minister of Education, admits to the greatest sense of alienation during the last two years of his thirty-year teaching career in Ireland, but that was (as transcribed by Bernstein) 'because of the increasingly reactionary social climate in Britain and Ireland'. Asmal defines exile as 'being cut off from the area of your sustenance, your emotional sustenance', but, because he had a family and continued to work for political change while in Ireland, he never did feel 'the loneliness, the alienation, that exiles felt'.

Bernstein's transcriptions also record the words of the otherwise faceless and voiceless participants in the South African democratic struggle. Even among friends they still experienced alienation. A South African who became an organiser for the Canadian Communist party complained of being unable to 'get the pulse of people' because he had not grown up there, so that, although he felt ideologically at home, he still was a stranger. His wife agreed: 'You are neither fish nor fowl nor good red herring and I felt an ache for South Africa.' Gemma Cronin reported expecting to find London 'vaguely familiar', but in the end feeling totally estranged. Horst Kleinschmidt, arrested with Breytenbach, experienced double isolation, extreme emotional trauma through a period in solitary confinement, and, in prison, also rejection by the adherents of the Black Consciousness movement. In sum, interviews with South African political exiles (much like the narratives of Boer prisoners of war at the beginning of the twentieth century) indicate a psychological profile comparable with Ovid's portrayal of his own exiled *persona*. Such comparison neutralises the fictionalising element that we have postulated in both Ovid and modern authors in similar straits, leaving in the end a clearer picture of exilic alienation, and leading us to greater appreciation of the emotional content of Ovid's exilic poetry.

6.2.4. Displacement voiced: a comparison

Facts: As we know, Ovid gives very few facts about his banishment. His hints convey a sense of injured innocence without giving concrete details about either his departure from Rome or his arrival at Tomis. *Tr.* 1.3 offers an emotional evocation of the eve of his departure but nothing about practical arrangements for his comfort. Ovid's journey to Tomis is depicted in subsequent poems in such a way as to confuse the serious seeker after literal facts. Mood, not detail, is what the poetry conveys.

6. Ad nostra tempora: *Ovid today*

Some meagre details may be read from *Tr.* 1.5.83 (perpetual banishment); 1.7.15-40 (he left his masterpiece, the *Metamorphoses,* unfinished); the whole of 3.5 spells out his innocence and indignation; 3.8.43-0 describes physical lassitude; 3.10.4 depicts his sterile, barbaric surroundings as a metaphor for his sterile life; 3.12.33-4 tells of a constant search for news of home; *Ex P.* 4.7.7-12 portrays Tomis as icebound – and dangerous. Initially, his overwhelming emotion was shock (*Tr.* 1.3.11). The factual narratives of modern exiles are usually more detailed.

Time: The mood of Ovid's exilic poetry grows increasingly dark as time passes, so that *Ex P.*4 seems most consistently despairing. Ovid himself frequently refers to the passage of time and its inability to alleviate his pain. At Tomis time is frozen, while it passes at a normal rate in Italy. 'Time passes so slowly you would think it is standing still' he says in *Tr.* 5.10.5-6, where the third winter of his stay seems longer than the first two. Passage of time features in: *Tr.* 4.8 (he is old); *Tr.* 5.8.31-2 (he counts the periods of sunshine and rain); and *Ex P.* 4.10.1-2, heralding his sixth summer at Tomis, held fast, like Odysseus on an enchanted island. Breytenbach comments on the elasticity of one's conception of time while incarcerated: 'Some periods are far longer than others' (*True Confessions,* 126). When his wife was allowed to visit him, 'time would stop ... only to flow away with a painful rush' (189). 'Time itself became the grey matter of my existence', he says (210). Dennis Brutus in his *Letters to Martha and other poems from a South African prison* (London, 1968: 38) writes of life on Robben Island: 'one [is] locked in a grey gelid stream/ of unmoving time', but (39) 'on Saturday afternoons we were embalmed in time/ visiting time:/ until suddenly like a book snapped shut ...'. Edward Said (*Elsewhere,* 149) speaks of exile as 'Life outside the calendar'. The journalist Ruth First in her prison memoirs (*117 Days,* Harmondsworth, 1965: 69) told of finding imprisonment 'an abandonment in protracted time'. Other South African women report on the great loss they experienced by missing out on up to ten years of their children's lives.

In an extended comparison Ovid illustrates how time works to inure animals to any hardship. Over time, he says, a bull will learn to draw a plough, a horse to accept the bit, lions and elephants grow tame, grapes ripen and ears of corn swell, acid fruit grows sweet; over time a ploughshare is blunted by wearing away hard rocks; even anger and grief are lessened by time. Yet his sorrows only grow, and a second year brings more pain than the first (*Tr.* 4.6.1-22). Cronin, in a memoir titled *Inside* (London, 1987: 31), has an almost similar metaphor: 'Times/ parcelled/ in separate/ brown paper packets .../ time that walks in circles .../ or drips from taps ....' Ovid's poem continues (verses 29-38) with another extended comparison showing how novelty makes any new challenge more bearable. Familiarity has brought him only greater misery: famil-

217

iarity with pain has added to his burden. His only comfort is that isolation has brought him so low that an early death will end his miseries (39-50). Elsewhere Ovid asserts that he had changed in a short period from a fairly sprightly forty-nine-year old into an 'old and grey quinquegenarian', with a similarly ancient wife (*Ex P.* 1.4.47-52). In similar vein Ngugi wa Thiong'o writes in *Detained: a writer's prison diary* (London, 1981: 188): 'I have "aged" considerably, for I have lived several years in six months.' Isolation causes time both to freeze and to accelerate.

Time as space: Time, for the isolated Ovid, equals space. The distance from Tomis is so great that a year is needed for a single cycle of correspondence, he says. When consoling a friend on the loss of his wife, he notes that his letter of sympathy may reach Rome only after the friend has happily remarried, so slow is mail between the two (*Ex P.* 4.11.15-22). Modern exiles and those isolated by imprisonment experience this same conflation of time with space. An exile excerpted in *Elsewhere* (219) explicitly refers to exile as 'cutting you off from time as well as place'. Another (p. 38) speaks of time as standing in for space, producing a 'literature of nostalgia', where lost time stands in for loss of the author's homeland. For Breytenbach, 'to be living and writing elsewhere' is [to experience] 'an absent presence, absent time or questioned time ... writing is like breathing, but more painful ... [you are always] an outsider' (*Elsewhere*, 16). The poet and musician Abdullah Ibrahim writes: 'Where loneliness' still waters meet nostalgia ... I'm hemisphered' (in C. Pieterse, ed., *Seven South African Poets*, London, 1971: 6). For Ngugi '... time is sluggish, space static and action a repetition of non-action' (*Detained*, 127). In Bernstein's collection of oral narratives a young South African activist speaks of escaping to Botswana, at first feeling great relief at his new freedom from persecution, but then, 'feeling the distance that is slowly creeping between you and family and [holding] the knowledge that you can't just shout and be in contact with them'. When he at last met up with his sister, his long absence had made them strangers: they had nothing to talk about. Distance and time had broken family bonds.

Loneliness: Ovid complains of desertion by friends (*Tr.* 1.9.5-16), only one or two remaining loyal (*Ex P.*2.11.9-12). At Tomis he experiences an all-encompassing loneliness (*Tr.* 5.10). He writes and reads his works aloud to himself, with no one else to judge them (*Tr.* 4.1.91-2), but he is often 'too miserable' to write (*Tr.* 5.7.7), 'sad' (*Ex P.* 2.7.16), 'debilitated by an immense series of ills' (1.4.19-21), and 'incapable of taking decisions on his own' (4.12.43-8). He imagines his wife to be equally lonely (*Tr.* 4.3.21-30), but sometimes petulantly berates her for insufficient sympathy, fearing that she is ashamed of him (*Tr.* 4.3.33-4, 51-2). The centre of his being is empty, hollow, without constant feedback from his Roman readership. The South African Arthur Nortje in a poem entitled

'Waiting' comments: 'It is not cosmic immensity or catastrophe/ that terrifies me/ it is solitude that mutilates.' Similarly, Cselaw Milosz saw himself as a 'writer censored by exile' and hence without readers (*Elsewhere*, 36), and Said speaks of the 'crippling sorrow of strangeness ... [a] constant estrangement' (ibid., 137-8). Yet when new friendships are forged, the exile experiences a new type of alienation. Having a new home brings new unhappiness, termed by Hannah Arendt (ibid., 36) the 'hopeless sadness of assimilation'. This is the Jewish experience. The South African poet Es'kia Mphahlele reports the characteristics of African exiles, where exile becomes 'a condition of the mind' (ibid., 122).

More often, though, exiles related to Bernstein their feelings of being 'strangers and outsiders', and 'terribly, terribly lonely'. For exiles, Bernstein comments, there were 'enormous problems', both social and psychological: loneliness experienced by their wives and children, who were cut off from the usual family support system. Jeremy Cronin commented to Bernstein on frequent breakdowns of marriages among exiles. Cronin's first wife died while he was in prison and his inability to have closure through 'the [usual] social rituals' plunged him into depression. Others mourned leaving sick parents. The child of exiled activists felt her parents 'loved the cause, not me'. Young children who had fled after the 1976 Soweto student uprising had no parent substitutes. Some tried to fit in elsewhere, but experienced new, intense psychological suffering when they found themselves rejected by the prevalently tolerant racism of Europe or Russia. Loneliness is the most salient feature of isolation.

Anxiety: Ovid's fears come and go (*Tr.* 2.147-8): fears of death (*Tr.* 1.2.51-2; 1.4.23; 3.3.83; *Ex P.* 2.1.65-6), but also of the awful, unnamed deed of which he stands accused, its memory a 'raw wound' (*Tr.* 3.6.28-9). Earlier, Cicero in exile wrote of himself as 'the effigy of a breathing corpse' (*Q.Fr.* 1.3.1). Most often Ovid experiences a vague anxiety of the mind (*anxietas animi*, *Ex P.* 1.4.7-8; 1.10.36), caused by the fact that he has suffered in the past: 'like animals that have suffered, I'm afraid' (*Ex P.* 2.7.5-16). An expert on prison literature cites the so-called 'DDD syndrome' (debility, dependence, dread) as an acknowledged by-product of the mental torture occasioned by solitary confinement. This is a typical characteristic of the depression caused by isolation, as described by Dennis Brutus: 'How deadly an enemy is fear!', calling for 'pity [for] the frightened ones' (*Letters to Martha*, 23-4). South African exiles very often continued to have an obsessive fear of a knock on the door that would herald police arrest. Exile exacerbates fear.

External threat: For Ovid, nature becomes imbued with intelligence. At *Tr.* 5.5.29-30 the pathetic fallacy reflects his own emotions: on his wife's birthday the smoke of his sacrificial fire tends toward Italy. Personalised, malevolent nature is also a reflection of his fears: the

219

barbarous, fierce Getans are like wild animals, representing all that is bad about his isolation from civilised life (*Tr.* 5.7.15-20); the area is a frozen waste with stunted trees (*Tr.* 2.12.16); a perpetual wasteland and frozen sea surround him, the Getans use poisoned arrows and he lives in constant danger (*Ex P.* 3.1.7-28; 4.7.5-16). A South African refugee, physically safe in England, commented to Bernstein 'Britain is cold in more ways than one' – nature and people shared the same unfriendly characteristics. For exiles, everything around them is a threat.

Physical illness: Ovid's mental suffering is reflected in physical symptoms. He is emaciated and haunted by insomnia (*Tr.* 3.8.27-8, 33-4). 'My spirit lies sick' (*Tr.* 5.2.7), and this leads to an all-encompassing lethargy (*Ex P.* 1.5.5-34) which becomes the norm: 'My talent is used to sadness' (*Ex P.* 3.4.45-50). Ovid's exilic poetry appears symptomatic of severe depression. His *Ibis* has been ascribed to the manic stage of bipolar disorder. The Zulu poet Mazizi Kunene, on a scholarship to England, and working as an ANC organiser, reports severe depression, being able to fall asleep only after drinking (*Rift*, 355). Many South African exiles did not long survive the 'alcoholic fog' with which they tried to dull their suffering, or degenerated into mental disorder. An exiled psychiatric social worker in Glasgow designates alcoholism as the 'disease that attacks us in exile' (ibid., 30). This is epitomised in: 'Brother now I play the bottle' by Kgotsitsile in 'Quest (memories of township tennis)' (from *When the clouds clear*, Fordsburg, 1990: 35).

Ovid's debilitating physical symptoms reflect his debilitated interior. Physical illness becomes a metaphor for mental and emotional suffering, as when he says 'a bottled-up sadness chokes me' (*Tr.* 5.1.63). The symptoms described in *Ex P.* 1.10 include lassitude, lack of appetite and general querulousness. Other poems describe a psychosomatic malady, listlessness and insomnia. He recognises these as interdependent ('for I have developed a sickly contagion of the mind in my body', *Tr.* 5.13.3), resulting in a pain in his side. On occasion he deplores the strength of his body in contrast to his weakness of spirit (5.2.5-6) but later admits that enforced idleness has weakened his whole body (*Ex P.* 1.5.5). *Ex P.*1.3 contains an extended medical metaphor. A sick man knows his condition better than his doctor. The letter from a friend has worked as medicine for Ovid's sick soul, but his wound nevertheless remains 'too raw to touch'. Memories of his lost fatherland serve to undo the good that his friend's comforting words had wrought.

Similarly, many South African exiles saw their longing in terms of illness. One reports of herself, 'I am having home disease' (*Rift*, 113). His wife says of the composer Todd Matshichika, 'His soul started to die' in London (ibid., 227). On his deathbed he imagined himself back at home. A medical doctor who left South Africa because 'there was more future outside' told Bernstein of 'two, three years of mourning, of deep mourning for South Africa ... and being depressed'. After many years of happy assimilation in Canada he still could assert: '[There] was a part of me that was cut off and I mourn that, I really miss that.' Similar intertwining of mental and physical suffering with Boer prisoners on Ceylon is documented by J.N. Brink (*Recollections of a Boer Prisoner-of-war at Ceylon,* Amsterdam, 1904: 181). He reports (201) the conviction among Boer prisoners that it was their 'duty to keep this wound open' – the knowledge that loved ones had died at home. Much later, the South African Ruth Weiss spoke to Bernstein about German-Jewish exiles that she met in America: 'they were so sick, I don't mean mentally sick, but they were so torn ...'. In isolation, mental and physical ills merge.

Depersonalisation and loss of a sense of self: Yet greater than physical symptoms lies the central malaise of exilic alienation, loss of a sense of self. It breaks Ovid's heart to think what he is now, in comparison with what he once was (*Tr.* 3.8.38; 3.11.25). We have seen Ovid declaring himself no longer human, but a 'thing', a work of art 'created' by his patron Sextus Pompeius (*Ex P.* 4.1.27-36). *Ex P.* 4.15.41-2 reflects total self-surrender as the poet proposes to go into willing slavery, the possession of his patron. In Roman law a slave was *res,* a thing, not a person (Gaius *Inst.* I.119-20). The degree of self-surrender here goes beyond any normal patron-client relationship. 'Self-alienation' amounts to depersonalisation, virtual 'metaphysical and literary voyeurism of the self', whereby the isolated author can almost dispassionately examine and report on his condition. A similar disruption of personality is expressed in the first poem of Dennis Brutus' anthology that, being forbidden to write poetry, he dubbed '*Letters*': 'My heart, my lost hope love, my dear/ Absence and hunger mushroom my hemispheres/ No therapy, analyses, deter my person's fission' (1968: 1).

A critic wrote of Breytenbach in similar vein: the poet experiences 'alienation from his ego ideal' and becomes the 'embodiment of the deconstructed self ... [he] resurrects himself textually as a shifting signifier ... a subject in process ... a chameleon' (B.F. Doherty, *Contemporary Literature* 36, 1995: 226-48). Objectification as a disintegrative coping mechanism is a central aspect of writerly alienation. The 'thing' is a creation of the disoriented self. Although Breytenbach should, in theory, have been reconciled by his adherence to Zen Buddhism to the loss of self, he still needs literature to make sense of this loss. We have seen that the hero of his *Memory of Snow and of Dust* (the fictionalisation of his prison experience) is called 'Mano', clearly a play on 'No Man'.

In his analysis of the Greek experience within Roman culture, Simon Goldhill explains the disorientation of a writer in exile as stemming from 'loss of a place from which to speak authoritatively'. This loss can include disruption of the basis of formerly-experienced authority, also the authority of accepted beliefs. Such loss of a sense of identity is a concomitant to all exile. Joseph Brodsky speaks of the pain of exile , 'but also the pain-dulling infiniteness, forgetfulness, detachment, indifference' (*Elsewhere*, 269 and 11). The South African Robyn Slovo (daughter of Joe Slovo and Ruth First) attests a feeling of 'very little identity of my own'. Hers was an extreme case, yet other children of exiles, some born abroad, speak of 'broken relationships', of not knowing their grandparents, loss of adolescence, deprivation (*Rift*, 450, 466), loss of a sense of identity (476, 490). Such is the result of dislocation.

Identification of author and works: Despair alienates Ovid from the one thing that works to sustain him, his poetry (*Ex P.* 4.13.41-2). Yet author and works become one – perhaps part of the process of objectification. Ovid's suffering is reflected in the sufferings of his manuscripts as 'the children of an exile', banished 'from birth' (*Tr.* 3.1.74). James Joyce, whose books were banned in his native Ireland, considered himself equally an exile, *persona non grata* (*Elsewhere*, 53). The South African Christopher Hope says, 'Banning a person's work is highly effective ... a person and his work simply disappear' (*Rift*, 348). For Jeremy Cronin (*Inside*, 76), his writings in prison became himself: 'Tonight is an envelope/ .../ the letter I, flesh made paper.' So closely are poets and their work associated.

Language as part of the self: Linguistic dislocation and changes in language usage are perhaps the most salient characteristics of the alienated, whether exile or prisoner. An expert on prison literature explains that physical pain destroys language, the first step being confession in words dictated by the warder. Conversely, an own voice in autobiographical narrative restores language. This would partly explain the almost consistent resilience shown by the various writers we are considering, who were used to expressing their thoughts in writing. With Ovid, the poet's sense of loss may in some measure be deduced from small, subtle changes of style. We have seen that where Latin poetry lends itself to intricate hyperbatic weaving of nouns and adjectives, in a passage that spells out his loneliness, the distinct lack of any sounding-board for his verse, and loss of control over language (*Tr.* 3.14.39-42), Ovid uses a more prosaic word-order, apparently an indication of extreme emotion. Here (43-52) he asserts that he is often at a loss for words, and that his Latin has a good admixture of Getic. This is not literally true: the poet's Latin remained both grammatically and metrically correct and consistently versatile. Ovid's claim to loss of language recurs at *Tr.* 5.7.51-8, where he also claims that his Latin is fraught with barbarisms (59-60). A claim to speechlessness indicates alienation.

Linguistic dislocation is well-attested by modern exiles quoted in *Elsewhere*. Heinrich Heine was fairly comfortable in Paris but refused to be naturalised, for he could not imagine himself as a 'German poet and naturalised Frenchman' (*Elsewhere*, 132). Breytenbach is content to be 'the only Afrikaans-writing Frenchman', yet 'being an exile means speaking all languages with an accent, even your mother tongue' (ibid., 180). Czelaw Milosz sensed his 'native tongue in a new manner' (40). This contrasts with Brodsky's assertion, 'like a dog hurled into outer space ... in the capsule of your own language ... an exiled writer is thrust or retreats into his mother tongue' (10). The exiled Marina Tsevetaeva, writing in Russian, found she had no readership (269). Their mother tongue represents an urgent need for exiles, so William H. Gass (224). It, however, continues to evolve at home, whereas the long-exiled author is limited to the version he knew before his departure; so Lion Feuchanger (256). Breytenbach on occasion asserts: 'each day I remember less of [my] language' (quoted in A.J. Coetzee, ed., *And Death White as Words*, London, 1978: 29). For Breytenbach, to carry one's language with one is '[to have] the bones of one's ancestors in a bag ... white with silence, they do not talk back' (*Rift*, 324). For Dennis Brutus linguistic displacement is a metaphor for physical and emotional displacement: '... the brackish waters of alienation/ lie like dust on heart and throat/ .../ unspeaking and meaningless/ as a barbarous foreign tongue' ('By the waters of Babylon', in *Seven South African Poets*, 18).

We have seen Ovid averring in *Ex P*. 4.13.17-22 that he has learned to write in Getic, celebrating the emperor who exiled him. He continues racked with uncertainties. At Tomis *he* is 'the barbarian', an object of misunderstanding and derision (*Tr.* 5.10.37). The issue of bilingualism in exile is fraught with ambiguities. The authors in *Elsewhere* recount divergent experiences of this phenomenon. Eva Hoffman learned academic English as an adult, but felt strange without true facility in neighbourly conversation, titling her autobiography *Lost in Translation* (*Elsewhere*, 229). Vasily Aksynow refers to a bilingual writer as 'an amphibian' (234-5). Stanislav Baranczak refers to the 'tongue-tied helplessness' of one who cannot translate jokes (244). Biruté Ciplijauskaité spoke of exilic literature as both 'hermetic and conservative', isolated from the culture of the writer's adoptive country (*Books Abroad* 50, 1976: 295-302). The transposed writer finds autobiography difficult and literary fiction a better medium (*Elsewhere*, 247-8). He feels gagged at home and tongue-tied abroad; writing in 'international English' prevents nuancing; translating an original work runs the danger of 'slipping and falling stylistically' (ibid., 250). The Czech author Jan Novak writes of 'linguistic schizophrenia' (261-5). Linguistic alienation is epitomised by Iain Crichton Smith in his collection of poems, *The Exiles* (London, 1984: 10): 'There is no sorrow ... worse than this sorrow/ the dumb grief of the exile .../ until he suddenly feels the "foreign clothes" are his.' Yet, elsewhere Smith complains: 'A world with a different language is a world/ we find our way about with a stick/ half deaf, half blind ...' (ibid., 46). Loss of ease in communication is central to exile.

Self-hatred: Together with speechlessness and loss of a sense of self come self-hatred and hatred of all the writer had formerly held dear. In his long 'speech for the defence' Ovid claims that he himself was his own greatest enemy (*Tr.* 2.82) and that he regrets his devotion to poetry (316). This sentiment frequently recurs, as in *Tr.* 4.10.63-4, where he reports having burned some of his works before his departure, enraged by the art that had brought on his downfall; yet 'I curse my songs but cannot do without them' (5.7.31-4). The solidarity of influence can work in two directions: like Ovid's 'dying Vergil burning his poems', D.H. Lawrence in his semi-autobiographical *Kangaroo* has his *alter-ego* Somers burn all his manuscripts before leaving Cornwall.

Self-hatred takes many forms. Thomas Mann, exiled from Germany during the Second World War, found that he both loved and hated his country, explaining that it is '[T]errible when one's own country is the enemy place' (*Elsewhere*, 100-4). Hannah Arendt speaks of the self-revulsion of Jews with a 'mania for refusing to keep our identity' (118). The isolation experienced by black South Africans in a country like Sweden with its tolerant racism led to considerable loss of self-esteem in many. When 'the body is sent away', the soul retreats into the 'cell of the self'; so William H. Gass (225). This leads to hatred of the self.

Tears: Naturally an exile's tears flow frequently. Ovid admits that there is a 'certain pleasure in crying' (*Tr.* 4.3.37). In many poems he reports weeping when remembering what he has lost, e.g. *Tr.* 1.3.1-4 (recalling the night of his departure), 5.4.3 (the poem itself 'reports' watching its weeping creator), *Ex P.* 1.2.27-30 (he is a Niobe, endlessly weeping). A South African exile Thoko Mafaje explains: 'You have to cry it out. You have a right to cry' (*Rift*, 432). Nevertheless, surprisingly few speakers in this 500-page volume of interviews confess to tears. Perhaps this relates to different social expectations in the Rome of two thousand years ago, as opposed to modern societal norms. The poet Kgotsitsile expresses this reticence: 'Baby baby baby/ there is no point in crying/ just because I'm not at home' ('Red song' in *When the Clouds...*, 35), and again: '... I know the anguish of loneliness/ is a dangerous luxury' ('Ask for the keys', ibid., 37). Modern exiles dared not cry.

Exile as death: In all cultures exile is frequently equated with death. We have seen Ovid feeling himself already dead (*Ex P.* 1.9.55-6). He reports thoughts of suicide, a 'love for death' (*amor necis*, *Tr.* 3.8.39) and 'knocking on death's door, that never would open for him' (3.2.23-4). An exiled South African mother who had no contact with her children explained why suicide is so attractive: 'This is how it is when you are dead – because you don't know' (*Rift*, 436). Breytenbach describes prison life as '[being] buried ... You are buried to what you know as normal life outside' (*True Confessions*, 108). We have noted that the title of his prison-work, *Mouroir*, punningly combines the French for 'mirror' and 'to die'. Kgotsitsile (*Clouds*, 39) addresses his dead sister: 'It is not you/ but us/ shrouded in gloom'. It was said of a South African exile dying abroad, 'His wife has been a widow for many years now' (*Rift*, 193). The bodies of such exiles were not allowed to be repatriated, eliciting the bitter comment from one such serial widow: 'His body was exiled' (419).

Death can offer escape, but only if the exile can die at home. A Boer prisoner of war on Ceylon reported his constant longing for South Africa: 'There he wants to live, there to die, and there to be buried!' (*Recollections of a Boer Prisoner-of-war*, 55). Betty Du Toit, a trade union activist who fled South Africa in the 1960s, longed to return, if only 'to die at home' (*Rift*, 61). Death-wishes signal the lowest point of exilic despair.

Defiance: With Ovid, death-wishes and morbid depression on occasion give way to an almost childish petulance. The *Leitmotiv* of the whole of *Tr.* 3.3 is a defiant 'They'll be sorry!'. Missives to his wife (3.3.25-6) and friends (5.13) often degenerate into bitter reproach. Occasionally Ovid admits to uncertainty about how he wants his wife to feel – happy, even without him, or sad, as he is (4.3.11-34). Defiance masquerades as continued patriotism, even in a political *persona non grata*. Exaggerated 'fear' of the displeasure of his imperial opponent over such patriotism amounts to a taunt (*Ex P.* 2.1.11-12). Edward Said, the incumbent of a professorial chair at Columbia University, cannot be regarded as 'dispossessed', but he acknowledges the exile's 'right to refuse to belong' in his new milieu, and his 'right to wilfulness, exaggeration and overstatement' (*Elsewhere*, 145). This theme is dominant in Gray's poem, quoted above, which has placed Ovid in the Eastern Cape of the twentieth century: 'Power is awesome, but what those who have none/ admire is the power that is wary of them, even their last independence/ ... Because I am relegated I rail against them although they look after me .../ ... O Caesar, see how reduced I am .../ ... I cast them off as you do me and I vilify/ these dirty-nailed fellows whom to my advantage I betray./ Great Caesar's all, from whom we are all banished' (*Gabriel*, 80). Such defiance is another facet of the love-hate relationship between persecuted and persecutor.

Hope and despair: In his almost total isolation the Roman Ovid lived doggedly on. Hope it was, he says, that kept him alive (*Ex P.* 1.6.35-41) but against this there always was the counterpoint of despair: the realisation that the better circumstances which he envisioned were forever lost (3.7.19-24). Breytenbach and various imprisoned South African journalists all reported on the fluctuations of hope and despair they experienced. C.H. Benbow (*Boer Prisoners of War in Bermuda*, Bermuda, 1982[2]: 10) says of these prisoners: 'Hope ... keeps body and soul together.' Benbow quotes an American newspaperman's comment that for these Boers, suffering of the mind was more intense than physical suffering (ibid., 19). This is the central malady of exile.

6.2.7. Poetic resistance and resilience

These, then, are the symptoms of Ovid's exilic alienation that we have compared with the emotions of modern exiles. We may safely conclude that they are universal and not unique to the Roman era, nor to this particular Roman author. The question remains: what, in any era, makes the protagonist's awareness of alienation at all bearable?

For a poet, the key lies in his literary pursuits; in the case of Breytenbach, these pursuits are considered by a critic as both keeping him alive and preparing him for death, as well as helping him to resist. These three factors are discernible in Ovid's relationship with Augustus as reflected in his self-revealing poetry. Ovid's resilience stems from his mental activity. As we have seen, some poems clearly reflect attempts at entertaining himself: so, for example, his joking designation of a gift of images of his imperial oppressors as 'present gods' (*Ex P.* 2.8), reducing a Euripidean drama to a fifty-four-line vignette (3.2.43-97) or a fantastic description of the apparition of *Amor*, who totally vindicates his 'former teacher' (3.3). Ovid's imagination soars with the creative impulse that fuels his poetry; letter-poems keep him occupied and bind him to family and friends. Assertions of mental travel and seeing with the 'mind's eye' increase in frequency over time. In *Ex P.* 4.9.41-4 Ovid explicitly states 'the mind alone is not an exile'. The South African I Chanoora says much the same, 'Inward is the only asylum/ after the womb' (*Seven South African Poets*, 40).

Poetry sometimes fails. Kgotsitsile asks in his 'Childhood of dreams': 'What happens when feeling/ moves down so deep/ even the poet lacks the word ...?' C.J. Driver comments: 'All this is guess work .../ It will not break one bone of exile' (*Seven South African Poets*, 61). Yet poetry works as resistance, as in Benbow's story of the Dutch Reformed minister on Bermuda who regularly memorised confiscated letters (written in Dutch) and rhythmically recited these, interspersed with Dutch Psalms, to Boer prisoners of war instead of delivering sermons. Cronin (*Inside*, 73) was able to write lyrical love songs to his wife in isolation: 'I found ... in solitude solidarity'. His memory was an inner retreat (87): 'part of me still deeply alive .../.../.../ I still go there, I mean/ A small room/ Behind my eyebrows' and (89) '... pools ... where the old pronoun/ I, the swimmer behind eyelids/ Isiqiqumadeva dreams ....' Memory can be a powerful antidote to loneliness. Crichton Smith (*Exiles*, 37) writes of a snowy scene: 'All is transmuted/ into the tracery of memory.' Goldhill, cited above, speaks of a 'slide between exile as a socio-political exclusion and exile as longing for a lost and idealised intellectual topography', with the implication that memory is transmuted into idealisation. Cuza Male remembers 'fleeing from nothingness', from her homeland, where 'only customs officials believe in the efficacy of poetry', and yet 'I live from my nostalgia' (*Elsewhere*, 252-4). Prisoners of war on Ceylon kept up their national customs, thereby experiencing the same phenomenon: 'The body may have been made prisoner, but the spirit is yet free!' (*Recollections of a Boer*, 128).

Bernstein in her Introduction to *The Rift* notes that South African exiles' memories were selective: they could remember 'only what is tolerable'. Abdullah Ibrahim captures the essence of such memory: 'The southern spring winds/ myself in two/ one wintered in cold steel ... the other/ a dimming summer/ camera'ed in youth' (*Seven South African Poets*, 8). Imaginative transcendence is also reflected in Ben J. Langa's 'struggle'-poem, 'For my brothers (Mandla and Bheki) in exile': 'In all our pain and agony we rejoice,/ For the tensile steel strength of our souls/ Transcends border and boundaries./ However far apart our bodies may be/ Our souls are locked together in perpetual embrace' (in A. Brink & J.M. Coetzee, eds, *A Land Apart: a South African reader*, London, 1986: 74). In similar vein Kgotsitsile (*Clouds*, 52) asserts '... boundaries and oceans merely separate people bodily'. Ovid would have concurred. His salvation was his imaginative life and the poetry that kept pouring out of him. It kept him occupied, and it alleviated his pain. Although banned from the public libraries in Rome, it was apparently privately circulated, serving as a subtle tool of polemic against the emperor. Crichton Smith asserts: 'Without light poetry would rise in the dark' (*Exiles*, 38). The isolated authors that we have considered would find poetry welling up unsought, expressing in stylised form the same feelings of desperation and alienation that all exiles experience everywhere, but cannot always express. Ngugi wa Thiong'o says of his prison writings (*Detained*, 98): 'I had to find ways and means of keeping my sanity.' In personal poetry and imaginative memory a poet can transcend the isolation of imprisonment or exile.

6.2.8. Conclusion

In exile the personal and the political are inextricably intertwined. The Roman Ovid was expressing the same longings that today are felt by all those dispossessed by the machinations of the politically powerful. In interviews by the critics Goddard and Wessels, published by the National English Literature Museum (Grahamstown, 1992: 70) Dennis Brutus speaks of writing 'at two levels, personal, and the larger or political', but Kgotsitsile (*Clouds*, 81) calls for the 'private voice' to take over, to liberate literature from new political pressures and the call to produce 'political tracts' (ibid., 88).

Ovid's solution to his physical travails was recourse to mental travel. In this, too, he was pre-empting the ultimate resource of an ANC psychiatrist who told Hilda Bernstein of the therapy he applied to those victims of torture who had fled South Africa and were then walking around the refugee camp at Mazimba in Tanzania 'like zombies' – to him a sign that in their minds they wanted to go back 'to take revenge'. He would put them into a 'semi-hypnotic state' and induce them to visualise their torture, but also to visualise finding a weapon with which to fight back, and hence to experience a cleansing catharsis. This visualisation made them receptive of therapeutic healing. Almost two millennia earlier, Ovid, too, had found a weapon with which to hit back: his poetry, recording in his own emotional outpourings the universals of exilic suffering experienced by all outcasts everywhere. That timeless connection seals the significance of his poetry. The feelings of alienation that Ovid voiced are the feelings of the isolated and dispossessed in all eras.

Excursus

Ovidian studies today

This excursus comprises a *satura* of diverse Ovidian topics that have also engaged my critical interest in the last two decades, starting with the scholarly interest elicited since the late nineteenth century by the meagre collection of ascertainable facts of Ovid's exile, as well as other material of historical interest. Its larger part reworks recent reviews written for critical journals, some longer than others, ending with some new material on important recent publications. The various parts together hopefully convey some idea of the diversity of modern Ovidian scholarship, without pretending to be exhaustive.

1. Historicist interest

1.1. 'The fiction of Ovid's exile'

From internal evidence, that is, omission of all reference to occurrences after AD 17, it is assumed that Ovid died in about 17 and was buried at Tomis. Tacitus' *Annals* do not mention Ovid's death. Nor does Seneca the Elder, who quotes him frequently, and whose son (the Gallio of Acts 18) was adopted by one of Ovid's correspondents, Junius Gallio.

Sources are equally silent on Ovid's relegation, leading to much controversy, even a view of the exile as literary fiction: 'Ovid was never exiled, or, if he was, not to Tomis.' This theory, first mooted by J.J. Hartmann in 1913, was taken up or refuted in turn by various scholars. Some forty years later, a Dutch Classicist, Otger Janssen, based his argument that the exilic works were poetic fiction on three observations: first, Augustus' condemnation of the *Ars Amatoria* was too tenuous, and too belated, to have elicited such heavy punishment; second, the vagueness of Ovid's much-vaunted error; and finally, the impossibility of fixing upon a single political explanation that would fit. Evidence in the poems themselves is by turns vague, erroneous, conventional, hyperbolic or jocular. Janssen argued that, as much of the poet's whole oeuvre is fictitious, this part may well be too, concluding that 'the poet invented exile as an excuse for failing literary powers'. Here Janssen's argument falls down, for he accepts as its basis one of Ovid's postulated 'fictions': the 'mediocrity' of his exilic works. A better argument would have been that the author had associated himself to such a degree with his works that, when his *Ars* was banished from public libraries, the poet pretended that he, too, was sent into exile.

A. Fitton Brown (*Liverpool Classical Monthly* 10.2, 1985: 19-22) in the face of severe criticism revived the idea of 'Ovid's exilic fiction', which was subsequently taken up by A. Schmidt and H. Hofmann of Groningen. This beguiling theory has some merit, but in the end there is too much against it, even if association of poet and works is so much part of Ovid's autobiographical stance. This present volume has attempted to show that Ovid's poetic skill remained as brilliant as it ever was, turning the dross of his harsh circumstances into poetic gold. The theory may be dismissed. Next we turn to other historicist approaches to Ovid's exilic works.

1.2. The search for Ovid's tomb

The possibility of finding Ovid's tomb has in the past offered much in the way of romantic archaeological excitement. A late source, St Jerome (Euseb. *Chron.*, ed. Schoene, p. 147), refers to Ovid's 'death and burial at Tomis' during the year AD 17, possibly deriving his information from Suetonius' lost work on the Roman poets, via Eusebius. The problem was enlarged by uncertainty as to the whereabouts of ancient Tomis. Although placed fairly precisely by Strabo, Pomponius Mela and Pliny the Elder, Tomis had been lost in vague mediaeval geography. Constanza, a Romanian city on a small peninsula jutting into the Black Sea, was first suggested by A. de la Motraye at the beginning of the eighteenth century, and finally identified by Bruto Arnaute in 1884. Its hinterland is the Dobroudja, a flat plain bounded on the west and north by the coils of the Danube, and on the south-east by the Black Sea itself. The Italian city of Sulmona, Ovid's birthplace, and this town have close ties, even displaying similar statues of Ovid (dating from 1887).

Both Romanians and Italians, particularly Sulmonians, have searched in vain for Ovid's tomb. Their searches, sometimes with recourse to dubious mediaeval authors, have intrigued scholars and the general public alike. An exciting 'discovery' was reported from Bucharest in the British *Daily Telegraph*, 29 July 1931: 'the finding of the poet's skull' by a certain Professor Braetescu. The sarcophagus involved was soon shown to be Hellenistic and the excitement died down. 'Professor Braetescu' did not publish his findings. Similarly, a Roman 'Ovidian tomb' later proved to be the third-century tomb of a Q. Nasonius Ambrosius and his wife Nasonia Urbica.

Ovid's epitaph for himself, *Tr.* 3.3.73-6, is as interesting for what it leaves out as for what it pretends to offer posterity. With no reference at all to the *Metamorphoses*, or any of Ovid's other apparent attempts at conformity to the Augustan ideal, it reaffirms the exile's paramount position as the composer of love-poetry. Eastern-European scholarly interest in epigraphy interpreted the existence of second- and third-century sepulchral inscriptions containing echoes of the first words of verse 73 (*hic ego qui iaceo ...*) as 'proof' that the grave 'must have been' in lower Moesia, where this epitaph 'must have been inscribed on his tomb', consequently serving as 'inspiration for similar epitaphs'. More sober scholarship has refuted this assumption. Ovid's words are clearly a poetic rendering, adapted to his purposes, of well-known epitaphic formulae often used elsewhere.

Legends about the tomb were not confined to Moesia. Ovid's popularity gave rise to many conflicting legends about possible places of burial, ranging over the far north (Polesia in Poland), to the north-east (Kiev or the mouth of the Dnestr), east (Georgia) and south (Varna in Bulgaria) or elsewhere on the Black Sea coast. The Russian author Pushkin associated himself strongly with Ovid when he was himself exiled to the Crimean Peninsula, to the north-east of Constanza. Mediaeval legends had a 'talking tomb of St Naso' that interrogated passers-by on the 'best and worst' verses ever written by the poet. Another story, based on an early tradition of a tomb in the area, asserted that Ovid travelled as far as Transylvania (Pannonia) in order to meet 'kindred souls'. An eighteenth-century drama by one Judzo Szemlly places 'Ovid' at Losonc, where he has a humorous 'conversation' with a Getan in nonsensical Latin rhyming couplets.

Ovid's bimillennium in 1958 sparked renewed interest in his personal life. For some Romanians, Ovid was the 'first national Romanian poet', particularly the 'first national to oppose a totalitarian regime'. Romanians who fled the country under Communist rule saw in Ovid's longing for Rome a parallel to their nostalgia for the Pontic regions. Some of these exiles found refuge in Italy. The editor of the Rome-based Romanian Classical journal, *Acta Philologica*, in 1958 wistfully explained: *exsules laudes maiorum atque virtutes illorum excolunt, apud quos studium libertatis maxime viguerit. Idem humanitatem unam atque unicam, quae nullo modo neque opprimi ... possit, voluit confirmare* ('The exiles cherish praise of their predecessors and their virtues, (predecessors) in whose works a thirst for liberty waxed most strongly. That same thirst for liberty wanted to strengthen this singular and unique humanity which in no way could be suppressed'). Clearly this is reaction against the Soviet oppression of the time.

N.I. Herescu, editor of the bimillenniary Festschrift, *Ovidiana* (Paris, 1958), soberly described the poet's 'epitaph' in *Tr.* 3.3 as a 'protest against arbitrary condemnation', the 'affirmation of Ovid's liberty as an artist'. Other past manifestations of Romanian national fervour should be read with greater caution, such as the contribution in the same volume of E. Lozovan (396-403) on the so-called 'bilingualism' of Ovid, taking as literal Ovid's various statements about the 'decline of his Latin' and his writing in Getic. This assertion is open to doubt, given the Greek antecedents of Tomis and the geographical situation of the Getic tribes, farther north.

Ovid's exilic works have long been used as source for proto-Romanian anthropological studies. Romanian scholars tended to judge the exilic oeuvre with nationalistic standards, finding signs of ultimate rapport between the poet and their own ancestors. Ovid's most stringent criticism of the people and the place was interpreted as 'slight exaggeration'. G. Salceanu (*Pontica* 4, 1971: 221-33) saw Ovid's words as proof of 'our' precedence in the area in prehistoric times: that is, of either members of the Germanic group as opposed to Slavs, or, more likely, Thracians as opposed to Greeks or Romans. The Proto-Romanians were in fact Thracians, that is, Indo-Europeans from the north-east who settled in the area in the Middle Bronze Age.

A polemic spread over nineteen years offers an amusing illustration of Romanian nationalist fervour. Scarlat Lambrino (*Ovidiana*, 1958: 379-90) deduced from Ovid's information on Getic customs (use of long bows, an assembly to listen to the 'Getic poem' on Augustus' apotheosis at *Ex P.* 4.13.23-32 and other references to Getae) that Tomis was a 'double community', epitomising mutual toleration of institutions and costume. The natives had converted to a new civilisation, showing a fusion of two peoples, Getae within Hellenistic walls. E. Lozovan supported this view (cited above and later repeated elsewhere). D.M. Pippidi at length replied to them with a thorough refutation based on archaeological observations, ridiculing the idea that the Tomitan agora was used for 'judiciary duels' (*Athenaeum* 55, 1977: 250-6). Pippidi conceded that there may have been a 'Getic ghetto', but nothing more. A later monograph by A.V. Podossinov (*Ovids Dichtung als Quelle für die Geschichte des Schwartzmeergebiets*, Konstanz, 1987) thoroughly established the poetic, hence fictional, nature of Ovid's depiction of ancient Romania, and decried all use of the exilic works as a source of literal information, emphasising the essentially literary nature of Ovid's depiction of the area and its inhabitants.

1.3. Theories about Ovid's relegation

Another area for historicist research has been the insoluble mystery of the reasons for Ovid's relegation. This was, as indicated in the Introduction, thoroughly covered by Thibault in his *The Mystery of Ovid's Exile*, the standard work on the topic. In 1992 Raoul Verdière provided an update (*Le secret du voltigeur d'amour ou le mystère de la relégation d'Ovide*, Brussels). Critics' interpretation of the two reasons Ovid gives for his banishment, the *carmen* and *error* of *Tr.* 2.207, are widely divergent, as Verdière amply shows. His chronological approach gives readers an opportunity to view fashions in interpretation of the poet after Thibault over a period of nearly thirty years.

Verdière discusses twenty-four authors' theories on the reasons for Ovid's exile. Each theory is re-argued, with copious quotations from Ovid, and from the author in question, and then refuted, with reference, too, to other critics' reaction to the thesis propounded. Thibault's work is sixth on the chronological list, preceded by five papers which, Verdière explains, the master himself had apparently been unable to obtain: authors such as one 'Baligan' had published in an obscure and almost unobtainable journal. Baligan's theory was that Julia Minor had been 'Corinna', Ovid's heroine of the *Amores*.

The usual thrust of theories is rehearsed, from the idea that Ovid had discovered some crime 'committed by another' (that is, that he had become involved in a political plot spearheaded by Julia the Younger, her lover Silanus and her brother Agrippa Postumus), to Carcopino's view of Ovid as a Neo-Pythagorean martyr. L. Herrmann turns Ovid into a 'second Clodius,' intruding on the Roman Bona Dea festivities while doing field-work for the *Fasti*, and A.W. Holleman portrays Ovid as proto-feminist champion of the woman's point of view and opponent of Augustus' arrogation of deity.

Verdière's own theory is based on the correlations '*Corinna* = *ingenium* = *poena* = *fuga*' (*sic*). He finds Ovid's Corinna in 'one of Augustus' many mistresses', to wit, Terentia, wife of Maecenas (whose indubitable involvement with Augustus actually dates to some thirty years before the poet's banishment). The abortion Ovid deplores in the *Amores* would then have been of a child of Augustus', which, had it been allowed to live, 'could have saved the dynasty'.

Sometimes Verdière's *ira et studium* obtrudes. He is honest enough to quote Syme (*History in Ovid*, Oxford, 1978) on Thibault's (and others') earlier attempts at unravelling the 'mystery' as 'a misdirection of the labour force', but he waxes indignant about both Syme's acerbic tone and the essentials of his criticism (90-3). Clearly, the then (1992) recently defunct doyen of British ancient historical research did not enjoy unalloyed Belgo-Gallic favour.

A final chapter, entitled 'La faute secrète,' gives the author's considered opinion of the various and conflicting theories surveyed, ending with another allusion to 'Corinna's abortion', further candidly exploring 'the possibility that Ovid lied' (133-5). Even this concession is confusing poetic truth with literal fact. Ovid is always the poet of 'imagined reality'. Whether he was exiled or not, and why, is as immaterial to his poetic purpose as it should be to our purpose as readers of his poetry. What Ovid's poetry of exile conveys, the anguish of loss and alienation felt by all exiles everywhere and in every era, is even more relevant in the twenty-first century, with its final solutions, ethnic cleansings, total onslaughts and aeronautical mobility, than ever it was in an era of ships and swords and the emperor's displeasure.

Yet Verdière makes it possible for readers to come to an own conclusion. I largely agree with Peter Green (cited in my Introduction): no other explanation than a political one can make sense of Ovid's exile. Verdière ends by quoting Thibault: 'The many ... attempts to solve this mystery have ... clarified the terms of the problem ...' [potentially leading to] 'an hypothesis which will be cogent ...'. Undoubtedly the terms of the problem have become clearer, but I maintain that no ultimate solution is attainable – or, for that matter, necessary. To read Ovid's poetry solely for the sake of discovering the reasons for his relegation is to read beautiful poetry for the wrong purpose.

1.4. Ovid's Rome

Far more satisfactory than historicist speculation on an insoluble puzzle is A.J. Boyle's recourse to archaeology that places Ovidian texts within their Roman contexts (*Ovid and the Monuments: a poet's Rome*, Bendigo, 2003), with introduction and commentary. Boyle has collated all passages in which Ovid refers to either Rome or its monuments. English translations face each excerpt, Loeb-style. The texts are based on well-known predecessors' work, but with Boyle's own suggestions and emendations. The translations are either new and by the author, or adapted slightly from the Penguin translation of the *Fasti* that he published together with R.D. Woodward (Harmondsworth, 2000). Of interest for our present discussion are Ovid's references to Rome in the exilic poems.

Such a catalogue could perhaps run the danger of being no more than a mechanical compilation of place names occurring in a variety of Ovidian texts, but in Boyle's able hands it is much more than that. It is useful as valuable reference text, or as capable review of recent theories on the relationship of Ovid with Augustus, or even as handy guidebook to the splendours of ancient Rome for eager travellers. It also works as a bedside book, a fascinating source for random dipping at idle moments. The book has three parts: a long introduction on 'Ovid and Rome'; texts and translation of passages arranged by topographical situation; and a commentary combining detailed historical information with concise literary criticism on each passage. A neat cross-referencing system points us either forward to a passage that will recur under the name of another topographical feature, or back, to one already quoted.

No work on Ovid's Rome can escape also being a work on the Rome of Augustus. Boyle's fifty-page introductory essay, liberally illustrated with quotations, gives a good overview of the relationship between the two men, the Augustan building programme, the reasons for Ovid's banishment (Boyle's preference is for a political explanation relating to factions within the imperial family), Ovid's rewriting of imperial Rome into a romantic setting for the dalliance which his *praeceptor amorum* encouraged young Romans to enjoy, and, finally, what Boyle calls the 'ideology of place': the locus of the clash between emperor and poet. Boyle makes the point that 'topography is a generator of meaning' (36). The meaning that Ovid ascribed to the monuments of Rome was a far cry from the meaning with which Augustus hoped to imbue his renovated city. The author on occasion takes issue with the opinions of other established critics such as Kennedy and Galinsky on the vexed question of Ovid's active 'anti-Augustanism' (a view that he convincingly supports against their opposition of the concept).

Boyle's erudition is both deep and wide-ranging. Historical, cultural and architectural information provided on each monument is backed by appropriate references to historical and/or contemporary sources. A comfortable, readable style disguises the depth of scholarship that the book represents. Perspicacious comments offer the author's own insights on often-neglected aspects. So Boyle points out that Augustus' vaunted building programme was 'in a sense a form of architectural "catch-up" with the rest of Italy', where axial layout and monumental temple and bath buildings had long since been the norm (42). Boyle coins the term 'palimpsestic city' (48) for the phenomenon of architectural and cultural layering that has obtained in Rome since the time of Augustus to the present.

Boyle's monumental work is a useful addition to any Classical library and a *sine qua non* for Ovidian scholars. I have seldom enjoyed a reference work more.

1.5. Socio-political criticism: a comparative reading

It is almost impossible, rich as Ovid's exilic poetry is, to read it in isolation. Hence the almost inevitable conjunction by scholars of Ovid with other ancient exiles. It is generally accepted that Cicero created the Latin genre of 'laments from exile' (partly derived from Greek precedents), and that Ovid gave this genre its poetic form. Hence works that cover both authors must be included in discussion of modern trends in Ovidian criticism. The following comparison of the two authors, is, however, more socio-political than literary.

Sandra Citroni Marchetti in her *Amicizia e Potere nelle Lettere di Cicerone en nelle Elegie Ovidiane dall'Esilio* (Firenze, 2000), joins her colleagues at the University of Firenze (Degl'Innocenti Pierini, Narducci) in her pursuit of the ramifications of Roman exile as a political tool. She sets out, as the title indicates, to discuss the relationship between friendship and power in Roman politics, as reflected in Cicero's correspondence and Ovid's exilic elegies. She offers some interesting new insights on the topic, suggesting intriguing lines of relationship.

After an Introduction giving a brief survey of its argument, the book is divided into four main 'Parts', with subdivisions. The two chapters of Part I are devoted to Cicero, describing, first, the centrality of the concept of consensus, that is, unity of *voluntas* in the relationship between friends, whether personal or political, and second, the necessity for a stable equilibrium in the exercise of interpersonal exchange. There can be, for English-speaking readers, a problem in understanding parts of the author's argument. The Italian *volunta* (more so than its Latin equivalent *voluntas*) works as the equivalent of a whole range of English terms, from 'need', 'want' or 'will', to 'wish', 'desire', 'urge', but also 'obligation', or even 'having to' do something. The shifting nature of this useful word renders the author's premise very broad, but it serves to indicate how much her interpretation of power relationships between different sets of friends could vary and still fit into her basic argument.

The first chapter stresses the importance of commonality of consent ('agreement of will'), with detailed recourse to Cicero's own thoughts on the matter. Friendship ends when consensus is abandoned. Where 'commonality of will', good feelings from one friend toward another, is lacking, conciliation involves the restoration of such feelings and the reinstitution of an equilibrium of power between two equally powerful protagonists. For Cicero, exile meant a crisis in the state of his *amicitia* with others. Restoration of the *bona voluntas* toward him of the powerful Pompey was all-important for bridging that crisis. The argument of Chapter II, on the restoration of equilibrium in power relations, is illustrated among others by discussion of Cicero's relationships with his freedman Tyro. This part ends with an analysis of Cicero's attempts to exploit the dynamics of political friendship in order to reach a common goal, even if that goal finally could be no more than achieving a *beata mors* ('blessed death', 98).

The second and third parts each carry a preamble (*'premessa'*), setting out its theoretical point of departure. The first chapter of Part II compares in detail the exilic writings of Ovid and Cicero with those of Theognis (the sixth-century Athenian aristocrat who suffered exile in a vaguely similar political situation). The argument next relates to essential changes in the kind of equilibrium of power between the late republic and early principate, observable in the altered nature of society (as reflected in the letters of the Younger Pliny, as compared with Cicero's letters). 'Good will' was still the *Leitmotiv*, but now between the emperor as dispenser, and his subjects as recipients, no longer between members of the ruling aristocracy in an equal distribution of power. *Voluntas* becomes the will of the emperor, to which his friends must bend theirs.

Citroni Marchetti's third Part at last concentrates on Ovid, particularly on precedents for Ovid's appeals for mediation by his friends between himself and the emperor Augustus. Her *'premessa'* discusses the practice of intermediation as essential to Roman life, also datable from earlier times (with Euripides' *Herakles* as example). The author carefully spells out differences between Cicero and Ovid. With Ovid, a degree of *metus* (fear) colours his requests for the intervention of friends. She traces Greek tragic precedents for Ovid's appeals for support (first, Ovid as a 'Prometheus', next, 'tragedy and justice'), then returns to Cicero's relationship with other exiled anti-Caesarians, with emphasis on his timidity as an intellectual.

The fourth and last Part deals at last solely with Ovid, concentrating on the names (either suppressed or revealed) of his friends, the ability of poetry to impart an immortal name, Ovid's fear of the harm that revelation of a friend's name could entail, and the looming presence of Augustus as *'Il terzo personaggio'* in all that Ovid wrote. In this the work may be compared with Boyle's Introduction, discussed above. Citroni Marchetti's work is both solid and wide-ranging.

We next turn to reception of various kinds.

2. Literary studies

2.1. Reception of Ovid's Metamorphoses

In nova fert animus mutatas dicere formas
corpora: di, coeptis (nam vos mutastis et illa)
adspirate meis primaque ab origine mundi
ad mea perpetuum deducite tempora carmen. (*Met.* 1.1-4)

I have a mind to say how bodies were changed into new shapes: gods (for you yourselves changed them), breathe your blessing upon the works that I have begun, and stretch out my song from the earliest beginning of the world until my own times.

Changing perceptions of the exilic works have found their counterpart in changes to the reception also of Ovid's other works. Hence I start with a brief overview of a fairly recent collection of essays on the *Metamorphoses*, edited by Philip Hardie, Alessandro Barchiesi and Stephen Hinds, *Ovidian Transformations* (Cambridge, 1999). Eighteen essays cover a broad range of issues, of which reception forms the *Leitmotiv*. The title of the book is an obvious pun on both its topic and its

theme, that is on the *Metamorphoses* itself, and on its intertextual rela-
tionships with other works, both backward-looking (where did Ovid get
his material and what did he do with it?) and forward (what was its influ-
ence on subsequent literature?). That this material already influenced
Ovid's own exilic work was the topic of my Chapter 5.

The editors have mustered a broad panoply of scholars. Hinds is
himself an influential critic of Ovid's exilic poetry and of intertextuality
in Ovidian context. His chapter, 'After exile: time and teleology from
Metamorphoses to *Ibis*' (48-67), takes up themes from earlier papers. He
argues that the concept of 'time' is loaded in the exilic poetry, and that it
is coloured by the poet's own reception (and editorial revision during
exile) of both those earlier works that had 'time' as a major ordering prin-
ciple: diachronic in the *Metamorphoses*, synchronic in the *Fasti*.
Similarly, in '*Mea tempora*: patterning of time in the *Metamorphoses*' (13-
30), Denis Feeney speaks of a 'dialogue of time and beginnings between
the *Metamorphoses* and the *Fasti*' (26). Both authors stress the signifi-
cance of Ovid's rewriting of the *mea tempora* of his famous prologue as
(the Augustan) *tua tempora* in *Tr.* 2.560.

These two critics' papers, when read in succession, set up an inter-
esting dialogue. Feeney emerges as the greater optimist, arguing that in
the *Metamorphoses* Ovid has succeeded in defeating the Augustan time-
frame, that Ovid's use of the word *perennis* in *Met.* 15.875 shows his
continued awareness of his 'chronological superiority to the Caesars –
his time is always now' (27). For Hinds, Ovid has accepted defeat at the
hands of Augustus. Time as an ordering principle of life stopped for Ovid
with his relegation; secondary meanings of *tempora* as 'tempests' and as
'a (clouded) brow' took over. Hence the *Ibis*, datable to his fourth year of
exile (when he was 54) still obsessively portrays the exile as a fifty-year-
old, pinning him to the age at which the blow fell, and time stopped for
him.

Another dialogue may be traced between the optimistic view of certain
mythical figures in the *Metamorphoses* as metaphors for the poet's
success in defeating the erosions of time or power play, and a negative
view of the final message that Ovid conveys through these same figures.
Elena Theodorakopolous opens her paper ('Closure and Transformation
in Ovid's *Metamorphoses*', 142-61) with the statement that 'brutal
attacks on the human body in the *Metamorphoses* relate to Ovid's view of
writing poetry and the creative and political anxieties involved' (142). For
her, the dismemberment of the poet Orpheus, and the unintelligible
murmuring of his tongue as his disembodied head floats down the
Hebrus (*Met.* 11.52-3) reflect the dissipation of Orpheus' poetic power
and its ultimate silence. Against this, Joseph Farrell ('The Ovidian
corpus: poetic body and poetic text', 127-41) takes up another word from
the programmatic first two verses of the *Metamorphoses*: *corpora*. From

the earliest times the word in its singular form has denoted a collection of works by a particular author. Farrell finds in the *Metamorphoses* a 'material correlative of the poet's own body' (128). In a footnote (159, n. 53) Theodorakopolous admits 'Farrell in this volume reads a triumph where I read defeat'. For Farrell, *Met.* 15.871-9 signals the possible destruction of the physical book as a 'body', whereas 'the voice goes on' – the ancients read aloud. The boundaries of the triadic arrangement of the *Metamorphoses* are marked by characters in some way representing the poet, starting with the Arachne-Minerva weaving contest in *Met.* 5 and 6. The tale of Orpheus (*Met.* 10.1-85, 11.1-66) transcends the second triadic break and in the end the survival of the poet as a voice serves as 'potent symbol of a singer whose voice outlives his body' (p. 138). This, for Farrell, stands for the exiled poet too, whose disavowal in the exilic poetry of the transcendence of his *Metamorphoses* is undercut by the fact that his disembodied poetic voice discernibly continues to speak.

Most of the contributors are reticent about the now acceptedly moot topic of the anti-, pro- or non-Augustanism of Ovid's *Metamorphoses*, except in passing allusions to power as having a voice; the powerless being mute. Karl Galinsky, the trend-setting critic for the acceptance of an idiosyncratic Augustanism in the *Metamorphoses*, reprises his thesis of the last thirty years: Ovid was never an intellectual saboteur of a mooted fully-worked-out programme of ideologised literary oppression. Galinsky's perhaps purposely radicalised arguments deconstruct the attitudes of scholars who read nuanced criticism of the Augustan regime into the flippant parody, if not outright opposition, underlying most of Ovid's works. Galinsky's arguments are, as always, sound, and he makes out a case for reading the *Metamorphoses* as 'creative interaction' (p. 111) with 'Augustan cultural thematics', his term for the 'highly ideologised' concept of 'ideology' (p. 105).

The Ovidian tradition and his influence in diverse genres are treated by various other scholars. Each offers much of interest, but space precludes detailed discussion. The final section ('Scholars and poets') comprises two papers on Ovidian reception that are unusual for differing reasons, and are *mutatis mutandis* also applicable to the exilic poetry. Richard Tarrant discusses 'Nicolaas Heinsius and the rhetoric of textual criticism' (288-300). Examples quoted illustrate both the man and his critical and exegetical principles. The eighteenth-century scholar appears as both erudite and humane. To read a foremost modern textual critic on a great predecessor is a rewarding experience: both scholars loom through the apparently dry material as fellow-travellers on the pleasant highway of verbal play first paved by Ovid.

And finally, Protean Ovid would (had he learned English as well as Getic) have admired the verbal pyrotechnics of John Henderson's post-modern critique of two volumes of modern poetry in his unusually titled

'Ch-ch-ch-changes' (301-23). Henderson's selective appreciation of both the versatility of a collection of translations by over forty poets (M. Hofmann and J. Lasdun, *After Ovid: New Metamorphoses*, 1994) and the aptness of Ted Hughes' versification of individual episodes (*Tales from Ovid*, 1997) ranges widely through modern works, from Pound and Eliot to David Bowie. As always, Henderson's good-natured demolition of icons is both entertaining and profound, his dense and elliptical English prose as enjoyable as Ovid's rapid Latin verse. Of the two, Ovid is the easier to understand.

2.2. Ovid's own metamorphosis

This leads us directly to consideration of the structure and music of Ovid's poetry as it serves to illustrate Ovid's personal metamorphosis during his exile. An Argentinian scholar, Éléonora Tola, has reworked her 2000 Sorbonne dissertation as a monograph, titled *La métamorphose poétique chez Ovide:* Tristes *et* Pontiques: *Le poème inépuisable* (Louvain, 2004). Tola explores the 'dissolution of Ovid's exiled self' and its recreation through his writings. Her central thesis (that Ovid's poetic metamorphosis while in exile is conveyed by a deliberately fragmentary distribution of topics) is elucidated in three parts, each comprising various chapters of thematic, close textual readings, with detailed study of metre and structure, intertextuality and 'autotextuality'. Major points are clarified in statistical tables underpinning Tola's interpretations of perceived 'metamorphosis'.

Part One discusses in turn the way alternation and 'undulation' dispose central themes throughout the exilic oeuvre: contrasts in time, the themes of death, shipwreck, voyaging, tears and storms. The first chapter typifies such 'undulation' as contrast between fluidity and stasis, tears and death, voyaging and petrification, also emphasising differences in approach between the *Tristia* and the *Ex Ponto*. Next Tola discusses the 'autotextual metamorphosis' of the poet's corpus. Concepts from *Metamorphoses* 1.1-2 are redistributed in *Tr*. 1.1.117-22 and 1.7.13-14 and *Ex P*. 1.2.27-36, but with variations in metrical patterning, word placement, verse forms and case endings.

Fluidity features next, starting with portrayal of liquids (from tears to the ocean) in Ovid's other works, then showing how, in the exilic poetry, tears and dialectic fluctuation are central to the theme of change to both the poet's body and his corpus. This leads to discussion of Ovidian lamentation, ambivalence and personal dissolution. Whereas the *Tristia* depicts the poet's gradual fluidification, the poetic 'I' loses all sense of identity within the Pontic collection. Here a petrifying torpor has seized Ovid's body; his poetry reduced to ineffectual rhetoric, as signalled by the tears of exile.

Tola's second part discusses 'the metamorphosis of a topic into frag-
ments' through Ovidian *inventio*. Three chapters trace in turn the poetic
distribution of the topics of voyaging, storms and shipwreck.
Fragmentation of these topics conveys the displacement of Ovid's body,
and, ultimately, of himself, the disintegration of the poetic 'I'. Detailed
close readings and statistical tables again illustrate both inter- and auto-
textuality, showing fluctuations between reality and fiction. Discussion
of storms and shipwrecks in Ovid and his models compares references to
the helplessness of navigators in the face of the storms of *Tr.* 1 to Ovid's
own jaunty metaphor from the *Ars Amatoria*. Shipwreck is the supreme
metaphor for the poet's personal disintegration.

This leads to the third part, the 'poetics of metamorphosis'. Ovid's
Metamorphoses is the 'inexhaustible poem' that underlies all metamor-
phosis in the exilic poems, providing the centrally important myths
whereby the poet can typify his changed situation (in particular,
Odysseus/Ulysses and Medea). Tola's final chapter discusses Ovid's exilic
poetics, characterised by metaphorical movement within his words
versus 'petrification' of his person, resulting in an 'oxymoronic dialectic'
involving contrast (between change and fixity, life and art, physical and
poetic bodies) as its most important element.

Tola concludes with a recapitulation of Ovid's paradoxical superimpo-
sition of literature on life. Metamorphosis is the basis of Ovid's exilic
poetics and of his life as an exile. Change of direction from all he wrote
before, pointed by both inter- and autotextuality, is signalled by changes
in acoustic play, in syntax, metrics, rhetoric and genre. A poetics of the
imaginary signals the ultimate metamorphosis of Ovid's poetic voice. The
Tristia illustrates Ovid's active metamorphosis into a poet in a changed
state; the *Ex Ponto* his passive change into a disembodied voice. Tola
concludes with the statement that Ovid did not lose his creativity, but
profoundly changed what he had, in a 'metamorphosis of metamorphoses'
(342). Like the voice of decapitated Orpheus, Ovid's voice continued to
resound.

Tola's critical insight is profound, her arguments cogent, discussion of
texts illustrating her various points meticulous and persuasive, and her
comparative tables and statistics impressive. The work offers a valuable
contribution to appreciation of the stylistics of Ovid's exilic poetry.

2.3. A recent commentary

There are very few recent commentaries on Ovid's exilic works. In
English we have Green's monumental Penguin translation of and
literary commentary on both the *Tristia* and *Ex Ponto* cited in my
Introduction. For the *Tristia* there are Luck's two volumes of text and
commentary in German (Heidelberg, 1967, 1977). From the same era are

J. André's French-language *Tristia* and *Ex Ponto* (Paris, 1968, 1977). Della Corte's Italian versions also date from the 1970s. The Black Sea letters have, until recently, been particularly poorly served. L Galasso's fairly recent Italian commentary on Book 2 (*Epistularum ex Ponto Liber 2*, Firenze, 1995) followed the commentary by M. Helzle on parts of Book 4 (*Publii Ovidii Nasonis Epistularum ex Ponto Liber 4. A Commentary on Poems 1-7 and 16*, Hildesheim, 1989). Helzle's *Ovids Epistulae ex Ponto: Buch I-II Kommentar* (Heidelberg) appeared in 2003. Most recent is an English-language commentary, again on the first book of the Pontic epistles (the reworking of his 2001 Oxford dissertation), by Jan Felix Gaertner: *Ovid, Epistulae ex Ponto, Book 1* (edited with Introduction, Translation and Commentary, Oxford, 2005). It includes Gaertner's own revision of aspects of J.A. Richmond's 1990 Teubner edition of the text and Richmond's own subsequent emendations. A fairly literal prose translation accompanies the text on opposing pages, Loeb-style.

The work attests to detailed scholarship, but is limited in scope. It aims to 'explain the text of Ov. *Pont.* 1 and to advance our understanding of some connected broader issues, namely the relation of Ovid's exile poetry to his pre-exilic works and its function within its historical context' (p. 1). Gaertner does not offer much in the way of literary analysis or comment, but has provided a vademecum for literary critics or other readers eager to examine the lexical connotations of the exiled poet's emotional outpourings. He offers an extensive philological examination of Ovid's diction as compared to that 'of his day', providing, in a lengthy Introduction, an overview of matters relating to the text, but largely peripheral to the emotional thrust of the poetry.

The Introduction runs to just under forty pages, starting with a short exposition of the author's aims and method (p. 1) and the arrangement of the poems (2-6). Addressees and readers come next (6-8). *Vos*, so often addressed by the poet, was more than the immediate addressee of a particular poem with his household. *Vos* may mean 'all his friends at Rome', indicating that the Pontic epistles are not merely private letters set to verse. *Vos* is also the general public, or any reader at any time. This 'draw[s the reader] into the spell of the *Epistulae ex Ponto*' (p. 8). The third rubric (8-24) derives its title from Syme's famous *History in Ovid* (1978). It covers aspects such as 'Rome under Augustus'. A long excursus on *clementia* and *ira* precedes discussion of emperor-worship, followed by an overview of the concepts *crimen* and *poena*. On Ovid's 'crime', Gaertner tends toward the general modern consensus: Ovid may have been a scapegoat in some crisis in 'dynastic politics' (Syme's term). *Poena* is elucidated with reference to common Roman practices of Ovid's day, and with copious reference to the poet's own assertions (15).

A long discussion of Ovid's place of exile (16-24) starts with the geography, climate and vegetation of Tomis, followed by an exposition of its early history. Next comes Tomis during the conjectured time of Ovid's stay (given as AD 8-18), with extensive reference to both primary sources and archaeology, epigraphy and numismatics. The discrepancy between archaeological and Ovidian information, Gaertner stresses, 'should not blind us to pieces of information of historical value' (23). This rubric ends with the suggestion that Ovid's palpable exaggerations and 'false statements' about the barbaric state of Tomitan civilisation were 'never meant to deceive his Roman readership' or cajole them into pitying the despairing exile. The poet intended '[to] render the epistles more captivating (*sic*) for his readership' (24). This would also have underlain Ovid's identification of Augustus with Jupiter: hyperbole served to turn a simple enactment of *relegatio* into 'an extraordinary event worthy and reminiscent of epic' (ibid.). Direction to the commentary on 1.4.29 (p. 290) brings the reader to a succinct summary of the manner in which our poet combined 'an autobiographical detail (Ovid's banishment) and a historical fact (the various degrees of emperor worship) with the literary topos of divine anger ...' as found in the themes of the *Iliad*, *Odyssey* and *Aeneid*.

Just over a page of discussion (24-5) elucidates what Gaertner terms 'non-autobiographical material', including historical references, comparisons and digressions, material from philosophical consolations on exile and death, and myth. Discussion of myth is tantalisingly brief, especially as Ovid very frequently himself seems to enter that world (see my Chapter 5 above). Equally brief is discussion of Ovid's allusions to his own earlier poetry, and his likening of himself in turn to a series of victims from the *Metamorphoses*. This short 'non-autobiographical' (*sic*) rubric ends with the conjecture that Ovid's allusion to Daedalus' 'ultimately unsuccessful plea to leave Crete' indicates Ovid's resignation to remaining at Tomis.

The final three rubrics of the Introduction are centrally important for the approach of Gaertner's commentary: 'Diction and Style' (25-34), 'Metre and Versification' (34-8) and 'Transmission, Text and Translation' (39-41). 'Diction' includes vocabulary, grammar and syntax, stylistic devices and imagery. Gaertner emphasises (25) that Ovid's diction in the exilic poetry is generally more prosaic and colloquial than in his earlier works, as requisite for letters. However, 'different levels of speech ... suit the respective context' (*sic*, 26). Gaertner carefully refutes those critics who still consider that the colloquial feel of the exilic poetry indicates a decline in Ovid's genius. Three Appendices cover, respectively, poetic and prosaic words, usages and *iuncturae*, and imagery.

The rubric on metrics treats of prosody (35), with interesting figures for the frequency of elision and prodelision in the *Ex Ponto* as compared to Ovid's earlier works or to those of other authors. Next Ovid's hexameters and pentameters are examined, including the frequency of monosyllables (36-8), often an indication of colloquial style. Gaertner argues (as I do in Chapter 3) that Ovid's increasing use of polysyllabic pentameter endings is not a sign of 'weakening powers' in our poet, as some assert. The last rubric covers text transmission and reception and Gaertner's use and adaptation of Richmond's edition and sigla.

Gaertner's translation, largely based on Richmond's text, reflects his own suggested emendations, as, for example, *'nimis hoc seu vis'* for *'vis hoc seu vis'*, at *Ex P.* 1.3.31, translated (in context) as 'Whether you want to call this too loyal or womanish ...' (63). It is Gaertner's stated intention to offer a translation that is 'literal rather than literary', and which can clarify questions not treated in the commentary (41). Hence the translation is adequate, but not exciting. Occasionally a more colloquial translation (e.g. 'bore / bears' for Gaertner's 'carried / carry'; for *'tuli'*, 1.1.26, / *'fert'*, ibid. 35) would have been more appropriate.

Commentary comprises the largest part of the work (93-527), some forty pages for each of ten poems. A short general introduction is followed by detailed comment which is mainly lexical and comparative, categorising words or phrases as 'poetic' or 'prosaic', citing other occurrences in Ovid, mostly followed by parallels in other authors, sometimes with references to secondary literature. Literary comment is also comparative or lexically-based (e.g. the apparent self-deprecation of 1.1.4 is compared with Catullus' similar *Carm.* 1.8-9; secrecy and fear are hinted at by choice of words like *'audent, latere, tutius'*, p. 98). Occasionally Gaertner's comment appears laboured; for example, (*ad* 1.1.11): *'nullo* for *nemine* is poetic (1.3.83n)'. Reference to the latter produces *'nulli*: the present usage of *nullus* for *nemo* is absent from Cicero, but occurs in other prose writers ...' etc., referring back to a comment on 1.3.56: *'nemo* is generally avoided in poetry ... Interestingly, it is used more frequently in Ovid's exile poetry' (255). Why not say of the first *'nullo'* at 1.1.11: 'a poetic abbreviation for the usual prose *"nullo homine"* – *"nemine"* is very rare'?

Gaertner is bold in proposals for deletion, and acceptance of those of others. For example, from poem 1 he proposes to excise verses 41-4, first suggested by Merckel. Earlier English editors Postgate and Owen do not consider this. Green's Penguin Translation and Commentary (1994: 295) persuasively argues against it (citing Némethy, Wheeler-Goold, Richmond). The passage adds illegal remuneration of worshippers of Roman Diana to an example citing reward for the followers of the Magna Mater. Next follow two verses likening the Julian names to a rattle or Phrygian flute. Gaertner (115) accepts Merckel's deletion on lexical grounds: the words *'vaticinator, ipsa, credulitate'* are 'oddities' indicating late interpolation, also, the 'rhetorical thread' between verses 37-40 and 45 is 'broken' by this passage. Yet rhetorical overkill is a frequent Ovidian device: the verses complete a common Ovidian over-extension of examples. The whole passage is suggestively laden with subtle subversion. Reference to the unnamed divine power that moves men to action carries political as well as religious implications, so Green, ad loc.

With no precedents, Gaertner proposes deletion of 1.4.15-18, arguing (282) that the verses are 'internally feeble' (offering some lexical justification) and that the extension of a series of exempla from agriculture to horse racing and shipping is 'strange'. He again ignores the Ovidian penchant for metaphorical overkill and for intertextual nuancing (boating and racing as metaphors predominate in the *Ars Amatoria*: the exemplum of over-use occurs at *AA* 3.81-2). Elsewhere (at 1.2.148) Gaertner (221) rejects a suggestion by Heinsius that a verse is spurious, arguing that both its form and sense are plausible.

The usual appendices feature: a 'Select Bibliography', a 'General Index', a brief 'Greek Index' and longer 'Latin Index' comprising all the words commented upon individually (for '*nullus*' we have two of the three references discussed above). Finally, an Index links reference to individual passages (from Ovid's other works or other authors), to Gaertner's commentary on the particular poem and verse that each entry relates to.

This is a generally useful reference tool, even if it tends to neglect exploration of the feeling that Ovid's exilic poetry conveys in favour of describing what the poems consist of. Gaertner is strongly persuaded of the paramount importance of literary tradition, seeming most comfortable within the German tradition of *Quellenforschung*, with little or no analysis of emotional content (which it seems to be his stated intention to avoid). In his Introduction to his edition of a collection of papers that resulted from a Corpus Christi seminar on exile held at Oxford during 2001 (*Writing Exile: the discourse of displacement in Greco-Roman antiquity and beyond*, Leyden, 2007), Gaertner restates the paramount importance of literary tradition, trenchantly opposing 'the notion of a distinct, psychologically conditioned "genre" or "mode" of exile literature'. The description of the collection in the Brill catalogue asserts: '... ancient and medieval authors perceive and present their exile according to pre-existent literary paradigms, style themselves and others as "typical exiles" and employ "exile" as a powerful trope to express estrangement, elicit readerly sympathy, and question political power structures.' While agreeing that this is so, I maintain, however, that Ovid also imbued his work with the urgency of intensely-felt personal experience and that analysis of such emotional content is a legitimate, worthwhile – and necessary – critical exercise.

2.4. Literary criticism

Of a far higher critical order is the reworking of his Cambridge dissertation by Gareth Williams (now of Columbia University), published as *Banished Voices: readings in Ovid's exile poetry* (Cambridge, 1994). It is perhaps the most influential of recent critical works on Ovid. A brief Introduction and Conclusion frame four discursive chapters that deal, in turn, with: 'The "unreality" of Ovid's exile poetry', 'Ovid's pose of poetic decline', 'Friendship and the theme of artistic motivation' and 'Ovid's treatment of Augustus in *Tristia* 2'. Sub-headings within chapters serve as indications of the author's train of thought. For example, the fourth chapter (on Augustus) deals consecutively with: the problem of approach, Ovid's 'mischievous Muse', *otium* and *recusatio*, 'Ovid on literature' and intertextual allusion to the *Ars Amatoria* in *Tr.* 2.

Williams makes the important point in his Introduction (p. 2) that '[a] sense of uncertainty over the "reality" of Ovid's physical and social environment in a desolate extremity of the Roman empire was very possibly as disconcerting for his contemporary reader as it is for his modern audience'. Williams' subsequent chapters go on to show how 'Ovid exploits this discomfort by constructing a body of verse which, on one reading, confirms every conceivable assumption about the attritional effects of Tomitan exile; [and shows how] on another reading, the exile poetry undermines those very assumptions' (ibid.).

Williams' first chapter explores what he terms Ovid's 'dissimulation' in the manner in which he presents the facts of his exile. Williams underpins his observations with concise recourse to the geography and political history of the area. Like Gaertner, Williams considers that Ovid's portrayal of Tomis and its surroundings is literary rather than literal. He illustrates this with critical analyses of Ovid's sources, leading to brief discussion of *Tr.* 5.7 and a more extensive 'close reading' of *Tr.* 5.10. Williams' critical observations are incisive: about Ovid's debt to Vergil, he speaks of our poet's 'creative involvement with the *Aeneid*' as being 'pursued with the same emphasis on supplying a new context for the Virgilian text which had characterised Ovid's method in the *Metamorphoses*' (p. 25). This chapter next examines – and demolishes – the 'factual information' about the Pontic region supplied by Ovid in *Ex P.* 1.8 and 4.7. Williams is similarly sceptical about Ovid's reminiscences of youthful travels with his friend Macer in *Ex P.* 2.10. Again a series of close readings indicates how much of what is conveyed as 'fact' is literary, and again these literary associations are carefully traced, with emphasis on Ovid's transformation of epic themes and terminology by setting them within an elegiac framework.

Williams' concise and easy style invites copious quotation: 'The intricate poetic mechanism of [*Ex*] *P.* 1.8 distinguishes and harmonises contrasted generic stereotypes in a way which integrates what has been thought to be a digression on Aegisos (11-24) into a structured and unified whole ... entail[ing] the narrative's subservience to a poetic structure ... [so that] it would be unwise to try to fix the boundaries of Ovidian invention' (pp. 33-4). Ovid purposefully 'undermines his [own] credibility' with 'protestations of trustworthiness'; so Williams, who suggests that Ovid in *Ex P.* 4.7 'enters into something like a reciprocal arrangement with his addressee', Vestalis, who is thereby put in 'an impossible situation', being obliged either to corroborate Ovid's exaggerated claims about their warlike environment or be complicit in casting doubt on 'the veracity of his own deeds as recorded by the poet' (35-6). Again Williams' close reading involves recourse to Ovid's epic sources and analysis of the manner in which conceptual and verbal allusions are adapted to Ovid's poetic purpose, part at least of which is 'impos[ing] on his readers' credulity'. Williams' answer to the inherent oxymoronic nature of Ovid's exilic poetry is acceptance of the poems as 'fundamentally ironic' (41).

Williams' close reading of *Ex P.* 2.10 similarly combines careful examination of Ovid's sources with explication of what he does with these literary precedents, drawing suggestive lines of connection from Ovid's ostensibly factual reminiscences of youthful enjoyments shared with his friend Macer. As Ovid tells it, the two young poets travelled together to Asia Minor, the original seat of martial epic, and thence to Sicily, retracing the journey of Aeneas, which included seeing not only Mount Etna with its Vergilian association of an (unspecified) giant struck by Jupiter's thunderbolt, but also Henna, with intertextual reminiscences of Ovid's own (two) portrayals of the rape of Persephone. Williams' unpacking of Ovid's allusive techniques is intricate, but can be summarised by saying that, *pace* Williams, in this poem Ovid presents both Macer and himself as 'literary identities' and their journeys as representative of the characteristics of the generic preferences of each.

This same technique is followed throughout: carefully relating individual poems (as case studies which illustrate his various points) to their literary sources, Williams spells out Ovid's innovative and often ironic adaptations of these sources. The reader is finally left with an enlarged impression of the elusive breadth of artistry of our poet, whose words on second reading seldom seem to mean what they initially appear to say. Williams' four chapters give important insights into the most salient aspects of Ovid's exile as I have also identified them (and tried to show throughout this book): the fantasy-world of his exile, his pretence at weakening powers that is portrayed in brilliant versification, friendship – also with his Muse – as consistent *Leitmotiv* in his exilic poetry, and Ovid's essentially ironic attitude to Augustus. Williams' readership is helped to become 'alive to the potential which poetic vocabulary has to be polysemic in its suggestiveness and interpretative possibilities' (212, from Williams' concluding paragraph).

After publication of this tour-de-force Williams next turned his attention to Ovid's most difficult and elusive poem. *The Curse of Exile: a study of Ovid's* Ibis (Cambridge, 1996) displays the same incisive scholarship. Ovid's amazing and baffling tirade is traditionally assigned to the period between the publication of *Tr.* 5 and *Ex P.* 1-3. It appears *sui generis* within the Latin literary canon. I, for one, have not had the courage to attempt to unravel its intricacies. Williams' five chapters as carefully relate Ovid's poetry to literary sources as in the work discussed above, but his most important contribution, that helps to make sense of Ovid's apparently random ranting, is to ascribe (with some recourse to modern medical sources) the poem to Ovid's deliberate portrayal of the ravings of a 'deranged *persona*' (126) in the grip of the manic phase of bipolar affective disorder – the opposite pole to the profound 'state of melancholy' that 'Ovid's exilic *persona*' conveys in most of his other exilic poems (113-14). Williams' allusive analysis of this manic rant serves both to make the poem accessible and to encourage our renewed admiration for Ovid's endless ingenuity.

3. Modern Ovidian fictions

So much for scholarship. Reception of Ovid's works takes many forms. My Chapter 6 considered Ovidian precedents for the poetry of modern exiles, some of whom were aware of him as a spiritual forebear, but also his 'natural heirs', those political exiles who voiced their woe in terms reminiscent of the timelessness of Ovid's despairing poetry. Ovid's exile has also provided a wonderful springboard for creative writing. I deal briefly below with some diverse examples.

Beside excursions into what may be termed historicist fantasy, and the analysis of the literary reception of some of his works as touched on above, Ovid's exile has sometimes been used as the base for totally fictitious literary works of widely divergent kinds. For example, in the 1930s John Masefield wrote a long narrative poem featuring an imaginary liaison between Ovid and Julia Minor, linked to a daring production of his *Medea* (the only drama we know of that Ovid composed). This play was lost some time after the appearance of Seneca's drama of the same name, which may have been quite closely based on it.

In the 1950s came the novel *Dieu est né en exil*, by Vintila Horia, a Romanian exile in Paris, which was translated and published in English in 1961. I have discussed this work in my *Displaced Persons* (London, 1999), as also the novel by the Australian, David Malouf, *An Imaginary Life*, which appeared in the late 1970s. In contrast with Horia's monotheistic, 'Christian' Ovid, Malouf's 'exiled poet' develops a new religion along pagan lines: he meets up with a proverbial 'wild child' whom the hero tames. Malouf's hero has very little resemblance to either the historic or the literary Ovid, but offers another illustration of the strong hold that the exiled genius has exercised for two millennia over the imagination of scholars and public alike across the western world. My Chapter 6 notes the theory that Malouf (as an Australian ill-at-ease with European culture) in a surge of 'colonial cringe' found in the exiled and alienated Ovid a kindred spirit.

A work I also touch on in my earlier monograph is *Die Letzte Welt* by the Austrian Christoff Ransmayr (rendered into English by J. Woods as *The Last World*, 1990), an ambitious post-modern construct created through skilful and timeless blending of the known facts and conjectured fictions of Ovid's life with some of Ovid's own characters, the pathetic victims of irrational change from his *Metamorphoses*, contrasted with the prototypical arrogance of all despotic rulers anywhere. The 'singular myth' that Ovid creates in exile is exploited in Ransmayr's tour de force, which finally collapses the limits between myth and metaphor by making a search among the denizens of a post-modernised, fantastic Tomis for a lost Naso (by his erstwhile bosom friend and frequent correspondent Cotta) the central theme of an allegory of the corrupting influence of absolute political power and the freedom afforded by the poetic imagination.

Ransmayr's work merits detailed critical attention, not only for what it does (put at its simplest, universalising the vain suppression of the arts by powerful political or financial factions), but for whence it derives. What needs particular analysis is Ransmayr's choice of names for his characters, who do not always appear to be exact parallels for their ancient counterparts. For example, the epileptic 'Battus' displays few of the characteristics of his Ovidian counterpart, but in the end, both are turned to stone. Or, why is 'Naso's' wife called Cyane, after Ovid's water-nymph who in vain tried to prevent the rape of Proserpina and in the end dissolved into her own pool of water? Why does Ransmayr's 'Echo' have a 'scaly patch of skin that wanders about her body' or his 'Cyparis' have a hunch-back? The garrulous 'Fama' is more obvious, as are 'Tereus' the butcher and his wife 'Procne' with her mutilated sister 'Philomela', who cringes at the approach of men, but the boy 'Itys' merely hurts a finger in the fan of a film projector. Drops of his blood are sprinkled over the projector. 'Marsyas' is never flayed, but mourns the disappearance of 'Echo'. 'Phineas' is not petrified by a 'Perseus', but lives over a cave, selling whisky and taming snakes.

Equally in need of analysis (or explication) is the symbolism inherent in Ransmayr's fantasy-landscape of high mountains of iron, salt mines and the slugs that cover the menhirs of a 'ravaged garden or a cemetery' (p. 27) that 'Cotta' visits in his search for vestiges of the poet. These the spry old servant 'Pythagoras' proceeds to destroy (the name a fitting comment on the pompous and wordy teacher of Numa in book 15 of the *Metamorphoses*). 'Pythagoras' kills the slugs by pouring vinegar on them and they respond by giving out a windy song, a sigh of death. When (significantly) fifteen stone columns have been exposed, 'Cotta' reads on them an incised translation of *Met.* 15.871-6 (*iamque opus exegi ...*', 'I have completed a work ...'). Whatever the significance of the slugs in Ransmayr's creative imagination, the certainty of Ovid's continued fame looms out from under them.

More straightforward (or perhaps less layered) is the last work we shall consider. The prolific author of stories set in ancient Rome, David Wishart, somewhat unimaginatively titled his excursion into Ovidian conjecture merely *Ovid* (London, 1995). This work ingeniously ascribes the poet's banishment to his discovery of a plot by the empress Livia to use the Germanic renegade auxiliary officer Arminius to enhance the reputation of her son, a plot that went horribly wrong and led to the Varian disaster. This conjecture need not be taken seriously, but the novel makes for entertaining reading. The hero in this case is young 'Corvinus', the grandson of Ovid's patron Messalla Corvinus, son of Messalinus, Ovid's correspondent and the nephew of Cotta Maximus (hence, too – to draw lines of relationship between the protagonists of two completely different fictional worlds – the nephew of the hero of Ransmayr's novel).

Again there is a search for Ovid's mortal remains. Young 'Corvinus' is approached by 'Perilla Rufia', Ovid's stepdaughter (familiar to us from *Tr.* 3.7), to help her to obtain the poet's ashes. While still (unhappily) married to Publius Suillius Rufus, Ovid's correspondent in *Ex P.* 4.8, 'Perilla' encourages the advances of young 'Corvinus' and the tale ends, predictably, with the prospect of their living happily ever after. The novel alternates between first-person narrative by 'Corvinus', in a jocular, racy slang, and the dispassionate 'diary' of Varus, Augustus' legate in Germania. 'Varus' explains, in a series of short notes, his plans to betray the Roman cause 'for the good of Rome'. Wishart makes this character anticipate and answer a not unreasonable quibble that no traitor would be so foolish as to put down his intended treachery in black and white. He is writing a justification for his own edification, 'Varus' writes, which he will destroy when it has been completed. Of course, circumstances beyond his control in the end ensure the 'survival' of the document.

The main thrust of the novel is the various vicissitudes that our young hero undergoes before he at last uncovers the ramifications of a conspiracy devised by Livia to put Augustus' legate in the wrong and provide her son Tiberius with an opportunity to show his mettle as general and saviour of the state. Further intricacies of the conspiracy need not concern us here: suffice it to say that Ovid had formerly partially uncovered and unwisely reported it to Livia. Hence his relegation, on the strength of 'Livia's' portrayal of the poet to the emperor as a libertine (of the kind that Wishart's 'Augustus' had not had the courage to be himself; so 'Livia'). Wishart's plot is ingenious, happily blending known facts about the era with informed conjecture, interlaced with evocations of the scenes and sounds of a Juvenalian Rome at its most unsavoury, a Rome in which our playful poet would have perhaps felt uncomfortable, but which fits with the promises of opportunities for dalliance featured in the first several hundred verses of Book 1 of the *Ars Amatoria.*

The value of Wishart's *Ovid* lies perhaps in its lively evocation of Rome, but more certainly in its ensuring that another generation will be intrigued by the undeserved lot of our endlessly versatile poet and may consequently turn to his verses to find out more. And when a reader has once encountered our poet's sense of fun and his effortless versification, Ovid becomes a lifelong friend – or so has been my experience.

Appendix I

Examples of personification and depersonalisation not cited in Chapter 1

Abstractions

dolor: *Tr.* 4.9.8; *Ex P.* 1.10.23; *ira*: *Tr.* 4.9.10; *decor*: *Ex P.* 2.3.13-14; *timor*: *Ex P.*
2.3.88; *cura*: *Ex P.* 2.4.4.

gloria: *Ex P.* 1.5.57; *voluntas*: *Ex P.* 2.5.31; *gratia*: *Ex P.* 2.6.32; 4.1.23; *virtus*: *Ex
P.* 4.8.47.

Fortuna: *Tr.* 5.8.15; *Ex P.* 2.3.51; 4.3.29-32; 4.9.121.

Apart from the fully personified and embodied apparition of *Amor* in *Ex P.* 3.3,
personification of *amor* is non-erotic at *Ex P.* 1.9.8 and 4.12.18.

Age is personified at *Tr.* 3.7.35-6; 4.8.13; *Ex P.* 1.4.2, and youth at *Ex P.* 1.10.12.

Geographical and meteorological terms

The Bear constellations: designation varies in the following allusions: *Tr.* 1.3.48;
1.4.1; 1.11.15; 2.190; 3.4.47; 3.11.8.

Ovid's place of exile: *Ex P.* 1.10.24; 4.10.57-8.

'Neutral' personifications of places: *Germania*: *Tr.* 3.12.47-8; 4.2.43; the poet's
own farm: *Tr.* 4.8.9-10.

Personified images and thought as vicarious travellers

Imago: *Tr.* 3.4.59; *Ex P.* 1.2.49; 1.9.7; 2.4.7.

'Inner vision' is presented variously: *Tr.* 3.4.61; 3.8.35; 4.2.61; *Ex P.* 1.8.34;
2.10.44, 3.4.20; 4.9.33.

Mens: *Tr.* 4.2.57; 5.2.7; *Ex P.* 2.4.8; 3.5.48; 4.4.45; 4.9.33 and 41; 4.15.37.

Poetry

Poetry as surrogate for himself: *Ex P.* 1.5.71-76; 1.7.1-2; 4.5.1-4; 4.9.7-8.

Identification of poet and poems: *Ex P.* 1.2.69; 2.5.33-6; 2.7.1.

Extension of the exile's sense of identity, often indicated by the
conscious blurring of limits between the man and his natural functions
by means of casual ('petrified') personification: His tears have no end,
*fine carent, Ex P.*1.2.27 – the verb *careo* is primarily applied to living
creatures in the allied senses of 'wanting', 'being deprived of' (Lewis and
Short). When the exile is ill, his vein 'does not follow its usual path': that
is, his blood will not flow normally: (*nec*) *peragit soliti vena tenoris iter,*

Ex P. 1.10.6. Food does not carry out its *officium, Ex P.* 1.10.22. His voice wins through, *pervenit Ex P.* 2.2.95. When writing poetry, his heart warms, *fervet*, to its work, *Ex P.* 3.9.22. Mental vision is a substitute for what the exile's eyes could not enjoy, *frui, Ex P.* 4.4.44.

Synecdoche (part for whole): in Ovid's prophecy of a triumph, a wreath can know (*nosse*) the head of the general that is used to it, *Ex P.* 3.4.102.

Relaxation of distinctions between human and non-human extended to others: At *Ex P.* 4.7.38 Vestalis' shield is depicted as covered in 'wounds', *vulnera*. Sextus Pompeius' treasure-chest never denied (*negavit*) him aid, *Ex P.* 4.1.24.

Depersonalisation: *inhumanos ... Getas*: *Ex P.* 1.5.66; 3.5.28; 4.13.22.

Appendix II

Literal translations of three poems featured in Chapter 2

Ex Ponto 3.2: To Cotta

1 I pray that the greetings which you read, sent to you from me, Cotta, as 'good health', may arrive as 'good health'; for you, a happy man, greatly relieve my torments, and you help to make a good part of me safe. Also, when some people give in and let go their tattered sails, you alone remain as anchor to my battered ship.

7 Your faithfulness is therefore to be thanked. I forgive those who, along with my fortune, turned their backs on me as I fled. When lightning bolts strike one man, they do not terrify only one person, and the crowd that is related to the stricken one is usually also afraid. Also, when a wall has given signs of future crumbling, the place empties because people are afraid. Who of those timid people would not avoid coming into contact with a sick person, out of fear of contracting a contagious illness?

15 Some of my friends also deserted me: because they were much too terrified, and not because they hated me. What was lacking wasn't loyalty, nor the will to do their duty; they feared the angry gods. And although they can be seen as rather cautious and timid, they did not therefore deserve to be called 'bad'. Either way, candidly, I should excuse my dear friends: and it is in their favour that they have nothing to reproach me with. I hope they'll be content with my forgiveness, and it will be a good thing if they hope that my testimony will clear them.

25 Those few of you who have not thought it disgraceful to bring aid in difficult times are the nobler party. Therefore then, my gratitude for your deserts will die only when I have become ashes, when my body has been consumed by fire. I'm wrong: my gratitude will also survive, even beyond the span of my life, if I should after all be read by a posterity that remembers me. Bloodless corpses belong on sad funeral pyres: name and honour survive the stacked bonfire. Theseus died, and so did that friend who accompanied Orestes, but both will live on through their fame.

35 But you, later generations will often praise you, and you will enjoy great praise in my works. Here even the Sauromatians and the Getae know you, and the barbaric crowd approves of such an attitude. And when I referred recently to your virtue (for I have learnt to chatter in Getic and Sarmatic), by chance a certain old man, standing in that throng, replied with these words in answer to my broken stammering:

43 'We also know the name, good guest, of friendship, we whom the Ister keeps far away from you folk. There is a place in Scythia (the ancients called it Taurus) which does not lie so very far from the Getic soil. In this land I was born (and I am not ashamed of my fatherland). That nation worships the goddess-twin of Phoebus. Her temple is still there today, supported by large columns, and the way to it leads right up forty steps.

50 'The story goes that there was a portent that came from heaven: and, lest you doubt my tale, the base still stands there, but now despoiled of its goddess. And the altar which had been white, the natural colour of the stone, changed its colour to red from all the blood that had been shed on it.

55 'A woman who has not experienced the marriage torch carries out the rites, someone who comes from a more noble family than the ordinary Scythian women. It is a form of sacrifice which our ancestors instituted, where any stranger that arrives is killed with a sword wielded by the virgin priestess.

59 'Thoas, a king famous in Homer's lays, ruled the kingdom, and there was nobody else more famous in the whole of the Black Sea. They say that while he wielded the sceptre, a certain Iphigeneia made the journey thither, flying through the liquid air. It is believed that she was wafted in a cloud through the air by the breezes and that Artemis put her down in these places.

65 'She had presided over the temple ritual for many years, carrying out the grim rites with unwilling hand, when two young men came with a sailing ship and landed, standing on shore. These two were equal in age and bound by mutual love. One was Orestes, and the other Pylades: fame is attached to their names. Immediately they were led to the altar of Trivia, both of them with their hands tied behind their backs. The Greek priestess sprinkled them with lustral water and tied the long ribbons round their hair. And while she prepared the sacred rite, while she veiled their temples with ribbons, and while she kept on finding reasons for slowly delaying, she said,

77 ' "I am not cruel: forgive me, young men, I'm preparing for a ritual that is even more barbarous than this place where it will be performed. It is the custom of this tribe. From what city do you, however, come, or what route are you following with your luckless ship?" She spoke, and when she heard the name of her own fatherland, the pious young girl found that they were fellow-citizens of her city.

83 ' "Let only one of you two fall as a victim to the sacred rite, and let the other go as messenger to our beloved homeland." Pylades was determined to die, and so ordered his dear friend Orestes to go, but he refused, and so the two battled among one another to see who should die. (This was the only thing about which the two could not agree; for the rest they were always one of heart and never argued.)

89 'While the young men were waging this altruistic battle of love, she wrote a note to her brother. She entrusted it as a message to her brother: and the person to whom it was given (just consider the lot of humankind) was her brother! And immediately they laid hands on the statue of Diana, and departed secretly by ship, travelling over the vast ocean. Although so many years have passed, the wonderful love of the young men now still has a great name in Scythia.'

97 After this well-known story had been told by him, all the Getae praised the

deed and the friends' loyalty. Certainly even on this shore, (and there is none wilder than this) the name of friendship moves barbarian hearts. What ought you to do, born (as you were) in the city of Rome itself, if such deeds touch even the hardy Getae? Add to this the fact that your attitude is always kind and your high principles show an indication of your nobility, the sort of nobility which Volesus, the founder of your family name, would acknowledge, and Numa (your ancestor on your mother's side) would admit is like his own; and the Cottae also approve them (Cotta was added to your family name, as a house that would have died out if you had not existed).

110 O great man, worthy of such a family, please consider that aid to your fallen friend is worthy of such principles.

Ex Ponto 3.3: To Maximus

1 If you have a little spare time to give a fugitive friend, o star of the Fabian line, o Maximus, come here, while I tell you what I saw (although I don't know whether this was an incorporeal shadow, or a picture of reality, or whether it was a dream).

5 It was night and the moon entered the double-opening windows, shining as she usually shines about the middle of the month. Sleep, mankind's rest from care, held me fast, and my limbs were sprawled all over the bed, when suddenly the air, shaken by winds, shuddered, and the window moved with a small creaking sound.

11 Terrified, as I lay stretched out on my left side, I moved my limbs, and sleep was driven from my trembling heart. Love stood there with an expression which he had never worn before, sadly holding the maple-wood foot of the bed with his left hand. He didn't have a collar on his neck, nor a hairpin in his hair, and his hair wasn't neatly arranged, as formerly.

15 Soft hairs hung down over his bristling face and his bristling feathers appeared before my own eyes, rather like on the back of a pigeon in flight, which many hands have handled and touched. As soon as I recognised him (and no-one else was better-known to me) my tongue grew loose and I spoke the following words:

23 'O Boy, you are the reason for the exile of your poor deluded teacher, (you whom it would have been better for me not to have taught); have you also come here, where there never ever is peace, and where the barbarian Ister joins the frozen sea? What was the reason for your journey, unless it was to see my misfortunes, which are, if you don't know it yet, hateful to you? You first dictated my juvenile songs to me: and with you as guide I added the five-foot line to the hexameter. And you did not allow me to rise to Homeric-type epic or to sing of the deeds of great leaders. Perhaps your bow and fires even diminished the slight powers of my talent, whatever there was of it.

35 'For while I sang of your realm and of your mother, my mind did not have any leisure for elevated work. But this had not been enough. I also stupidly in a poem enabled you to become sophisticated through knowledge of my Art. And for these deeds, a reward of exile was given to miserable me, and exile to the ends of the earth, at that, where there is no peace.

41 'But Eumolpus, son of Chion, did not act like that toward Orpheus, and

256

Olympian Zeus did not react like that to the Phrygian Satyr (Marsyas) *and Chiron did not get such a reward from Achilles, and they say that Numa did not harm Pythagoras. I shan't recount all the names piled up through the ages: I alone perished through my pupil's doings. While I was giving weapons to you, and while I was teaching you, wanton, I, as master, with you as pupil, I got such a reward.*

49 *'But you know very well, and you can say (swearing with a clear conscience) that I never tampered with other men's legitimate marriages. I wrote these things for those fast girls who don't wear a young girl's ribbon in their hair nor the long matron's* stola *over their ankles. Say, pray, when did I ever teach married women to deceive, and to bring forth illegitimate offspring through my blandishments? Or isn't every woman, whom the law prevents from having secret liaisons with men, strictly safeguarded from these books? What use is it, if I am believed to have composed precepts for adultery, which is forbidden by a very severe law?*

59 *'But you – may you have the kind of arrows that can strike anything, and may your torches never be without a flickering flame, and may Caesar rule the empire and control all countries, he who, through your brother Aeneas, is your descendant – please make his anger less implacable towards me and let him want me to be punished in a more comfortable place!'*

65 After I dreamt that I had said this to the winged boy, I dreamt that he said these words to me in reply: *'By my weapons, my torches, and by my weapons, my arrows, and by my dear mother, I do swear, and by the head of Caesar, I do solemnly swear that I learnt nothing, except what was allowed, when you were my teacher, and that there is nothing criminal in your* Ars.

71 *'And I wish that you could defend yourself on the other count as you can on this! You know that there is another thing which harmed you more. Whatever it is (and not even the pain itself ought to be mentioned) you cannot say that you are free from blame. Even if you are concealing a crime under the excuse that it was only an error, the anger of the Avenger was not greater than it deserved.*

77 *'But my wings have flown a tremendous way, so that I might see you and console you as you lie prostrate. I first saw these places at the time when, on my mother's request, the Phasian girl* (Medea) *was transfixed by my arrows. You, boon companion from my barracks, you are the reason why I now should revisit this place, after such a long age. Let go of your fear therefore: the anger of Caesar will grow mild, and a kinder hour will come as answer to your prayers.*

85 *'And don't fear a delay, the time is at hand which we are looking for, and a triumph has filled everything with happiness. While his house and his sons and his mother Livia rejoice, while you yourself are glad, great father of your fatherland and of the general, while the population congratulates itself, and throughout the whole city, each altar glows with fragrant fires, and while the venerable godhead (or: temple) offers easy access, it is to be hoped that our prayers may also prevail.'* He finished speaking, and then he either disappeared into thin air, or my senses started waking up.

95 If I should doubt that you stand favourably towards these words, o

Maximus, I should have to think that swans are as black as Memnon. But milk could not change to black pitch, nor glowing ivory turn into worm-wood. Your whole family is in accord with your attitude of mind: for you have a noble heart, as guileless as that of Hercules.

100 Envy, a lazy fault, does not touch high principled characters, and, like a hidden snake, it creeps along, low on the ground. Your sublime mind even stands above your whole family, and you have a name that is no greater than your natural talent. Therefore, let others harm unhappy people and hope to be feared: let them carry pikes tinged with back-biting gall: but your house is used to helping supplicants, and amongst their numbers, I pray, I should like to be recorded.

Ex Ponto 3.4: To Rufinus

1 These words, carrying no vain greeting to you, your friend Naso sends to you from the Tomitan city, Rufinus, and he entrusts to your favour his 'Triumph', if ever it should come into your hands. It is a slight work and does not measure up to your expectations; but I ask that you look after it, what-ever it may be like.

5 Strong things prevail on their own and do not need any doctoring: a sick man, uncertain of help, resorts to medicine. Great poets do not need a calm reader: they hold everybody spellbound, even those that are unwilling and resist them. I, whose talent a long period of troubles has diminished (or perhaps I never had any before!), weak in power, I grow strong under your approval, and if you should take that away from me, I should think that everything has been taken.

15 And although all my affairs are supported by your well-disposed favour, that book has a special right to your indulgence. Other poets wrote about a triumph they had seen; it is something else to write things 'seen' by the hand of memory. I wrote these things which in the past could scarcely be absorbed in public by my eager ears, and now Rumour was my eyes. Does a similar enthusiasm or the same impression truly come from things heard as it does from things seen?

23 Further, I complain because the glitter of silver and gleams of gold and purple which you saw, did not come my way; but, seeing the places, and the tribes arranged in their thousands, would have fed my song, and so would the battles themselves. The faces of kings, the most certain representatives of their tribes, would especially, perhaps, have helped that work, at least to a certain extent.

29 From the applause of the populace itself and their joyful excitement, any kind of talent could have been fired up; and I would have derived such vigour from such a clamour, as a common soldier does when he has heard the bugle call to arms. Well, even if my heart had been colder than snow and ice or than this place which I have to suffer, that triumphant face of the general standing in his ivory chariot would have shaken all the cold from my senses.

37 I, lacking these, and having used uncertain authorities, come rightly to ask the favour of your aid (lit.: *aid from your favour*). I am unfamiliar with the

names of the generals and the names of the places: my hands had hardly any material to work with. How much of such great things could rumour bring me, or could someone write to me? How much more, dear reader, oughtn't you to forgive if there is any error, or if I left out anything?

45 Add further that my lyre, which is used to harping on the complaints of its owner all the time, is scarcely tuned for a happy song. Happy words scarcely occurred to me when I looked for them, after such a long time, and to be glad seemed like something completely new to me. And, as one's eyes, when they are unused to the sun, draw back in fear, so my mind was slow to turn towards joy.

50 Freshness is the most precious of all things, and thanks for a favour which long delay retards simply disappears. I guess that other writings about such a great triumph have long ago already been eagerly read aloud by people. The thirsty reader drank those goblets first, mine only when he was already full; that water was drunk fresh, mine has grown lukewarm.

57 I didn't flag, and laziness did not make me tardy: the furthest shore of a vast gulf retains me here. In the time that the story is still on its way here and songs are hurriedly written and, after completion, go to you, a whole year can have passed. It makes a great difference, too, whether you are the first to pluck from an untouched rosebush or whether you pick by hand when scarcely a few late roses are left. Is it therefore a wonder, after the flowers had been plucked from a garden already stripped bare, that a wreath was made which was not worthy of your general?

65 *I pray that no poet should think that this was said against his own songs: My Muse spoke on her own behalf. I have sacred community with you, o poets, if unhappy people are allowed to be part of your choir. And, as a great part of my mind, you have lived with me, my friends; now in this part too, although far away, I still cherish you. May my songs therefore be commended by your favour, as I cannot myself speak on their behalf. An author's work usually pleases after his death, because envy is used to harming the living and to carping at them with unjustified backbiting. If living unhappily is a kind of death, the earth awaits me, and only my funeral is still lacking to my end.*

77 Finally, although my work is blamed on all sides, there will be no one who would blame my devotion to duty. Although my powers should be lacking, my will to do it could still be praised: I foretell that the gods will be pleased with that. Such willingness has the result that a poor man can also come favourably to their altars, and a sacrificial lamb pleases them no less than a slaughtered bullock.

83 The subject was also so great, that it would have been a great labour to undertake even for the very great poet who wrote of Aeneas. My gentle elegiacs could not carry the vast weight of the triumph on their lop-sided wheels. I cannot make up my mind which foot I now should use: for another triumph, about you, O Rhine, is at hand. The prophecies of truthful prophets are not deceptive: the next laurel should be given to Jove while the previous one is still green.

91 And you are not reading *my* words only, while I am removed far away to the Ister, waters that are drunk by the half-pacified Getae: *what you read*

is the voice of a god: a god is in my heart, and with the god as guide I predict and prophecy these things.

95 *Why do you stop preparing the chariot and formal procession for the triumphal processions, O Livia? No wars are delaying you. Perfidious Germany has thrown away its spears and lost them: you should say that my omen has weight. Believe me, and in a short while the truth of my words will appear: your son will double his honour, and, as before, sally forth behind a pair of horses.*

101 *Bring out the purple, which you will place on the victor's shoulders: the wreath itself can recognise a head that is used to it. But shields and helmets will gleam with gems and gold, and the trophy tree will still loom over chained soldiers. Ivory villages will be encircled with turreted walls, and people will think that this battle, as it is portrayed, is being waged in real earnest. The Rhine, all muddy, will carry its hair hanging down under broken reeds, and its water all tainted with blood. Even captive kings demand their barbarous insignia and tapestries too rich for their lot: and so, too, all the other things (which it has often prepared for you) the unconquered courage of your people will again need to prepare.*

113 *O gods, under whose tutelage I spoke of things to come, I pray that you will prove my words by fulfilling them quickly.*

Vocabulary Table
Absolute and relative frequency of specialised vocabulary

Note: 'Relative' represents number of occurrences per 100 verses.

	Books		Phase 1 *Tr.* 1, 2	Phase 2 *Tr.* 3, 4	Phase 3 *Tr.* 5	Phase 4 *Ex P.* 1,2, 3	Phase 5 *Ex P.* 4
	Total verses		**1280**	**1466**	**800**	**2264**	**930**
a	*clementia*		1	4	1	3	1
	iustitia, iustus		2	-	1	8	5
	moderor		1	1	1	3	-
	Total:	Absolute	4	5	3	14	6
		Relative	0.31	0.34	0.37	0.62	0.64
b	*pater patriae*		2	1	-	2	-
	parens		2	1	-	1	2
	Total:	Absolute	4	2	-	3	2
		Relative	0.31	0.14	0	0.13	0.21
c	*imperium*		6	-	1	5	5
	triumphus		-	5	-	13	-
	pax		1	2	2	13	1
	hostis		5	10	7	23	8
	Total:	Absolute	12	17	10	54	14
		Relative	0.93	1.15	1.25	2.38	1.50
d*	*amicitia*		1	6	-	5	1
	amicus		13	12	11	40	7
	Total:	Absolute	14	18	11	45	8
		Relative	1.09	1.22	1.30	1.89	0.86
e*	*amor* (non-erotic)		4	2	3	3	2
	pius, pietas		12	9	9	16	13
	Total:	Absolute	16	11	12	19	15
		Relative	1.69	0.58	1.50	0.83	1.61

(contd)		Phase 1	Phase 2	Phase 3	Phase 4	Phase 5
f*	*fides*	10	5	5	14	7
	fidelis	1	1	1	2	2
	foedus	2	1	-	3	1
	Total: Absolute	13	7	6	19	10
	Relative	1.01	0.40	0.70	0.80	1.07
***	(d+e+f)					
	Total: Absolute	43	36	29	83	33
	Relative	3.36	2.46	3.62	3.67	3.55
g	*officium, officiosus*	3	4	6	16	11
	studium	6	10	10	15	6
	favere, favor	6	6	2	16	2
	Total: Absolute	15	20	18	47	19
	Relative	0.93	1.36	2.25	2.07	2.04
h	*fateor*: Absolute	11	2	5	15	8
	Relative	0.85	0.13	0.62	0.66	0.86
i	*crimen*: Absolute	23	17	3	7	7
	Relative	1.79	1.15	0.37	0.31	0.75
	error: Absolute	4	8	-	5	3
	Relative	0.31	0.54	0	0.22	0.32
	culpa: Absolute	8	6	7	5	2
	Relative	0.63	0.40	0.87	0.22	0.21
j	*exsul, exsulare*	7	10	6	8	1
	exsilium	2	4	1	13	1
	relegatus	3	-	2	2	2
	Total: Absolute	12	14	9	23	4
	Relative	0.93	0.95	1.12	1.01	0.43
k	*sodalis*	3	6	-	5	2
	vates	1	5	4	8	6
	Total: Absolute	4	11	4	13	8
	Relative	0.31	0.75	0.50	0.57	0.86
l	*carmen* Absolute	40	24	18	34	33

	Phase 1	Phase 2	Phase 3	Phase 4	Phase 5
Relative frequency relating to his earlier works					
Rel. negative	4.7	2.7	3.7	2.6	3.2
Rel. positive	3.9	2.7	2.7	1.3	1.1
Relative frequency relating to the present (exilic poetry)					
Rel. negative	2.3	2.0	2.5	1.6	3.2
Rel. positive	0	2.0	5.0	2.2	7.0

(contd)			Phase 1	Phase 2	Phase 3	Phase 4	Phase 5
	Musa	Abs. negative:	4	3	0	0	0
		Abs. positive	3	5	4	8	7
	Total:	Absolute	47	32	22	42	40
		Relative	3.67	2.18	2.75	1.85	4.30
m	*deus*:	Absolute	33	25	21	57	19
		(Relative)	(2.57)	(1.70)	(2.62)	(2.51)	(2.04)
	Jupiter (Jov-)		12	10	2	9	2
	divus		1	3	-	1	-
	numen		15	5	6	28	9
	Total:	Absolute	61	43	29	95	30
		Relative	4.77	2.93	3.62	4.19	3.22
n	*fortuna*		9	13	11	13	6
	fatum/fata		4	17	9	16	6
	fatalis		1	-	3	1	-
	Parcae		-	-	2	1	-
	sorores		-	-	2	-	1
	sors		3	4	2	1	1
	Total:	Absolute	17	34	29	32	14
		Relative	1.32	2.31	3.62	1.41	1.50
o	*mitis*		7	5	5	14	7
	lenis		2	2	3	3	3
	Total:	Absolute	9	7	8	17	10
		Relative	0.70	0.47	1.00	0.75	1.07
p	*ira*		18	18	8	28	6
	iratus		3	3	-	-	-
	irascor		1	-	2	1	-
	Total:	Absolute	22	21	10	29	6
		Relative	1.72	1.43	1.25	1.28	0.64
q	*precor*		17	17	4	32	11
	oro		3	-	-	2	2
	preces		2	2	1	13	3
	Total:	Absolute	22	19	5	47	16
		Relative	1.71	1.29	0.62	2.12	1.72
r	*queror, querula*		2	4	6	6	9
	fleo, flebilis, fletus		3	7	7	7	-
	lacrima		7	11	1	16	4
	litura		1	1	-	1	2
	Total:	Absolute	13	23	14	30	15
		Relative	1.01	1.56	1.75	1.32	1.61

(contd)			Phase 1	Phase 2	Phase 3	Phase 4	Phase 5
s	*miser*		16	14	10	17	12
	sollicitus, attonitus		2	7	3	3	3
	tristis, infelix		10	21	7	20	3
	pudet		1	3	1	5	7
	Total:	Absolute	29	45	21	45	25
		Relative	2.26	3.06	2.62	1.99	2.68
t	*desero,*						
	desiderium		5	4	5	7	4
	procul, longe		11	19	5	14	6
	extremus, ultimus		8	12	3	11	3
	diversus		2	3	-	3	-
	peregrinus, profugus		6	4	3	7	1
	Total:	Absolute	32	42	16	42	14
		Relative	2.50	2.86	2.00	1.85	1.50
u	*imago*		4	3	2	8	-
	oculi mentis		-	1	-	4	4
	Total:	Absolute	4	4	2	12	4
		Relative	0.31	0.27	0.25	0.53	0.43
v	*mens*		11	18	5	24	9
	ingenium		14	13	7	19	9
	Total:	Absolute	25	31	12	43	18
		Relative	1.95	2.10	1.50	1.90	1.93
w	*corpus*	Absolute	-	6	1	4	-
		Relative	0.00	0.40	0.12	0.17	0.00

Myth Tables: The Pattern of Myth in the *Tristia* and *Epistolae ex Ponto*

Table 1. Figures that occur once only in the *Tristia* (first stage, AD 9-12) and are then discarded

Name	Tr.	Ex P.	Ib.	Met.	Fasti	Her.	Am.	AA	Rem.
Oedipus	1.1.114			15.429					
Teucri	1.2.6				4.40	3.130 7.140			
Althaea (Thestias)	1.7.18		601	8.304, 434, 446, 452, 473	5.305				721
Alcathous	1.10.39			8.8				2.421	
Actaeon	2.105			2.554 3.198, 230, 720, 721		20.103			
Endymion	2.299					18.63		3.83	
Iasion	2.300			9.423					
Helen of Troy	2.371			13.200 14.669		5.75 8.99 16.281, 287 17.134		2.359, 365, 371, 699 3.11, 253, 759	65
Pelops	2.380		179 585	6.404, 411		8.47 17.54	3.2.15		

Table 1 contd.

Name	Tr.	Ex P.	Ib.	Met.	Fasti	Her.	Am.	AA	Rem.
Hippolytus	2.383			15.497, 544	3.265 6.744	4.36, 164 21.10	2.4.32 2.18.24, 30	1.338 1.511	
Canace	2.384		357	3.217		11			
Hippodamia	2.387			12.210, 224		8.70 16.266 17.248	3.2.16	2.8	
Tereus	2.389			6.424-682 (10 X)	2.629, 856 6.697		2.14.33		61
Aerope	2.391								
Scylla (d. of Nisus)	2.393			8.91, 104					
Electra	2.395				4.31, 32, 174,177 6.42				
Aegisthus	2.396					8.53			161
Atalanta (*Schoeneia virgo*)	2.399			10.565, 598		4.99	3.2.29	2.185 3.775	
Danae	2.401			4.611 6.113 11.117			2.19.27, 28 3.4.21	3.415	
Haemon	2.402	561							

Table 1 contd.

Name	Tr.	Ex P.	Ib.	Met.	Fasti	Her.	Am.	AA	Rem.
Iole	2.405			9.140, 278, 394		9.6, 113		3.156	
Pyrrhus	2.405		303	13.155, 455	6.732	3.136 8.3, 8, 42, 82, 103, 115			
Hylas	2.406							2.110	
Calliope	2.568		482	5.339	5.80				
Danaus	3.1.62					8.14 14.15, 79			
Antigone	3.3.67			6.93					
Elpenor	3.4.19		485	14.252					
Eumedes	3.4.27								
Merops	3.4.30			1.763 2.184					
Irus	3.7.42		417			1.95			
Perseus	3.8.6			4.611-770 (6 X) 5.16-248 (13 X)		15.35		1.53	
Absyrtus	3.9.10								
Minyae	3.9.13			7.1, 115, 120					
Leander	3.10.41					19.1, 40, 150, 185		2.249	

Table 1 contd.

Name	Tr.	Ex P.	Ib.	Met.	Fasti	Her.	Am.	AA	Rem.
Acontius	3.10.73					21.103, 209, 229			
Semele	4.3.67		278	3.261, 274, 278, 293, 520 5.329, 9.641	3.751, 6.485, 503		3.3.37	3.251	
Gorgo	4.7.12			4.618, 699, 779, 801 5.180, 196, 202, 209 8.543	3.450	9.165		2.700 3.504	
Cerberus	4.7.16			4.450, 501 7.413 9.185, 14.65		9.94			
Harpyiae	4.7.17								
Sphinx	4.7.17		378						
Minotaur	4.7.18							2.24	
Gyas	4.7.18						2.1.12		
Aoniae	4.10.39			5.333 6.2	4.245		2.18.26		
Halcyone	5.1.60			11.384-674 (14 X)	4.173	18.81 19.133			
Lycurgus	5.3.39		503 607	4.22	3.722	2.111			

Table 1 contd.

Name	Tr.	Ex P.	Ib.	Met.	Fasti	Her.	Am.	AA	Rem.
Pentheus	5.3.40			3.514-712 (7 X) 4.22, 429					
Aegides	5.4.26			8.174, 405, 560 12.237, 343					
Eetion	5.5.44			12.110	4.280				
Echioniae arces (Thebes)	5.5.53								
Pelias	5.5.55			7.298, 305, 329, 346		2.101 12.129			
Palinurus	5.6.7		594						577
Automedon	5.6.10							1.5 1.8 2.738	
Podalirius	5.6.11							2.735	313
Dardanus	5.10.4								
Protesilaus	5.14.40			12.68		13.12, 16, 84, 156			

269

Table 2. Figures that occur more than once in the *Tristia* only (first stage: AD 9-12)

Name	Tr.	Ex P.	Ib.	Met.	Fasti	Her.	Am.	AA	Rem.
Phaethon	1.1.79 3.4.30 4.3.66			1.751, 755, 777 2.34-369 (8 X)	4.793				
Argolic fleet	1.1.83 2.439			13.659 15.337	4.72		2.6.15		
Caphereus	1.1.83 5.7b.36			14.472, 481					735
Icarus	1.1.90 3.4.22			8.195, 204, 231, 232, 233 10.450	4.284		2.16.14	2.76, 93, 94, 95	
Turnus (Rutulus)	1.2.7 1.5.23 1.9.33		631	14.451-573 (7 X) 15.773	1.463 4.879, 880, 883, 891				
Callisto	1.3.48; 14.1; 1.11.15; 2.1.190; 3.4b.47; 3.11.8			8.207	2.153, 156 3.107, 108 4.580	18.149 152			
Aeolus	1.4.17 1.10.15			1.262; 4.487, 512; 6.681; 7.672; 9.507; 11.444, 573, 748; 13.26; 14.103, 232	2.456	10.66 11.5, 34, 65, 74, 95 15.200	3.12.29	1.634	

Table 2 contd.

Name	Tr.	Ex P.	Ib.	Met.	Fasti	Her.	Am.	AA	Rem.
Euryalus	1.5.23; 1.9.33 5.4.26								
Nisus	1.5.24 1.9.33		362	8.8, 17, 90, 126 (n.a: the father of Scylla)	4.500 (ditto)				68
Dulichium	1.5.60, 67 4.1.31		386	13.107, 425, 711 14.226		1.87			272 699
Helle	1.10.15 3.12.3			11.195	3.857	18.141 19.123, 128			
Eteocles	2.319; 5.5.34								
Briseis	2.373 4.1.5					3.1, 137 20.69	1.9.33 2.8.11	2.713 3.189	777 783
Chimaera	2.397; 4.7.13			6.339; 9.647					
Daedalus	3.4.21 3.8.6			8.159-261 (6 X) 9.742		18.49		2.23, 33, 74	
Priam (Dardanius)	3.5.38 5.1.55 5.4.11 5.12.7			11.757 12.1, 607 13.201, 404, 409, 470, 520 14.474	6.431	1.4, 34 3.20 5.82, 83, 95 16.48, 98, 209 17.58 211	2.14.13	1.441, 685 3.440	

Table 3. Figures from the *Tristia* that recur once in the *Epistolae ex Ponto* (both stages, AD 9-17, or later)

Name	Tr.	Ex P.	Ib.	Met.	Fasti	Her.	Am.	AA	Rem.
Telegonus	1.1.114	3.1.123			3.92 4.71				
Laodamia	1.6.20 5.5.58 5.14.39	3.1.110				13.2, 35, 36, 70		2.356 3.138	724
Thoas	1.9.28 4.4.66	3.2.59	384						
Telephus	2.20 5.2.15	2.2.26		12.112					
Anchises	2.299	1.1.33		9.425 13.640, 680	4.35	7.162 16.203			
Seven against Thebes	2.320	4.8.53							
Telamonian Aiax	2.525	4.7.41		13.2-356 (15 X)			1.7.7	3.111, 517, 523	
Erichthonius	2.294	2.9.20		2.553 9.424	4.33				

Table 3 contd.

Name	Tr.	Ex P.	Ib.	Met.	Fasti	Her.	Am.	AA	Rem.
Cupido	2.385 4.10.65	1.4.41		1.453 4.321 5.366 7.73 9.482, 543 10.311	2.463	15.215 16.115	1.1.3 1.2.19 1.6.11 1.9.1 1.11.11 1.15.27 2.5.1 2.9a.1 2.9b.33, 47, 51 2.12.27 3.1.41	1.233, 261	3 139 157 555
Clytaemnestra	2.396	3.1.121							
Philomela	2.389	1.3.39		6.451-658 (9 X)			2.6.7		61
Procne	2.389 5.1.60	3.1.119		6.428-653 (15 X)	2.629 2.855				
Hermione	2.399	2.11.15				8.59 16.256		1.745 2.699	771
Phyllis	2.537	4.16.20				2.1, 60, 98, 105, 106, 138, 147	18.22, 32	2.353 3.38, 460	55, 591, 606, 607
Danaides	3.1.62	3.1.121				1.3 14.15	2.2.4		

Table 3 contd.

Name	Tr.	Ex P.	Ib.	Met.	Fasti	Her.	Am.	AA	Rem.
Latona	3.2.3	4.14.57		6.160-336 (8 X) 13.635	5.543				
Croesus	3.7.42	4.3.37							
Triptolemus	3.8.1	4.2.10		5.646, 653	4.550				
Busiris	3.11.39	3.6.41		9.183		9.69		1.649, 651	
Capaneus	4.3.63, 5.3.29	3.1.51		9.404				3.21	
Evadne	4.3.64 5.5.54 5.14.38	3.1.112							
Tiphys	4.3.77	1.4.37				6.48		1.6, 8	
Iphigenia	4.4.67 80	3.2.62		12.31					

Table 3 contd.

Name	Tr.	Ex P.	Ib.	Met.	Fasti	Her.	Am.	AA	Rem.
Amor	5.1.22	3.3.13		1.480, 532, 619, 540 5.374, 10.26, 29		4.11, 148 7.32, 59 15.179 16.16 20.28, 30, 146, 226, 230	1.1.26 1.2.8, 18, 32 1.3.12 1.6.34, 37, 59 1.10.15 2.1.38 2.9b.34 2.18.4, 5, 18, 19, 36 3.1.20, 43 3.4.20	1.7, 8, 17, 21, 23, 83, 232 2.17, 229, 708, 497 3.559	1 39 148 198 246 346 530 551 612 759
Niobe	5.1.57 5.12.8	1.2.29		6.148, 156, 165, 273, 287			3.12.31		
Alcestis	5.5.57 5.14.37	3.1.106							
Admetus	5.14.37	3.1.106	442					2.239	
Iphias	5.14.38	3.1.111						3.22	

Table 4. Figures from the *Tristia* that recur more than once in the *Epistolae ex Ponto* (AD 9-14 or later)

Name	Tr.	Ex P.	Ib.	Met.	Fasti	Her.	Am.	AA	Rem.
Castor	1.1.45 4.5.30	2.2.83 2.11.15		12.401	5.709		2.16.13 3.2.54	1.746	
Aeneas	1.2.7 2.261, 262, 533	1.1.33, 35 3.3.62 3.4.84		13.665, 681 14.78-603 (11 X) 15.437-861 (8 X)		7.9, 25, 26, 29	1.8.42 1.15.25 2.14.17 2.18.31 3.9.13	1.60 3.86 3.337	
Theseus	1.3.66, 1.5.19 1.9.31 2.403	2.3.43 3.2.33 4.10.71, 78	412 495	7.404, 421, 433 8.263, 268, 303, 547, 566, 726 12.227, 356, 359 15.492, 856	3.460, 473, 487, 491 6.737		1.7.15	1.509, 531, 551 3.35, 457, 459	
Pirithous	1.5.19	2.3.43 2.6.26		8.303, 404 12.218, 229		4.112		1.744	
Orestes	1.5.22 1.9.27 2.395 4.4.69, 87 5.4.25 5.6.25	2.3.45 3.2.33, 69, 85		15.489			8.9, 15, 59, 101, 115	1.7.9 2.6.15	589 771
Pylades	1.9.28, 5.6.26	3.2.70, 85						1.745	589

Table 4 contd.

Name	Tr.	Ex P.	Ib.	Met.	Fasti	Her.	Am.	AA	Rem.
Hector	1.6.19 1.9.30 1.10.17 3.11.27	2.11.15 4.16.19 4.7.42	564	11.758, 760 12.3, 69, 77, 447, 448, 591 13.82, 178, 279, 426, 487, 512, 666		1.14, 36 3.86, 126 7.144	1.9.35 2.1.32 2.6.42	1.15, 694 2.646, 709, 778	
Penelope	1.6.22 5.5.52 5.14.36	3.1.107 4.16.13		8.315, 13.511		1.1 84	1.8.47 2.18.21, 29 3.4.23	1.477 2.355 3.15	
Pollux	1.10.45, 4.5.30	2.2.83 4.5.30			5.711, 715		2.16.13 3.2.54		
Giganto-machia	2.71, 333	2.11.12 4.8.59		10.150					
Hercules	2.405 3.5.43	4.13.11 4.16.7	253 293 605	7.364; 9.135, 162, 256, 264, 278, 286; 11.627; 12.554, 574; 13.23, 52; 15.8, 47, 231, 284, 711	1.584 2.237 5.632, 696 6.65, 78, 209, 521	9.18, 27, 57, 129, 149	3.6.36	1.68 3.168	47
Numa	3.1.30	3.2.106 3.3.44 4.16.10		15.4, 481, 487	1.43; 2.69 3.262, 276, 300-85 (7 X) 4.641, 652, 667 5.48, 6.264		2.17.18		

Table 4 contd.

Name	Tr.	Ex P.	Ib.	Met.	Fasti	Her.	Am.	AA	Rem.
Orpheus	4.1.17	2.9.53 3.3.41	600	10.3, 64, 79 11.5, 22, 23, 44, 66, 92			3.9.21	3.321	
Cadmus	4.3.67	1.3.77 4.10.55		3.3-174 (7 X) 4.70, 572, 591, 592	1.490 6.553				
Artemis	4.4.63	1.2.78 3.2.64,71	384						
Medusa	4.7.11	1.2.35, 36 3.1.124	447 553	4.655, 743, 781, 783 5.69-312 (6 X) 10.22	3.451 5.8	19.134		2.309	
Scylla (monster)	4.7.13	3.1.122 4.10.25	385	7.65 13.730, 900, 967 14.18, 39, 52, 59, 70	4.500	12.123, 124	2.11.18 3.12.21		
Philoctetes	5.1.61, 5.2.13 5.4.12	1.3.5, 3.1.54		13.329					
Satyrs	5.3.37	3.3.42 4.16.35	81	1.193, 692 4.25 6.110, 383, 393 11.89 14.637	1.397, 411 3.409, 737, 745, 757 6.323, 703 14.142	4.171 5.135		1.542, 548 3.157	

| Table 5. Figures that occur only in the *Epistolae ex Ponto* (second stage, after AD 12-14, or later) | | | | | | | | | |
| 5a. One occurrence each in the *Epistolae ex Ponto* | | | | | | | | | |
Name	*Tr.*	*Ex P.*	*Ib.*	*Met.*	*Fasti*	*Her.*	*Am.*	*AA*	*Rem.*
Atreus		1.2.19		15.855		8.27	3.12.39		
Diomedes		1.2.119				9.6.7			
Theromedon		1.2.119	383						
Asclepius		1.3.21							
Tydeus		1.3.79	350, 428		1.491	9.155			
Enceladus		2.2.11					3.12.27		
Sybil		2.8.43			3.534 4.875				
Cassander		2.9.43	461						
Arethusa		2.10.27		5.409-642 (6 X)	4.423, 873				
Amphiaraus		3.1.52			2.43				
Amazons		3.1.95		15.552		4.2		2.743 3.1	
Dionysius		4.3.39							
Thyestes		4.6.47	359, 545	15.462				1.327	
Aurora		4.9.3		1.61; 2.113, 144; 3.150, 184; 4.81, 630; 5.440, 6.48; 7.100, 209, 703, 721, 835; 11.296, 598; 13.576, 594, 621	5.733	4.95 15.87 16.201 18.112	1.13.3 2.4.43	1.330	

5b. More that one occurrence in the *Epistolae ex Ponto*

Name	Tr.	Ex P.	Ib.	Met.	Fasti	Her.	Am.	Ars	Rem.
Jason		1.3.75 1.4.23, 36 3.1.1				6.37, 77, 119, 139 12.151 16.347 17.229 19.175			546
Bistonius		1.2.110 1.3.59 2.9.54 4.5.35	379	13.430		2.90 16.346			
Machaon		1.3.5; 3.4.7						2.491	
Nestor		1.4.10; 2.4.22		8.313; 12.169; 13.63, 64	3.533	1.38		2.736	
The Cyclops Polyphemus		2.2.113 4.10.23	387	13.744-772 (9 X) 14.167, 174, 249	4.473				
Antiphates		2.2.114 2.9.41		14.234, 239, 249 15.717					
Eumolpus		2.9.2, 19, 20 3.3.41		11.93					
Alcinous		2.9.42 4.2.10		14.565			1.10.56		
Thersites		3.9.10 4.13.15		13.233			2.6.41	482	
Pegasus		4.7.52 4.8.80		4.786, 5.262					

Name	Tr.	Ex P.	Ib.	Met.	Fasti	Her.	Am.	AA	Rem.
Asclepius and Machaon (= healers)		1.3.5 1.3.21 3.4.7							
Philoctetes	5.1.61 5.2.13 5.4.12	3.1.54 1.3.5		13.329					
Achilles	1.9.29, 2.411, 3.5.37, 4.1.15 5.1.55	1.3.74 1.7.51 3.3.43	627	8.309 11.265 12.73-615 (14 X) 13.30-597 (17 X) 15.856	2.119	3.25, 41, 137 8.45, 85 20.69	1.9.33, 2.1.29 2.8.13 2.18.1 3.9.1	1.11, 441, 689, 701, 711, 743	381 477 777 473
Patroclus	1.9.29, 5.4.25	1.3.73 2.3.41		13.273		1.17 3.23		1.743	
Orestes and Pylades	1.5.21, 1.9.27 4.4.69, 87 5.4.26 5.6.26	2.3.45 2.6.25 3.2.33, 70, 85	527				2.6.15		589
Theseus and Perithous	1.3.66 1.5.19 5.4.2	2.3.43 2.6.25 3.2.33		8.303 12.227		4.111			
Agamemnon and Clytaemnestra	2.396; 5.6.25	2.6.25 3.1.121 4.8.51	527	13.184, 444 15.855		3.38, 83	3.13.31		485

Table 6. Dominant or thematic use of mythological figures throughout the exilic works, AD 9-17?

Table 6 contd.

Name	Tr.	Ex P.	Ib.	Met.	Fasti	Her.	Am.	AA	Rem.
Medea	2.387, 526 3.8.3 3.9.9, 15, 34	3.1.120 3.3.80 4.10.52	603	7.11, 41, 70, 285, 298, 406	2.42	6.75, 103, 108, 127, 128, 151 16.347 19.176		2.103 2.382 3.333	261
Jason		1.3.75 1.4.23, 36 3.1.1				6.37, 77, 119, 139 12.151 16.347 17.229 19.175			
Phalaris of Agrigentum	3.11.42, 51 5.1.53	2.9.44 3.6.42	439					1.653	
Busiris	3.11.39	3.6.41		9.183		9.69		1.649 651	
Ulysses / Odysseus	1.2.9 1.5.57 2.376, 3.11.61 5.5.51	3.1.53 3.6.19 4.10.9 4.14.35 4.16.13		13.6-773 (16 X) 14.71-671 (7 X)	6.433	1.1, 35, 84 3.129 19.148	2.18.21, 29	2.103, 123, 355	285

Table 7. Statistical play
Trends in provenance, possibly indicating Ovid's shifting interests over time

Summary of Tables with approximate dating	Absolute number of figures		Repeated use of figures in the exilic works from the three pentads of *Metamorphoses*			Relative frequency of all earlier occurrences for every one occurrence in exilic works, indicating Ovid's preoccupations?				
	Known	New	M 1-5	M 6-10	M. 11-15	Tr.	Ex P.	Met. + Fasti	Her.	Love poetry
Tab. 1: AD 9-12, one occurrence in *Tr.* only	46	9	18	18	8	1	-	1.1	0.8	0.5
Tab. 2: AD 9-12, more than once in *Tr.*	14	2	4	11	13	1	-	2.44	0.9	1.18
Tab. 3: AD 9-14, or later, in both stages	22	6	7	12	4	1	0.7	1.2	1.2	2.3
Tab. 4: AD 9-14, or later, more in *Ex P.*	18		6	11	20	1	1.1	3.2	0.6	2.6
Tab. 5: After AD 12, only in *Ex P.*	6	4	2	15	-	-	1	1.2	1.6	0.33
Tab. 6: AD 9-17?, dominant throughout	11 sets or individuals	1 set	3	11	1	1	1	1.4	1.5	2.3

Index

addressees (friends): Albinovanus Pedo, 27; Atticus, 23, 136; Brutus (his editor), 17, 21, 24-6, 119; Carus, 16, 27-8, 93, 106, 137, 179; Cotta Maximus, 18, 20, 21-2, 23, 24, 25, 28, 33, 36, 59, 61, 63, 104, 137, 172, 249, 250, 254-6; Cotys, King of Thrace, 23, 38, 58, 125, 170, 182; Fabius Maximus, 21, 24, 26, 60-2, 66, 71-2, 74, 104, 118-19, 123, 137, differentiation from Cotta, 21-2, 25; Flaccus, 22, 27, 143-4, 182; Gallio, Junius, 27, 229; Graecinus, 22, 23, 27; Macer, 24, 58-9, 140, 179, 246-7; Messallinus, 18, 22, 36, 57, 62, 131; 'Perilla' as his stepdaughter, 16, 250; Rufinus, 21, 24, 60-1, 139, 258; Rufus (his wife's uncle), 24; Salanus, 23; Severus, 22, 26, 46, 106; Sextus Pompeius, 26, 28, 46, 50-1, 83, 116, 204, 221, 253; Suillius, 26-7, 37, 132, 250; Tuticanus, 27-8, 178; Vestalis, 26, 44, 83, 247, 253; possibly also: Hyginus (keeper of Palatine Library), 62, 137, 161
Aeneid: 8, 46, 65, 73, 121, 149, 181, 185, 195, 199, 243, 246
alienation through isolation: 185, 200, 212-28; characteristics of: loss of sense of identity, 50, 213, 221; loss of sense of power, 213; loneliness, 218; anxiety, 219; fear, 219; physical illness, 220; identification by author with works, 222; linguistic dislocation, 222-3; self-hatred, 224; tears, 224; association with death, 224; sublimation, 214, 226-7; defiance, 225; alternation of hope and despair, 225-6; nostalgia, 227
amicitia: use of word, 96-7, 115, 118; nature of, 119, 121, 236; duties of, 22-3, 121, 128, 174, 182; gift-giving in, 83; utility of, 25, 121, 154; *Ex P.* 1-3 as '*Ars amicitiae*', 119, 121, 134
Augustus: as 'god' (Jupiter), 14, 15, 19, 22, 29-33, 39, 44-5, 66, 75, 84, 87, 115, 117, 120, 125-6, 128, 154, 155, 162, 175, 177-83, 194, 203, 254, 257; as 'all too human', 19, 20, 32, 42, 43, 182, 203; oscillation between human and divine, 177-8; attempts to restore religion and morality, 3, 32-4, 39-40, 142, 186; attitude to Ovid and vice versa, 7, 32-3, 37, 73, 123, 200; attributes listed in *Res Gestae* 34.2: 32-3, 203; *clementia*, 30, 32, 102, 116, 133, 242; *iustitia* (sense of) justice, 31-2, 116-17, 120, 133, 136, 164; *moderatio*, 32, 116-17; *pater patriae (parens)* 32, 72, 104, 116-17, 120, 203; adoption of Tiberius: 35, 37, 61, 72, 117, 154, 203; banishment of members of his family, 2, 15, 30, 48; capriciousness, also of Livia, 32, 35-6, 75; fondness for games of chance, 15, 204; 'games' to celebrate his birthday as new deity, 27, 44; marriage laws, 3, 34, 188; compared with his own marriages, 34, with South African laws, 186-8; Ovid's *error* as personally affecting, 31, 40, 200; his power, 10, 21, 32-3; powerlessness to protect citizens, 33; Livia as 'power behind throne', 34
Augustus' family: Julian *gens* (names, line): 8, 21, 22, 23, 34, 35, 37, 166, 244; Claudian *gens,* 23, 34, 35, 37; exiled members, 20, 29, Ovid's barbed (veiled) allusions to, 20, 29, 34, 37-8, 87, 172; pervasive divine metaphor for, 32, 33, 34, 35, 37, 104, 110, 125, 126, 134, 226, 259; Agrippa, 34, and Vipsania, 39; Agrippa Postumus, 39, 233; Agrippina and Levilla, 37; Drusus the Elder, 37; Drusus, son of Tiberius, 37, 61; Gaius, 39, 139; Germanicus, 22, 23, 26-7, 29, 37, 61, 62, 96-7, 127, 132, 134, 139, his divine status, 37, 127; Julia Maior, 34,

www.ingramcontent.com/pod-product-compliance
Lightning Source LLC
Chambersburg PA
CBHW071449110726
47908CB00003B/567